CONQUEST OF THE FOUR QUARTERS

Also by Jonathan Bader

Meditation in Śaṅkara's Vedānta

Conquest of the Four Quarters

Traditional Accounts of the Life of Śaṅkara

JONATHAN BADER

ADITYA PRAKASHAN
New Delhi

First Published: 2000

ISBN 81-7742-002-X

Published by Aditya Prakashan, Delhi – 110 009
and printed at Rajkamal Electric Press, Delhi – 110 033.

ॐ श्री गुरुभ्यो नमः

CONTENTS

Preface

Some seven hundred years or more after Śaṅkara's day, a series of hagiographies began to emerge which were instrumental in establishing him in popular culture. Until the present century these works were composed exclusively in Sanskrit. One in particular stands out from the rest, the *Śaṅkaradigvijaya* of Mādhava. This text, composed between 1650 and 1800, skilfully brought together materials from several earlier hagiographies. Its popularity grew to such an extent that it eventually eclipsed the other works, which have languished in relative obscurity ever since. The Śaṅkara hagiographies have so far failed to attract much scholarly attention largely because they are of little historical value. Yet, the authors of these works had no intention of writing history. They sought to eulogise Śaṅkara and, to this end, mythography was far more powerful than biography as a medium of expression. Indeed, the hagiographers succeeded in creating a fluid and dynamic image of Śaṅkara which became celebrated throughout the whole of the subcontinent. This study focuses on the hagiographies composed prior to and including the *Śaṅkaradigvijaya*, i.e., eight texts in all.

My primary aim is to consider how Śaṅkara has been received in India, and in particular to examine the conceptual models upon which his life story is constructed. The work is organised along the lines of the features that stand out most prominently in the hagiographies. Firstly, there are the mythic structures which provide not only the peaks but also the foundation of the narrative. The Śaṅkara story is cast firmly within the framework of Śaiva mythology: the protagonist is, above all, an *avatāra* of Śiva. Secondly, I have attached considerable importance to the sense of place. Śaṅkara's grand tour of sacred sites proves to be a quest for the throne of omniscience, and also demonstrates the complementarity of royal and ascetic paradigms in traditional India. Thirdly, there are the debates, through which the wanderings characteristic to a renouncer are transformed into a *digvijaya*, a conquest of the four quarters. It is through the *digvijaya* that Śaṅkara fulfils his mission of restoring harmony to a divided land, and eventually comes to be recognised as a national hero. Finally, I have paid much attention to the legacy of Śaṅkara as well as the continuity of the Advaita *sampradāya*, in order to emphasise that theirs is a living tradition.

This study was originally presented as a PhD thesis at the Australian National University in 1991. For the past eight years the manuscript has remained virtually hidden away, while my own pursuits in Advaita Vedānta have been oriented more towards practice than to theoretical concerns. It is only through the repeated prompting of my wife, Erica, that I have finally decided to bring the work into the public domain.

I am very grateful to a number of people who provided much help in the preparation of this study while I was at the Australian National University: Tissa Rajapatirana, Luise Hercus, Professor J. W. de Jong, and Michael Comans. I also wish to acknowledge the Faculty of Asian Studies for their overall support and the generous facilities afforded me in my research. I am especially grateful to Dipesh Chakrabarty, who first encouraged me to undertake this project. Yogendra Yadav and Sudha Joshi helped me through some of the Hindi materials.

There are a number of people I would like to thank for their help and cordiality during my visits to India. In the first place, I am most grateful to the Śaṅkarācāryas who showed me that the rich tradition they represent is still very much alive. The *ācāryas* and their staff welcomed me and graciously answered my many questions: at Kānchipuram, His Holiness the late Jagadguru Candraśekharendra-Sarasvatī and A. Kuppuswami; at Sringerī, His Holiness Jagadguru Bhāratītīrtha and Shankar Sharma (private secretary to the late Jagadguru Abhinavavidyātīrtha); at the Kumbha Melā, His Holiness Jagadguru Svāmī Svarūpānanda, *pīṭhādhipati* of the Dwārkā and Jyotir *maṭhas*, and Michael Mavro who arranged for me to meet Svāmījī. In Bombay Dr. W. R. Antarkar generously provided me with various materials for my research. In Madras Professor N. Veezhinathan spent several hours patiently replying to my queries about the *Śaṅkaravijaya* of Anatānandagiri, and the late Swāmī Tapasyānanda of the Śrī Rāmakrishna Order set aside time to discuss the Śaṅkara hagiographies at length.

Two other people deserve special mention for strongly encouraging my pursuits in India, both practical and theoretical. The late Swami Narikutti provided a powerful demonstration of how life could be lived according to traditional knowledge. Over the years we spent much time in his cave on Aruṇācala, the sacred mountain at Tiruvannamalai. We enjoyed numerous cups of his superb chai, over which Swami Narikutti spoke with much insight on the teachings of the greatest 20th century exponent of Advaita, Śrī Ramaṇa Maharshi. Swami Narikutti also took the trouble to read through the whole of the manuscript with his jackal's eye of discrimination. Swami Satyananda of Tiruvannamalai also took great interest in my work and provided inspired satsang.

This study has benefited considerably from the critical comments of Professor Hermann Kulke, Professor Sheldon Pollock, Phyllis Granoff and Greg Bailey. As well, Phyllis Granoff gave generously of her time in suggesting numerous improvements for my translations of some of the more difficult verses. However, for any mistakes which remain, I take sole responsibility.

My final and greatest debt is to my wife Erica, who has had to live with one so distracted by the details of research these many years. Her support, and more especially her honesty, has kept me from losing the plot. To her is due the larger part of whatever fruits may arise from the work.

ABBREVIATIONS

ALB	*Adyar Library Bulletin*
AŚV	Anantānandagiri 's *Śaṅkaravijaya*
BṛŚV	*Bṛhat-Śaṅkaravijaya*
CŚV	Cidvilāsa's *Śaṅkaravijayavilāsa*
GŚC	Govindanātha's *Śaṅkarācāryacarita*
GVK	*Guruvaṃśakāvya* of Lakṣmaṇa-Śāstrī
IIJ	*Indo-Iranian Journal*
JAOS	*Journal of the American Oriental Society*
JIP	*Journal of Indian Philosophy*
JUB	*Journal of the University of Bombay*
MBh	*Mahābhārata*
PC	Patañjalicarita of Rāmabhadra-Dikṣita
PEW	*Philosophy East and West*
PrŚV	*Praācīna Śaṅkaravijaya*
RŚA	Rājacūḍāmaṇi-Dīkṣita's *Śaṅkarābhyudaya*
ŚDV	*Śaṅkaradigvijaya* of Mādhava
TŚA	Tirumala-Dīkṣita's *Śaṅkarābhyudaya*
VŚV	Vyāsācala's *Śaṅkaravijaya*
WZKS	*Wiener Zeitschrift für die Kunde Südasiens*

Introduction

On the fifth day of the bright half of the month of Vaiśākha, April 21, 1988, a select crowd gathered in the rarified atmosphere of the Vigyan Bhavan in New Delhi. They had come to pay tribute, long due, to a national hero. The President of India, the Prime Minister and various other dignitaries stood on the podium before the freshly garlanded figure of a young *saṃnyāsin* clad in ochre robes. This was no Hindu militant, but an apostle of unity. He was, in the words of President R. Venkataraman,

> a unique personality who gave to Bharat its identity. The Vishnu Purana describes the country south of the Himalayas and north of the ocean as Bharat. This puranic ideal of a unified country has remained with us from time immemorial. The architect who gave practical shape to this ideal and achieved the cultural unity of the country was none other than Sankara Bhagavat Pada.[1]

In this august gathering, the name of Śaṅkara was finally entered into the ledger of national history. The seal of approval came in the form of a year-long festival, the "Rāṣṭrīya Śaṅkara Jayantī Mahotsav", proclaimed by the Government of India in commemoration of the twelve hundredth anniversary of his birth.

This was a historic occasion and a celebration of history. In his address at the inaugural function, Professor K. Satchidananda

---

[1] The speeches of President Venkataraman (in English) and Karan Singh (in Hindi) were published in *Sanskriti Bharati*, vol. 1.1 (1988), a quarterly journal of the Department of Culture, Ministry of Human Resource Development, Government of India, pp. 7-9; 35-36.

Murty reminded the audience of the great esteem in which Śaṅkara was held by the leaders of modern India, from Rammohan Roy right up to Indira Gandhi; and "her greatest historical hero, she stated, was Shankaracharya".[2] Yet the weight of history had been long denied to this cultural hero. For more than a hundred years controversy had raged over the dates of Śaṅkara. The voluminous and tiresome literature this debate has generated, seems to suggest that there is no personality in the absence of a precise chronology. In the end it was the government which rescued Śaṅkara from the uncharted waters of history. This was achieved by steering clear of the treacherous snares, on the one side, set by the opposing forces in the debate on Śaṅkara's chronology,[3] and on the other, the powerful pull of the bureaucratic imperative for recording essential statistics. The Rāṣṭrīya Śaṅkara Jayantī Mahotsav Committee, headed by Rajiv Gandhi, saw to it that the figure of Śaṅkara was clearly cast as a national monument, but that no dates were to be

---

[2] K. Satchidananda Murty, Inauguration address, printed as a separate booklet by the Rāṣṭrīya Śaṅkara Jayantī Mahotsav Committee, New Delhi, p. 4.

[3] The academic participants in the debate were lightweights in comparison to the traditional scholars who appealed to the sense of national pride. These nationalists argued that Indian culture goes back far earlier than that of the brash Europeans who were temporarily in the ascendant. According to one such argument, Śaṅkara lived in the 6th century B.C. This means the dates of the Buddha must also be pushed back—to 1800 B.C.! This was propounded by T.S. Narayana Sastry in *The age of Śaṅkara* ([1916] 2nd ed.; Madras, B.G. Paul & Co., 1971). His friend and colleague, M. Krishnamachariar, takes a similar line in the introduction to his *History of classical Sanskrit literature* ([1937] reprinted, Delhi: Motilal Banarsidass, 1974), p. cx. For a useful survey of the scholarly arguments on the subject, see K. Kunjunni Raja, "On the date of Śaṃkarācārya and allied problems", *Adyar Library Bulletin*, 24 (1960), pp. 125-148.

inscribed on the pedestal.[4] President Venkataraman explained just why Śaṅkara cannot be dated:

> Adi Sankara lives in time; but is timeless. He was born in Bharata-varsha; but his vision is universal, all-encompassing. And so India, which treats history not in terms of centuries or even millennia but in *yugas*, prefers to think of Adi Sankara not as one who moved from event to event in life but as one who gave us a vision that transcended all limitations of time. Chronologies lose their significance with one like Sankara.[5]

This was truly a historic occasion: the meeting of time and the timeless.

The official addresses at the inaugural function stressed that the festival was more than a national affair.[6] Śaṅkara's teachings were universal. Perhaps they even held the key to world peace: "Nations armed to the teeth with weapons of annihilation...may well turn to Śaṅkara for enlightenment".[7] While it is questionable whether his profile extends into the sphere of international politics, there is no doubt that Śaṅkara has secured a place in the global academic culture. The proliferation of scholarly studies inspired by Śaṅkara's thought are ample testimony of this. Indeed his emergence as an international figure derives from an unusual cultural collaboration. Both the early spokesmen of Indian nationalism

---

4 The three inaugural addresses skilfully avoided any mention of chronology. Nevertheless, the labours of the many scholars who had sought to establish the dates of Śaṅkara were not without some reward. The years 788-820, which had been widely (but by no means unanimously) accepted for some time were tacitly approved by the government.

5 *Sanskriti Bharati*, vol. 1.1 (1988), p. 7.

6 An international seminar on Śaṅkara was held in the same venue on 9-12 January 1989.

7 President R. Venkataraman, *op. cit.*, p. 7.

and some of the orientalists who were patronized by Imperial Britain found in Śaṅkara the epitome of the true Indian psyche. The outstanding figures in this coalition were Swāmī Vivekānanda and F. Max Müller. They sought to establish Śaṅkara at the apex of a "Brāhmanism" which partook of the essence of Indo-European culture and thus stood apart from what both the nationalists and the imperialists saw as the garish idolatry of "later Hinduism".

The corridors of power in New Delhi were not to be the only venue for a Śaṅkara festival. An organization was formed in Kerala which envisaged the whole of India as the setting for a celebration. This was in the hope that "commemorating the Vijaya Yātrā of Ādi Śaṅkara [which took place] 1200 years ago will further kindle the spirit of national integration, cultural unity and spiritual renaissance".[8] The reenactment of Śaṅkara's tour of victory began in Kālaṭi, Kerala, which is believed to be his birthplace. It was to end in Kedāra in the Himālayas, the place of his *mahāsamādhi*, according to some accounts of his life. Despite the traditional backgrounds of the convenors, they too were subject to conditions which are virtually universal in the latter part of the 20th century. There is no longer time for walking. The *yātrā* would proceed via a motorized chariot, bearing the items for ritual worship. Nevertheless, this was a project which would touch the lives of many as the chariot made its stops in the cities and pilgrimage places en route to its destination.

The great interest shown in recreating his journey to the four quarters of the subcontinent demonstrates that Śaṅkara still holds a place in the thoughts of many individuals as well as in the country's intellectual history. Although they are largely restricted to educated Hindus, his teachings have directly affected

---

8 Letter distributed by the Ādi Śaṅkara Jyoti Digvijaya Yātrā Committee, Kālaṭi, Kerala, dated 9 November 1988.

people's lives. Perhaps Śaṅkara's presence makes itself most strongly felt when old age approaches, and people find it difficult to avoid the fact of their own mortality. At this time the atavistic call of the forest *ṛṣis* is more easily heard, and there is impetus for reflection on the ancient ascetic values which Śaṅkara represents.

There are many images which the name Śaṅkara brings to mind. He may appear in the guise of an exegete, a metaphysician, a guru, a wandering mendicant, or an incarnation of the great god whose name he bears. These are but a few of the portraits to be found in the substantial body of literature devoted to Śaṅkara's life. There are some twenty Sanskrit accounts which were composed prior to 1900, and several more have been written in the 20th century.[9] One text stands out from the rest, the *Śaṅkaradigvijaya* of Mādhava, composed between 1650 and 1800. This work skilfully brought together materials from several of the earlier hagiographies. The result was a single coherent version of the Śaṅkara story which gained almost universal acceptance, eventually eclipsing the other Sanskrit texts. In this century there have been many renderings and adaptations of the *Śaṅkaradigvijaya*, in various vernaculars and in English. However, I have been unable to find any vernacular accounts of his life which are more than a hundred years old. This suggests the extent to which Śaṅkara was limited to the sphere of Sanskritic culture prior to the nationalist period. Once he became a national hero his portfolio was considerably expanded. Since 1947 the Śaṅkara story has been still more widely disseminated through school textbooks, a comic book and a feature film.[10]

---

9 The sources are described in Chapter One. A list of the printed editions of these texts is provided separately in the Bibliography. There is also a list of 20th century compositions.

10 These are discussed in Chapter One.

In contrast to the enormous body of literature devoted to Śaṅkara's work, there has been very little scholarly interest in his life story.[11] This is largely because the Śaṅkara hagiographies, written more than seven hundred years after his death, cannot be treated as historical records of his life. But we cannot afford to dismiss popular religious texts solely on historical grounds. It is not just the Śaṅkara story which has been neglected on this account. The vast body of hagiological literature extant in India is only just beginning to attract serious attention. Since 1983 Phyllis Granoff has led the way into this largely unexplored territory through a series of important studies, primarily devoted to the life stories of classical Indian philosophers.[12] In this study I hope to bring to light some of the rich materials that the Śaṅkara hagiographies have to offer for anyone interested in the study of Indian culture. I have chosen to focus on the Sanskrit accounts of Śaṅkara's life composed prior to (and including) the *Śaṅkara-digvijaya*, i.e., eight texts in all.[13] Until the *Śaṅkaradigvijaya* assumed its preeminent place, there were fewer boundaries within which the narrative of his life had to be sketched. This diversity promises the greatest potential for exploration. Since seven of these hagiographies have not as yet been translated into English,[14] I

---

11 See Chapter One, notes 7, 8 and 10 for details of the research which has been done.

12 See the Bibliography for details of the nine articles she has contributed on the subject. She is also the co-editor (along with Koichi Shinohara) of *Monks and magicians: religious biographies in Asia* (Oakville, Ontario: Mosaic Press, 1988).

13 Details of the eight texts are listed at the beginning of the Bibliography.

14 The only translation in a European language is Paul Deussen's German rendering of the first chapter of Mādhava's *Śaṅkaradigvijaya*. For details see note 73 in Chapter One. There are two rather free translations of the *Śaṅkaradigvijaya* in English, see the the first page of the Bibliography for details.

have included here my own translations of numerous passages from the texts.

In this study I refer to the Sanskrit sources for the Śaṅkara story as hagiographies instead of using terms such as 'religious biographies'. This is to emphasize that the authors of these texts had little interest in presenting what we would regard as a "true" account of a life. In contrast to the positivist approach which seeks an ineffable truth value in empirically verifiable facts, the hagiographers take the Śaṅkara story as true in itself. For the hagiographers what is sacred *is* true. Thus their concern is primarily with locating Śaṅkara in the realm of the sacred (*hagios*). By inserting him into mythic narrative structures Śaṅkara is best placed for attaining identity with the forces of the divine. Moreover, mythography was (and probably remains) a far more potent force than biography in establishing the reputation of a religious leader in India. For this reason, the mythographic perspective from which the Śaṅkara story emerges cannot be ignored. Yet its study poses a serious problem for critical scholars. Since the time of the Enlightenment, European thought has been so thoroughly dominated by a humanistic orientation that it is difficult for contemporary critics to grant an equal place to a perspective in which man is not the object of study. Indeed, my own reading of the hagiographies has not been able to escape some of the positivist perspectives which stubbornly persist in the present day. The narrative structures I examine here are conditioned by a world view in which truth is discovered through the perception of the equivalences that are written into the very nature of things. It is therefore inevitable that my own project will be in some tension with that of the hagiographers.

My primary aim in this study is to consider the ways in which Śaṅkara has been received in India. However, I do not pretend to occupy an objective place, outside the discourse of my own analysis. It is with this in mind that I intentionally speak in the first person. While the texts are necessarily mediated by my own perceptions, I have endeavoured to at least ensure that the primary Sanskrit sources—and what I believe to be *their* concerns—maintain a constant presence throughout this study. The diversity in the eight hagiographies, which are the focal point of my research, makes it possible to measure the texts against each other. While some consideration is given to the evolution of the Śaṅkara story, I have tried to limit the introduction of truth values from outside the texts. For this reason I have, for the most part, refrained from addressing historical questions concerning Śaṅkara's life. Similarly, I do not intend to argue that one text is inherently better than another. Although I have my own aesthetic preferences, I have sought to treat all eight texts as equally valuable examples of the ways in which Śaṅkara has been represented.

This study is organized along the lines of the features which stand out most prominently in the hagiographies. In the first place are the mythic structures which provide not only the peaks but also the foundation of the narrative. Secondly, I have attached much importance to the sense of place and to Śaṅkara's great journey which lends continuity and cohesion to the story. Thirdly, there are the debates through which the wanderings characteristic to a renouncer are transformed into a *digvijaya*, a conquest of the four quarters. It is through the *digvijaya* that Śaṅkara accomplishes his mission of restoring unity to the land. Finally, I have paid special attention to the legacy of Śaṅkara and the continuity of the Advaita tradition (*sampradāya*), particularly with a view to emphasize that this is a living tradition. To this end, I have also included the texts of personal interviews with the current Śaṅkarācāryas. These appear in Appendix A.

In drawing the boundaries of this project, I have had to exclude several important considerations. The sheer volume of the hagiological literature of India—and the fact that it is largely uncharted—posed great difficulties for my research. To define the Śaṅkara hagiographies alone has required much in the way of time and resources. For this reason, I have not attempted comparisons with other hagiographies, even those which called out most loudly for attention, namely the stories of Rāmānuja and Madhva. Similarly, I have decided to leave aside questions in literary criticism. Now Daniel Ingalls has pointed out the imperative to examine the methods and concerns of Sanskrit literary criticism prior to introducing concepts alien to their own cultural milieu.[15] It does appear that the Śaṅkara hagiographers worked within the framework of traditional literary conventions; some of the writers even identify their compositions as *kāvyas*. But it is not at all clear what indigenous critics expected of a hagiography, if it was seen to constitute a recognizable genre at all.

A further problem arises in determining the circumstances surrounding the composition of the Śaṅkara hagiographies. Some seven hundred years elapsed between the death of Śaṅkara and the first appearance of our Sanskrit sources. There must surely have been oral traditions which provided the raw materials for the texts. Comparisons between the hagiographies reveal certain absences which point to the existence of such oral materials. Moreover, there are stories told today which are not found in the existing hagiographies.[16] What was it, then, that

---

15 Daniel H.H. Ingalls, *An Anthology of Sanskrit court poetry: Vidyākara's "Subhāṣitaratnakośa"*. (Harvard Oriental Series, vol. 44. Cambridge, Mass.: Harvard University, 1965), pp. 49-53.

16 The Paramācārya of Kānchipuram relates, for example, the story of how Śaṅkara learned a *mantra* from the toddy tappers which would make a coconut palm bend down. This was how he entered the locked compound of Maṇḍanamiśra (Candraśekharendra Sarasvatī, *Adi Śaṅkara: his life and times*,

prompted a shift from an oral transmission to a written one? This is a question I can only tentatively address. The shape of oral traditions is notoriously difficult to define. The haziness of the frontiers which mark off the earliest hagiographies leaves much uncertainty about the emergence of the written texts as well. Little is known about the authors of what appear to be our oldest sources, the *Śaṅkaravijayas* of Anantānandagiri and Vyāsācala, nor can their dates be specified.

Ancient India provides ample evidence of the power which attaches to oral traditions. Indeed in Hindu culture writing tended to be looked down upon—at least where sacred traditions were concerned—until well after the beginning of the Common Era.[17] It is beyond the scope of this work to explore the larger question of how the book eventually secured a place of respect in many streams of Hinduism. But I will briefly touch upon the fact that this shift is especially conspicuous in the Purāṇas,[18] and that there is a strong connection between the (Śaiva) Purāṇas and the Śaṅkara hagiographies, in terms of content, mood and sometimes even style.[19] I would suggest that the relationship between the Purāṇas and the hagiographies was a bilateral one. If Śaṅkara was to be admitted to the realm of the sacred, there was no better way than via the open-ended traditions of the Purāṇas. On the other hand, the Purāṇas were probably a major factor in encouraging the composition of the Śaṅkara hagiographies.

---

tr. T.M.P. Mahadevan [(1980). Reprinted, Bombay: Bharatiya Vidya Bhavan, 1988]), p. 159.

17 For a survey of the discussion on the subject see C. Mackenzie Brown, "Purāṇa as scripture: from sound to image of the holy word in the Hindu tradition", *History of Religions* 26 (1986), pp. 68-86.

18 *Ibid*., p. 71.

19 This is discussed in conjunction with the examination of the eight individual hagiographies in Chapter One.

The nexus of this relationship derived primarily from the *bhakti* traditions, and to a lesser extent from the notion of the book. It is in the Purāṇas that the (ritually pure) *bhakti* cults found their legitimacy, as well as their medium of propagation. So pervasive were the currents of *bhakti* that even the Advaita *sampradāya* could not but imbibe some of this devotional fervour. Theirs was an ascetic tradition. While Viṣṇu was not necessarily excluded, Śiva, the lord of ascetics, was the more likely focus of devotion. The great teacher in the Advaita *sampradāya* who bore the name of Śaṅkara was a logical link between the divine and mortal realms. In this way he became a figure of devotion. Still more equivalences came into play. The hagiographies devote much attention to establishing the connection between Śaṅkara and Vyāsa. The two actually meet on one or more occasions in all versions of the narrative. According to the Advaita tradition, Vyāsa composed the *Brahmasūtra*. In the hagiographies it is he who must approve Śaṅkara's authoritative commentary on the work. As the figure of Vyāsa is indistinguishable from the sacred texts he is believed to have written, so too, the person of Śaṅkara is identitified, and eventually merges with the sacred texts on which he has commented. Vyāsa is of course traditionally regarded as the author of the great Purāṇas. Although the hagiographies do not emphasize this aspect in demonstrating his connection with Śaṅkara,[20] the association implicitly brings Śaṅkara further within the ambit of the Purāṇas.

---

20 This is because they are classed as *smṛti* and as such must remain subservient to the *śruti*, which is Śaṅkara's primary concern. The *Brahmasūtra* constitutes a rather special case. Although it too is a *smṛti* work, it gains a greater place in that it is a concordance of the Upaniṣads. Nevertheless, the hagiographers seek to establish Śaṅkara as an authority figure in the Purāṇa tradition by portraying his reorganization of the devotional cults. This is discussed in Chapter Six.

The notion that a Purāṇa is a sacred substance, in the form of a book, may well have been an impetus for the mythographers to give substance to the Śaṅkara story. Several Purāṇas proclaim the merit which accrues from both the copying and making a gift of the text.[21] These are not only pious actions but an expression of devotion towards the deity who is glorified in the text. By analogy, one who writes, recites or copies the text of the Śaṅkara story performs the worship of Śiva/Śaṅkara. In this way, the text became a means of spiritual practice. Since Śaṅkara was seen to be an embodiment of Śiva,[22] the composition of the text which would tell his story was the equivalent of sculpting a holy image. (But with the brahmin orientation of the Advaita tradition, the writer's tools were the more viable medium of expression). Some of the hagiographies are structured in a manner which is conducive to a daily reading. One of the texts makes it explicit that the recitation of its contents, preferably as a daily practice, helped to remove the perception of duality.[23] The identification of

---

21 C. Mackenzie Brown, "Purāṇa as scripture", p. 77-78.

22 It is not clear when this first happened. Paul Hacker has described the striking Vaiṣṇava characteristics prevalent in the earliest period of the Śaṅkara tradition, "Relations of early Advaitins to Vaiṣṇavism", *Wiener Zeitschrift für die Kunde Süd- und Ostasiens* 9 (1965), pp. 147-154. But the obvious connection between Śiva and Śaṅkara has been made since the time in which Padmapāda's *Pañcapādikā* was composed. In the third introductory verse of the *Pañcapādikā*, Śaṅkara is praised in an elaborate figure of speech, a *viruddha-śleṣa*, which suggests that he is and yet is not Śiva himself: "I salute the incomparable Śaṅkara who is not possessed of serpent coverings, who is bereft of ashes, who does not have a body half of which is [comprised of] Umā, who is not terrible, whose dark blue marking is erased and who is not together with Vināyaka", *namāmy abhogi-parivāra-sampadaṃ nirasta-bhūtim anumārdha-vigraham / anugram unmṛdita-kāla-lāñchanaṃ vināvināyakam apūrva-śaṅkaram //.*

23 *Śrī Śaṅkaravijayavilāsa by Cidvilāsa-muni*. Edited by W.R. Antarkar. *Bhāratīya Vidyā* 33 (1973), pp. 1-92, verse 4.55.

Śaṅkara with the substance of the sacred texts is apparent in the way later Advaitins tend to refer to him as simply the *bhāṣya-kāra*, the author of the commentary (on the *Brahmasūtra*). Moreover, his exegetical efforts required the medium of the book. The commentaries were far too complex for an exclusively oral composition and transmission. Śaṅkara is a writer of texts. Therefore, his is a life which should be written.

Thus far I have spoken only of some of the religious conceptions which were fundamental to the writing of Śaṅkara's life. The texts were also the product of powerful political influences. The emergence of the hagiographies seems to correspond directly to the rise of the Śaṅkara institutions.[24] The most prominent of these was the monastic centre (*maṭha*) at Sringerī, which was patronized by, and closely allied to the Vijayanagara kings. But not enough is known about the early history of Sringerī—and still less about the other Śaṅkara *maṭhas*—to provide precise definitions of the relationship between the institutions and the texts. One thing is certain however. The stories which glorified Śaṅkara would well serve the interests of the *maṭhas*. The institutions could only stand to benefit from the prestige accruing to the deified figure of the man who was perhaps the outstanding teacher and writer in their ascetic lineage. It would be better still if the stories were embodied in written form. The written text surpasses the oral one as a medium for the edicts of an institution. The text would also take its place along with the costly ritual objects which were a sign of the power inherent in the *maṭha*. Once the institutions made him an object of adoration, the name Śaṅkara began to resound in the air. The learned ones outside the *maṭhas* would soon hear the call, and the poet would find in him the stuff of a mythic drama.

---

24 This is discussed in detail in Chapters Six and Seven.

There was possibly an even more urgent need for the Śaṅkara story to be written, in the face of attacks from the Madhva sect which had broken away from the fold of Advaita. There are two hagiographies of Madhva, whose colophons state that they were composed by the son of his direct disciple.[25] These texts require careful examination to determine their precise position in their own tradition and *vis à vis* the Advaita *sampradāya*. But I must leave this task for a separate study. Suffice it to say that the Madhva hagiographies make a vicious attack on Śaṅkara's reputation, as well as that of a later Advaitin, whom they refer to as Padmatīrtha. The proximity of Uḍupi, the centre of the Madhva cult, to the Advaita stronghold at Sringerī, made it almost inevitable that conflict between the two would arise.

The immediate political issues which encouraged the writing of the Śaṅkara story were, in the hands of the hagiographers, the base metals to be transmuted into the purer form of myth. Therefore, the hero would appear as a divine *avatāra* and his quest would take the shape of a *digvijaya*, through which the primordial unity of the golden age would be restored. From well before the time of Śaṅkara, the *avatāra* and the *digvijaya* were paradigms of royalty that were invoked to legitimize imperial rule.[26] The fact that these conceptual structures are an integral part of the Śaṅkara story reflects the interrelationship of royal and ascetic models. These complementary values are also responsible for the rendering of Śaṅkara's figure in the mould of an austere, conquering hero.

---

25 *Maṇimañjarī by Nārāyaṇa-paṇḍita*. Edited by T.R. Kṛṣṇācārya. Bombay: Nirṇayasāgara Press, *śaka* 1834 [=1912], and *Sumadhvavijaya by Nārāyaṇa-paṇḍita.* Edited by T.R. Kṛṣṇācārya Bombay: Nirṇayasāgara Press, *śaka* 1834 [=1912].

26 Ronald Inden demonstrates the special importance of the *digvijaya* to the formation of imperial kingdoms in his *Imagining India*, (Oxford and Cambridge, Mass.: Basil Blackwell, 1990), pp. 228-262.

There is little place for tenderness or human warmth in such a narrative. Although the writing of the hagiographies is an expression of *bhakti*, it is an austere devotion. The rich emotional expression which is characteristic to the description of the Vaiṣṇava saints—and even to the stories of the Śaiva Nāyaṉārs—is largely absent from the Śaṅkara hagiographies.

In the narrative structure within which the life of the royal hero was invariably set, the only leading female role was that of Rājyaśrī, the personification of regal glory.[27] V. S. Pathak has described two possible unfoldings of this narrative.[28] In the one, the world conqueror (*cakravartin*) seizes the princess, who is actually the goddess of royal fortune, from a rival king. However, in the more common pattern it is the goddess herself who chooses the one who would be king. The writers of the Śaṅkara story embraced both possibilites. The goddess was cast not as Rājya-Lakṣmī but as Sarasvatī. This modification was essential because Śaṅkara's quest was for the throne of omniscience, and this could be obtained only through winning over the goddess of learning. While Śaṅkara does not overtly seize the goddess, he does defeat his leading rival, Maṇḍanamiśra, who is her husband. True to the terms of the contest, Maṇḍanamiśra must abandon his wife to become an ascetic follower of Śaṅkara. The extent that she now belongs to Śaṅkara is shown by those hagiographers who relate how he bids her to follow him to Sringerī, where he instals her as the presiding deity of the temple. The motif of the bride's choice is developed in the incident in which Sarasvatī herself tests Śaṅkara's intellectual strength in debate. It is only upon her acknowledgement of his superiority that Śaṅkara is permitted to ascend to the throne of omniscience.

---

27 See V.S. Pathak, *Ancient historians of India: a study in historical biographies* (Bombay: Asia Publishing House, 1966), pp. 27-28; 49-50.

28 *Ibid*., pp. 74-75.

Although she is kept hidden from the public gaze, within the temple's inner sanctum, the goddess exerts a powerful force upon the Śaṅkara tradition. She is worshipped by the Śaṅkarācāryas today as Śāradā, Kāmākṣī and Rājarājeśvarī. The metaphysics of the Advaita *sampradāya* remain non-dualistic;[29] the ritual practice still conforms to Vedic norms. But in this exclusively male ascetic order there is a place for tantric worship, albeit very chaste, and the mystic union of the sexes. The hagiographies provide intriguing glimpses of the private sphere, wherein the Devī resides. A remarkable, little known incident related in the *Guruvaṃśakāvya*, tells of Śaṅkara's visit to the goddess Siddheśvarī in Nepal. Hers was a living presence which welcomed him immediately he arrived:

> Sitting the *muni* on her lap, she touched him, as though he was Skanda, with words which were like nectar. The group of *siddha*s [living there], who looked on with jealousy, showered stones upon them. The efforts of the *siddha*s were in vain. The yogi stopped their shower, warding off the stones which surrounded them. Even now she appears there in splendour. Then, being thirsty, he begged Siddheśvarī sweetly for buttermilk (*takra*), as though she was his mother. She produced a river of buttermilk, which burst forth from her thigh. That [river] is famous even now as the Takrā.[30]

I leave this episode without comment as an example of the wealth of materials the hagiographies have to offer, and as an open invitation for further exploration of the Śaṅkara story.

---

[29] In the course of personal interviews, I questioned the Śaṅkarācāryas about this, and the special place of the Devī in the Advaita tradition. Their answers appear in Appendix A.

[30] *Guruvaṃśakāvyam by Kāśī Lakṣmaṇa-Śāstrī* (Śrīraṅgam: Śrī Vāṇīvilās Press, 1966), 3.64-66.

CHAPTER I

Sources for the Life of Śaṅkara

It is an appropriate irony that the foremost exponent of nondualist metaphysics left behind few, if any, clues about his life. He scarcely refers to himself in his works. We learn only that they are composed by Śaṅkara, a pupil of Govindapāda. His direct disciples give us virtually no specific details about him. He was not, so far as we know, associated either with a particular place or an important king. Hence he does not figure in any inscriptions, [1] and we are left without a historical frame of reference for his life.

What we do know about Śaṅkara is that he is the author of commentaries on ten of the older Upaniṣads, the *Bhagavadgītā* and the *Brahmasūtras* His are the oldest extant commentaries on these fundamental texts. Such was the importance of his work that most of the later commentators were compelled to refer to him. Of the remaining three hundred odd works traditionally ascribed to Śaṅkara, very few are likely to be his own

---

1 There is a Cambodian inscription, dated 877/878 A.D., concerning the foundation of a Śiva temple by King Indravarman, who had a teacher (*ācārya*) named Śivasoma. This Śivasoma is said to have learned the *śāstras* from Bhagavat Śaṅkara, and to have also had a teacher (*śāsaka*) named Bhagavat Rudra. In his discussion of the inscription, G. Coèdes remarks: "Il n'est pas impossible qu'il s'agisse du célèbre Śaṅkarācārya dont l'activité dans l'Inde se place au début du IX e siècle." Although this is certainly possible, it would be difficult to prove that the inscription refers to one and the same Śaṅkara. Like the reference to a teacher named Rudra, who is not known as a contemporary of *the* Śaṅkara, it may be that Śivasoma learned from two Śaiva teachers, who were both designated with names of Śiva. See G. Coèdes, *Inscriptions du Cambodge*, vol. 1, (Collection de textes et documents sur l'Indochine III, Hanoi: École Française d'Extrême-Orient, 1937), pp. 37-46.

compositions. But one major independent treatise, the *Upadeśasāhasrī*, has been proved an authentic work.[2] This text and the commentaries comprise a substantial and coherent body of work from which we can derive a clear picture of the nature of Śaṅkara's thought, but not of his life.

There remains some uncertainty even about Śaṅkara's dates, which can be fixed only in relation to other important figures. In the *Upadeśasāhasrī*, he cites a passage from Dharmakīrti (600-660), which defines his earliest limits. His upper limits are fixed by Vācaspatimiśra (active c. 840) who wrote a subcommentary on Śaṅkara's *Brahmasūtra-bhāṣya.* For some time, many scholars have held that Śaṅkara lived from 788-820 A.D.[3] It was on this understanding that the Indian government sponsored a year long tribute—the *Rāṣṭrīya Śaṅkara Jayantī Mahotsav*, which began in April 1988—to commemorate the twelve hundredth anniversary of his birth. Hajime Nakamura has sparked some reappraisals in proposing to push back Śaṅkara's dates to the period 700-750.[4] But more recently, Tilmann Vetter has maintained that we can claim only that his

---

[2] Sengaku Mayeda, "The authenticity of the Upadeśasāhasrī ascribed to Śaṅkara", *JAOS*, 85 (1965), 178-196. For discussion on the authenticity of Śaṅkara's commentaries, see the studies of Paul Hacker and Sengaku Mayeda, cited in the Bibiliography.

[3] See K. Kunjunni Raja, "On the date of Śaṅkarācārya and allied problems", *ALB*, 24 (1960), 125-148, and Allen Thrasher, "The dates of Maṇḍana Miśra and Śaṃkara", *WZKS*, 23 (1979), 117-139.

[4] Hajime Nakamura, *A History of Early Vedānta Philosophy*, tr. Trevor Leggett et. al. (Delhi: Motilal Banarsidass, 1983, [first published in Japanese, 1950-56]), p. 87. His suggestions have been accepted by Karl Potter, *Encyclopedia of Indian Philosophies. [vol. 3] Advaita Vedānta up to Śaṃkara and his Pupils* (Princeton: Princeton University, 1981), p.18, and also by Daniel H. H. Ingalls, "Śaṃkara's arguments against the Buddhists", *PEW*, 3 (1954), p. 292n.

dates fall somewhere within the period 650-800.[5] Even in traditional circles, there is some disagreement on this matter. There are, at present, five major *maṭha*s, i.e., monastic centres, which trace their lineage directly back to Śaṅkara. The present pontiff of the Sringerī Śaṅkara *maṭha* holds that he lived about twelve hundred years ago. However, the heads of the Dwārkā and Kānchipuram *maṭha*s claim that Śaṅkara was born in 509 B.C.[6]

There are some twenty accounts of Śaṅkara's life extant in Sanskrit (see bibliography for details). These sources certainly do not take what could be regarded as an historical approach to Śaṅkara's life. Instead, they seek to glorify him by recounting numerous miraculous phenomena, and deify him as an *avatāra* of Śiva. If they are to be assigned to a literary genre, one would have to say that they are hagiographies, not biographies. It must also be noted that none of these works are known to have been composed prior to the 14th century. The task of determining the extent to which these sources—composed some seven hundred years or more after Śaṅkara's life—represent actual historical details seems a rather hopeless one. It is understandable that historians have despaired at the utility of the Śaṅkara hagiographies. In fact, the reaction of scholars outside

---

5 *Studien zur Lehre und Entwicklung Śaṅkaras* (Publications of the De Nobili Research Library, vol. 6, Vienna: Indological Institute University of Vienna, 1979), p.11.

6 Personal interview with H. H. Śrī Abhinavavidyātīrtha Bhāratī in Sringerī, on 4 January 1989. When I told him of my plan to meet the Dwārkā *ācārya* (H.H. Svāmī Svarūpānanda) after leaving Sringerī, he commented "You will find that he does not agree with us on Śaṅkara's date, he holds it to be 509 B.C." The date of Śaṅkara's birth is also given as 509 B.C. in A. Nataraja Aiyer and S. Lakshminarasimha Sastri, *The traditional age of Sri Sankaracharya and the maths* ([1962] Madras: Rajan and Co., 1988), p. 143, written under the auspices of the Kānchipuram Śaṅkara *maṭha*.

of India to these texts has, with few exceptions, been rather negative.[7]

Indian historians and philosophers have generally paid scant attention to the Śaṅkara hagiographies[8]. However, there is in India a large body of literature, written for the most part by non-academics, concerning these texts.[9] Their primary aim is

---

[7] Mario Piantelli in his *Śaṅkara e la rinascita del Brāhmanismo* (Fossano: Editrice Esperienze, 1974) provides an extensive summary of Śaṅkara's life, with reference to eight hagiographies. Because he is primarily concerned with providing an overview of Śaṅkara's life and thought, Piantelli has not examined the hagiographies themselves. Other scholars have, for the most part, restricted themselves to one source, the ŚDV. David Lorenzen has written a very useful, but brief study based primarily on the ŚDV: "The life of Śaṅkarācārya", in *Experiencing Śiva: encounters with a Hindu deity*, ed. Fred W. Clothey and J. Bruce Long (Colombia, Mo., 1983), pp. 155-175. Karl Potter has responded strongly to this article, and more generally, against giving credence to the hagiographies, "Śaṃkarācārya: the myth and the man", *Journal of the American Academy of Religion. Thematic Studies*, 48 (1982), 111-125. Phyllis Granoff has examined the ŚDV in two studies on Sanskrit hagiography: "Holy warriors: a preliminary study of some biographies of saints and kings in the classical Indian tradition", *JIP*, 12 (1984), 291-303, and "Scholars and wonder workers: some remarks on the role of the supernatural in philosophical contests and Vedānta hagiographies", *JAOS*, 105 (1985), 459-467. Yoshitsugu Sawai has discussed the image of Śaṅkara in the ŚDV in "The faith of ascetics and lay Smārtas: a study of the Śaṅkaran tradition of Śṛṅgerī", Ph.D. thesis, Harvard University, Cambridge, Mass., 1984.

[8] Among the very few critical works on Śaṅkara's life by academics in India is the lengthy Hindī study by Baldev Upādhyāy, *Śrī Śaṅkarācārya. Śrī Śaṅkarācārya ke jīvancarita tathā upadeśoṃ kā prāmāṇika vivaraṇa* (Allahabad: Hindustānī Ekeḍemī, 1950).

[9] These works display a peculiar combination of affirmation and denial of the validity of historical sources. The writers tend to appeal to history when the data proves amenable to their viewpoint, but place an equal reliance on tradition when historical evidence is lacking or unfavourable. See especially T. S. Narayana Sastry, *The Age of Śaṅkara* ([1916], reprinted Madras: B.G. Paul, 1971).

in furthering the claims of one Śaṅkara *maṭha* against another. For them, the texts become sources of authority on which to base claims regarding the nature and relative standing of the *maṭhas*. Hence, we find attempts to demonstrate that Śaṅkara did, or did not, as the case may be, leave his mortal frame at Kānchipuram; that he did, or did not, establish four *maṭhas*, etc. I do not wish to enter into such disputes, nor would I wish to argue that the Śaṅkara hagiographies should be construed as historical sources.

If we can agree to forgo the search for the historical context of Śaṅkara's life and the expectation that we may discover biographical details which will illumine our understanding of his work, we may indeed find that the Śaṅkara hagiographies have other rewards to offer us. In the first instance, we can expect that our stories of Śaṅkara must, like any good story, capture the imagination of the reader, if they are to succeed. Our accounts are, after all, primarily literary works and can be enjoyed as such. But there is no dearth of material in the hagiographies conducive to a serious study of the way in which Śaṅkara is received in India. Our texts have moulded the raw materials of oral traditions and recast the outlines of earlier sources in creating the legendary life stories by which Śaṅkara is now known in India. Moreover, the texts provide us with valuable insights into important conceptual models in traditional Hindu thought.

I must reiterate that in this study the accounts of Śaṅkara's life are not seen as histories. By this, I do not mean to suggest that ancient India is without a true history, nor that Indians fail to represent themselves as historical entities. Rather, I would urge that we must sometimes go beyond the sense of complacency we feel when we can accurately define dates and draw up elaborate historical schemas. There are certain significances which remain elusive to purely empirical perceptions. The human spirit can ill afford to lose touch with symbols, myths and legends.

The Principal Sanskrit Hagiographies

While it does not strike me as a fruitful enterprise to construe the stories of Śaṅkara's life in terms of their historicity, I do think some purpose may be served in an analytical examination of the texts themselves. In particular I would like to establish, insofar as it is possible, the nature of the relationship between some of the Sanskrit texts which are the primary sources for the legendary life of Śaṅkara.

Our study of the Śaṅkara hagiographies is much indebted to W. R. Antarkar who has made these texts his life study. He has located six previously unknown manuscripts, three of which he has edited and published. He has also brought out an edition of the CŚV, which had hitherto been virtually unavailable in print. In his unpublished thesis he has described twenty texts which recount the life of Śaṅkara.[10] Antarkar's invaluable contribution in the collection and description of these texts has been the very basis on which I have begun this study. But insofar as his primary aim has been to examine the texts in terms of their authenticity as historical sources for the life of Śaṅkara, I have had to turn away and follow a different approach. Of the twenty Śaṅkara hagiographies, one text, the *Śaṅkaradigvijaya*, has come to completely overshadow the rest. Indeed most references nowadays to Śaṅkara's life, whether

---

[10] W. R. Antarkar, "Śaṅkara-Vijayas: a comparative and critical study", University of Poona, 1960. He has published three articles, based on the thesis: (1) "Bṛhat-Śaṅkara-Vijaya of Citsukhācārya and Prācīna-Śaṅkara-Vijaya of Ānandagiri A/S Ānanda-Jñāna", *JUB*, 29 (1960), 113-121; (2) "Śaṅkara-Vijaya of Anantānandagiri", *JUB*, 30 (1961), 73-80; (3) "Saṅkṣepa Śaṅkara Jaya of Mādhavācārya or Śaṅkara Digvijaya of Śrī Vidyāraṇyamuni", *JUB*, 41 (1972), 1-23.

scholarly or popular, are based solely on the ŚDV. Once this version of Śaṅkara's life had established its reputation, perhaps towards the end of the eighteenth century, subsequent writers were satisfied to largely restate its contents.[11] For this reason, and for the sake of convenience, I have used the ŚDV as the cut off point, which limits to eight the number of Sanskrit sources which will be examined here.

Of these works, the four earlier ones are extremely difficult to date, even in relation to one another. In the case of three of them—the AŚV, CŚV and TŚA—it will be shown that they were probably not composed prior to the 14th century. The other early work, the VŚV, has little in the way of specific details which would allow us to fix its date. Yet there is no reason to assume that it is earlier than the 14th century, either. There is a definite, athough somewhat complex, relationship between the eight texts. In contrast to Antarkar's attempts to establish a linear chronology of the texts,[12] I have sought to define the nature of the relationship between the texts. This can be seen in the following table.

---

11 There are two exceptions. The *Ācārya-digvijaya-campu*, by Vallīsahāya (MSS. held in the Sarasvati Mahal Library, Thanjavur, and the Madras Government Oriental MSS. Library), closely follows the AŚV, according to Antarkar (Thesis, p. 39). He places the work at the end of the 19th century. The second exception is the *Bṛhacchaṅkaravijaya* by Brahmānanda Sarasvatī. Antarkar inspected the single MS. at the home of its owner in Kumbakonam. From Antarkar's description of the text, it is clear that its extensive and idiosyncratic elaboration of stories is outside of the MS. traditions to which the other hagiographies belong.

12 He places the texts in the following sequence of priority: (1) the no longer extant BṛŚV, (2) the no longer extant PrŚV, (3) AŚV, (4) VŚV, (5) CŚV, (6) GŚC, (7) TŚA, (8) RŚA, (9) ŚDV, (10) Sadānanda's *Śaṅkara-digvijayasāra*, (11) GVK. (W. R. Antarkar, Thesis, pp. 89-95). Sadānanda's work is not considered in this study because it is largely derivative of the ŚDV. The two no longer extant texts are discussed in Appendix B.

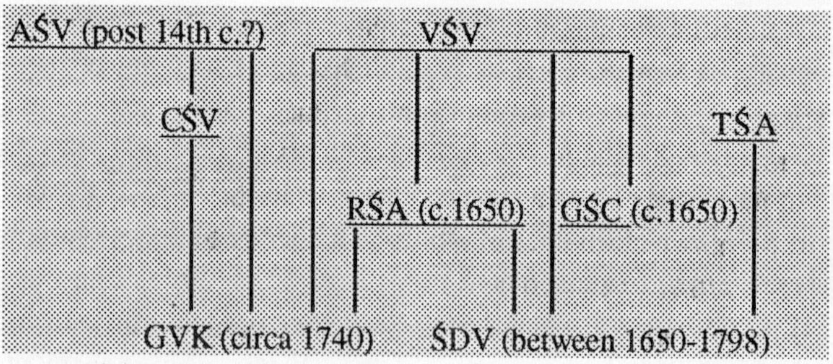

AŚV Anantānandagiri's *Śaṅkaravijaya*
20 MSS., 3 printed editions-prose/verse, 74 chs, 209pp.

CŚV Cidvilāsa's *Śaṅkaravijaya-vilāsa*
4 MSS., 2 printed editions, 1655 verses, 32 chapters

VŚV Vyāsācala's *Śaṅkaravijaya*
6 MSS., 1 printed edition, 1191 verses, 12 chapters

RŚA Rājacūḍāmaṇi-Dīkṣita's *Śaṅkarābhyudaya*
4 MSS., 2 printed editions, 552 verses, 8 chapters

GŚC Govindanātha's *Śaṅkarācāryacarita*
3 MSS., 2 printed editions, 549 verses, 9 chapters

TŚA Tirumala-Dīkṣita's *Śaṅkarābhyudaya*
1 MS.(incomplete), 1 ed., 634 verses, 7 chapters

GVK Lakṣmaṇa-Śāstrī's *Guruvaṃśa-kāvya*
1 MS., 2 printed editions, 205 verses, 3 chapters

ŚDV Mādhava's *Śaṅkaradigvijaya*
30 MSS., 3 printed editions, 1834 verses, 16 chapters

The AŚV and CŚV are clearly related in that they share some common verses and contain similar descriptions of several major episodes in Śaṅkara's life. It is likely that the AŚV is the earlier of the two compositions because it is lacking a number of incidents which occur in the CŚV. There is no indication that either of the authors of these two texts were aware of the existence of the VŚV. Similarly, there is no evidence that Vyāsācala, the author of the VŚV, knew of the AŚV or CŚV. Nor can we tell what sources Vyāsācala did draw upon. But the influence of the VŚV on the four later texts is readily apparent. Vyāsācala is openly acknowledged in the GŚC, which closely follows his work. Mādhava, the author of the ŚDV, actually incorporates some five hundred verses from the VŚV into his own work. It is most probable that the authors of the RŚA and GVK also had the VŚV before them, for they follow much of the material in this older work. The TŚA stands very much apart from the three other earlier sources, with which it holds little in common. Its relationship is only with the later ŚDV which has borrowed nearly five hundred of its verses.

In addition to the problems in dating the hagiographies, there are difficulties in determining their place of origin. It is only possible to locate with certainty the places in which three of the hagiographies were composed. Govindanātha, the author of the GŚC, lived in south Kerala. Rājacūḍāmaṇi-Dīkṣita, who wrote the RŚA, was attached to the court at Thanjāvūr (Tamil Nadu). Although he does not mention his own native place, Lakṣmaṇa-Śāstrī states that he composed the GVK at the behest of an incumbent *ācārya* at the Sringerī *maṭha* (Karnataka). Geographical references in the other five texts suggest that their authors were all resident, at least for some time, in south India. A detailed consideration of the individual texts and their authors follows.

1. Anantānandagiri's *Śaṅkaravijaya* (AŚV)

The influence of this work is second only to that of the ŚDV in the number and distribution of manuscripts throughout India. The Paramācārya of the Śaṅkara *maṭha* at Kānchipuram held it to be the best account of Śaṅkara's life.[13] A good deal is known about this text. But many questions remain, especially in regard to the identity of its author and his date. The first printed edition of the work was brought out in 1868 in Calcutta.[14] Another almost identical edition was published in Calcutta in 1881.[15] Both the Calcutta publications give the author's name as Ānandagiri, despite the fact that the author identifies himself as Anantānandagiri in the opening verse and colophons. A third edition was prepared by N. Veezhinathan, at Madras University in 1971, on the basis of 16 manuscripts and the 1881 Calcutta text. (My citations of the AŚV follow this edition unless noted otherwise). Although the Madras edition attributes the work to Anantānandagiri, T. M. P. Mahadevan, who contributes a lengthy introduction, tries to leave open the possibility that Anantānandagiri may be identical to Ānandagiri.

A good part of the confusion about the author's identity stems from the opening lines of the AŚV: "I, Anantānandagiri, a disciple of Bhagavat, whose commands are without

---

13 Personal interview at Kanchipuram, 18 December 1988. See Appendix A for further details.

14 Ānandagiri, *The Śaṅkaravijaya, or the life and polemics of Śaṅkara Ācharyya*, ed. Jayanārāyaṇa Tarkapañcānana ("Bibliotheca Indica" series, no. 46, Calcutta: Baptist Mission Press, 1868; reprinted Osnabrück: Biblio Verlag, 1982). The edition was prepared on the basis of three MSS., in three different scripts: Devanāgarī, Telugu and Bengali.

15 Ānandagiri, *Śaṅkaravijaya*, ed. Jīvānanda Vidyāsāgara Bhaṭṭācārya (Calcutta: Sārasudhānidhi Press, 1881). It is virtually the same as the 1868 edition, save that it has been reset, without the variants.

impediment, shall describe the purpose of the advent of my *paramaguru*".[16] This could be easily understood to imply that the author is a direct disciple of Śaṅkara. But there is no reason why we need assume that the term *paramaguru* refers to the actual guru of the writer. He may simply be referring to Śaṅkara as a supreme guru in the Advaita lineage, to which he too belongs. There is, of course, a renowned commentator on Śaṅkara's work named Ānandagiri, who probably lived in the latter part of the 13th century.[17] In some of the colophons of his works, Ānandagiri cites his guru's name as Śuddhānanda. According to tradition, Śuddhānanda is the guru of the commentator, Ānanadagiri, although both are believed to have lived closer to Śaṅkara's time. If this same Ānandagiri is taken to be the author of the AŚV, it is not possible—on either historical or traditional grounds—to claim that he was a direct disciple of Śaṅkara.[18]

The attempts to identify Anantānandagiri with the commentator Ānandagiri can be dismissed on two accounts. In the first instance, the level of philosophical discussion which is maintained in the AŚV rarely reflects the considerable scholarship of the learned commentator, Ānandagiri. It is possible that the author of the AŚV intentionally limited the depth of philosophical argument so as not to make the work inaccessible to a wider audience. But, to cite just one objection,

---

16 *anantānandagirir aham apratihatājñasya bhagavataḥ śiṣyaḥ* [sic] *mama paramaguror avatāra-prayojanaṃ varṇayāmi*, p. 1 (Madras edition).

17 *New Catalogus Catalogorum*, vol. 2, Madras, 1966, pp. 99-100.

18 Moreover, it is risky to jump to conclusions about the identity of the author, or the names of Śaṅkara's direct disciples, just on the basis of the text. For the AŚV refers in one place to Śuddhānantānandagiri as a direct disciple of Śaṅkara (p.17, Madras ed.). Do we take this person to be the same as Śuddhānanda, Ānandagiri or Anantānandagiri? There is also a reference to Anantānandagiri being a direct disciple (ch. 66, p.189). Are we to understand that this is the author?

it is difficult to imagine how someone who has commented on Śaṅkara's *Brahmasūtra-bhāṣya*, in which certain Buddhist views are fairly well represented, would present such a vague account of a Buddhist opponent.[19] Secondly, as K. T. Telang has shown,[20] the author of the AŚV quotes from the *Vaiyāsika-nyāya-mālā*. This text is attributed to Bhāratītīrtha, who lived in the 14th century.[21] While we can reasonably accept this as the earliest possible date for the AŚV, we can only speculate that Anantānandagiri may have composed the work not long after the time of Bhāratītīrtha.

There seems no reason to doubt that Anantānandagiri was a *saṃnyāsin* in the Śaṅkara lineage. It is likely that he had strong affiliations with Kānchipuram in Tamil Nadu. For in the AŚV, this city looms large in Śaṅkara's life. Anantānandagiri relates Śaṅkara's foundation of what are actually adjacent cities, Śiva-kāñcī and Viṣṇu-kāñcī. He is said to have consecrated a *śrī-cakra* there, and set up a *maṭha* as well. Still more significant is the author's portrayal of Kānchipuram as Śaṅkara's final earthly abode. Anantānandagiri's primary concern is in depicting Śaṅkara's successful establishment of Advaita-Vedānta as the pre-eminent traditional doctrine of India: "he made all the brahmins and the rest [of the twice-born] who inhabit the lands

---

19 See AŚV ch. 28.

20 "The Śaṅkaravijaya of Ānandagiri", *Indian Antiquary*, 5 (1876), 287-293.

21 The *Vaiyāsika-nyāya-mālā* has been published as an appendix to the Bibliotheca Indica edition of the Brahmasūtras, *The aphorisms of the Vedānta*, by Bādarāyaṇa, Calcutta 1863 (reprinted Osnabrück: Biblio Verlag, 1981), under the title *Vyāsādhikaraṇamālā*. The work consists of a series of verses, with commentary, which summarises the discussion in the *Brahmasūtras*. Since there is no colophon citing the author of this work, the editor's attribution of the work to Bhāratītīrtha is presumably on the basis of the first verse in which the author pays his respects to Vidyātīrtha. The AŚV quotes a verse concerning BS 1.1.1 from this work in chapter 11 (p. 69, Madras ed.) and another on BS 3.4.23 in chapter 47 (p. 160).

from Rameśvara to the Himālayas and in between, highly prized for their devotion to pure Advaita".[22] We see this accomplished through his debates with more than fifty opponents belonging to as many different sects. The description of these disputations occupies 48 of the 74 chapters comprising the work. Several other chapters focus just on Śaṅkara's exposition of Advaita. There is not much emphasis on his life story. Indeed, there is far less than in the other seven sources. In chapter three, for example, nearly five and a half pages are devoted to a description of the precocious teachings of the eight year old Śaṅkara. Yet the events which precipitate his leaving home to find his guru, Govindapāda, are dispensed with in just a few lines:

> Renouncing [worldly life] when he reached his eighth year, on account of the seizure by the crocodile in the river which flowed near to his village, and departing from his village, called Kālaṭi, he arrived at the illustrious Vyāghrapura [i.e., Chidambaram]. In that place, the all-knowing Śrīmat Śaṅkara-Bhagavatpādācārya was accepted [as fit to enter] the stage of the *paramahaṃsa* because of the true teachings of Govinda, chief of yogis.[23]

The remainder of the chapter concerns itself with a discussion on the justification of renunciation, normally the fourth and final stage of life, directly from the first stage, studentship. There is no further description of what transpired between Śaṅkara and his guru. This also suggests that the story of Śaṅkara's life must have been sufficiently well known by the time of Anantānandagiri so that he could, in good conscience, abbreviate these events.

---

22 p. 194, last two lines.

23 p. 16, lines 3-6.

A brief look at the catalogue of opponents in its table of contents might lead one to expect the AŚV to be largely philosophically oriented. This is not the case. The AŚV was clearly composed for a wider audience. There is more emphasis on the behaviour and dress of the opponents than their doctrines. What *is* described about their doctrines probably reflects a popular understanding of their views. For it is often difficult to identify their views with reference to the authoritative texts of their respective sects. Śaṅkara is not depicted here with the sense of decorum he maintains throughout his attacks on rival philosophical viewpoints in his own compositions. Instead he is shown to take an approach more likely to appeal to a more general audience. While the opponents are, for the most part, shown to address him politely, Śaṅkara treats them with some disdain. A good illustration of this occurs in his meeting with a Vaiṣṇava *bhakta*, who engages in simple devotional practices, without following any of the obligatory Vedic ritual. Śaṅkara asks him:

> "How many years have you been remaining in such a state, Viṣṇuśarman?" He said," I heard in my childhood that seven generations[24] have been like me [but] my forefather prior to that was somewhat disposed to ritual duty." Having heard that, he who is the all-guru, feeling distressed from anger and astonishment, said to Viṣṇuśarman, "Get away from me". [Viṣṇuśarman,] whose mind was filled with anguish, saying, 'please forgive all my offences' made a full prostration and stood rigid, his hands cupped together [in supplication], along with his attendants. Thinking, with compassion, 'I should protect Viṣṇuśarman who has come for refuge, even though he is attached to the wrong path', he commanded his disciples, Hastāmalaka and

24 This is a tentative translation for *saptama-puruṣaḥ*.

> the rest, in regard to carrying out the ritual atonement (*prāyaścitta*) for him and his attendants.[25]

But Śaṅkara is only occasionally shown to manifest such compassion. More often he refers to his opponents as fools (*mūḍha*). Sometimes Anantānandagiri himself interjects a few derisive comments: "Then a Saugata with a fat body and a tiny head said to Śaṅkara..." [26]

Anantānandagiri does betray a marked sympathy for the Śaiva opponents. They are the first to be met by Śaṅkara in debate, and they are permitted to expound their arguments at greater length than any of the other sects. Śaṅkara must patiently listen to an extensive doctrinal exposition from the first of his Śaiva opponents which takes up nine full pages of text. When he is at last allowed to reply, Śaṅkara says:

> Those *śrutis* which you recited are also recited by me, because their purport is one [and the same]. But this much is contrary, being without the authority [of *śruti*], i.e., the [sectarian] marking of the branded *liṅga* which must be worn [in your sect]...For one whose body has been purified by correct *dharma*, which begins with the *garbhādhāna* rite, as is stated in the Vedas and is customary for a brahmin, there is no basis for branding.[27]

Despite the obvious bias towards orthodox Śaivas here, this reply encapsulates the position Śaṅkara upholds in the AŚV. The *vaidika-dharma* must be followed by all the twice-born, in particular the brahmins. Extreme practices involving the branding of sectarian markings are not permitted. A great deal of the argument found in the AŚV is concerned with this very

---

25 p. 45, lines 6-13.

26 p.110, line 14.

27 pp. 27, last 4 lines; p. 28 lines 1-4.

point. But the devotionally oriented sects are allowed to continue, provided they acknowledge the supreme authority of the Vedas (as interpreted in Advaita-Vedānta), and carry out the obligatory ritual practice.

There is one major textual problem in the AŚV. The work appears to have been transmitted in two different recensions. The first is preserved in the two editions published in Calcutta, while the second recension is adopted in the Madras edition. For the most part, there is little significant variation betweeen the two. But there are two entirely different versions of the second chapter, which describes the circumstances and place of Śaṅkara's birth. According to the first recension, he was born in Chidambaram, Tamil Nadu. The second recension describes his birth at Kālaṭi in Kerala. The other seven sources examined here (and virtually all the later accounts as well),[28] are unanimous in agreeing that Śaṅkara was born in Kālaṭi. It is not easy to explain how the two versions of the AŚV arose. But let us first examine them. This is the version in the Calcutta editions:[29]

> [1] Then the God, whose nature is that of the whole, became celebrated in this world, dwelling in the city of Cidambara, in the form of the *ākāśa-liṅga.*[30]
>
> [2] Multitudes of brahmins are dwelling in that place. In the family of [one of these,] the learned Mahendra, [a son] was born, named Sarvajña, chief of a brahmin family.
>
> [3] His wife, Kāmākṣī, was marked by all the auspicious characteristics. Having meditated on the lord of Cidambara, the couple obtained a daughter.

---

28 Antarkar, unpublished thesis, p. 237.

29 pp. 9-10 of the 1868 Bibliotheca Indica ed.; pp. 8-9 of the 1881 ed.

30 Literally, "dwelling in Cidambara with the name of *ākāśa-liṅga* ".

[4] The girl, named Viśiṣṭhā, was celebrated in the world. She was ever fond of meditation and devoted to [the path of] *jñāna*.

[5] In her eighth year, her father, Sarvajña, himself gave her to a brahmin named Viśvajit, who was free from passions and wonderful in his deeds.

[6] [But] she, who was discriminative, was meditating always on the non-dual Śiva, whose nature is that of *ākāśa*, as her lord, and worshipped him with great intensity.

[7] Surprisingly enough, rejecting even such a one, Viśvajit went to the forest, mentally determined to practise *tapas*.

[8] From that time, she continued to please Cidambara-Maheśvara with *pūjā*s and with meditation, centred on the Self.

[9] That God, although, complete in himself, (*sarva-pūrṇa*), entered the lotus of her face, causing astonishment to all the others gathered there.

[10] Viśiṣṭhā was favoured (*juṣṭa*) as was Ambikā, by [Śiva's] extremely powerful *tejas*. She was honoured continuously by all the people, and worshipped by her parents and the rest [of her family].

[11] The months passed, and the foetus grew, day by day. The best of the brahmins, making the lord of Cidambara the *yajamāna*,

[12] performed the [requisite] rituals, according to the Vedas, beginning from [the time of] the third month. When the tenth month was reached, from the sphere of Viśiṣṭhā's womb,

[13] Mahādeva came forth, having the name Śaṅkarācārya. Then, the host of *deva*s sent forth a shower of flowers, divine *dundubhi*s resounded, and

the heavenly region remained happy for a long time.

The Madras edition reads as follows:[31]

[1] In the eminent village, known as Kālaṭi, an ornament of Kerala, there was [a man named] Śivaguru, the wise son of Vidyādhirāja.

[2] Sadā-Śiva Śambhu, who was intent on blessing the world, by means of his *tejas*, entered into the wife [of Śivaguru] because of the greatness of her *tapas.*

[3] That faithful wife bore a foetus whose *tejas* was equal to that of the sun. He was born at an auspicious time, when the five planets were exalted.

[4] All of the relatives were delighted by the rain of flowers streaming down from heaven. It is said that Śivaguru, the father, having obtained a boon from Śambhu,

[5] although knowing that his son would be short-lived, did not say anything [about it]. [Śivaguru] was remembering what Śiva had said about him, [i.e., that the boy would be possessed of] excellent qualities such as omniscience.

[6] It seemed amazing that the darkness of night was turned away by the *tejas* of that child [even while] he was in the birth chamber of the house.

[7] At that time, trees were everywhere laden with fruit and flowers. All the quarters were bright and the waters were clear.

---

31 See pp. 8-10. The editor indicates manuscript variants in the sequence of some of the verses here. I have taken the liberty of placing the verses in what seems the most logical order.

[8] The snake and the mongoose, the dog and the deer, the lion and the elephant, eschewing their enmity for each other, were gifted with tranquillity.

[9] People of the highest, the lowest and middle [classes] from a multitude of countries all came in order to see the one who was of golden lustre.

[10] Women, brahmins, *śūdra*s, children, the elderly, and others as well, seeing that beautiful one, thought, 'he is verily Śambhu'.

[11] At that time, a book, which was respected by his creed, fell from the hand of a Buddhist in an assembly and dropped down to the ground.

[12] There were a good many discourses on Veda and Vedānta.

[13] The heart of Veda-Vyāsa obtained unequalled joy from the production of the desired meaning of the words [in the discourses, he being] the knower of their application.

[14] Thereupon, Śivaguru named him 'Śaṅkara'. Perceiving the aptness of the meaning of his [name], the great seers rejoiced.

[15] With [the passing of] days, fortnights, months and years, the boy grew. In his fifth year, he was [already] learned, on account of having grasped [his lessons], beginning with the letters [of the alphabet].

[16] [But] his honoured father died without having performed his initiation. His faithful wife performed the funeral rites, together with the relatives.

[17] The mother arranged for the *upanayana* to be done by a virtuous and learned *gotra* relative of hers.

[18] In his fifth year, he, whose mind was steady, mastered the four Vedas. Although just a boy, he plunged into all the *śāstras*.
[Śaṅkara], who performed superhuman deeds, [also] undertook service to his mother.

After these divergent accounts of Śaṅkara's birth, both recensions revert to almost identical versions of his precocious teachings which comprise the third chapter. The remaining chapters betray only minor variants. We must bear in mind that among the very few points of agreement on Śaṅkara's life in the hagiographies, there is a clear consensus in identifying his place of birth as Kālaṭi, and the name of his father as Śivagurú. This makes the Calcutta version of the AŚV all the more conspicuous as the sole dissenter in maintaining that Śaṅkara, the son of Viśvajit, was born in Chidambaram. What is more, this version of Śaṅkara's birth gives great emphasis to Viśiṣṭhā and casts her in the role of single mother. Her husband, Viśvajit, has disappeared from the scene some time prior to Śaṅkara's birth. Once the father leaves home to practise *tapas* in the forest, we hear no more of him.

It is difficult to judge which of the two versions of the text is the earlier. I have not been able to inspect the numerous manuscripts of the AŚV, which might suggest an answer. However, N. Veezhinathan has provided some useful information on the manuscript variants, in the preface to his Madras edition of the AŚV. He has adopted the version which places Śaṅkara's birth at Kālaṭi, on the basis of seven of the manuscripts he has consulted. Yet the remaining nine manuscripts he utilized support the reading of the Calcutta editions in citing Chidambaram as Śaṅkara's place of birth.

While it is possible that the two versions represent two distinct traditions, it is perhaps more likely that an interpolation has occurred.[32] It is not difficult to imagine that the absence of the father from the scene of Śaṅkara's birth may have appeared too likely to generate malicious comments from opponents of the Śaṅkara lineage. Indeed two hagiographies of Madhva make an all out attack on Śaṅkara's reputation in portraying him as the incarnation of the demon Maṇimat, born to a widow.[33] In view of this, it may have seemed desirable to revise the account of Śaṅkara's birth so as to make it tally with the tradition which holds that his father was very much present until the time of his initiation. This, after all, is the story the other hagiographies record.

On the other hand, there is no popular tradition in Chidambaram, so far as I know, which claims Śaṅkara as a native son. While we cannot place too much reliance on this, it must also be noted that there is a popular tradition that Patañjali taught Gauḍapāda, the grand-guru of Śaṅkara in the thousand-pillared hall of the famous Sabhānāyaka (Naṭarāja - Śiva) temple of Chidambaram.[34] Both editions of the AŚV locate Śaṅkara's guru, Govindapāda, in Chidambaram. In the Calcutta version, then, Śaṅkara does not leave home in order to find his guru as he does in the Madras reading and the other hagiographies. But this may be connected with the absence, in the AŚV, of the poignant scene of Śaṅkara's departure from his mother, and likewise, the omission of the episode in which he

---

32 This may have stemmed from the dispute between the *maṭhas*, discussed in Chapter Six.

33 *Maṇimañjarī* and *Sumadhvavijaya.* Both works are by Nārāyaṇa, the son of Trivikrama, a direct disciple of Madhva (13th c.). See the Bibliography for details.

34 See Rāmabhadra-Dīkṣita's *Patañjali-caritam* ("Kāvya-māla series no. 51, Bombay: Nirṇaya-sāgara Press, 1895); S. Meyyappan, *Chidambaram: Golden Temple* (Chidambaram, 1987), p. 49ff.; *The history of Nataraja temple,* (Chidambaram, n.p., n.d.), p.13.

returns as a *saṃnyāsin* to perform her funeral rites. These incidents figure prominently in all the other hagiographies.

2. Cidvilāsa's Śaṅkaravijaya-vilāsa (CŚV)

This work has not enjoyed the wide distribution of the AŚV, although the two have much in common. A printed edition, edited by W. R. Antarkar, on the basis of three of the four extant manuscripts, is now fairly accessible.[35] The text is written in a style resembling that of the Purāṇas. It is set in the frame of a dialogue in which a guru, Cidvilāsa, narrates the story of Śaṅkara's life to his disciple, Vijñānakanda. The colophons identify the author as Cidvilāsa, an ascetic (yati). Perhaps the author chose to honour a predecessor in the lineage, who bore the same monastic name, as the authoritative narrator of the story. It is likely that the author was affiliated with the Sringerī maṭha, for he devotes a three chapter excursus to a description of Sringerī, which he identifies as the site of the ancient sage Vibhāṇḍaka's āśrama. But it is not possible to determine further details about the author or his date.

Cidvilāsa's fundamental concern seems to be in the construction of an edifying narrative poem which will glorify the Advaita lineage and thus promote the transmission of its doctrines. This concern can be seen in the short dialogues between teacher and student which conclude each chapter. Two examples will make this amply clear:

> Vijñānakanda said: "Oh illustrious teacher, be compassionate to your student whose mind is far away from the impediments (*pratyūha*) of worldly activity. If your mind is not disquieted, thinking that this [student], who while standing says 'do tell

---

[35] Cidvilāsa-muni, *Śaṅkaravijaya-vilāsa*, ed. W. R. Antarkar, in *Bhāratīya Vidyā*, 33 (1973), pp. 1-92.

> *me* ', [in spite of] having accepted the [teachings on the] oneness of *jīva* and Īśa along with the phrase (*dhiṣaṇā*), 'I am that, the *haṃsa* ', then do tell me directly, benevolent one, [what happens next in the story]" (3.51).
>
> Cidvilāsa said,"Oh, wise Vijñānakanda, the famous dialogue between Vidhi and Śarva, which I related [to you], is constantly sought out. He who recites it every day, out of respect and with devotion, will be freed from distinction. By virtue of the unity of *jīva* and Īśa, he will live as a liberated one and strive even more for the highest good"(4.55).

While some attention is given to Śaṅkara's debates against sectarian opponents in the CŚV, they do not dominate the narrative as do the much lengthier descriptions of argument in the AŚV.

Since the CŚV contains several incidents which are not found in the AŚV, it is probable that the CŚV is a later work. The CŚV elaborates, for example, on the episode in which Śaṅkara is seized by a crocodile and the subsequent scene surrounding his departure from home. Another significant addition found in the CŚV is the reference to Śaṅkara's establishment of four *maṭhas*. The only other of our hagiographies which mentions this incident is the GVK (c. 1740). But it must also be pointed out that the CŚV parallels the AŚV in the absence of some episodes found in the other six sources. There are many instances where the CŚV definitely follows the AŚV. Moreover, Cidvilāsa has taken a number of verses from the AŚV and incorporated them in his composition.[36] The relationship between the CŚV and AŚV is

---

[36] Some examples are: CŚV 2.60/62, 14.32, 14.36, 15.3ff., 24.34, 25.36ff., 27.36 and 28.5ff. These verses are found in the AŚV on p.3, p.169, p.171, p.18, p.183, p.188, p.104 and pp.81-82.

discussed further in Appendix B in conjunction with an examination of fragments from two lost texts: the "Prācīna-Śaṅkaravijaya"and "Bṛhat-Śaṅkaravijaya".

3. Vyāsācala's *Śaṅkaravijaya* (VŚV)

Although there are only some six extant manuscripts of this work,[37] it has been very influential on the later writers. There is no doubt that the VŚV is one of the earliest available hagiographies of Śaṅkara, yet it is difficult to even speculate on the date of the text. It is possible that the VŚV is as early, or even earlier than the AŚV. But there is no evidence that Anantānandagiri was aware of Vyāsācala, or vice versa. It is clear that the VŚV must have established itself, at some point in time, as an authoritative source on Śaṅkara's life. Four of our hagiographies appear to have relied on this text. Of these, the GŚC and ŚDV clearly acknowledge their debt to Vyāsācala. Govindanātha refers to him in this way: " I salute the poet Vyāsācala who encompasses the whole tradition. He was a wave [on the ocean] of Śaṅkara's fame. Because [of his being able to] penetrate the entire surface of the earth, I am unable to grasp the blossom of the meaning of that lofty mountain of poetry" (GŚC 1.6-7). Mādhava, the author of the widely distributed *Śaṅkara-digvijaya*, praises him and describes the nature of his work as follows:

> Fortunate is the excellent poet Vyāsācala, the author of the poem in which Maheśa, under the name of [Śaṅkara-] Bhagavatpāda appears as the hero; in which *śānti*—which has subsidiaries by way of the [other moods] such as the erotic—is

---

[37] Details of the printed edition are as follows: Vyāsācala, *Śaṅkaravijaya*, ed. T. Chandrasekharan (Madras Government Oriental Manuscripts Series, no. 24, Madras: Government of Madras, 1954).

> manifest as the [predominant] mood (*rasa*); in which the destruction of ignorance is the fruit [of the poem]. And those who are knowers of his work are also fortunate (ŚDV 1.17).

It is well that Mādhava is lavish in his praises. For he has included some 500 verses from Vyāsācala's work in his ŚDV.

Unfortunately, very little can be said about the author of the VŚV. In the text he mentions his name variously as Vyāsācala (on four occasions), Vyāsādri (twice), Vyāsagiri (once) and once as Vyāsaśaila-muni.[38] This latter designation suggests that the author may have been an ascetic. It is probable that Vyāsācala had affiliations with Kānchipuram. For he pays special attention to this city, which he glorifies in a lengthy *māhātmya* (7.102-144). However, it does not seem possible that Vyāsācala occupied the seat of the Kāmakoṭi-*pīṭha* at Kānchipuram as has been suggested by Ātreya Kṛṣṇa-Śāstrī.[39] Otherwise, one would expect some reference in the text to the establishment of a *maṭha*. Moreover, according to the VŚV, Śaṅkara never actually visits Kānchipuram. Instead, the city is described in conjunction with the visit of his disciple Sanandana. Unlike the other hagiographers, Vyāsācala does not provide us with an introduction to his text. He commences the story in the very first verse. It is left to the reader to determine his intentions.

Vyāsācala does not seem to take much interest in relating the specific details, such as the names of the places where the various events in Śaṅkara's life unfold, which are found in the

---

[38] In the final verse of each of the twelve chapters, the author presents a concise summary of that chapter's contents. In eight of these final verses he incorporates his own name in the verse.

[39] He makes this claim in *Śaṅkara-guru-paramparā*, in Tamil. I have not seen this work but it is cited by the editor of the printed edition of the VŚV, pp. iv-v.

other hagiographies.[40] His attentions are instead concentrated on the creation of a true *kāvya* work which will effectively evoke the various moods appropriate to the different episodes of the narrative. He places particular emphasis on the story of Śaṅkara's youth, for which he devises a special frame, in the form of a sub-story. The tale of Upamanyu's boyhood penance—because of which he receives a visit from Śiva and the boon of the ocean of milk—occupies two of the work's twelve chapters. The poignancy of Śaṅkara's parting from his mother echoes the episode as first described in the story of Upamanyu:

> ...[Upamanyu,] who was firm-minded, although only five years old, asked permission to perform *tapas*, "I should wander about a little. You should [stay here and] pray to all the gods". As soon as he said this, his mother swooned. And [then], recovering a little and embracing her son, she said,"...My dear, do not wander far. You do not have the capacity to perform *tapas*. Will they not say to me, 'What kind of mother [are you]? It is the wrong time.[41] He is only five years old, his [milk] teeth have not [yet] fallen out'. Living here [in this very place] you should perform *tapas* according to your own ability, if it pleases you. I will become your companion in *tapas*, according to my ability. Abandoning you, I am not able to remain here" (VŚV 2.10-13).
>
> ...[Śaṅkara] said to her, "mother, a crocodile...has taken me. I am now unable to carry on my life. In assuming the garb of a *saṃnyāsin*, my life may continue". [She reflected,] 'in this world, there is no

---

40 Of the eight hagiographes, the VŚV provides the shortest list of pilgrimage places visited. See the table in Chapter Four.

41 This is a tentative translation for the last *pāda*: *māṃ kiṃ vadeyur jananīm akāle*.

> way that a mother with only one son would cause her son to take up renunciation.[42] [But] giving [him] up is preferable to me than losing [him] entirely, for then these eyes would not be seeing [him at all]. Having thought it over, she resolved on [allowing] her son's renunciation. Then she said, "you may undertake renunciation". He uttered the statement, "I have renounced". Thereupon, he was freed from the jaws of the crocodile and happily reached the shore of the river. After he had spoken, his mother swooned and fell to the ground. Sprinkling her with water, he revived her. He said, "mother, do not be subject to grief..." (4.45-48).

Vyāsācala retells the story of Śaṅkara's boyhood later on in the text (11.111-138). Here, the story serves another function, in drawing together the threads of the narrative. Indra prompts his guru to tell the Aśvins of Śaṅkara's birth, to show that he is no ordinary mortal, so as to convince them that it is permissible for them to heal him of a serious affliction.

As is characteristic of a *kāvya* work, we find in the VŚV considerable description of both scenic places and the seasons. Most of the tenth chapter and half of the eleventh are devoted to a portrait of the region around the Sahya mountains and an elaborate description of the passage of the six seasons[43]. It is during this time that the disciples carry out a search for physicians capable of healing Śaṅkara's illness. Despite these descriptive interludes Vyāsācala never loses touch with the narrative, which moves along in a lively fashion, unencumbered by excessive metaphorical devices.

---

42 I have followed the alternate reading in 4.46.

43 See 10.18-130 and 11.1-78.

4. Rājacūḍāmaṇi-Dīkṣita's *Śaṅkarābhyudaya* (RŚA)

It is fortunate that a second printed edition of this work has recently become available, the first edition being very rare.[44] In the case of this text, we *do* have reliable information on the author and his date. Rājacūḍāmaṇi-Dīkṣita, who composed numerous Sanskrit works, was patronised by the Nāyaka king, Raghunātha of Thanjāvūr (reigned 1614-1633).[45] In the opening verse of the RŚA, the author refers to his father, Śrīnivāsa-Dīkṣita, who was himself a poet of some renown, and was the father-in-law of the Vedāntin, Appaya-Dīkṣita. In verses two through five of the RŚA, Rājacūḍāmaṇi-Dīkṣita cites the titles of seven of his previous works. One of these, "Tantra-śikhā-maṇi", a work on Mīmāṃsā, contains a verse in which the author has himself supplied the date of the composition — 1636.[46] It is for this reason that I have placed the date of the RŚA at c.1650.

The circumstances surrounding the composition of the RŚA are in themselves something of a story. In RŚA 1.6, Rājacūḍāmaṇi-Dīkṣita describes having seen Indra in a dream. The author takes this apparition to be his own guru, whom, he

---

44 The first edition appeared in *The Sanskrit Journal: Sahṛdayā*, 17-18 (1914-15?), published in Srirangam. Details of the second edition are: Rājacūḍāmaṇi-Dīkṣita, *Śrī Śaṅkarābhyudayam*, ed. S. V. Rādhākṛṣṇa-Śāstrī (Śrīraṅgam: Śimili Śrī Veṅkaṭarāma-Śāstrī Trust, 1986).

45 In RŚA 1.5, Rājacūḍāmaṇi-Dīkṣita mentions that he has written scores of *kāvya*s. For an informative essay on this writer, see the introduction by V. Gopala Iyengar to Śrī Rājacūḍāmaṇi-Dīkṣita, *Ānandarāghavam*, ed. P. M. Padmanābha-Śarmā (Tanjore Sarasvati Mahal Series no. 134, Thanjavur: Tanjore Maharaja Serfoji's Sarasvati Mahal Library 1971), pp. 1-16. See also M. Krishnamachariar, *History of Classical Sanskrit Literature* ([1937], reprinted Delhi: Motilal Banarsidass, 1974), pp. 234-236.

46 Cited in the introduction to *Ānandarāghavam* (see previous note), p.2.

states, was commanding him to compose the work.[47] Rājacūḍāmaṇi-Dīkṣita does not tell us what sources he has relied on. However, from a comparison of the main incidents in the story and the places Śaṅkara is said to have visited, it seems that he has followed the VŚV.[48] Like Vyāsācala's work, the RŚA is fundamentally a *kāvya* composition. But in the RŚA, the narrative is quite compressed and to some extent subordinated to elaborate stylistic devices. Some obscure and unexpected references occur in the text. For example, when Śaṅkara is *en route* to Kānchipuram he is described as "looking towards the place which was truly auspicious and fit to be the abode of the sacrificer, Maṇikheṭa" (7.44). Here the poet manages to bring his own father into the story, playing on the words of his honorary title, "Ratnakheṭa". In this way, he cleverly arranges for Śaṅkara to bless with his glance the place where his father is to be born.

For the most part, the life story in the RŚA is not fundamentally different from that of the VŚV. Rājacūḍāmaṇi-Dīkṣita does, however, add a couple of incidents. The story of Śaṅkara's reviving a dead child, and his restoring from memory the lost works of Padmapāda and King Rājaśekhara, first occur in the RŚA. The verses describing these two episodes are taken, almost verbatim, into the *Śaṅkara-digvijaya*, by Mādhava. In all, some 130 verses from the RŚA are incorporated into the ŚDV.

---

47 *śarvaryāś carame yāme śayānas sa kadācana / gīrvāṇendra-gurum buddhyā gīrvāṇendram alokata // kṛpayā coditas tena kṛpaṇānujighṛkṣuṇā / sa eṣa kurute kāvyaṃ śaṅkarābhyudayābhidham //* (1.6; 1.10).

48 See the table of incidents in Chapter Two, and the table of pilgrimage places in Chapter Four.

5. Govindanātha's *Śaṅkarācārya-carita* (GŚC)

Govindanātha is the only one of our eight hagiographers known to be from Kerala.[49] Indeed, the GŚC is sometimes referred to as the "Keralīya-Śaṅkara-vijaya".[50] According to K. Kunjunni Raja, Govindanātha flourished in southern Kerala during the first half of the 17th century.[51] Govindanātha openly acknowledges his debt to Vyāsācala (1.6-7), and closely models his work on that earlier composition, which is the only apparent source for his work. The GŚC is, in fact, a summary of the longer and more sophisticated VŚV. To cite just one example, the GŚC retells in just twenty-two verses the important sub-story of Upamanyu, which figures largely in the VŚV. Vyāsācala has devoted one hundred and thirty odd verses to this story which occupies two full chapters in his work. However, Govindanātha omits two episodes which are found in the VŚV: Śaṅkara's encounter with the Kāpālikas, and the story of Śaṅkara's illness. Although it is difficult to say why Govindanātha has chosen to delete these incidents, we can more easily imagine his motivation in making one of the few significant variations he introduces in the story. In the VŚV the last we hear of Śaṅkara is that he has gone to a place which is

---

49 The printed edition I have used is, Govindanātha, *Śrī Śaṅkarācāryacaritam*, ed. Narmadāśaṅkar Methā (Puṇe: Citraśāla Press, 1931). I have seen a reference to an earlier printed edition—Trichur: Kerala Publishing House, 1926—which I have not been able to obtain, cited by Sengaku Mayeda, *A thousand teachings: the Upadeśasāhasrī of Śaṅkara* (Tokyo: University of Tokyo, 1979), p. 7n.

50 W. R. Antarkar has found that the so-called "Keralīya-Śaṅkara-vijaya" is actually the same text as the GŚC, see his thesis, p. 26. Antarkar is presently preparing a new edition of the GŚC.

51 *The contribution of Kerala to Sanskrit literature* (Madras: University of Madras 1958), pp. 205-206. The information derives from a commentary on another of Govindanātha's works, *Gaurīkalyāṇa*, a Yamaka poem.

pleasing to him.[52] Govindanātha does not hesitate to specify Śaṅkara's final mortal abode—Vṛṣācala, in Trichūr, Kerala—which, he adds, is the Mt. Kailāsa of the south.[53] By having Śaṅkara end his days in the very spot in which his parents had practised the austerities which secured his birth, Govindanātha is able to glorify his own native place.

If it is true that Śaṅkara was born in Kerala, as all our sources agree,[54] we might expect to find some record of local traditions about his life. Yet the GŚC does not have anything substantial to add to what is found in the other texts, nor does it appear to be an important source for later writers. Neither does the GŚC convey a flavour specific to Kerala. A far more extensive description of Kālaṭi, Śaṅkara's native place, is provided by Cidvilāsa, for example. This is yet one more indication that Śaṅkara is not bound to a particular region. He is rather a figure who belongs to the whole of India, as we shall see.

6. Tirumala-Dīkṣita's *Śaṅkarābhyudaya* (TŚA)

There is only one extant manuscript of this work, and it is incomplete. The text has, however, been made more readily available thanks to W. R. Antarkar, who has prepared an edition from this single manuscript.[55] The text breaks off early in the seventh chapter at a rather exciting point in the narrative.

---

52 *rucita-deśam ayaṃ jagāma* (12.82).

53 *...krameṇa śiṣya-saṃyukto vṛṣācalam avāptavān // tatra dakṣiṇa-kailāse nivasann ekadā guruḥ / jñātvā nija śarīrāntaṃ sa-śiṣyaiś ca prasanna-dhīḥ //* (9. 18-19).

54 With the exception of one recension of the AŚV. See the discussion on the AŚV, above.

55 The MS. is held in the Mysore Oriental Research Library. The printed edition is edited by W. R. Antarkar, *Śri Śaṅkarābhyudaya-mahākāvya*, in *JUB* 34 (1965) 138-187. Antarkar has recently informed me (September 1989) that he has been unable find another MS. in the course of his extensive search throughout India for MSS. on the life of Śaṅkara.

Śaṅkara is about to be beheaded by a Kāpālika. His faithful disciple, Padmapāda, has just transformed himself into a manifestation of Nṛsiṃha, in the hope of saving his guru. In order to get at least a rough idea of the extent of the missing verses in the TŚA, we may make some comparison with the ŚDV and the VŚV, which have similar descriptions of this incident. Both works place the Kāpālika episode at a point which is two-thirds of the way through the text. On this basis, we can assume that the sole remaining manuscript of the TŚA is lacking appoximately the last third of its text.

The date of the TŚA is uncertain. In the table on page 24, I have somewhat arbitrarily placed the TŚA as though it were contemporaneous with the CŚV. The text may actually be situated anywhere in the period between the CŚV and the ŚDV. It is most unlikely that the text is earlier than this, and indeed it may well be as late as 1650. The problem in dating the TŚA is that the work bears no definite relationship to any of our hagiographies prior to Mādhava's *Śaṅkara-digvijaya.* Tirumala-Dīkṣita does acknowledge that other poets have sung the praises of Śaṅkara,[56] but he does not specify, nor is it apparent from the text, which sources he has relied upon. There is some possibilty of a relationship between the TŚA and RŚA for there are a few similarities in the way the two texts treat certain incidents.[57] But even if this is so, it would be very difficult to determine which text influenced which. It is due to the widely distributed ŚDV that the otherwise little-known composition of Tirumala-Dīkṣita has been perpetuated. For Mādhava has incorporated in his work nearly 500 verses from the TŚA. This amounts to more than 75% of the available text of the TŚA.

---

56 *stutaḥ kaviḅhir apy asmat-kṛtyā tuṣyatu śaṅkaraḥ* (1.7).

57 Both relate Śaṅkara's creation of a river, while the other texts say he merely moved the river. It may be significant that both authors are Dīkṣitas. But not too much reliance can be placed on this.

In the colophons of the TŚA, Tirumala-Dīkṣita tells us that he is the son of Tirumala Koṇḍopādhyāya and that he is devoted to serving Paramaśivendra, who is presumably his guru. There is a famous Paramaśivendra who was the guru of Sadāśiva Brahmendra of Kānchipuram. The Śaṅkara *maṭha* at Kānchipuram claims that this Paramaśivendra occupied the Kāmakoṭi *pīṭha* in the period 1539-1586.[58] The Kāmakoṭi *pīṭha* chronicles are not wholly reliable as historical documents, but if there was *a* Paramaśivendra who headed the *maṭha* at this time, it is within the realm of possibility that he was the guru referred to by Tirumala-Dīkṣita. *If* this were the case, we would have to place the TŚA in the latter part of the 16th century.

As far as Tirumala-Dīkṣita's motivation in composing the work is concerned, we know only that he has written the *Śaṅkarābhyudaya* "in order to publicize the lineage of the teachers of the Advaita viewpoint" [59] Tirumala-Dīkṣita has succeeded in his purpose to the extent that he was the first to record—or may have even been the original creator of—a number of significant episodes which have become an integral part of the popular conception of Śaṅkara's life. There are four such incidents. These have been made current because of the wide distibution enjoyed by the ŚDV, which presents Tirumala-Dīkṣita's version of the four episodes almost verbatim. Nowhere else do we read of the incident in which Śaṅkara is tested by Śiva, disguised as an outcaste.[60] This episode has become one of the best known stories on Śaṅkara's life. Nowadays in India, the tale is repeatedly cited to demonstrate

---

58 A. Nataraja Aiyer and S. Lakshminarasimha Sastri, *The traditional age of Sri Sankaracarya and the maths* ([1962], reprinted Madras: B.G. Paul, 1988), p. 131.

59 *advaita-darśanācārya-sampradāya-prasiddhaye śaṅkarābhyudayaṃ kurmo*...(1.5).

60 See TŚA 3.65ff. The same is repeated in ŚDV 6.25ff.

that Śaṅkara, in bowing down to one of lowly birth, was above "casteism". Similarly it is only in the TŚA and ŚDV that we find the young Śaṅkara imploring Lakṣmī to confer wealth on a poor but pious householder.[61] The other new episodes concern the visit of five sages who foretell Śaṅkara's future, and his stopping a river in flood and thereby saving his guru.[62] The TŚA stands apart from the other hagiographies in the conspicuous absence of one very popular story. Tirumala-Dīkṣita is the only author to omit the tale in which the eight year old Śaṅkara is seized by a crocodile. Without resorting to this excuse to become a renouncer, Śaṅkara must plead more directly with his mother:

> (2.95) "I see no happiness whatsoever, mother, for those who are ignorantly wandering in the course of worldly existence. Having become a renouncer, I shall set forth in order to be liberated from the bonds of worldly existence...(2.101-102) Allow me [to follow] the renouncer's life. Give up this grief. Whenever you remember me, mother, in that very moment I will be before you". On account of such true, dispassionate statements, she was consoled to some extent, and sent forth the wise one. Having fallen at his mother's feet, he just went out of the house".[63]

---

[61] See TŚA 2.21ff; ŚDV 4.21ff. According to tradition, this incident inspired Śaṅkara's first poetic composition, the *Kanakadhārā-stotra* .

[62] See TŚA 2.77ff.= ŚDV 5.36ff.; TŚA 3.20ff.= ŚDV 5. 135ff.

[63] Verse 2.95 reads *bhramatāṃ bhava-vartmani bhramān na hi kiṃ cit sukham amba lakṣaye / tad avāpya caturtham āśramaṃ prayatiṣye bhava-bandha-muktaye*. This verse is repeated in SDV 5.54, but Mādhava, like the other authors, feels it necessary to introduce the crocodile incident (ŚDV 5.61ff.) as the instrument by which Śaṅkara secures his mother's permission. The text of the TŚA continues: (2.101) *purato bhavito'smi tat kṣaṇaṃ tava mām amba yathā smariṣyasi / paritāpam amuṃ jahīhi mām anujānīhi yatīndra-vṛttaye //* (2.102) *amṛṣoktibhir evam ādibhiḥ kavir āśvāsitayā kathaṃ ca saḥ /* [the text

Another notable ommission from the TŚA is the episode in which Śaṅkara's first disciple, Sanandana, miraculously walks across the waters of a river. The lotus blooms, which appear underfoot at every step, are a sign of his intense devotion, enabling him to quickly reach his guru. Five of the other hagiographies cite this as the reason he is renamed Padmapāda[64]. In the TŚA, Sanandana and Padmapāda are actually treated as two separate individuals. When Tirumala-Dīkṣita details the divine origins of his cast of supporting characters, he describes Padmapāda as a manifestation of Nārāyaṇa and Sanandana of Aruṇa.[65] Tirumala-Dīkṣita would presumably have known, at least from oral tradition, of both the incidents he omitted. We can only speculate on the reasons he decided to reject them. It is certainly not due to an aversion to miracles, for these are not lacking in the TŚA. Perhaps he found the crocodile story too undignified, or too weak an excuse for Śaṅkara's renunciation. The story of Padmapāda may be a later development in Śaṅkara's hagiography since it is not found in the VŚV either. But it is also possible that there are two streams of traditional stories about the disciples.

---

reads *sā*, but this must be incorrect] *prahitaḥ praṇipatya mātaraṃ niragad eva grahādviruktibhiḥ* //The reading *grahādviruktibhiḥ* is probably an error in the MS. It is difficult to tell just what the correct reading should be here. In the introduction to his edition of the TŚA (*loc. cit.*, p. 141), Antarkar notes that the MS. contains numerous errors.

64 The AŚV does not include this or any other story about the disciples. Sanandana is not mentioned as a disciple, but Padmapāda does occupy a prominent place in the AŚV. Vyāsācala only refers to Sanandana.

65 In 2.2 he writes, "The one who dwells with Lakṣmī was born on earth—from a Brahmin known as Vimala, a repository of the arts—as one called Padmapāda" (*kamalā-nilayaḥ kalā-nidher vimalākhyād ajaniṣṭa bhū-surāt bhuvi padmapādaṃ vadanti yaṃ*). In 2.6. he says, *aruṇa samabhūt sanandano*.

7. Lakṣmaṇa-Śāstrī's *Guruvaṃśa-kāvya* (GVK)

This work describes the lineage of *ācārya*s at the Sringerī Śaṅkara *maṭha*.[66] The first three of the text's nineteen chapters deal with Śaṅkara himself, the founder of the line. In the colophons of the GVK we learn that the poem was composed at the behest of the *ācārya*, Saccidānanda Bhāratī, the disciple of Nṛsiṃha Bhāratī. According to the archaeological report which first described the manuscript, Saccidānanda Bhāratī occupied the seat at the Sringerī *maṭha* from 1705-1741.[67] Since the GVK ends with a description of the incumbency of this *ācārya*, the work can be dated c.1740.

In the colophons of the GVK, Lakṣmaṇa-Śāstrī describes himself as the boy-scholar (*vidvat-bālaka*). This appears to be an honorary affix, perhaps bestowed on him by Saccidānanda Bhāratī. It is obvious that the author was resident at Sringerī for some time, but we know nothing more about him. Lakṣmaṇa-Śāstrī acknowledges earlier writers on the subject: "the lineage of the noble ones has been described by the foremost poets" (1.6). In his own commentary on the GVK, he specifies "Ānandagiri and others". By this Lakṣmaṇa-Śāstrī undoubtedly means the AŚV. It is clear that he has also used the CŚV, VŚV and RŚA. For incidents from these four works are repeated in the GVK. But there is nothing to indicate that Lakṣmaṇa-Śāstrī knew of the ŚDV or TŚA. The incidents unique to these two works are not found in the GVK.

The GVK stands out from the other hagiographies in that it was apparently commissioned by the head of a Śaṅkara

---

66 Kāśī Lakṣmaṇa-Śāstrī, *Guruvaṃśa-kāvyam* (Śrīraṅgam: Śrī Vāṇīvilās Press, 1966). The same publisher brought out an earlier edition, ed. Kunigal Rama Sastrigal (Sri Vani Vilas Sanskrit Series no. 12, n. d.), which contains only the first seven chapters but has a commentary by the author.

67 Mysore Archaeological Department, *Annual Report for the year 1928*, Bangalore, 1929, pp.15-20.

institution. Contrary to what we might expect, however, there is no special glorification of Sringerī in the section of the work concerning Śaṅkara. What is said about Sringerī in the text is quite similar to what is already found in the CŚV. There is one other significant point on which Lakṣmaṇa-Śāstrī follows the CŚV—Śaṅkara's founding four *maṭhas* in the four quarters of India. The other six hagiographies do not mention this popular tradition.

Lakṣmaṇa-Śāstrī also relates two incidents which are unique to the GVK. The first concerns Padmapāda. [68] In the course of begging alms, he is attacked by a king. In order to protect himself, Padmapāda assumes the form of Narasiṃha. The king offers him his palace and the whole of his kingdom in reverent tribute. The story forms a prelude to the Bhairava episode in which Padmapāda again takes on the form of Narasiṃha, this time to save the life of his guru. The second new episode concerns Śaṅkara's visit to the goddess, Siddheśvarī, in Nepal. She accepts him as her own son and grants him a river of milk.[69]

8. Mādhava's *Śaṅkara-digvijaya* (ŚDV)

This is by far the most widely distributed of the hagiographies. The incumbent Śaṅkarācāryas of the Sringerī, and Dwārkā/Jyotir *maṭhas* maintain that the ŚDV is the most authoritative account of Śaṅkara's life.[70] There are some thirty available manuscripts

---

[68] The name of this disciple is variously spelled Padmapada or Padmapāda in the different hagiographies. The story appears in GVK 3.41-47.

[69] See 3.63-66.

[70] Personal interview with Śrī Abhinavavidyātīrtha in Sringerī on 4 January 1989, and a personal communication from Śrī Svāmī Svarūpānanda Sarasvatī (who heads both the Dwārkā and Jyotir *maṭhas*), dated August 1988. See Appendix A for further details of the interviews.

of the ŚDV, distributed in various parts of India. A good printed edition of the text, with two Sanskrit commentaries has been available for the past hundred years.[71] There is also an edition of the text with a Hindi translation and commentary,[72] and there are two complete English translations.[73]

The editor of the Anandāśrama edition of the ŚDV has taken the liberty of altering not only the title of the work but the name of its author as well. The colophons at the conclusion of each of the ŚDV's sixteen chapters state that the work, entitled *Saṃkṣepa-Śaṅkara-jaya*, was written by Mādhava. Although some may find it rather annoying, the modification of the title does not strike me as a particularly serious problem. The alteration of the author's name is another matter altogether. Here the editor has made two very dubious assumptions. To begin with, he assumes the identity of Mādhava and Vidyāraṇya, which remains in question.[74] Secondly, and this is

---

71 Vidyāraṇya, *Śrīmacchaṅkaradigvijaya. Advaita-rājyalakṣmī-ṭīkāntargata-viśeṣa-vibhāga-ṭippaṇībhis tathā Dhanapatisūri-kṛta-ḍiṇḍimākhya-ṭīkayā ca sametaḥ*, ed. Mahādeva Cimaṇājī Āpṭe (Poona: Ānandāśrama Press, 1891). I have not seen the very first printed edition, brought out by the Gaṇapati Kṛṣṇajī press in 1863 (*śaka* 1786).

72 Mādhavācārya, *Śrī Śaṅkara-digvijaya*, translated [into Hindi, with additional comments] by Baldev Upādhyāy, ([1943], third edition, Haridvār: Śrī Śravaṇanāth Jñān-mandir, 1985).

73 (1) Madhava-Vidyaranya, *Sankara-dig-vijaya: The traditional life of Sri Sankaracharya*, tr. Swami Tapasyananda (Madras: Sri Ramakrishna Math, 1978). (2) Vidyaranya, *Srimad Sankara Digvijayam*, tr. K. Padmanaban (2 vols., Madras [published by the author], 1985/86). It should be noted that both of these translations are quite free. Moreover, both translators often incorporate material from the commentaries in the text, or even add some of their own comments. Paul Deussen has published a German translation of the first chapter of the ŚDV in his *Allgemeine Geschichte der Philosophie*, I 3 (Leipzig: F. A Brockhaus, 1908), pp. 181-189.

74 The identities of Mādhava and Vidyāraṇya remain problematical. T. M. P. Mahadevan argues that Mādhava-Vidyāraṇya is the pupil of Bhāratītīrtha -

far more serious, even if we allow the designation "Mādhava-Vidyāraṇya", there is no evidence in the text that connects the Mādhava named in the colophons with "Mādhava-Vidyāraṇya". The ascription of the work to Vidyāraṇya has been widely, but by no means universally, accepted in India. This is despite several objections which make it clear that Vidyāraṇya could not possibly be the author of this text.[75] However, the revised title of the work has well and truly stuck. For this reason, I will continue to refer to the text by its popular title, *Śaṅkara-digvijaya*.

I have already referred on several occasions to the fact that the ŚDV incorporates numerous verses from other works. One of these, the RŚA can be reliably placed at c.1650. This is the earliest possible date for the composition of the ŚDV. The upper limit for the work is 1798, the year in which Dhanapatisūri's commentary on the ŚDV was written. If we can assume that the GVK was composed c.1740, at the behest of the incumbent *ācārya* of the Sringerī *maṭha*, as is asserted in the colophons of the text, it follows that the ŚDV had not come into prominence at this time. It is even possible that Mādhava composed the ŚDV after 1740.

In the opening verse of the ŚDV Mādhava salutes Vidyātīrtha as the embodiment of the *paramātman*. It is presumably on this basis that the ŚDV is (incorrectly) ascribed to Vidyāraṇya, for the *Jīvanmukti-viveka*, attributed to

---

Vidyāraṇya, *The philosophy of Advaita* ([1938] 4th ed. New Delhi: Arnold Heinemann, 1976), pp.1-8.

75 One of the first to question the ascription of the ŚDV to Vidyāraṇya was T. S. Narayana Sastry (*op. cit.*) in 1916. He cited the appearance of numerous verses in the text which were borrowed from other works. More recently, W. R. Antarkar has argued convincingly against the claim of Vidyāraṇya's authorship (*JUB*, 41, [1972] 1-23). Yoshitsugu Sawai has enlarged on Antarkar's discussion, "On a legendary biography of Śaṅkara", *Journal of Indian and Buddhist Studies*, 34 (1985), 454-459.

Vidyāraṇya, also commences with a similar salutation to Vidyātīrtha. It seems that Vidyātīrtha is another name for Vidyāśaṅkara, in whose honour a temple was consecrated at Sringerī in 1356 by Bhāratītīrtha, the guru of Vidyāraṇya.[76] Because Vidyātīrtha is considered the greatest guru in the Sringerī lineage, it is not surprising for him to be evoked by one such as Mādhava, the author of the ŚDV, who, we may assume, was affiliated to that tradition. It is difficult to say much more about the identity of Mādhava. The name is not an uncommon one, nor is the epithet "Nava-Kālidāsa", which he ascribes to himself in ŚDV 1.9.

In the second half of the opening verse, Mādhava states that he has collected together the essential matter in the old work on Śaṅkara, *prācīna-śaṅkara-jaye sāraḥ saṃgṛhyate sphuṭam*. Acyuta, the second commentator on the ŚDV, identifies this as the work by Ānandagiri, i.e., the AŚV.[77] We do find three verses in the ŚDV which also appear in the AŚV, but these may have come down to Mādhava through oral tradition. Overall, there is scarcely any sign of material specific to the AŚV in the ŚDV. Mādhava relies instead on three other hagiographies—VŚV, RŚA and TŚA—many of whose verses are directly incorporated in the ŚDV. He refers to only one of the authors of these three texts directly, Vyāsācala, whom he praises highly in 1.17.[78] Although he has taken nearly as many verses from the TŚA, I can only assume that Mādhava has a special regard for Vyāsācala, whom he appears to take as the foremost of the

---

76 See A. K. Shastry, *A history of Śriṅgeri* (Dharwad: Prasaranga, Karnatak University, 1982), pp. 16-21. This beautiful Hoysala/Dravidian style temple remains in excellent condition today.

77 *śaṅkarasya bhagavato...ānandagiryabhidhas tasya tat praśiṣyasya vāk-sāraḥ*, p.3 (Ānandāśrama ed.). It is possible that Acyuta might mean the PrŚV here, for he, like Dhanapatisūri, does not clearly distinguish between the AŚV and the PrŚV. The PrŚV is discussed in Appendix B.

78 See the discussion of the VŚV above.

earlier poets on the subject. Hence, the allusion to the old work in the opening verse of the ŚDV may well be to the VŚV.[79]

It is esssential that we are very careful in considering Mādhava's substantial borrowings from earlier works. To impose our notion of plagiarism here would be well and truly foreign to the context of Sanskrit traditions. Lambert Schmithausen clarifies this issue precisely:

> To expect a classical Indian author to distinguish expressly between what he has conceived or at least formulated himself and what he has taken over from earlier works of his line of tradition is to attribute to him a modern historical sense and to assume that he set great store by originality. For a traditionalist author, "originality" would have been a serious charge...but "plagiarism" a nonsensical one. Of course, an author will be inclined to expressly quote from a highly authoritative or canonical source...but in the case of a work which has not (yet) reached such a status he will more probably simply make use of it.[80]

Mādhava should not be belittled for his use of other works. In skilfully assembling a compilation of diverse materials,

---

79 There remains a problem in the interpretation of the title of Mādhava's composition which appears in the colophons, *Saṃkṣepa-śaṅkara-jaya*. It seems rather odd to speak of an abridgement (*saṃkṣepa*) here, since the ŚDV is substantially longer than the VŚV. The question also arises as to whether the verb *saṃgrah* in the opening verse is meant to be understood in the same sense as *saṃkṣepa*. The possibility cannot be ruled out that Mādhava may want to suggest that there was a great, ancient work which is the authority on which his composition rests. There may have been a tradition which told of the existence of such a work.

80 *Ālayavijñāna: on the origin and early development of a central concept of Yogācāra philosophy* (2 vols. Studia Philologica Buddhica Monograph Series IVa-b, Tokyo: International Institute for Buddhist Studies, 1987) part II, p. 476.

supplemented with his own elaborate verses, he has produced a substantial literary work. I would go so far as to suggest that he has succeeded in creating the "Essential Śaṅkara-vijaya", which is what is perhaps implied by the original title of the work, "*Saṅkṣepa-Śaṅkara-jaya*".

It is only on this understanding that I can, in good conscience, examine the way in which the ŚDV has been constructed from the components of other works. The table below identifies the verses from earlier texts which Mādhava has incorporated in the ŚDV (see Appendix C for precise details of the borrowed verses).

SOURCES FOR THE ŚDV		
Total number of verses in ŚDV:		1843
Verses composed by Mādhvava:		662
Total verses borrowed from:		
	VŚV	505
	TŚA	495
	RŚA	136
	PC	14
	AŚV	3
		1153

In addition to the material drawn from the three hagiographies discussed above—VŚV, RŚA and TŚA—there is a fourth work, the *Patañjali-carita* (PC), by Rāmabhadra-Dīkṣita, who was active c.1700.[81] Mādhava uses some fourteen verses from this text, which weaves together traditional

81 See T. S. Kuppuswami Sastri, "Rāmabhadra-Dīkṣita and the southern poets of his time", *The Indian Antiquary*, 33 (1904), pp. 126-142; [continued on] pp. 176-196. Refer especially to p.179.

stories on the life of Patañjali. The last two chapters of the PC briefly relate the life of Śaṅkara, who according to the traditions recorded here, is placed in an illustrious lineage extending from Patañjali to Gauḍapāda and to Govindapāda, the guru of Śaṅkara.

It is likely that the ŚDV contains more verses from the TŚA than the table indicates. Since the latter third of the text is missing in the only extant manuscript of the TŚA,[82] it is not possible to determine the exact nature of the additional borrowings. But there is a strong clue which points to this further connection between the ŚDV and TŚA. It is found in the famous episode (described only in these two works) in which Śiva appears before Śaṅkara in the guise of an outcaste, in order to test his understanding of non-duality. Once Śaṅkara succeeds in recognising his true form, Śiva deems him fit to carry out the various tasks which are envisaged for him. In TŚA 3.83 (=SDV 6.50), Śiva reveals to him that he will triumph over Bhāskara, Abhinavagupta, Nīlakaṇṭha and Maṇḍana. When the text breaks off in the sole remaining manuscript of the TŚA, only the task of Maṇḍana's defeat has been carried out. What transpires after this must, for the time being, remain a mystery to us. However, we do find an elaborate account of Śaṅkara's triumph over Bhāskara, Abhinavagupta and Nīlakaṇṭha in Chapter 15 of the ŚDV. As can be seen in the table on the preceding page, the fifteenth chapter of the ŚDV is the only one in which no borrowed verses have been identified. Since the anachronistic story of Śaṅkara's encounters with these three figures does not occur in the other hagiographies, it seems reasonable to assume that the TŚA has provided Mādhava with the inspiration—if not the very verses—for his account of these episodes.The borrowed verses in the ŚDV frequently show minor variations from those in their original sources. It is

---

82 See the discussion of the TŚA, above.

sometimes difficult to be certain when the differences are simply due to variant manuscript readings and when Mādhava has himself made these alterations. However, in most of the cases where the variants are significant, I have noted this by the designation [var.] in the detailed table on p. 351.

Sometimes Mādhava is compelled to make revisions simply for the sake of consistency. In ŚDV 5.90, for example, he repeats *Patañjali-carita* 8.19, which describes Śaṅkara, already in ascetic dress, entering the abode of his guru Govindapāda. But Mādhava changes one *pāda* so that Śaṅkara meets his guru in the forest on the banks of the Indubhavā [=Narmadā] river, and not in the city of Kāśī, as the original verse has it. For here Mādhava is primarily following the TŚA's version of this meeting, according to which, Govindanātha sends him to Kāśī, where he is to carry out his teaching work, *after* his training is completed.

In composing the ŚDV, Mādhava generally relies on the earlier sources to provide the details of the major incidents in Śaṅkara's life story. He frequently combines the materials of two or more sources in order to more fully elaborate these episodes. Sometimes Mādhava himself adds a few points. But for the most part, his contribution consists in the addition of ornate descriptive verses—in metres such as *sragdharā* and *śārdūlavikrīḍita*—with which he connects the borrowed verses into a coherent structure. In the seventh chapter of the ŚDV, Mādhava demonstrates his skills in weaving together three different accounts of Śaṅkara's meetings with Vyāsa and Kumārila-Bhaṭṭa. As a result of this creative editorial work, these important episodes are invested with a richness of detail which far surpasses that of the earlier versions. There are only a few occasions on which Mādhava's careful attention to detail lapses in combining disparate sources. For the most part, the resulting inconsistencies are not very serious. One of the more obvious mistakes occurs when Mādhava repeats the verses from the TŚA on the celestial origins of the main characters in the Śaṅkara story. As was noted above, Tirumala-Dīkṣita has described distinct divine emanations for Sanandana and Padmapāda, whom he takes as separate individuals. Having apparently forgotten about using these verses from the TŚA, Mādhava, later presents the popular story—as it is narrated in the RŚA—in which Sanandana and Padmapāda are one and the same person. But aside from a few such inconsistencies, the ŚDV stands as a well integrated account of Śaṅkara's life.

It is no accident, then, that the ŚDV is considered the last word in the Śaṅkara hagiographies. Mādhava has managed to include more incidents and provides a greater elaboration of most of these episodes than any of our other accounts. With his editorial skills, reflected in his deliberate and judicious use of materials, Mādhava has produced a work which contains the best of the earlier sources. I would suggest that these are the primary factors for the prominence the ŚDV has achieved. There is no doubt that the wide distribution of manuscripts, and more especially of printed texts, has also contributed greatly to establishing the pre-eminence of this work.[83] But wide circulation alone is no guarantee of success. It must be remembered that there are also numerous manuscripts of the AŚV. In fact, the publication of Anantānandagiri's text preceded the appearance of the "standard" edition of the ŚDV by some twenty years.[84] Yet the AŚV, lacking as it is in details of

---

83 There is every possibility that there was a concerted effort, probably on the part of one or more of the Śaṅkara institutions, to ensure the proliferation and distribution of manuscripts of this work throughout India. The question of the precise means by which such a text has been propagated is an important issue which, unfortunately, must remain beyond the scope of this study.

84 The first printed edition of the ŚDV in 1863 was, so far as I can tell, never very readily available. The Ānandāśrama edition did not appear until 1891. This has become the "standard" edition of the ŚDV and has achieved

Śaṅkara's life story, has not been as influential as the ŚDV.[85] It is Mādhava's work which has become the "Essential Śaṅkara-vijaya".

Additional Sources

There are various other works which refer to Śaṅkara's life. While time and space preclude an exhaustive survey, I would like to mention some of the more significant sources. One brief Sanskrit text should be considered here, insofar as it stands very much apart from the principal hagiographies. This rather curious work, *Śaṅkaravijaya-saṅgraha*, by Puruṣottama Bhāratī,

---

fairly wide distribution. There were, no doubt, several writers who must have utilised instead the AŚV, which first appeared in 1868 (in the Bibliotheca Indica Series, Calcutta), simply because of its accessibility. One notable example is Hariścandra (1850-85), an important figure in the establishment of Hindi literature. He has relied almost exclusively on the AŚV for his description of Śaṅkara's life in his essay "Śrī Śaṅkarācāryya", collected in *Bhāratendu granthāvalī*, vol. III, ed. Vrajaratnadāsa (Kāśī: Nāgarīpracāriṇo Sabhā, *saṃvat* 2010 [1953]), pp. 42-50. Thus, he writes that Śaṅkara was born in Cidambaram to Viśvajit and Kāmākṣī (p. 44). This account of Śaṅkara's birth, although preserved in the Calcutta version of the AŚV, was not destined to receive lasting acceptance.

85 Even the Paramācārya of the Kānchipuram Śaṅkara *maṭha*, who has stated his preference for the AŚV (see Appendix A for details), is compelled to make frequent references to the ŚDV when discussing the life of Śaṅkara. A series of talks he gave in Madras in 1932 (originally published in Tamil in 1933) were translated into English: *Ādi Śaṅkara: his life and times*, tr. T.M.P. Mahadevan, ([1980] Bombay: Bharatiya Vidya Bhavan, 1988). In this work, the Paramācārya sometimes cites episodes of Śaṅkara's life as they are related in the better known ŚDV. On p. 79, for example, he mentions that Maṇḍanamiśra's residence is in Māhiṣmati, as is stated in the ŚDV. According to the AŚV Maṇḍana is said to live in Vidyālaya or Vijilabindu, depending on which recension is consulted.

is difficult to date.[86] According to W. R. Antarkar, who has edited the text, one of the two available manuscripts bears the title, *Kūṣmāṇḍa-Śaṅkaravijaya.* The alternate title refers directly to the peculiar description of Śaṅkara's birth from a pumpkin. The text comprises 108 verses, largely in *śloka* metre, and one isolated prose paragraph which occurs in the fourth of its six chapters.

The first chapter describes Śiva's visit to earth, in the garb of a wandering ascetic. Perceiving the degenerate state of the world during the *kali yuga*, Śiva decides to become manifest in order to destroy the wicked. He visits Kālaṭi, which he considers to be the right place for his mortal manifestation. There he sees a pious widow whom he asks to take a seed of the *kūṣmāṇda* plant, which she is to place at the foot of a pillar, and water. But she must not pluck its ripe fruit. She looks after the plant as instructed (2.1). A single ripe fruit develops and falls to the ground in front of the pillar. A child emerges from the fruit. She takes him home and looks after him. When the people question her about the child, she relates the story of the ascetic's visit. Needless to say, they do not believe the story and abuse her angrily. However, all is shortly made well again when Bṛhaspati himself arrives to instruct the child in the sacred lore (2.8-9). The rest of the text more or less conforms to the details of Śaṅkara's life given in the better known hagiographies. The ending of the story is reminiscent of the GŚC, in that Śaṅkara last visits Vṛṣācala, sings a hymn to Viṣṇu and thereupon attains the realm of Śiva (5.15-16).

What is most noteworthy about the *Śaṅkaravijaya-saṅgraha* is not simply the story of human birth from a pumpkin seed—a common theme in Hindu mythology—but rather the suggestion of Śaṅkara's immaculate conception. There is a similar

---

86 Edited by W. R. Antarkar, in *Oriental thought* [Poona], 6 (1962), pp. 1-16

implication in the Calcutta recension of the AŚV, which describes Śaṅkara's conception—directly from Śiva—in the absence of his natural father.[87] It is possible that there was a stream of traditional stories which presented such an account of Śaṅkara's birth.

Antagonistic portrayals of Śaṅkara

While tales of an immaculate conception would certainly magnify Śaṅkara's glory, they could also, without much difficulty, be turned against him by the opponents of his Advaita doctrine. This is precisely the course of attack taken by the followers of Madhva, the 13th century founder of a rival school of Vedānta. Highly abusive accounts of Śaṅkara's life appear in two Sanskrit hagiographies of Madhva, *Maṇi-mañjarī* and *Sumadhvavijaya*, both written by Nārāyaṇa-paṇḍita, the son of Trivikrama, a direct disciple of Madhva.[88] In these texts, Śaṅkara is presented as the incarnation of the demon Maṇimat, who is born as the bastard son of a widow. To underscore this ignominious birth, his name is cleverly and ironically twisted to "Saṃkara".[89] In a sardonic reference to Śaṅkara's Advaita, the *Maṇimañjarī*, relates that as a child "Saṃkara" could only

---

87 See the discussion of the AŚV, above.

88 The more extensive account is found in the former work: *Maṇimañjarī by Nārāyaṇa-paṇḍita*, ed. T.R. Kṛṣṇācārya (Bombay: Nirṇaya-sāgara Press, 1912), which devotes two of its eight chapters to "Saṃkara's" life. The *Sumadhvavijaya* (identical details of publication to *Maṇimañjarī*), also describes the life of Śaṅkara in its first chapter. For a description of these two texts, and the Mādhvas in general, see G. A. Grierson's article "Mādhvas, Mādhvāchārīs", in the *Encyclopaedia of Religion and Ethics*, ed. James Hastings (Edinburgh, 1908-26), vol. VIII, pp. 232-235. Another useful reference is C. N. Krishnaswami Aiyer, *Sri Madhwa and Madhwaism: A short historic sketch* (Madras: G.A. Natesan, n.d. [191-?]).

89 S̲aṃkara is literally, 'the defiled one', in contrast to Ś̲aṃkara, 'the auspicious one'.

enumerate one thing at a time, because he was so poor that he never beheld more than a single object at any one time. It is "Saṃkara's" mission to carry out the demons' intentions of destroying Vedānta, by subverting its doctrines. He propagates the doctine of "*śūnya-mārga*", and eventually becomes a Buddhist, although he continues to pose as a Vedāntin. The celebrated tale of Śaṅkara's encounter with Maṇḍanamiśra and the subsequent debate with his wife is also savagely parodied. "Saṃkara" is said to seduce his Brahmin host's wife. Madhva's ultimate task is to destroy the false Brahmasūtra commentary perpetrated by this demon incarnation.

Śaṅkara's life is grist to the mill of some Buddhist writers as well. Tāranātha (b. 1575), the Tibetan scholar-monk, grants him a prominent place in his chapter on Dharmakīrti in the *History of Buddhism in India*.[90] Indeed, Śaṅkara is here accorded an unusual degree of respect. He is said to have obtained skill in debate from Mahādeva himself, and is credited with victories which bring twenty-five Buddhist centres into his fold. His disciple, Bhaṭṭācārya , who was taught by Sarasvatī, [91] was similarly successful. However, the most famous Brahmin

---

90 Tāranātha, *History of Buddhism in India*, translated by Lama Chimpa and Alaka Chattopadhyaya, ed. Debiprasad Chattopadhyaya (Simla: Indian Institute of Advanced Study, 1970), pp. 225-237. The Tibetan text was first published by Anton Schiefner in 1868, and translated by him the following year [*Tāranātha's Geschichte des Buddhismus in Indien*, St. Petersburg, 1869] Several scholars have remarked that Tāranātha's history does sometimes hit the mark in correctly identifying names and dates. In this regard it is interesting to note that he takes Śaṅkara and Dharmakīrti (c. 600-660) as contemporaries. For comments on Tāranātha and Dharmakīrti, see D. Seyfort Ruegg, "Towards a chronology of the Madhyamaka school", in *Indological and Buddhist studies: Volume in honour of J. W. de Jong on his sixtieth birthday*, ed. L. A. Hercus *et. al.* (Canberra: ANU Faculty of Asian Studies, 1982), pp. 505-530; esp. 515ff.

91 This may be a variation on the accounts in the Śaṅkara hagiographies of the Śaṅkara-Maṇḍanamiśra encounter, in which Sarasvatī plays a major role.

scholar of the day was, it seems, Kumāralīla [=Kumārila-Bhaṭṭa?] It was to him that Dharmakīrti went, in the guise of a sincere believer, in order to learn the secret teachings which would enable him to defeat the *tīrthika*s [i.e., Hindus]. The parallel with the Śaṅkara hagiographies is striking, even though the tables have been turned. All our texts agree that Kumārila-Bhaṭṭa studied directly under a Buddhist teacher, which enabled him to soundly thrash the Buddhists in debate. In atonement for the sin of repudiating his Bauddha guru, Kumārila-Bhaṭṭa later chose to immolate himself. It was at this very time that the Śaṅkara-Kumārila meeting is said to have occurred. Returning to Tāranātha's narrative, Kumāralīla, angered by Dharmakīrti's triumph over numerous Brahmins, confronts his former pupil. Dharmakīrti, of course, is victorious, and Kumāralīla embraces Buddhism.

Tāranātha next relates Śaṅkara's challenge to the monks of Nālandā. They postpone the debate for a while, so as to allow Dharmakīrti time to travel there to represent their case. The contest took place in Vārāṇasī, in the presence of a large audience. Prior to the debate, Śaṅkara stipulated the following terms:

> 'In case of our victory, we shall decide whether to drown him in the Gaṅgā or to convert him to a *tīrthika*. In the case of his victory I shall kill myself by jumping into the Gaṅgā'...Dharmakīrti defeated Śaṃkarācārya repeatedly. At last he was reduced to a position where there was nothing more to say. When Śaṃkarācārya was about to jump into the Gaṅgā, the *ācārya* tried to stop him. But he did not listen to this. He told his own disciple Bhaṭṭa Ācārya, 'go on arguing and defeat this man with shaven head. Even if you do not win, I shall be

> reborn as your son and shall go on fighting him'.
> Saying this, he jumped into the Gaṅgā and died.[92]

The following year Śaṅkara was reborn as Bhaṭṭācārya's second son. Despite seven years further preparation, Bhaṭṭācārya himself is defeated by Dharmakīrti, whereupon the two sons flee. Eventually, the second Śaṅkara comes of age and again confronts Dharmakīrti at Vārāṇasī, where an identical scenario repeats itself. Śaṅkara is reborn for a third time (to Bhaṭṭācārya's eldest son). Śiva himself tutors the boy, who feels ready for debate at the tender age of twelve. Fortunately, Dharmakīrti at last shows the good sense to put Śaṅkara out of his misery, and so brings this cycle of drownings to an end. *He* now stipulates the terms of the debate: the defeated must accept the creed of the victor. The thrice defeated Śaṅkara finally embraces the Buddhist *dharma*.

I have so far reserved comment on the conspicuous lack of Indian vernacular sources for Śaṅkara's life. Indeed, I have not as yet found a single vernacular work which is more than a hundred years old devoted to the subject.[93] This may, at first glance, seem surprising. However, it must be remembered that Śaṅkara is above all an exponent of traditions which have been

---

92 Tāranātha, *op. cit.*, p. 233.

93 There may, of course, have been some minor compositions or translations of Sanskrit texts which have not survived. But I have found no evidence for the existence of an old, influential vernacular work on Śaṅkara's life. There are, however, vernacular works which do have some references to the subject. One prominent example is the Hindi compendium of brief hagiographies, the *Bhaktmāl*, of Nābhādās (Gosvāmī Śrī Nābhājī, *Śrī Bhaktmāl,* with the commentary of Priyādās, Lucknow: Tejkumār Press, 1962). Nābhādās devotes one *chappay* verse to Śaṅkara (see pp.316-322). According to R. S. McGregor, the *Bhaktmāl* was completed early in the 17th century; its commentary by Priyādās is dated 1712 (*Hindi literature from its beginnings to the nineteenth century,* vol. 8, fasc. 6 of *A history of Indian literature*, ed. J. Gonda [Wiesbaden: Harrassowitz, 1984], pp. 108-9).

transmitted almost exclusively in Sanskrit. He is not credited with any vernacular compositions whatsoever. Neither can the speakers of a particular regional tongue lay claim to Śaṅkara as their own son. He belongs only to a greater India whose lingua franca is Sanskrit. It is only fitting, then, that his hagiographers saw fit to glorify his deeds through the medium of Sanskrit.

In the absence of vernacular sources, one may well ask how Śaṅkara's life story has been popularized. The question can be easily answered for post-independent India, where Śaṅkara serves as an important representative of national values. To begin with, schoolchildren are given set texts which present an "official" account of his life. In Uttar Pradesh, for example, eighth standard pupils have been reading *Hamāre pūrvaja* since the 1950's.[94] The short chapters of this Hindi reader eulogize the mythical and historical ancestors of the Indian people, from Bharata and Bhīṣma to Śaṅkara and Śivājī. As well, Śaṅkara has his own place in the widely circulated educational series of comic books, "Amar Chitra Katha", published in Hindi and English. Number 60 in the series is entitled *Adi Shankara. The story of the expounder of the Advaita school of philosophy*. A citation from the edifying preface to the comic book will suffice to describe the way in which Śaṅkara is presented as a truly national figure:

> Then, as now, the disruptive forces of religion, race, caste and language threatened to weaken the fabric of the one nation that is India. Now, as then, the teachings of a man like Shankara, who believed

---

94 Kṛṣṇadev Prasād Gauṛ, *Hamāre pūrvja*, 3 vols. [reprinted many times]. The edition I have consulted—printed in a run of 350,000—has the following details: [*rājniyukt prakāśak*] Mathurā: Taiknīkal Prakāśan, 1980. The entry on Śaṅkara appears in vol. 3, pp. 56-60. I am indebted to Yogendra Yadav who supplied the text and read through it with me.

> in the One Undivided Self, can serve to awaken our country to a sense of unity.

More recently, in 1982/83, a major film on his life was released in India, entitled simply "Ādi Śaṅkarācārya".[95] This was, I believe, the first full length feature film to be made in Sanskrit, although a Hindi version was also produced. The film has since appeared on the Indian national television network in both its Sanskrit and Hindi versions. The textbook, comic and feature film are all clearly based on the depiction of Śaṅkara's life in Mādhava's *Śaṅkaradigvijaya*. Even though a Hindi translation of this work may well have been their more immediate source,[96] these three contemporary "texts", which have established Śaṅkara's place in popular culture, are direct offshoots from the Sanskrit text of the ŚDV.

I cannot offer a definitive description of how the Sanskrit accounts of Śaṅkara's life have been popularized during the millenium prior to Indian Independence. But I would suggest that the project of glorifying Śaṅkara's life, as well as the dissemination of his teachings, has been carried out largely by the Śaṅkara *maṭhas*, which are known to date back to at least the 14th century.[97] The *maṭhas* have, of course, recopied and preserved manuscripts of the hagiographies, along with the manuscripts of Śaṅkara's own compositions. The peripatetic life style of the present day *ācāryas* who head these *maṭhas* emulates the extensive wandering of Śaṅkara as is related in the hagiographies. We can, I think, assume that some of these teachers have, in keeping with Hindu ascetic traditions, been

---

95 The script and direction are by the Kannada film-maker, G. V. Iyer; music by Balmuralikrishna, a leading exponent of Karnatak music; production by N.F.D.C., Bombay. The details on the film are supplied in the *International film guide 1984*, ed. Peter Cowie (London 1983), pp. 178-79.

96 A complete Hindi translation of the ŚDV has been available since at least 1943. See note 72.

97 See Chapter Six for a discussion of the *maṭhas* and their *ācāryas*.

touring India since the time of the foundation of the Śaṅkara *maṭhas*. It is likely that in the course of their preaching, which was most probably in the vernacular, they have spread the accounts of Śaṅkara's life they knew from the Sanskrit hagiographies, and from oral tradition.[98] Even today the *ācāryas* draw sizeable crowds in the large towns and cities. They often attend major religious festivals, in particular the *kumbha melā*, where they can easily attract several thousand listeners to their talks. I was fortunate to be an eye witness to this continuing teaching tradition during the most recent *kumbha melā*, held at Allahabad in 1989, at which three chief *ācāryas* were present. The considerable efforts they made in promoting the knowledge of Śaṅkara's life and work must have made an impact on more than a few of the ten million participants at the festival.

---

98 Many talks of the present day *ācārya* s have been collected and separately published. I have seen such works in Tamil, Telugu, Kannada and Hindi. There are also some English translations of these texts. See note 85 above and the Bibliography for details.

CHAPTER II

The Construction of the Life Story

Perhaps the only certain biographical details we have for Śaṅkara are the the name of his teacher and identity of his leading disciples. In the absence of autobiographical statements, textual references to eye-witness accounts or even records preserved in inscriptions, we can only assume that the life story of Śaṅkara has been constructed on the basis of traditional stories which were circulated orally. This oral tradition must have grown substantially in the centuries following Śaṅkara's death. For the elaborate life story of Śaṅkara found in the Sanskrit hagiographies stands in strong contrast to the paucity of verifiable biographical data. The influences which encouraged the composition of these hagiographies cannot be identified with certainty. But it is likely that the emergence of the texts coincides with the development of major Śaṅkarite institutions.[1] The Śaṅkara story further expanded as later authors built upon the earlier textual materials. By the time Mādhava's *Śaṅkara-digvijaya* gained currency, probably by the end of the 18th century, there was a well established body of literature to facilitate the transmission of Śaṅkara's life story.

To some extent it is possible to trace the growth of the life story through the Sanskrit hagiographies. But it must be remembered that these texts, written hundreds of years after the time of Śaṅkara, cannot be construed simply as historical records. For this reason, there is little to be gained in attempting a comparative analysis of the hagiographies in terms

---

1 See the Chapter Six for a discussion of the Śaṅkara *maṭhas*.

of their historical accuracy.[2] Indeed it seems more appropriate to take the hagiographers as the creators of a life story—and not as its recorders. For this reason, I would prefer to recognise the validity of all the hagiographies insofar as they are viable literary structures for the representation of Śaṅkara's life. The numerous variations found in the texts probably tell us more about the predilections of their respective authors than about Śaṅkara himself. The different orientations of the hagiographers have already been discussed in Chapter One. Here I will concentrate instead on the points where the texts agree. In focussing on the incidents which all the hagiographers chose to include, it will be possible to examine the fundamental patterns of the life story.

Because of the lack of eye-witness accounts, it is possible that the hagiographers had to rely more heavily than they might have otherwise on already established models in order to construct a life story of Śaṅkara. Unfortunately, the study of religious biography in traditional India is still in a formative state.[3] For this reason, it seems premature to speculate on the extent to which the Śaṅkara life stories conform to principles inherent in Indian hagiography. While there is no doubt that

---

2 It is on this point which I must disagree with the approach taken by Dr. W. R. Antarkar in his unpublished thesis, "Śaṅkara-vijayas: a comparative and critical study", University of Poona, 1960.

3 Phyllis Granoff has made a very significant contribution to the field in a number of recent articles: "Holy warriors: a preliminary study of some biographies of saints and kings in the classical Indian tradition", *JIP* 12 (1984), 291-303; "Scholars and wonder-workers: some remarks on the role of the supernatural in philosophical contests in Vedānta hagiographies", *JAOS* 105 (1985), 459-467; "The miracle of a hagiography without miracles: some comments on the Jain lives of the Pratyekabuddha Karakaṇḍa" *JIP* 14 (1986), 389-403; "Jain lives of Haribhadra: an inquiry into the sources and logic of the legends", *JIP* 17 (1989), 105-128; see also her two articles in *Monks and magicians: religious biographies in Asia*, ed. Phyllis Granoff and Koichi Shinohara (Oakville, Ontario: Mosaic Press), 1988.

hagiography is (at least from our perspective) a distinct literary genre in India, few of the numerous available texts have yet been examined. Moreover, text critical problems in this genre are considerable, as can be seen above in Chapter One. This has made broad comparisons difficult. Even a more specific comparative project, utilising for example the Rāmānuja and Madhva hagiographies, is beyond the scope of the present study. It is my hope that this work may, however, provide materials useful to a wider study of hagiography in India.

The table on the following pages summarizes and compares the way in which our eight Sanskrit sources treat the life of Śaṅkara. The table lists virtually every major event in the life story which figures in two or more of the texts. The sequence of events listed is based largely on the order in which they occur in the most widely distributed hagiography, the ŚDV. Some of the more significant variant versions of individual episodes are indicated in the table with asterisks. Because the sole extant edition of the TŚA is incomplete,[4] the number of the later episodes which are included in this text remains in question.

It may come as a surprise to discover that some well known incidents are not found in many of the Sanskrit hagiographies. Only two of our sources relate how Śaṅkara worshipped Śiva in the guise of an outcaste (no. 17). Similarly, the foundation of the *maṭhas* (no. 42) is described in only two of the texts. However these episodes have since been popularized by the mass media. Both incidents can be found in the school textbook *Hamāre pūrvaja*, in the widely circulated comic book "Adi Shankara" and in G.V. Iyer's film "Ādi Śaṅkarācārya".[5]

---

4 See the discussion of the TŚA in Chapter One.

5 See Chapter One, under the heading Additional Sources.

	aśv	cśv	vśv	gśc	rśa	tśa	śdv	ġvk
1. Mythic setting for life story	X	X				X	X	X
2. Parents' *tapas* (at Vṛśācala*)	X	X*	X*	X*	X	X	X*	X*
3. Ś born at Kālaṭi in Kerala	X	X	X	X	X	X	X	X
4. Father dies when Ś is 5 or 6	X	X	X	X	X	X	X	X
5. Ś's prayer to Lakṣmī						X	X	
6. He moves river / creates river*			X	X	X*	X*	X	X
7. King of Kerala meets Ś					X	X	X	X
8. Five sages predict Ś's future						X	X	
9. Seized by crocodile in river	X	X	X	X	X		X	X
10. Crocodile is a Gandharva		X			X			X
11. Promises to return to mother		X	X	X	X	X	X	X
12. Saves Krishna statue			X	X			X	X
13. Meets his guru Govindapāda	X	X	X	X	X	X	X	X
14. Stops a flood, saving guru						X	X	
15. Given *liṅga*, or 5 *liṅga*s*	X*	X						X
16. Śiva comes out of *liṅga*	X	X						X
17. Meets outcaste who is Śiva						X	X	
18. Sanandana walks on water		X		X	X		X	X
19. Meets Vyāsa, gains approval	X	X	X	X	X	X	X	X
20. Meets Kumārila Bhaṭṭa	X	X	X	X	X	X	X	X
21. Debates Maṇḍana/Viśvarūpa*	X	X	X*	X*	X*	X	X	X*

	aśv	cśv	vśv	ġśc	rśa	tśa	śdv	ġvk
22. Tested by*/ debates Sarasvatī	X	X	X*	X*	X*	X	X	X
23. Enters body of king, Amaruka*	X*	X	X	X*	X*	X*	X*	X*
24. Narasiṃha saves Śaṅkara	X	X					X	X
25. Ś installs Sarasvatī at Śṛṅgerī	X	X				X	X	X
26. Sees serpent protecting frog		X						X
27. Ś sets out for *digvijaya*	X	X				X	X	X
28. Kāpālika tries to behead Ś			X		X	X	X	X
29. Ś revives dead child					X	?	X	
30. Ś makes the dumb speak		X	X	X		?	X	X
31. Ś makes the simple learned			X	X	X	X	X	X
32. Disciples jealous of Sureśvara			X		X	?	X	X
33. Performs mother's funeral rite		X	X	X	X	?	X	X
34. Ś curses people of Kālaṭi		X	X	X	X	?	X	X
35. Restores lost work of king					X	?	X	X
36. Establishes temple at Kāñcī	X	X				?	X	X
37. Bhairava approves of Ś	X	X				?	X	
38. Treated for illness by Aśvins			X		X	?	X	X
39. *Sarvajñapīṭha* at Kañcī/Kaśmir*		X*	X	X*	X*	?	X	X
40. Ś granted hot spring	X	X				?	X	X
41. Establishes 6 *bhakti* sects	X	X				?		X
42. Establishes 4 *maṭhas*		X				?		X

Another incident which finds a place in these three contemporary sources is Śaṅkara's prayer to Lakṣmī (no. 5). The role of the media in shaping the popular conceptions of Śaṅkara in recent times cannot be underestimated. But it is essential to first consider how the Sanskrit sources represent the life of Śaṅkara.

The model and perhaps the most fundamental theme of Śaṅkara's life story is that of the *avatāra*. His story follows a typical pattern in which a great god takes birth as a human in order to destroy demonic forces and restore order on earth. Phyllis Granoff has shown that the *avatāra* motif is common to the traditional biographies of both kings and saints in India.[6] Indeed, even in the case of authors who are eye-witnesses to the lives of their subjects, the hero is likely to be depicted as a god. The recasting of the hero in a divine mould is not simply a retrospective glorification. It is rather a paradigm chosen intentionally by the hagiographers.

Within the framework of the *avatāra* story, an underlying narrative tension is manifest in the shifts between the divine and human modes of the hero's actions. Śaṅkara is, on the one hand, depicted as the great god Śiva, particularly in the opening and conclusion of the narrative. In order to emphasize this, the author must introduce divine players in the drama. Numerous miracles will add further substance to the celestial mode. But Śaṅkara is, after all, a man who must suffer at least something of the human condition. This mode is developed through some poignant episodes, especially during Śaṅkara's childhood.

The mythological setting of the hagiographies will be discussed separately in Chapter Three. Here the emphasis is on the basic pattern of Śaṅkara's life story, as revealed in the incidents common to the eight Sanskrit hagiographies.

---

6 Granoff, "Holy warriors", esp. pp. 290-296.

Numerous quotations are used in order to reproduce some of the flavour of the original sources.

Circumstances of his birth and early years (nos. 2, 3, 4, 9, 13)

All the texts agree in describing the *tapas* which is undertaken by a pious but childless brahmin couple. The husband is invariably identified as Śivaguru while his wife usually remains unnamed or is simply referred to by the respectful epithet Āryā or Āryāmbā. [7] It is implied that the couple is past the usual age of procreation. For this reason, the *tapas* they perform is all the more impressive:

> The two of them, who were controlled and restrained, were engaging in *tapas*, wearing *rudrākṣa* beads and ashes. Sometimes they lived on [food which they] prepared, sometimes on water, sometimes on fruit, sometimes leaves, sometimes air, and sometimes on nothing. They bathed even in cold water, were scorched in the five fires, and meditated always on Vṛṣācaleśa in the lotus of their hearts. Although elderly, they were always engaged in worship and gratified with sweets thousands of brahmins, learned in the *śruti*. They made offerings to all the gods and obtained the blessings of the brahmins. [8]

Most of the texts specify the place of their *tapas* as Vṛṣācala, a Śaiva sacred site, usually identified with present day Trichūr in Kerala.

---

[7] The TŚA once refers to her as Viśiṣṭā (1.92). It is possible that this follows the Calcutta recension of the AŚV, which also uses this name.

[8] CŚV 2.34-38a. In 2.37 I take the alternate reading, *dvijān sahasrān*. Read *miṣṭānnaiḥ* for *miṣṭānaiḥ*.

Pleased with their *tapas*, Śiva decides to bestow on them the boon of a son. Disguised as a brahmin, he appears to Śivaguru in a dream and offers to grant his heart's desire. However there is a catch. He must decide whether he would prefer one son who is all-knowing but short-lived, or numerous sons who are undistinguished but long-lived. Śivaguru, of course, chooses the former. He awakens and informs his wife of the good news. The happy couple arrange for the feeding of a large number of brahmins. This is how the conception occurred:

> ...Having satiated the best of the brahmins with clothing, food, gold, and the like, the couple then obtained permission to depart from those brahmins, who had finished eating, and received their blessings. They were desirous of eating the food which those [brahmins] had left. [Meanwhile,] a light coming from Īśvara entered into the food which was [about to be] eaten. Delighted, the couple then ate the food with respect. Āryāmbā conceived a child, as the eastern quarter [does] the full moon.[9]

The couple return home. Although Āryā is emaciated from her austerities, a wonderful pregnancy ensues. The great power of the embryo she bears causes her some discomfort. But this is more than compensated for by the marvellous signs she witnesses:

> Asleep, she saw herself carried by a great, naturally white bull, and being praised by those such as Vidyādharas, foremost of those skilled in singing and the like, who approached with modesty. Obtaining the boon, she heard the words "victory,

9 CŚV 5.27cd-30.

> victory" and "protect [me]"; "look upon me with your glance".[10]

The dreams, the visions and voices she hears indicate the divine nature of the infant developing in her womb. There is no doubt that it is Śiva, although the texts vary in specifying the exact nature of the incarnation.

Our sources are nearly unanimous in naming Kālaṭi, a village in the Ernakulam district of Kerala, as the child's birthplace.[11] As would be expected, the birth occurs at an auspicious time. This is described as "a day in the spring season when the five planets were in exaltation".[12] The birth is accompanied by wondrous signs:

> On that day, numerous herds of creatures who were [normally] antagonistic—prominent among which are the deer and hyena, the elephant and lion, and the snake and rat—giving up their [mutual] enmity, went about together and were glad. They rubbed

---

10 VŚV 4.17-18; ŚDV 2.64-65.

11 A significant variant occurs in the Calcutta edition of the AŚV, according to which the birthplace is in Chidambaram, Tamil Nadu, see above, p. 22ff. A more minor variant which is sometimes found is the spelling Kāraṭi. The town of Kālaṭi has now become a place of interest for pilgrims and tourists. It is reached by road from Alwaye (Āluvāy) which is about 25 kms. north of Ernakulam on the main rail line. A memorial temple complex was constructed in 1910 by the Śriṅgerī Śaṅkara-*maṭha*, on what is said to be the actual site of his birth. The buildings are situated above the steep banks of the river today known as the Periyar. Closer to the town centre, another monument, a nine story *kīrti-stambha* which stands 46 metres high, was constructed by the Kānchipuram Śaṅkara- *maṭha* in 1978.

12 CŚV 5.37. See also VŚV 4.20, ŚDV 2.71, AŚV p. 8 (line 7), RŚA 1.26, GŚC 1.59, GVK 1.59; the TŚA does not provide any specifics. Although the texts give only quite general details, a number of writers have tried to derive the exact time of birth on the basis of this sketchy information. See, for example, T. S. Narayana Sastry, *The Age of Śaṅkara* ([1916], reprinted Madras, 1971), pp. 237ff.

> each other nicely and removed [each other's] itching. At that time, the trees and creepers released fruits and a multitude of flowers. The waters of all the rivers became clear. The oceans forsook their natural agitation and water rose up suddenly from out of the mountain ranges. Suddenly, excellent books, in the hands of those adhering to doctrines opposed to [that of] the proponents of Advaita, fell down loudly. The summits of the *śruti* [i.e., the Upaniṣads] were dazzling white [i.e., as teeth sparkle in laughing (*has*)], and the heart-lotus of Vyāsa bloomed....Beholding the birth chamber which was made bright by his body and which was illuminated in the night on account of his *tejas*, wonder was produced for all the people. The house, which was without a lamp, became free from darkness.[13]

This scenario is comprised of stock images which are widely used in *kāvya* literature in describing the circumstances attendant on the birth of a great being. Most of these images can be found in Aśvaghoṣa's *Buddha-carita* (esp. 1.21-26) and Kālidāsa's *Raghuvaṃśa.* [14]

Indeed, up to this point, the whole of the story is developed along the lines of conventional patterns for the advent of a great

---

13 VŚV 4.22-24; 28; and ŚDV 2.73-75; 82.

14 In *Raghuvaṃśa* 3.13-15, Kālidāsa describes the birth of Raghu in this way: "Then, at the appointed time, she bore a son whose wealth of good fortune was indicated by the five planets resting at the apex [of their orbits] without setting....That moment, the directions became clear. A pleasant wind blew. The sacrificial fire, whose flame went clockwise, accepted the offering. Everything was predicting that which is auspicious. For the birth of such a one is for the uplift of the world. On account of the innate lustre of that well born one, which was spreading all around the bed in the birth chamber, the night lamps were bereft of lustre..."

man. Now an incident occurs which sets in motion the events which give specific definition to Śaṅkara's life:

> His father, although an old man, was performing the ritual actions for him, according to the precepts of the *śruti*. Seeing that foremost of sons, he was pleased. Just when he was wishing to perform [the boy's] initiation, in his fifth year, he died. In this world, destiny is insurmountable.[15]

The grief-stricken widow carries out the funeral rites for her husband and manages to arrange for the *upanayana* of her son. The texts emphasize the special warm relationship which develops between the mother and her only child. But the forces of destiny do not allow much consolation for his mother:

> She was the refuge for Śaṅkara and he was [the refuge] for his mother. Separation from their relationship was unbearable for both of them. Nevertheless, because of his immortal nature, he did not want marriage. Does one who has gone to Meru wish for an inferior place?[16]

Śaṅkara is impelled to seek the immortal state which, in the Advaita tradition, is only possible for the renouncer. There is no scope for his following a householder's life. This creates a tension in the narrative, and much anguish for his aging mother.

Even this train of events follows a mythic model. The precedent of Śiva's boons to the legendary sage Upamanyu is cited as a motivating factor for the *tapas* undertaken by Śaṅkara's parents.[17] Upamanyu's tale provides the specific

---

15 VŚV 4.32.

16 VŚV 4.42; ŚDV 5.34

17 Āryā mentions the deeds of Upamanyu to her husband, Śivaguru, as an incentive to practise *tapas* in CŚV 2.43, GVK 1.45 and ŚDV 2.47. The entire

framework for the Śaṅkara story. At the age of five, Upamanyu felt the call to practise penance in the forest. His widowed mother tried in vain to dissuade her only son from leaving home. His sheer determination was the only factor in his departure. There is no promise of return, although a happy ending does, in fact, ensue.

Strong inclinations alone are insufficient reason, in the Śaṅkara story, for his renunciation. Fate must intervene in the form of a crocodile who seizes the young Śaṅkara while he is bathing in the river.[18] Following a tradition which allows renunciation in the face of a life-threatening calamity (*āpat-saṃnyāsa*), he asks his mother's permission to become a *saṃnyāsin*. She has little choice but to agree. The moment he declares his renunciation, he is miraculously freed from the crocodile's jaws. Before setting out on the road he makes a moving promise to his mother:

> "Mother, whether it is day or night, or in between, whether [you are] in control of your faculties (*svavaśaga*) or not, you should think of me. I will come there at that time, having left everything [else]. You should be confident [about this]. I will also carry out your [funeral] rites".[19]

This establishes an unusual bond for a renouncer. But in these circumstances it seems somehow appropriate.

---

story is related in the second and third chapters of the VŚV and GŚC 2.19-40. See Chapter Three for a translation of the VŚV's version of the story.

18 One very notable exception occurs in the TŚA, the only source which disallows the crocodile incident. See the discussion in Chapter One.

19 VŚV 4.52; ŚDV 5.71. The AŚV makes no mention of the promise. But this text has almost nothing to say on Śaṅkara's early years. The Madras edition makes only the briefest reference of the crocodile incident (p. 16 line 4). The Calcutta edition omits even this.

Now he is free to fulfil his destiny. Still he must first receive formal initiation as a *saṃnyāsin,* so he sets out in search of his guru. After a considerable journey,

> the great soul, desirous of learning that [doctrine] which was complete in all respects, reached Govindapāda, whose greatness was extensive. He had learned the supreme truth from Gauḍapāda, who was the pupil of Vyāsa's son, and was established in Brahman.[20]

Śaṅkara finds his guru and a place in the illustrious Advaita lineage which the tradition traces back not only to Vyāsa, but ultimately to Śiva himself. The texts also refer to a traditional story which links Govindapāda and his teacher Gauḍapāda to yet another lineage, descending from Patañjali:

> [Govindapāda], having entered a cave in the earth, and learned from the lord of serpents himself, who was manifest [as Patañjali], proclaimed to the world the *Śabda-bhāṣya* and the *Yoga* [*sūtra*] because he was intent on serving the world.[21]

---

20 TŚA 2.105; ŚDV 5.97.

21 TŚA 2.104; ŚDV 5.96. There may be a misprint in the TŚA which reads *prakaṭitam acalācale,* while the ŚDV has a clearer reading, *prakaṭitam acala-tale,* lit. 'proclaimed on earth'. A similar verse occurs in VŚV 4.64. An elaborate version of this story is found in the fifth chapter of the *Patañjali-carita* of Rāmabhadra Dīkṣita (Kāvyamāla Series no.51, Bombay: Nirṇayasāgara Press 1895). Patañjali teaches his divine grammar to a thousand students simultaneously in the thousand-pillared hall of the Naṭarāja temple in Chidambaram. He is able to accomplish this because he is the embodiment of the primeval serpent, Ādiśeṣa, who supports the world with his thousand heads. Since no mortal can gaze upon his true form, he is obliged to teach from behind a curtain. One day, curiosity gets the better of his students. They pull back the curtain and are immediately burned by his *tejas.* One student survives. This is Gauḍapāda, a rather dull-witted boy, who had left the hall without permission, just prior to the disaster. Although Patañjali must mete

Śaṅkara receives the mantle of traditional authority from Govindapāda. He is now qualified to assume his real work, the restoration of the true teachings of Vedānta. To this end, he must compose a commentary on the *Brahmasūtra*.

Meets Vyāsa who approves his work and extends his life (no. 19)

Surely there could be no one more qualified than Vyāsa, traditionally regarded as the author of the *Brahmasūtra*, to confirm the validity of Śaṅkara's commentary. It is presumably for this reason that all the texts relate Vyāsa's surprise visit to Śaṅkara, soon after he has completed the commentary. There are two very different versions of what happens at their meeting. In the more predictable account, he greets Vyāsa with great respect:

> Seeing the foremost of those whose speech is controlled, the guru of gurus, whose sight infused confidence, Śaṅkara, together with a host of disciples, rose up to meet him, with delight in his heart.[22]

Śaṅkara praises him at some length. Vyāsa approves of the commentary and grants an extension of his life, which is drawing to the end of the sixteen years originally allotted him. Śaṅkara is given another sixteen years in which to accomplish his mission.

In the other version of the meeting, related in the AŚV and CŚV, Śaṅkara treats Vyāsa rather disrespectfully and defeats him

---

out some punishment to his wayward student, he does directly give him the teachings. Gauḍapāda, in turn transmits the doctrine to Govinda.

22 TŚA 4.8; ŚDV 7.21; cf. VŚV 4.70ff., RŚA 2.1ff., GŚC 3.62ff., GVK 2.29ff.

in debate.[23] This might suggest that there was a tradition (an earlier tradition?) which held that Śaṅkara was fully capable of defending the truth of his *Brahmasūtra* commentary against *all* comers. In this light, Śaṅkara, who is after all none other than Śiva, must be at least the equal of Vyāsa. The ŚDV tries to combine both versions, but nonetheless depicts Śaṅkara behaving quite respectfully to the old brahmin. The two versions of the meeting converge in Padmapāda's calling an end to the debate: "Śaṅkara is Śaṅkara manifest [in bodily form], and Vyāsa is Nārāyaṇa himself. When a dispute occurs between the two, what am I, a servant, to do"?[24] This verse reasserts the divine mode of the narrative.

The reference to Śaṅkara's life span in this episode is conspicuous in a narrative which otherwise gives little scope to temporal concerns. The possibility that Śaṅkara may have lived a short life—only thirty-two years according to most of the hagiographers—cannot, of course, be ruled out.[25] But in view of the intervention of the immortal sage and the symmetry in the stipulation of two identical life cycles, I would be inclined to take the sixteen years in a figurative sense, rather than attributing chronological significance to it. Bearing in mind the notion that there are sixteen digits of the moon, the sixteen years may be read as a metaphor for the lunar cycle. Other significant numerical associations include the sixteen libations of the soma ritual and the sixteen items of worship employed in *pūjā*.

---

23 See Chapter V, above, for the account of the meeting in the AŚV.

24 AŚV p. 169, lines 8-9; CŚV 14.32; ŚDV 7.11.

25 The CŚV is the only one of the eight hagiographies which makes no mention of the 16 year life span, nor of Vyāsa's boon. In the penultimate chapter, Cidvilāsa refers to Śaṅkara's body being old and worn out: *jarā-jarjara-vigraha* (CŚV 31.32).

Meets Kumārila-Bhaṭṭa (no. 20)

The texts portray Kumārila-Bhaṭṭa as the man responsible for the defeat of Buddhism and the re-establishment of the Vedic path.[26] His victory is accomplished largely through debates. But two of the texts refer to more extreme encounters in which the Buddhists lose their heads as well as the argument.[27] At first, Kumārila is unsuccessful : "I was unable to defeat them, not knowing the secret meaning of their doctrines".[28] He then decides to learn the teachings from the inside, directly from a Buddhist (or Jaina) guru.[29] This enables him to triumph over his opponents, but he also incurs evil karma: "Even one who imparts a single syllable is a guru. How much more should be said of one who teaches the *śāstra*s? Having learned from an all-knowing guru, I have rebuked that guru and [so am guilty of] a great offence".[30] In order to atone for his sinful deed, Kumārila

---

26 He is referred to as Kumārila only in the RŚA (2.20ff.), TŚA (4.17ff.) and in those TŚA verses which are repeated in the ŚDV. The other texts refer to him simply as Bhaṭṭa, Bhaṭṭācārya or Bhaṭṭapāda. There are two somewhat different versions of this incident. One is found in the AŚV and CŚV which describe the Śaṅkara-Kumārila meeting in Ruddhanagara (or Rudranagara). The other six texts say the meeting was in Prayāga.

27 "An excellent brahmin named Bhaṭṭācārya, [who] arrived from the northern country, defeated countless Bauddhas and Jainas, who were clinging to evil doctrines (*duṣṭamata*), by means of various different sorts of knowledge and arguments (*prasaṅga*). Having cut off their heads with axes, and throwing them down into numerous wooden mortars, he made a powder [of them] by whirling around a pestle. In this way, he was fearless in carrying out the destruction of those who held evil doctrines. AŚV p. 173, lines 5-8. See also CŚV 16.20.

28 VŚV 5.24; ŚDV 7.93.

29 Several of the texts relate that he was found out. He is pushed from a great height by his Buddhist "colleagues" whom Vyāsācala refers to rather sarcastically as "those who practise the doctrine of *ahiṃsā*" (5.28). His faith in the Vedas miraculously protects him from injury.

30 VŚV 5.31.

resolves to end his life in a slow burning fire of chaff. When Śaṅkara arrives on the scene, the fire is already alight.

The relationship between Śaṅkara and Kumārila is rather complex. On the one hand, they are allied in their mutual adherence to the Vedic path. Indeed most of the hagiographies relate Kumārila's cordiality and respect for Śaṅkara. Nevertheless there is some underlying tension between them because of their differing perspectives. The former emphasizes the way of ritual action, while the latter, of course, teaches the way of knowledge as the sole means of liberation. The AŚV makes their differences explicit. On seeing Kumārila seated in the mound of burning chaff, Śaṅkara says:

> "How has [such a] state been reached by you, who are ignorant, oh brahmin? [It is] because, oh foolish one, you do not know the sacred texts which have hidden meanings such as, 'If the slayer thinks to slay it; or, slain, thinks it is slain, both of them do not know. This [Self] does not slay, nor is it slain' ".[31]

In the hagiographies Śaṅkara resolves the tension by asking Kumārila to write a sub-commentary for his newly composed *Brahmasūtra-bhāṣya.*[32] Kumārila cxprcsscs his admiration for the work, but is firm in his resolve to carry out his self-immolation. Instead he recommends his chief disciple for this task. He is "renowned in the world as a great householder who

---

31 AŚV p. 173, lines 16-19. The quote is from *Kaṭhopaniṣad* 2.19. See also CŚV 16.24-25.

32 In the AŚV Śaṅkara simply asks for a debate with Kumārila. What is most interesting here is that Kumārila initially mistakes Śaṅkara for a Buddhist: "...Why is it, you excellent young Bauddha, that you did not come here when I was in my normal state (*jāgrat-kāle*) and are [now] coming here causing me distress" (p. 173 lines 20-21).

is devoted to ritual action according to the Vedas".[33] Of course he will have to be first won over to the way of knowledge.

Debates Maṇḍanamiśra/Viśvarūpa, Sarasvatī adjudicates (no.21)

This debate is one of the focal points of the life story. While the hagiographies do not agree on the identity of the supporting actor in this episode, they are unanimous about his role.[34] He is the foremost of Śaṅkara's opponents. His reputation is perhaps greater than that of his guru, Kumārila. Their debate will determine who holds the supreme authority for the interpretation of Hindu traditions: the Vedic ritualist, who is necessarily a householder, or a renouncer who follows the path of knowledge. The hagiographers mark a major shift in the cultural code of orthodoxy. Their narrative accounts bring to life a transition of sacred authority from the brahmin householder to the *saṃnyāsin.*

Maṇḍana/Viśvarūpa's wealth is commensurate with his fame. He lives in an enormous mansion. So vast is his learning that it permeates the environs of his home. When Śaṅkara asks

---

33 VŚV 5.35; ŚDV 7.114.

34 Our texts are evenly divided on this point. Four texts refer to this great opponent as Viśvarūpa, while three name him Maṇḍanamiśra. The ŚDV uses both these names because Mādhava has borrowed verses from the VŚV and RŚA on the one side and TŚA on the other. Our texts are probably not very reliable for information on the question of the Maṇḍana-Sureśvara equation. For a useful discussion and clarification of the confusion between Maṇḍana and Sureśvara, see the introduction by S. Kuppuswami Sastri to his edition of *Brahmasiddhi by Acharya Maṇḍanamiśra* ([Madras, 1937] reprinted Delhi: Sri Satguru Publications, 1984) esp. p. lvii. It is interesting to note that VŚV 5. 37ff. and GVK 2.47ff. refer to an attendant and disciple of Kumārila named Maṇḍana who is quickly won over to Śaṅkara's side just prior to Śaṅkara's meeting Viśvarūpa.

a group of servant women the whereabouts of this celebrated abode, they reply most eloquently in a series of verses:

> Know that to be the abode of Maṇḍanamiśra where there are parrots kept in cages at the door, uttering words relating to different kinds of knowledge [beginning with] *pratyakṣa* and ending with *śabda*.[35]
>
> ...uttering words relating to different views such as the identity of the *jīva* and Īśvara and the difference between the two.
>
> ...uttering words relating to setting forth arguments about the correct suffixes at the end of words, roots, etc.
>
> ...uttering words with regard to the performance of deeds suitable for a brahmin, such ás [ritual] bathing...[36]

On the day of Śaṅkara's arrival Maṇḍana/Viśvarūpa is engaged, as always, in his ritual practice. But he is no ordinary ritualist: "in order to have a brahmin there, he summoned Vyāsa—who came because of the strength of his *mantra*—to the [sacrificial] place of the ancestors".[37] According to some of the texts, Jaimini is present as well.

Although one set of hagiographies describes a cordial and respectful meeting of the two great men, another dramatizes the conflict right from the outset. According to the latter, more colourful accounts, when Śaṅkara arrives at the house, he is at first unable to enter: "realising that the door was locked and that entry would be difficult, he entered from a path in the sky by

---

35 This is a tentative translation of *pratyakṣa-śabdānta-miti-prabhedaiḥ*. Another possibility is that the words express "different sorts of knowledge and have final terminations which are loud and clear".

36 AŚV p. 175, first 4 verses.

37 AŚV p. 175, lines 3-4.

the power of *prāṇāyāma* ".[38] Maṇḍana/Viśvarūpa is horrified at the inauspicious arrival of a *saṃnyāsin* in his ritual space. He rudely questions Śaṅkara, who sarcastically twists the meaning of his words to return his insults. The verbal sparring reveals more a conflict of lifestyles than doctrines, but it is a lively preview of the householder versus renouncer debate which will follow:

> [M:] "Where are you from, shaven-head"?
>
> [Ś:] "I am shaven as far down as the neck".
>
> [M:] "What? Have you been drinking"?
>
> [Ś:] "Yes, I have water when I am thirsty".
>
> [M:] "You must be drunk."
>
> [Ś:] "Drunkenness is normal for householders".
>
> [M:] "Are you being stupid?"
>
> [Ś:] "Those who identify with the body are stupid".
>
> [M:] "You must be down on your luck to come here begging."
>
> [Ś:] "One who does not know how to honour an ascetic is unlucky".
>
> [M:] "Your presence makes my home impure."
>
> [Ś:] "Householders who don't live properly make their homes impure."
>
> [M:] "You must be a thief to sneak into my home like this."
>
> [Ś:] "You mistake your own inner demons— desire, anger, greed, pride, delusion and jealousy— for thieves.[39]

---

38 AŚV p. 176, lines 18-19.

39 AŚV p. 177, lines 1-4. This is a very free translation.

Vyāsa intervenes to put an end to this banter. He advises Maṇḍana to receive Śaṅkara with the respect due a *saṃnyāsin*. When he is offered food, Śaṅkara insists that the only alms he seeks are those of debate. The two men make a wager, stipulating the terms of the debate. It is an all or nothing contest. The loser must give up his very way of life and follow that of the victor.

Both parties to the debate are pleased to accept Maṇḍana/Viśvarūpa's wife as the arbiter. Although she goes by different names in the texts: Sarasavāṇī, Bhāratī, Ubhaya-Bhāratī, etc., it will be more convenient to refer to her simply as Sarasvatī. For all the hagiographers present her as an incarnation of the goddess of learning. As such she is eminently qualified to adjudicate the debate. The hagiographers recount how the goddess Sarasvatī once laughed at the sage Durvāsas when he erred in a Vedic recitation. The notoriously angry sage cursed her to be born as a human. The story is most probably derived from the 7th century *Harṣa-carita* by Bāṇa. In the beginning of the work's first chapter, Bāṇa relates this same tale while narrating the history of his own family lineage. The hagiographers have only to change one small detail. Originally, the curse was due to end when Sarasvatī gives birth to a child. In our texts the curse terminates when she meets Śaṅkara in mortal form.

The great debate goes on for quite some time, anywhere from six to one hundred days, according to the various accounts. In some of the texts it is the withering of the fresh floral garland each of the combatants wears which will indicate the loser. But in the AŚV it is Sarasvatī herself who determines the outcome of the contest:

> When the argument, which ranged over all of the sciences, beginning with the Veda, was in its hundredth day, Sarasavāṇī, who was in the kitchen,

> heard the faltering of [Śaṅkara's] opponent. She, who was all-knowing, went to her husband and said, "my lord, Maṇḍana-miśra, come for alms".[40]

In calling Maṇḍana/Viśvarūpa by name, and asking him to take his food in the manner of a *saṃnyāsin*, Sarasvatī indicates that Śaṅkara has indeed defeated her husband. In accordance with the terms of the debate, Maṇḍana/Viśvarūpa humbly accepts Śaṅkara as his guru. He is initiated as a *saṃnyāsin* and is renamed Sureśvara. He will prove to be Śaṅkara's greatest disciple.

Debates Sarasvatī (no. 22)

Sarasvatī has now fulfilled her human destiny. Her meeting with Śaṅkara has released her from the curse which bound her to mortal life. There are two different versions of what happens at this point. In the one, she simply disappears from view and returns to her heavenly abode. While in the other, Śaṅkara restrains her from departing:

> In the moment prior to her husband's acceptance of the state of a renouncer, she took to the sky, [going] out of the kitchen window. Seeing Sarasavāṇī going towards the realm of Brahmā, the Parama-guru bound her in that region of the sky by means of the Vanadurgā *mantra*. Then he said, "Oh Sarasavāṇī, you are Brahmā's *śakti*. You are manifest (*pratiphal*) as the limiting adjunct in the guise of the wife of Maṇḍanamiśra, who is a part of that [Brahmā-*śakti*]. After [first] engaging in argument with me, you may go".[41]

---

40 AŚV p. 177, lines 10-12.

41 AŚV p. 177, lines 17-19; 178, lines 1-2

The debate between Sarasvatī and Śaṅkara has a very different basis to the contest which has just ended. The texts do vary as to whether Śaṅkara or Sarasvatī actually initiates the debate. Yet there is no doubt that what is at stake here is Śaṅkara's claim to omniscience. This is an issue essential to all the hagiographers. According to those texts which describe Sarasvatī's disappearance immediately after the defeat of Maṇḍana/Viśvarūpa, the issue is resolved when she later reappears to test him just as he is about to ascend the throne of omniscience. It is the goddess of learning who provides the conclusive testimony for Śaṅkara's omniscience.

The hagiographers present us here with a clear perspective of the way knowledge is measured in those Indian traditions which accept the authority of the Vedas. It is not so much a question of one's grasp of particular details, of the facts which are so dear to our own rationalist heritage. Neither is the ability to devise a coherent system for the analysis of a body of information indicative of knowledge. It is, above all, mastery of the *śāstra*s which marks one who truly knows. The *śāstras* comprise the rules which govern activity within the particular sphere of their respective jurisdiction.[42] Moreover, the *śāstra*s establish the models for human behaviour; and the paradigms are far more significant than the particulars of their application.

For the most part, the hagiographers resist the temptation to represent Śaṅkara's omniscience in terms of personal experience. In this respect, the texts remain true to the spirit of the Advaita tradition. As Śaṅkara himself insists in his *Brahmasūtra-bhāṣya*, "Brahman is the source, i.e., the cause of the great *śāstra*s, such as the Ṛg Veda, which are [themselves]

42 For a clear and concise study of the nature of *śāstra*, see Sheldon Pollock, "The theory of practice and the practice of theory in Indian intellectual history", *JAOS* 105 (1985) 499-519.

virtually omniscient...They reveal all things like a lamp".[43] Similarly, he argues that it is not mens' opinions but *śāstra*, and especially the *śruti*, which determines perfect knowledge.[44] In traditions such as Buddhism, which are not reliant on the transcendent authority of scripture, knowledge is more likely to be measured by personal experience. Hence there is no bar to describing Buddha's omniscience in terms of his remembrance of all lives past and future,[45] or as his knowing whatever he pleased.[46] The Śaṅkara hagiographies must, however, restrict themselves to proving his mastery of the *śāstras*.[47] A divine agency, namely Sarasvatī, will further validate his claim to omniscience.

The debate between Śaṅkara and Sarasvatī is a substantial one: "she undertook the full range of argument with him in all the *śāstras* and also in the Vedas, *itihāsas*, and Purāṇas".[48] But Śaṅkara proves his unshakable grasp of each and every subject. Then Sarasvatī hits upon a clever plan: "In order to defeat the ascetic she set her mind [on choosing a topic]—the elaboration of the distinctions of lovers and mistresses, in the *śāstra* of the erotic arts—which was difficult for him to enter into".[49] Since Śaṅkara has remained celibate from childhood, he is of course unable to respond to this query. After some reflection, he asks

---

43 *mahata ṛgvedādeḥ śāstrasya...pradīpavat-sarvārthāvadyotinaḥ sarvajña-kalpasya yoniḥ kāraṇaṃ brahma* (1.1.3). The great *śāstra*s are said to be "virtually" omniscient so as to distinguish them from Brahman, their source, which must be greater, according to Śaṅkara.

44 BSBh 2.1.11.

45 See the *Tevijja-Vaccagottasutta*, *Majjhima-Nikāya*, I 482.

46 See *Milindapañha*, 102 ff.

47 Even in the episode where Śaṅkara reproduces lost compositions he had heard but once (no. 35), his prowess points to skills which contribute to his mastery of *śāstra*.

48 AŚV p. 178, lines 6-7.

49 *Ibid*. lines 7-8.

for an adjournment of the debate. Sarasvatī graciously assents to his request.

Enters body of dying king to learn the erotic arts (no. 23)

This incident is included in all the hagiographies. Nevertheless, it is an episode some modern commentators would quite like to expunge from the story. In his account of Śaṅkara's life for the volume in the "National Biography Series", T. M. P. Mahadevan relegates the event to a footnote and refers to it as "an irrelevant interlude".[50] The verses describing Śaṅkara's erotic encounters while inhabiting the body of a king are particularly distasteful to those Hindus who have sought to reinterpret their traditions so that they will conform to a Victorian moral code. Of the two translators of the *Śaṅkaradigvijaya*, the first manages to provide "almost a full translation" of these verses, albeit with an apology,[51] while the second simply prints the Sanskrit text without translation.[52]

Through his superhuman vision, Śaṅkara perceives a king—whom most of the texts refer to as Amaruka—in the throes of death. Śaṅkara sees the opportunity to learn the subject of which he is ignorant and enters the king's body by means of his yogic power. Seeing the king suddenly restored to life, his wives and subjects are naturally overjoyed. With due ceremony, he is returned to the throne. As Anantānandagiri

---

50 *Sankaracharya* (New Delhi: National Book Trust, [1968] reprinted 1977).

51 *Srimad Sankara Digvijayam*, by Vidyaranya, translated by K. Padmanaban, (2 vols., Madras: K. Padmanaban, 1985/86), vol II, p. 71.

52 *Sankara-dig-vijaya. The traditional life of Sri Sankaracharya*, by Madhava-Vidyaranya, translated by Swami Tapasyananda, (Madras: Sri Ramakrishna Math, 1978), p.123n.

unabashedly describes it, Śaṅkara wastes no time in getting down to business:

> Having stayed there for a moment, the king went to his eldest wife. Because of [the king's] skill in amorous activity, he was experiencing the pleasure which arose from embracing her. Joining together mouth with mouth and her breasts with his chest, and pressing together (*saṃkuc*) navel with navel and feet with feet, making, in this way [his] body as though one [with hers], he was intent on embracing her tightly. Touching her in secluded places with his hands, he appeared like a bold [lover].[53]

Although the hagiographers are not averse to describing Śaṅkara's practical experiences while in the king's body, most insist that he learned the *Kāmaśāstra* of Vātsyāyana and composed either a commentary on that text, a *śāstra* or the *Amaruka-śataka.* For it is the literary composition which more properly marks his mastery of the subject. Having accomplished his aims, Śaṅkara re-enters his own body and returns to Sarasvatī in order to conclude the debate. Without much further ado, she acknowledges his supremacy in *all* branches of learning.[54]

---

53 AŚV p. 179, first three verses.

54 Most of the texts describe a further series of adventures here. Śaṅkara becomes so immersed in the pursuit of royal pleasures that he forgets to return to his own body, which is left in a cave, attended by his disciples. His followers decide to go to the court in order to bring him back. In the meantime, the chief wife—or the ministers—realise that the king is not quite his old self and that his body must be inhabited by a great yogi. Accordingly the decision is made to seek out and destroy the true body of the yogi who now dwells within the king. Soldiers are despatched to scour the surrounding area. They find Śaṅkara's body and consign it to the funeral pyre. By now the disciples have reached the court. They sing verses, "...waking [him] up with statements dealing with the ultimate reality (*parokti*): 'That which is conformable to the primary meaning of the word *satya*, thou art that, thou art

To a certain extent, Śaṅkara's erotic experiences can be seen as a reflection of the ascetic/erotic polarity inherent in the mythology of Śiva. After all, it is one and the same Śiva who burns up the god of love with his ascetic power yet indulges for countless years in erotic sport with Pārvatī.[55] But in the hagiographies Śaṅkara's erotic activities are confined to the human sphere.[56] Once again it is the opposition of the mortal and divine modes of his life that creates a dynamic tension and brings to life the narrative.

The ten incidents described above constitute the basic framework on which the Sanskrit hagiographies have been constructed. If we are to discover the models for these fundamental components of the narrative, as well as for many of the elaborate details chosen or created by the hagiographers, we must look to mythology and not to history. However tempting it might be to speculate on the historical veracity of the human elements in these common episodes, there is little

---

that, oh king. You are not this one, whose state is that of a renowned king, *tattvamasi*, *tattvamasi* , oh king. That which is the cause of the performance of such things as the production of the universe, *tattvamasi*, *tattvamasi*, oh king. That which is all, which is non-dual, which has the nature of all the Vedas, *tattvamasi*..." (AŚV p. 180, lines 13-18). Śaṅkara awakens and returns to the cave to find his own body aflame. He calls upon Narasiṃha who appears and heals his physical form. Most of the hagiographers refer to a further testing by Sarasvatī who questions him as to the purity of his conduct. He replies, "I have certainly not committed an offence (*kilbiṣa*) since birth, in this body, mother" (VŚV 12.81).

55 Thanks to the work of Wendy Doniger O'Flaherty the contradiction between Śiva's ascetic and erotic activities need no longer seem so confusing. See her *Asceticism and eroticism in the mythology of Śiva* (London and New York: Oxford University Press, 1973).

56 There is one notable exception. In an incident which appears only in the GVK (3.63ff.), Śaṅkara travels to Nepal, where he meets the goddess Siddheśvarī. He sits on her lap like a child and is given buttermilk from her thigh.

possibility for substantiating any conclusions which might be reached. Although the hagiographies do identify Śaṅkara's guru as Govindapāda—and this is the only certain point at which the texts converge with history—we have firmer evidence for his guru's name in the colophons of Śaṅkara's own work. There is not even unanimity on the identity of Śaṅkara's leading disciples in our texts. The AŚV, for example, does not mention Toṭaka, who is usually counted, along with Sureśvara, Padmapāda and Hastāmalaka, as one of the four chief disciples.[57] As well, there are some differences in the texts concerning Sanandana and Padmapāda.[58]

Like most of the elements from which Śaṅkara's life story is constructed, the tradition of Śaṅkara's four principal disciples is probably derived from a mythic model. This can be traced to the Purāṇic accounts of the *avatāra*s of Śiva. Several Purāṇas describe the pattern of his manifestations, which recur throughout a period of 28 eons (*kalpas*).[59] In the fourth and final age (*kali-yuga*) of each *kalpa*, Śiva appears on earth, accompanied by four disciples:

> "Then at the end of the [*kali-*] *yuga*, in that eon which has four periods, I will be born for the benefit of the world and the good of the

---

57 The AŚV lists the following disciples who accompany Śaṅkara in the early stages of his travels: Padmapāda, Hastāmalaka, Samitpāṇi, Cidvilāsa, Jñānakanda, Viṣṇugupta, Śuddhakīrti, Bhānumarīci, Kṛṣṇadarśana, Buddhivṛddhi, Viriñcipāda and Śuddhānantānandagiri (p. 17). Sureśvara and others later join his fold.

58 See the discussion of the TŚA in Chapter One.

59 Three Purāṇas contain almost identical material on the subject. See (1) *Vāyu-purāṇa* 23.107ff. (Veṅkaṭeśvara Press edition, reprinted Delhi: Nag Publishers, 1983); (2) *Śiva-purāṇa* 3.4.3ff. (i.e. *Śatarudrasaṃhitā*, Veṅkaṭeśvara Press edition, reprinted in 2 vols., Delhi: Nag, 1986); (3) *Liṅga-purāṇa* 1.24.10ff (Veṅkaṭeśvara Press edition, edited by J.L. Shastri Delhi: Motilal Banarsidass, 1980).

> brahmins...on that occasion I will have four disciples who are great souls, brahmins, with the [characteristic] tuft of hair, who have mastered the Vedas".[60]

It should not be surprising, then, that Śaṅkara too is portrayed with four disciples. In the long list of the various sets of Śiva's disciples, the Purāṇas mention a quartet better known from another story: Sanaka, Sanandana, Sanātana and Sanatkumāra.[61] These mind-born sons of Brahmā refuse to participate in the work of creation, preferring instead ascetic life. This is yet another of the mythical paradigms for the Śaṅkara story which are examined in the following chapter.

---

60 *tadā catur-yugāvasthe tasmin kalpe yugāntike anugrahārthaṃ lokānāṃ brāhmaṇānāṃ hitāya ca utpatsyāmi ...tatra siṣyāḥ śikhā-yuktā bhaviṣyanti tadā mama...catvāras tu mahātmāno brāhmaṇā vedapāragāḥ* ; *Liṅga-purāṇa* 1.24.10-15.

61 *Ibid.*, p. 24 (1.24.30).

CHAPTER III

The Mythological Setting

The Śaṅkara story is cast within the framework of Śaiva mythology. The hagiographers develop the narrative on the basis of a divine scenario. Whether it is constituted from within or is erected on the perimeter of the narrative, the mythological setting is fundamental to the story. In five of the hagiographies the curtain raiser is a celestial drama. The basic plot is drawn from a well known theme in the Purāṇas.

In the AŚV, CŚV and GVK the first character to appear on the stage is Nārada, the mediator between men and gods. Making one of his periodic world tours, he discovers that the *dharma* is in a serious state of decline. Nārada sees the brahmins neglecting their religious duties, necessary for the maintenance of the social order. Having misinterpreted or even abandoned the authoritative Vedic scriptures, they are instead following various heretical paths. Alarmed at the chaos which has ensued from the proliferation of non-Vedic sects, Nārada proceeds directly to Brahmā and reports on the situation:

> "I have looked today on all the quarters...Please hear the news of the earthly realm. The sacred scriptures are reviled. Some men are always attached to Śambhu, some are devoted to Viṣṇu. Some worship Bhairava; others follow the creed of Vighneśa. Some are established in the belief of Śakti, some are devoted to Kāma. Some are established in the belief of the Sauras, some are attached to the moon. Others worship the protectors of the quarters; others the planets, stars, etc. Some [worship] the Gandharvas and Sādhyas, others ghosts and goblins.

> Thus are the states of men, according to their desires, which are of various types. Although in breech of the *śruti*, they adhere to beliefs which depend [only] on themselves for their validity, and which, ignorant as they are, they believe to procure the supreme state. Absorbed in jealousy towards each other, each one striving for victory, filled with anger, each bearing the [sectarian] marks, formed according to his own desire, they are without knowledge of the Self, disregarding the eternal Brahman, unaware of the supreme. All [of those] people have become heretical (*pāṣaṇḍatā*)".[1]

Upon hearing this, Brahmā decides to consult Śiva as to what should be done. Nārada and Brahmā travel together to the realm of Śiva. After duly praising him, they inform him of the problems on earth and request his intercession. Śiva agrees to rectify the situation. He tells them that he will take birth as the son of a pious brahmin woman: "and having defeated those who hold false doctrines, however well known and widespread they are, I will roam about on earth with the name Śaṅkarācārya".[2]

The TŚA and, following it, the widely distributed ŚDV begin their story in the realm of Śiva. The great god is approached by the *devas* who request him to protect the world and re-establish the Vedic path. In these texts it is not only Śiva who is to take birth as a mortal. There are a host of divine beings who will accompany him in his mission.[3] Kumāra is to be born as Kumārila-Bhaṭṭa in order to defeat the Buddhists, the principal opponents of the Vedas. Brahmā becomes Maṇḍanamiśra, who in the hagiographies is the leading pupil of Kumārila-Bhaṭṭa and eventually becomes the chief disciple of Śaṅkara. Naturally enough, Sarasvatī is born as Maṇḍana's wife,

---

1 CŚV 2.55-63.

2 CŚV 4. 49.

3 See TŚA 1.39-42; 2.1-9 and ŚDV 1.45-55; 3.1-9.

Śaṅkara. Naturally enough, Sarasvatī is born as Maṇḍana's wife, Ubhaya-Bhāratī. As for the other of Śaṅkara's disciples to be, Nārāyaṇa takes birth as Padmapāda while Vāyu becomes both Hastāmalaka and Toṭaka.

What are we to make of this elaborate mythological setting? It is just too simplistic to read it as mere glorification of Śaṅkara or, worse still, as a crude attempt to vindicate his interpretation of scripture by an appeal to divine right. Of course, it cannot be denied that the hagiographers did intend to popularize the image of Śaṅkara. The construction of a suitable mythology would surely serve this end in a culture which has accorded—at least, until the present century—a prominent place to myth. But this is at best a partial explanation of the question. I would suggest two ways in which to approach the mythological element in the accounts of Śaṅkara's life. The first is in terms of a traditional preference for mythology over history. The second concerns the relationship of the mythic and social orders.

There has been a definite tendency in Hindu traditions to devalue historiography. This can be seen broadly in terms of what Mircea Eliade has so eloquently described as an attempt on the part of traditional cultures to abolish profane time.[4] In removing the temporal limitations which bind them to the mundane realm, it then becomes possible for a people to participate in the timeless reality of the divine realm. From this perspective, human activity can only be imbued with sanctity when it repeats the primordial actions of the great beings who live in the eternal mythic present. This becomes feasible when history is transformed or even replaced by mythology.

In contrast to Eliade's celebration of the efforts of traditional cultures to transcend history, it has been more

---

[4] Mircea Eliade, *The Myth of the Eternal Return or, Cosmos and History*, tr. Willard Trask (2nd ed., Princeton, 1965), especially pp. 34ff.

awareness which is manifest in traditional India. In a recent article, Sheldon Pollock has called for a re-evaluation of this common assumption.[5] Pollock argues that the Mīmāṃsakas, probably the most influential of the Vedic exegetes, intentionally suppressed the historicity of the Vedas. This is in keeping with the Mīmāṃsakas' insistence on the suprahuman authority (*apauruṣeyatva*) of the Vedas. Not only are the Vedas said to be without authors, they are also without beginning. Since temporal referents could only serve to negate the eternality of the Vedas, it is not surprising that the Mīmāṃsakas would seek to eliminate all historical referentiality in their interpretation of Vedic texts. There can be little doubt that the Vedas set the standard for scriptural authority in the Hindu tradition. For this reason it is certainly possible that the general lack of interest in historiography in traditional India stems from the precedent set by the Vedic exegetes.

It is not only the scriptures which stand outside of time. The all important lineage of the teachers who insure the continuity of the sacred traditions must also have its source in the mythic realm. The *Bṛhadāraṇyaka Upaniṣad*, for example, traces the line of teachers back to Āditya in one list, and to Prajāpati in another. The Śaṅkara hagiographies follow the same procedure in their description of the Advaita lineage. Śaṅkara's teacher Govinda is traced at least as far back as Vyāsa:

> Vyāsa, was the son of Parāśara and Satyavatī. His son was the *muni* Śuka, whose authority is well known. Gauḍapāda was his student, and the *muni* Govindanātha was his pupil.[6]

The GVK states that the line begins with Śiva himself:

---

[5] Sheldon Pollock, "Mīmāṃsā and the problem of history in traditional India", *JAOS* 109 (1989), pp.603-610.

[6] VŚV 4.63 and, following that ŚDV 5.105.

> Śiva is well known as the primal guru; after him was Nārāyaṇa, who has the knowledge of reality. The subsequent one was [Brahmā], whose seat is the lotus and who was entitled to his grace. His student was the *muni* Vasiṣṭha, who, manifesting brahmin strength, overcame [Viśvāmitra], the son of Kuśika. His pupil was Śakti, possessed of the power of *mantras*; and his pupil was Parāśara. Then there was Vyāsa...[7]

In this way, Śaṅkara is fitted into a lineage which has no temporal limitation. As further reinforcement of the authority of his most important work, the commentary on the *Brahmasūtra*, the hagiographies relate that Vyāsa himself appeared before Śaṅkara to test and then, of course, approve the validity of his interpretation of this fundamental Vedānta text.

Our own cultural expectations of verisimilitude make it difficult for us to imagine the viability of a biography which does not recreate "realistic" human experience. Similarly, we do not find a life story convincing if it is not firmly situated in its "correct" historical context. But we must recognize that mythography is often far more powerful than biography. Given the assumption of the transcendent nature of scripture in traditional India, it is more appropriate that the life story of a man who re-establishes the Vedic tradition should be constructed from mythic rather than historical materials.

The mythical context of the hagiographies can also be understood in terms of the relationship of the renouncer to the social order. Although a formal procedure for renunciation had already been in existence long before his time, Śaṅkara has come to represent one of the foremost of Hindu renouncers. According to tradition it is Śaṅkara himself who established the

---

[7] GVK 2.16-18.

ten orders of *saṃnyāsins.*[8] Great dramatic tension in the early part of his life story is created by the young Śaṅkara's urge to become a *saṃnyāsin.* As the only child of a poor widow, his desire for renunciation gives rise to enormous anguish for his mother. This highlights the underlying tensions that renunciation creates in Hindu society.

Louis Dumont has argued convincingly that the renouncer stands out as the only real individual in traditional India.[9] In a society which defines the individual solely on his family, caste and regional affiliations, the renouncer can only be an anomaly. That the renouncer is uncomfortable about the fact of his own individuality is, in Dumont's estimation, shown by his efforts to eliminate or transcend it. But how does the society overcome *its* anxiety about the *saṃnyāsin*? To a certain extent this is accomplished by including the *saṃnyāsin* in the scriptural code. While renunciation came to be formally accepted as proper to the final stage of life, controversy remained about the validity of renunciation prior to the completion of one's family duties. When the young Śaṅkara is accepted as a *saṃnyāsin* by his guru, the author of the AŚV raises a prima facie objection:

> "But surely the fourfold stages of life beginning with that of the celibate student (*brahmacarya*) are [customary] for brahmins...If, in this way, the [procedure] of accepting one [directly] into the stage of the *paramahaṃsa* [-*saṃnyāsin*] from the stage of *brahmacarya* is adopted, what would be the purpose of the other stages"?[10]

Anantānandagiri justifies Śaṅkara's renunciation with the often quoted passage from *Jābāla Upaniṣad* 4, "On whatever day he

---

[8] See Chapter Six for further discussion.

[9] Louis Dumont, "World renunciation in Indian religions", *Contributions to Indian Sociology*, 4 (1960), pp. 362.

[10] AŚV p. 16.

becomes dispassionate, let him go forth [as a renouncer] on that very day". Since different interpretations of the scriptural code on renunciation are possible, it is understandable that some uneasiness should remain about the *saṃnyāsin*, particularly in the case of early renunciation.

Mythology promises some resolution of this tension. In traditional India the realm of myth clearly parallels the social order. This is especially evident in the hierarchy of the divine and supernatural forces. Although the *saṃnyāsin* does not fit so easily into the social order, he finds a surer place in the mythic realm. There is a long tradition, persisting even in the present day, which links the *saṃnyāsin* to the supernatural. Popular stories abound of the miracles worked by swamis and yogis. They are said to intercede with the gods on behalf of their devotees, or even to directly grant their desires. According to a tradition recorded in the TŚA and ŚDV, Śaṅkara, as a young student, begged alms at the home of a poor brahmin family. The woman of the house graciously presented him with the only thing available, a small *āmalaka* fruit. Moved by this generosity in the face of poverty, he pleaded with Lakṣmī to grant the family some reward. The goddess filled the house with golden *āmalaka* fruits.[11] Although there may be a problem in defining Śaṅkara's relation to the social order, there is no question of his place in the realm of the gods. His is the abode of Śiva. In this way, by situating the *saṃnyāsin* in the mythic realm, the sense of order which was disrupted by his renunciation is restored.

While five of the hagiographies establish a mythological setting which functions as an external structure for the Śaṅkara story, the VŚV, and following it the GŚC, develop a

---

11 TŚA 2.21-31; ŚDV 4.21-31.

mythological framework from within the narrative.[12] In these two works, the story unfolds to the point where Śivaguru and his wife are faced with the dilemma of their childlessness:

> Śivaguru, who had done everthing which should be done, was feeling depressed. He said to his wife, "what will become of us, dear one? Our life is half over. Oh high-born one, [we] have not [yet] seen the face of a son, which is said, in this world, to be conducive to attaining a better world (*lokya*)".[13]

In order to illustrate the beneficence of Śiva, the (here nameless) wife narrates the story of Upamanyu to her husband Śivaguru. This is what inspires the course of *tapas* the couple undertake in the hope of obtaining a son. This sub-story story prefigures the major events which will occur in the early life of their own child, Śaṅkara. But what is more significant is the mythological paradigm which is set up.

Although the Upamanyu story portrays Śiva as the bestower of boons, there is no mention here of his granting offspring to his petitioners. Perhaps this is understood from the context of the tale of Upamanyu as it appears in the *Mahābhārata*.[14] The epic recounts the way Śiva grants Krishna the boon of a son. Arriving at Śiva's realm in the Himālayas in order to practise *tapas*, Krishna meets the sage Upamanyu. The sage assures Krishna that he will receive the desired boons and reassures him of Śiva's grace by narrating his own story. Other

---

12 The five works are the AŚV, CŚV, GVK, TŚA and ŚDV. The remaining hagiography, i.e., the RŚA, introduces its own special mythological dimension in the last four of its eight chapters. Here the focus shifts away from the Śaṅkara story. These chapters comprise a series of *māhātmya* s, in praise of the various pilgrimage places Śaṅkara visits. The narrative is transformed into a series of vignettes on the various deities, who are represented through the mythological stories associated with each sacred site.

13 VŚV 1.39.

14 MBh 13.14.

versions of this legend feature in the *Śiva-purāṇa* and *Liṅga-purāṇa*.[15] The myth also appears in the *Cidambara-māhātmya*.[16]

Vyāsācala devotes two of the VŚV's twelve chapters to this story. He elaborates on the rather spare narrative found in the *Mahābhārata* and the two Purāṇas. In these three earlier sources Śiva remains the focal point of the story. Almost every element in the narrative serves as further testimony to Śiva's glory. Vyāsācala shifts the emphasis to Upamanyu himself, and develops a relationship between Upamanyu and his mother which is scarcely implied in the earlier versions. In reshaping the story, Vyāsācala retains the image of Śiva as a granter of boons, while constructing a mythical paradigm for the life of Śaṅkara. This sub-story is an unexpected little gem hidden in an influential Śaṅkara hagiography. A complete translation of the story follows.[17]

---

15 *Śivapurāṇa* 3.32.1-78, in the Veṅkateśvara Press edition (reprinted in 2 vols. Delhi: Nag, 1986) pp. 333-335. *Liṅgapurāṇa*, 1.107.1-43, in the edition edited by J. L. Shastri (Delhi: Motilal Banarsidass, 1980), pp. 183-184.

16 Hermann Kulke has made a detailed study of this work: *Cidambaramāhātmya: Eine Untersuchung der religionsgeschichtlichen und historischen Hintergründe für die Entstehung der Tradition einer südindischen Tempelstadt* (Wiesbaden: Harrassowitz, 1970). See note 38 for further discussion.

17 Although the translation is for the most part quite literal, some verses are more freely rendered so that the delightful style of the original is not completely lost. The material in square brackets is not in the Sanskrit text, but has been added for more clarity in the translation. I am indebted to Phyllis Granoff for her many helpful suggestions in the translation of some of the more difficult passages.

A Mythical Interlude: Vyāsācala's *Śaṅkara-vijaya*, Chapters 2 and 3

1. It is said that long ago, Upamanyu, at the age of five, was pleasing Śiva with his meditation. The deity who is like a wish-fulfilling creeper was propitiated. Surely he would grant the desired rewards.

2. Upamanyu's emaciated, poverty-stricken mother, it is said, gave him [rice] flour mixed in water and a little breast milk. The boy consumed it, taking it to be milk.

3. Being a dependent, he once went with his mother to the home of his maternal uncle—the abode of all virtues, wealthy and rich in cows—and lived in the home of this uncle.

4. [There] he enjoyed food, milk and ghee. He played with the children and was free from infirmity. And then the boy returned to his poverty-stricken home with his mother.

5. Once again, his poor mother gave him wild rice flour, as before. The food did not please him. He left it and said, "Mother, this drink is not milk, it is water".

6. The distressed mother, weeping and wiping her son's tears which were welling up, quietly said, "My dear, such is the milk here in this house. I do not have the fortune to buy special things.

7. At some time or other, in another existence, I did not propitiate Īśvara, who is the wish-fulfilling tree, my dear. If the lotus feet of Īśvara had been worshipped, how could such [a state] be possible?

8. My dear, in this world, there are those who have attendants, fine clothing and ornaments and those who are entitled to enjoy the happiness of women, gems, cows and earth. Know that these men have worshipped Śiva in the three worlds. Otherwise, how could they be entitled to the glories mentioned?"

9. "If this is so, mother, then the ritual action which would put an end to my misery (*durvidhatā-apahantṛ*), ought to be considered and performed according to the precepts. Hara should be be propitiated. Without [his] compassion there is misfortune (*vipatti*). Abandoning my body [to the practice of *tapas*], on account of what is inauspicious [in our fate], there is no other [alternative] for me".[18]

10. Having said this to his mother, [the boy] who was firm-minded, although only five years old, asked permission to perform *tapas*: "I should wander about a little. You should [stay here and] pray to all the deities".

11. As soon as he said this, his mother swooned. And [then], recovering a little and embracing her son, she said, "You do not know [even] one of the quarters, not east, west or north.

12. My dear, do not wander far. You do not have the capacity to perform *tapas*. Will they not say to me, 'What kind of mother [are you]? It is the wrong time. He is only five years old, his [milk] teeth have not [yet] fallen out'.

13. Living here [in this very place] you should perform *tapas* according to your own ability, if it pleases you. I will become your companion in *tapas*, according to my ability. Abandoning you, I am not able to remain here.

14. It is clear that Śiva is here, there [and everywhere]. He is omnipresent like the air, but not in bodily form. The essential condition of *tapas* is steady devotion and an unwavering mind, not a change of place.

15. It is true that Śiva is omnipresent. But he is made to manifest his potency in particular places, just as fire which is omnipresent will become manifest in an individual tree"

16. "Mother, the home is not the proper place for *tapas*, nor is its neighbourhood which is filled with friends, etc., approved

---

[18] The translation of this verse is tentative.

[by the scriptures]. Were the ancient sages, who abandoned their homes and went to the ascetic groves, prone to foolishness?

17. *Tapas* is truly [best] in childhood, i.e., now, and not in adolescence or old age. The changes [which occur] because of adolescence are an obstacle to *tapas*; and the old man is unable to perform *tapas.*

18. Seeing a boy performing *tapas,* the gods were disposed to compassion. For he is a source of wonder. And men, for their part, seeing a child engaging in difficult deeds, feel pity and are sympathetic.

19. It is said that Dhruva (Auttānapādi), at the age of five, performed quite unbearable *tapas,* [which was done] in the name of Śrī Viṣṇu. He gained a position which was difficult to obtain. Have you not heard of this?

20. If I were to perform *tapas* in your presence, you would suffer each day, seeing me practise terrible *tapas.* Therefore it is better that I dwell far away.

21. Because of your sorrow on account of my going to another land, you are unable to save yourself or anyone else from sorrow. Therefore, stay here mother, endeavouring always to gain what is dear to me".

[Chapter 3]

1. Having thus won over his mother with rejoinders which were unanswerable, he set forth. His mother entreated [the boy] who was setting out to a distant place with these words:

2. "You should worship Śaṅkara, who is a wishing tree to those who bow down to him, and set forth as you wish. Having performed your duty, come back to me again. Śrī Pārvatī and Purahara, who are full of affection, should regard you as though you are their legitimate son.

3. My dear, you should worship Śiva, the ocean of compassion. Resort to the five syllable formula, with a pure mind. Because of the completeness of your mode of life, there is no [need] here for the obligation of being led [to the teacher]. The wise long for the one whose business is universal jurisdiction".

4. His mind was steady. He turned away his friends who followed, with the lotus of his face beautified by a smile. Abandoning his love for his home, he set out, with Śiva remaining in his heart.

5. The people on the road thought, 'Is this solitary one Agni or a forest deity'? He wandered and, although hungry, he did not ask for anything. He maintained his body by what was bestowed to him in accordance with the precepts.

6. Although questioned by the people on the road—"Where are you wandering, boy"? "From where have you come"? "What are you seeking"? "Who are your parents"?—he was unperturbed, giving no reply.

7. Having passed through rivers with abundant waters and certain mountainous countries, he remained on the road, casting his eyes around him. He saw a forest decked with trees.

8. On one side, it was filled with excellent deer [but] inhabited by herds of fearsome boar. On the other side, there were mischievous monkeys crying out "*kila-kila*", [but] it was terrifying because of the herds of elephants.

9. He left the road and entered into a dense grove, whose characteristics were as he desired. Then he saw a lake before him. The boy set his mind on dwelling [there].

10. Going to the shore of the excellent lake, whose waters were pure, he resorted to the base of a firm tree. For those who are firm-minded, the forest is considered a home. For those who are weak-minded, the home is considered a forest.

11. Immersing himself in the pleasant waters of the lake, and beautifully covering the earth at the base of the firm tree with blades of *darbha* grass, their [tender] shoots uppermost,

12. He sat there, facing the east, and uttered the Aiśvara *mantra* which was spoken of [by his mother]. [The boy,] whose garment was made of the long, spreading [aerial] roots of the banyan tree, took a creeper for his waistband.

13. He was directing his mind, which [by nature] goes out to sensory objects, towards the excellent *mantra* (*manu*), which is the form of the deity who is auspicious. He whispered the *mantra* as previously instructed, keeping his eyes half-opened.

14. Immersing himself in the lake, he performed the three ablutions, which practice is taught by the sages. Seated firmly in the cross-legged posture, he was satisfied with solitude as his (female) companion.[19]

15. He partook only of measured amounts of fruit. He did not ever leave [the place] for very long. He neither slept too long, nor passed too much time in wakefulness. The boy *muni* was a great knower of yoga.

16. A pride of hungry lions wandered towards the waters of the lake, desirous of drinking. Seeing the boy *muni*, they ran far away, as though frightened, roaring a little, their intentions broken.

17. Herds of deer, whose habitat was nearby, became familiar because of seeing [him there] for a long time. Unagitated, they surrounded the boy *muni*. Familiarity is indeed the cause of friendship.

18. Now at one time, a hyena (*tarakṣu*), who feeds upon deer approached, in pursuit of a herd of deer. Angered at the swiftness of the herd of deer, he howled right in front of the boy *muni*.

---

[19] This is a tentative translation of *vijanatā-vanitā-paritoṣitaḥ*.

19. A little fear rose up in the boy *muni*, who heard the ear-piercing howling. Then he called to mind the syllables, "Śiva Śiva". The hyena fell down dead, frothing [at the mouth].

20. Thirsty wild elephants approached the lake, trumpeting loudly. Having looked upon the moon-like face of the *muni*, they were freed from thirst because of their joyful state of mind.

21. Prior to the youth's arrival, there was a fire blazing here and there in the great forest. It was extinguished merely by his arrival. There was happiness in the forest which had many trees.

22. Deer, lions, hyenas, elephants and others, whose minds were the abodes of natural hostility, abandoned their eternal hostility and drank together at the waters of the lake.

23. At one time he gave up fruits and the like. The *muni* went on like that on alternate days. After that he took up [the same procedure] on a monthly basis. Then, after that, he gave up [eating] at all times for a year.

24. On account of the power of his yoga, the *muni* lived on water in the aforesaid way. Then the *muni* became one who lives like a serpent [i.e., only on air]. He was intent on the worship of the nectar of Śiva's lotus feet.

25. Then, having given up *mantra* recitation, the great one began to worship Śiva by means of meditation (*samādhi*). [He imagined Śiva] endowed with hands, feet, etc., with the waxing moon [on his crest], with luminous ashes and shining ornaments.

26. [He imagined Śiva] holding in his upraised hands an axe and an antelope, his lower arms [making gestures bestowing] fearlessness and boons. His seat was a great white-coloured lotus. He was clothed in the skin of a tiger.

27. He was beautiful, with the lotus of his face opening in a smile. His eyes were the sun, fire and moon. By means of his radiance, he was causing the quarters to remain undarkened

[although] his own neck was steeped in the blackness of the poison [he had swallowed].

28. [Then the boy adopted the posture of standing on one leg.] He placed one foot on the earth and the other was kept raised up. The child, whose arms were kept down, having fixed his eye on the sun, worshipped Śiva.

29. That child, who was practising *tapas*, excelled the ancient *muni*s in *tapas*. Even the *muni*s [themselves], having gone and seen the child intensely engaged in *tapas*, were quite amazed.

30. From his body there arose a powerful light which reached the three great worlds. The rays of the sun, facing downwards were struck by the *tejas* of the *muni* and went upwards.

31. In whatever quarter he placed his foot, the earth—with its oceans, forests, rivers and mountains—bowed down [to him] in that quarter. Indra (Harihaya) heard of this wonder.

32. He very much feared the boy *muni*, who was engaged in deeds surpassing the gods and demons, [thinking] 'With what desire is he practising *tapas*? Is he wishing for my supreme position'?

33. Harihaya spoke to the company of *apsarās*:" You [beautiful ones], with timid antelope eyes, should proceed to the place where the *muni* is practising *tapas*. There the three worlds are very frightened because of the strength of [the boy].

34. Śiva is obedient to the commands of those who worship his lotus feet. He will grant him everything, oh lotus-eyed women.

35. Having quickly approached the place of the youth's grove, you women should destroy his *tapas*, out of devotion [to me]. And having turned away the best of *muni*s from his *tapas* with a vengeance (*yātanā*), you should return here immediately".

36. The celestial ladies, who were spoken to thus by Hari, addressed a clear statement to Harihaya, "We here are obedient to your words, lord, hear our words attentively:

37. Where young men are concerned [women] such as us obtain a foothold. But he is only five years old. He does not know what is pleasing to young women, lord. He surpasses Dhruva in *tapas*. [Surely] he will curse us.

38. We do not wish to act like moths [who would go] into the terrrible, angry fire of the excellent *muni*. Having harassed *munis* engaged in *tapas*, many [*apsarās*] of former times were destroyed.

39. Why would that boy be concerned with you? He is not eager for your renowned place. Those who have no firm position are afraid of others. But this position belongs to you by natural right."

40. The destroyer of Vala heard these words and replied, his lower lip shaking: "Oh, you whose treasure is beauty (*bhaga-dhana*), by whose sweet and false words men's minds are captivated, having spoken wrongly, you should now obey me.

41. This renowned thunderbolt weapon of mine which is invincible to enemies and also that one [weapon] of yours—a beautiful body, whose appearance causes fear for the *munis* who are practising *tapas*—are now [both] blunted.

42. There is no benefit whatsoever in having attendants who are distinguished by standing apart at the time of need. Let those lovely ladies leave here immediately and not rove about in my sight [again]".

43. Having uttered these words, Purandara, accompanied by his attendants, entered the realm of Brahmā (Vidhi). He saw the four-faced one and pointed out the calamity which had arisen.

44. "Oh Lord, the boy *muni* is practising intense *tapas* which is superhuman. From that has arisen a great power which is oppresssing the earth. People are not [even] able to go about.

45. The creation of the world has been carried out by you, Lord. Surely a bit of protection ought to be carried out as well. But

no desire is given over to that by [you] who are engrossed in the recitation of the Vedas".[20]

46. Brahmā, who heard the speech uttered by Harihaya replied: "That one from whom the worlds have arisen and from whom all the scriptures shine forth,

47. That very Lord directed me to perform only the work of creation. He appointed Viṣṇu (Hari) to take care of it . Let us therefore go to see Hari who is reclining on the serpent [-couch] on the ocean of milk".

48. Obeying the words of Vidhi, [the gods,] first of whom is Purandara, together with Vidhi, went up to the ocean of milk, abounding in treasure, desirous of seeing Hari.

49. Hari, the equitable sovereign of the gods, was aware of what was indicated by the wishes of Śakra as soon as the gods arrived. Although continually reclining there, he was [ever] awake.

50. The host of gods, who were preceded by the most excellent god, beheld the irreproachable god, who grants what is desired. He was seated upon the coils of the serpent. His radiance was equal to the lustre of a rain cloud.

51. Then the venerable one who approached, knowing the importance of the duty at hand, spoke to the sovereign of the lotus: "Listen, oh Hari, we have made an effort to come here in regard to the calamity which has arisen.

52. Indeed we have not previously known of [such] calamities. And moreover, Lord, [it is even worse because] what is happening is imagined to be in accordance with correct behaviour.[21] For the [family] elders, endowed with great pity, do not expect an offence on the part of a child.

---

[20] This is a tentative translation of the verse.

[21] The translation here is tentative.

53. There is nothing in the three worlds which is unknown to you, dwelling in the secret abode within everyone's mind. Nonetheless I will tell you something of it. We are sorely troubled by an outsider.

54. [He is] the son of a *muni*, whose mind is steady. Although only in his early years, he is practising terrible *tapas*. It is known that no one has undertaken such a thing before, nor will someone try to do so again.

55. Having overcome even the great powers, he continues (*vas*) burning the three worlds with the *tejas* which has arisen from his body. Turning him away from his *tapas*, you should protect the world as [you have] before".

56. [Hari said] "Whether he desires something or whether he is [simply] practising the most severe and highest *tapas*, he is aiming at something beneficial. Only through Śiva can you turn him away from that. For even we are not able to distract him.

57. This is an incomparable [task] which is asked of me by the host of gods who are preceded by [Indra,] the enemy of Vala. In regard to the duty of protection which was spoken of, oh gods, I must go to Śiva, who is endowed with auspiciousness.

58. The act of creating is for the lotus-born one, and the work of destroying is set forth for Hara. Although the task of protecting is mine, nevertheless, I cannot do it alone".[22]

59. [Hari said] "Let Śiva govern my speech. Having approached the one who is the teacher of what is beneficial and what is not beneficial, we who are gathered together should tell Śiva about the present calamity which is giving us anxiety".[23]

---

[22] The translation of the last *pāda* is very tentative.

[23] In this verse, I have followed all the variant readings found in the Adyar MS.

60. Hari, who was eager for setting out, called to mind Garuḍa, who came [there]. Mounting him, he went together with the gods to the highest of mountains where the earth is made of silver.

61. Indra (Mādhava), preceded by Viṣṇu (Hari) and Brahmā (Viriñci), was pleased with the abode of Śiva which was filled with excellence. Then, having alighted from his own vehicle, he modestly went to the threshold of the doorway.

62. He questioned the bearer of the golden staff, the unrivalled Nandin, whose body is brilliant white, [about the situation]. [Nandin] said to Hari that [Hara is] always destroying, but at this particular time protecting is [also appropriate] for Hara".[24]

63. Having announced to Hara [the arrival of] Hari, [Nandin,] taking Hari's hand went before [Hara]. Then, Hara immediately rose up and clasped Hari's hand with his own.

64. Śiva attended to the lotus-born [Brahmā], together with his circle [of retainers], and the other gods in a suitable manner. Now the host of great sages heard of this meeting of the two objects of veneration, Hari and Hara.

65. [The great sages], whose minds were delighted, proceeded quickly in order to see the highest ones, Hari and Hara. The meeting of those two was a rare [event] here, even for the best of the gods.

66. Then the honoured host of *munis*, who were skilled in eulogy, respectfully eulogised Hari and Hara with eulogies.[25]

---

24 The second half of the verse is unclear. The translation is tentative.

25 The *munis*' hymn is as follows: (66.) "Oh, *deva* who is the protector of the world, salutations to you. Salutations, oh Hara, who is destroying the three worlds. (67.) Oh blue-necked one, salutations to him who consumes the poison. Salutations, oh lotus-eyed one, day and night. Oh Lord of Girijā, have compassion always. Oh lotus-eyed one, cast a glance in this direction. (68.) Salutations, salutations, hail to you, oh enemy of Mura. Salutations, salutations, hail to you, oh enemy of [Tri-] pura. Salutations, salutations to

73. Śaṅkara said to the host of gods who were praising him, along with the host of *munis*: "Why are you coming here? Tell me directly, without hesitation, what is the matter. [Surely, this] great assembly is for a reason".

74. Then the venerable one, who was following the intentions of Surendra, spoke: "Oh wise Paśupati, what your honour has asked about is confusing to me, but it is surely known to you on account of your omniscience.

75. [The situation] which has arisen is known to you who are dwelling here. There is no concealing [it]. The means of escaping from this calamity should be proclaimed. There is no one other than you who will get rid of this [calamity]".

76. After the venerable one had thus spoken, Śiva, who was desirous of performing the task [already] known to him, without [showing any] weakness said, "I must remove the fear caused by the child. While I am the protector [there should be] no fear on your part.

---

you whose vehicle is Garuḍa. Salutations, salutations to you, oh *deva*, whose vehicle is the bull. (69.) Salutations to you, oh *deva*, whose ornaments are serpents. Salutations to you who is reclining on the coils of serpents. Salutations to you whose diadem is the crescent moon. Salutations to you whose diadem has diverse gems. (70.) Salutations to you two, by whom masses of sins are destroyed merely by your being remembered, whose lotus feet are to be enjoyed by bee-like *munis*. Oh Hari and Hara, let there always be bowing to the two of you. Carry out what is desirable, you two auspicious ones, who are destroying what is not desirable. (71.) Let this bowing be to you who has the Gaṅgā issue forth from your lotus feet, oh you who are destroying the pain of those who are bent down [to you]. Oh Hara, you who have the best of rivers in the cover of your matted locks, you by whom death is defeated, salutations, salutations. (72.) Oh resident of the cemetery (*pitṛvana*), salutations to you. Oh resident of the forest of Badarikā, salutations to you. Oh *deva* who is the beloved of the [one born from] the ocean, salutations to you. Oh *deva* who is the beloved of the [one born from] the Himālaya, salutations to you".

77. Having turned away that *muni* 's son from *tapas,* I will deliver you from calamity. There is nothing to fear from a child who is practising *tapas.* You should proceed [back] to your abode in the same way that you came".

78. After the host of gods, preceded by the sovereign of the gods, had bowed to Śiva (Giriśa) and left, Paśupati went forth from the mountain [with the intention of] turning away the boy *muni*, possesed of *tapas*, from his *tapas.*

79. Approaching [the child] with his bull, Hara, who was desirous of testing the steadiness of the boy's mind,[26] transformed himself into Indra (Surapati). At the same time, his bull became the four-tusked [Airāvata], lord of elephants. And then [Śiva's consort] Girijā became Śacī.

80. [Śiva's] attendants became gods[27] and Gaṇapati became Nalakūbara.[28] The first of the artistic sentiments[29] became the handsome form of Jayanta, [Indra's son]. The women folk [of the attendants] became the wives of the gods.

81. The bow of Śiva (*ajagava*) appeared in the form of the thunderbolt weapon. The crescent moon [appeared] in the form of a mound of flowers. The mass of snakes became ornaments. [Śiva] was everywhere (*vibhu*) and everything. Like an actor or actress, he can put on any disguise.

82. That lord of Śacī approached the boy, but the child who was in *samādhi*, did not know it. Gazing gently on the boy's face, Hara, the ocean of compassion, was pleased.

83. And while at first the boy did not awaken [from *samādhi*], he [then] perceived him standing before him because of the trumpeting which came forth [from Indra's elephant]. At once

---

26 Following the alternate readings, *abhisaran* and *manasaḥ*.

27 Following the alternate reading.

28 He is the son of Kubera, a leader of the gods.

29 That is, *śṛṅgāra*, the erotic sentiment (*rasa*).

[the boy], whose splendour was like that of the newly risen sun, opened the lotus of his eyes and said, "What is this"?

84. Taking no further notice, the boy *muni*, whose *tapas* was intense, once again resorted to *samādhi*. [Indra,] perceiving the exceeding steadiness of the boy's mind, became greatly surprised.

85. The enemy of Vṛtra spoke [these] words to the child: "How [unsuitable] is the mortification of this lovely body and how [unsuitable] is your great state of dispassion when your age is reckoned to be [only] five years.

86. When your beautiful body is gone, dear one, what will you obtain? And while it exists, you should follow the aims [proper] to men. Seek happiness, abandon your very painful vow. What benefit is there in burning up your body with *tapas*?

87. If happiness is wished for on your part, you should approach my feet, which are worshipped by the most excellent gods. I will grant you riches (*vitta-gata*). How much more reward is there by deeds which are withering up your body?

88. Oh strict-vowed one, you should roam about together with my sons in my pleasant forests and groves. Their fragrance is made manifest by the breezes [bearing] the pollen of sweet-smelling flowers and a combination of perfumes.

89. If your desire is for anything on [this] earth, it can easily be obtained. Tell me directly and I will grant it now. Or if you are afraid of an unbearable enemy, child, I will slay [him]. There is no doubt about that either.

90. The sages do not recommend the kind of deed that leads to no good for oneself and does not bring hapiness to another. But what you are doing seems to be just such a deed.

91. You should open the double door of your eyes, child. Behold, I am Harihaya. This is my spouse. This is the handsome ruler of elephants.

92. The [reason for our] arrival is not in order to disturb your *tapas*[30], but because of the weight of our pity, having seen your youthfulness. You should tell [me] whether the *tapas* is in order to bring about something profitable or whether you are abandoning the fruits of your *tapas*.

93. On account of the *tejas* arising from your body, this world is enduring scorching pain. Action which is improper [to one's state of life] has unfavourable consequences for the world. The *muni*-folk are thought to be people who remove another's pain".

94. Then the child opened his eyes. Amazed, he saw the excellent gods. He uttered these words to the leader of the gods: "Of what concern to you is the fruitfulness of my *tapas* ?

95. Oh Harihaya, I do not long for the happiness which is cherished here by men as [the fruit of] ritual action. There is nothing at all for you to fear from me. You should proceed happily [back] to heaven, at your leisure.

96. Because both are produced from causes, how much difference is acknowledged (*iṣyate*) between the happiness of the gods and the happiness of men? The impermanence of what is born is certain. The superiority in regard to those two [kinds of happiness] is [merely] a distinction of days.[31]

97. Birth is understood [to occur] in the classes of [both] men and gods; and death is said [to occur] for that which is born. What is the use of the cherished positions of Hari and Viriñci, whose positions are impermanent, bound by limited [periods of] time.

98. That which is imperishable and indestructible, and which is free from [all] talk of birth and death, is what is to be desired.

---

30 Following the alternate reading.

31 The implication is that the only real difference is in the length of the celestials' day, which is equivalent to 360 human days.

Mankind is arisen from that. It is certainly not afflicted by [something] horrible (*ulbaṇa*) such as death, birth or old age.[32]

99. For one who has devotion to *tapas*, staying in a deserted place is preferable to association with crowds of people. For there is no unimpeded continuity [of *tapas* in the presence of crowds].[33] Bhagavān is disturbing me with his large entourage.

100. If you do not depart, Hari, and if you, who are allied with so many [people], continue causing disturbance to my *tapas*, I will hurl this supreme weapon at you and you will perish along with your entourage".

101. When the steadfast boy had spoken, [Śiva], having discarded his disguise, restored his own beautiful form, along with that of [his consort] Śivā and his attendants, and became visible to the child.

102. The child was stunned from seeing the appearance of [such] extraordinary people. Utterly amazed, [he thought to himself] 'Shall I bow to his feet or should I place his lotus feet on my head'?

103. Having perceived the stunned state of the boy *muni*, Nandin, who was standing beside Hara, said "You have not shown respect upon meeting [with Śiva]. You should approach and bow to the lotus feet of Īśvara".

104. The boy, who was thus addressed, immediately bowed to his lotus feet. The child bathed [Śiva's] form with tears of joy and was unable to speak.

105. Sadāśiva said to [the boy] who was bowing respectfully, "Come, *muni* 's child, be seated here in my lap. Ah, you are so emaciated from maintaining *tapas*. I will grant you whatever is desired right now.

---

32 This is following the two alternate readings in the first two *pādas*. The translation is tentative.

33 This is a tentative translation of *na hi samastyavighāta-paramparā* .

106. My spouse Girijā is also delighted with you. She wishes for you to be thought of as a son.[34] Today, I certainly have three sons: the two sons who were born previously and now this one".

107. Thus were the words uttered by Śiva. Rejoicing and drinking in [the sight of] Śiva, with both his eyes moist/fixed (*stimita*), the child, whose slender body was blooming [as it were], his hair standing on end, replied [with these] words:

108. "The two of you who are my parents are [alone] entitled to say what is good for their son. A son ought not speak [of it]. Nevertheless, I [would] really choose imperishable devotion for your lotus feet".

109. Having heard [these] words, Parameśvara took the *muni* 's son into his own lap. He kissed the face of the *muni* 's son and the *muni* was freed from the fear of worldly existence.

110. Śiva spoke of the *muni*s' deeds of old. Having granted the ocean of milk, which had risen up in delight, to the *muni* 's son, who was held close [to Śiva], the sickly appearance abiding in the *muni* disappeared.

111. The daughter of the mountain, for her part, took the *muni*'s son on her lap and gave him the milk of her breast. She said, "Henceforth you are my own son. You should roam about as you please, dear one".

112. [Śiva said] "Have you understood, child, the great *āgama*s which have issued forth from the lotuses of my six faces? They are enlightening the primary cause of all classes of things and are burning up worldly existence. They are easily obtained through the compassion of the guru".

---

34 Following the alternate reading.

113. At the command of Paśupati, a great ocean of milk, like thick autumnal moonlight, flowed near. It clearly[35] brought immediate contentment for the child.

114. The incomparable trees of the gods came to honour the child. They had numerous flowers and fruit [to offer]; their buds were shaken down by a gentle wind and they had warbling flocks of birds which gave pleasure [to the ears].

115. Whatever the child would remember of his past, that false conception would drop away from his mind. The child said, "Even for the host of *muni*s and gods, it is difficult to obtain the collection of great properties [which were received in conjunction with the ocean of milk]".[36]

116. Having attained fulfilment in [receiving the ocean of milk together with] the great properties, he went home with the permission of Śiva and Śivā. He bowed to the lotus feet of his mother. Seeing the boy, the mother, for her part, was delighted.

[End of the third chapter of the VŚV].[37]

---

35 Following the alternate reading

36 The collection of great properties (*mahā-guṇa-saṃhati*), may refer to some or all of the boons Upamanyu is said to receive from Śiva in the *Śiva-purāṇa* (*Rudra-saṃhitā*, 3.32.56-62): freedom from old age, suffering and death; fame; *tejas*; divine knowledge; great power; knowledge of the Pāśupata practice and its method; [the ability] to be teacher; cleverness; and his own realm. In addition to these, Pārvatī grants him the ocean of milk; yogic power; perpetual happiness; imperishable knowledge of Brahman and great riches (*Śrī Śiva-mahāpurāṇam*, reprinted in 2 vols. Delhi: Nāg Publishers, 1986. Vol. I, pp.334-335).

37 There is an additional verse which concludes the chapter: (117.) In the sweet and faultless poem written by Vyāsācala, the third chapter, alternately quick and slow [i.e., in *druta-vilambita* metre] has ended. It is naturally pure and was concerned with speaking of the greatness of the extremely zealous one (*upamanyu*), and it was pleasing because of the story.

In the *Mahābhārata* and *Liṅga-purāṇa*, Upamanyu's story ends with his receipt of the boons.[38] The narrative then reverts to the frame story in which Krishna practises austerities in order to obtain Śiva's blessing for a son. In the *Śiva-purāṇa*,[39] however, Upamanyu returns home to his mother after receiving the boons from Śiva and Pārvatī. Since Vyāsācala ends the story in the same way, it is possible that he relied on the *Śiva-purāṇa* in composing his own account. But where he differs from all three of the earlier sources is in creating a special relationship betweeen Upamanyu and his mother. Moreover, Vyāsācala adds that Upamanyu is specifically requested by his mother to return home after completing his task (3.2). This mythic model sets the scene for Śaṅkara's leaving home as a boy-renouncer and his eventual return to his mother, if only to perform her funeral rites.

The mythological framework of the hagiographies is fundamentally Śaiva in its orientation. For this reason, the Śaṅkara story is distinct from the (perhaps more familiar)

---

38 According to Hermann Kulke (*Cidambaramāhātmya*,Wiesbaden: Harrassowitz, 1970, pp. 34-36), the *Cidambaramāhātmya*'s version of the story, resembles that of the *Mahābhārata*, but there are some striking differences. The mother does not try to deceive her son by providing a mixture of flour and water instead of milk. Moreover, Upamanyu receives the ocean of milk without having to perform any *tapas*, since, Kulke argues, this composition aims at fostering the practice of *bhakti*. The *Cidambaramāhātmya* was almost certainly known to Vyāsācala who refers to some of its legends in his description of Padmapāda's pilgrimage to Cidambaram (VŚV 8.13-20). Indeed, Cidambaram features in five of the hagiographies.

39 For the Purāṇic versions of the story, I have consulted only the most readily available printed texts in *devanāgarī* , i.e., the reprints of the Veṅkaṭeśvara Press editions. It is quite possible that the various manuscripts may have different accounts. For a convincing argument as to why there is no *one* version of a Purāṇa, see, Ludo Rocher, *The Purāṇas* (vol.II, Fasc. 3 of *A History of Indian Literature*, edited by Jan Gonda, Wiesbaden: Harrassowitz, 1986), pp. 6; 59ff.

portrayals of the *avatāra* in Vaiṣṇava traditions. David Lorenzen, in one of the only analytical studies of the Śaṅkara hagiographies to date, argues that the "Śaivite bias" of the texts conflicts with Vaiṣṇavism which is "surreptitiously introduced through the implied comparison of the childhoods of Śaṅkara and Kṛṣṇa".[40] Lorenzen points to the tension between the householder model, which is essentially Vaiṣṇava, and that of the renouncer, which is Śaiva. I would agree that the householder/renouncer conflict is central to Śaṅkara's life story. But I am skeptical about the extent to which the hagiographies reveal, however "surreptitiously", a Vaiṣṇava component. While the Śaivas cannot but have been influenced by Vaiṣṇava traditions, some very real distinctions remain.[41] In the case of the Śaṅkara hagiographies, Śaiva materials, such as the paradigmatic story of Upamanyu, seem to have been far more influential than the legends of Krishna's youth.[42]

The differences in Śaiva and Vaiṣṇava mythologies are clearly manifest in their representations of the *avatāra*. Despite the existence of some early textual references to Śiva's mortal

---

40 David N. Lorenzen, "The life of Śaṅkarācārya", in *Experiencing Śiva. Encounters with a Hindu deity*, ed. Fred W. Clothey and J. Bruce Long, (Colombia, Mo., 1983, 155-175), p. 164. The discussion is based primarily on the ŚDV. While a focus on this one text is justifiable insofar as it is now the most widely accepted hagiography, there are some limitations to the conclusions which can be drawn on the basis of a single source. Several of the stories from the ŚDV, which Lorenzen cites as examples of the Śaṅkara-Kṛṣṇa parallels, are not necessarily typical of the Sanskrit hagiographies as a whole. Nevertheless, this is a concise and insightful study.

41 Lorenzen acknowledges the criticism he has received from Wendy O'Flaherty, who suggested that he did not pay enough attention to the "Śaivite archetypes" of the life story, *ibid*, p. 175, note 29.

42 In addition to the VŚV and GŚC (2.19-40), the Upamanyu story is mentioned in CŚV 2.43, GVK 1.45 and ŚDV 5.34.

manifestations,[43] the *avatāra* concept remains somewhat hazy in Śaiva traditions. The incarnations reflect the ambivalent and often frightening qualities of Śiva himself. This is in contrast to the more benign and approachable nature of Viṣṇu's *avatāras*, several of whom have their own well defined cults. There are not so many votaries of Śiva's incarnations. The long list of Śiva's *avatāras* cited in the Purāṇas include few who are important in their own right.[44]

Anger is probably the most characteristic feature of Śiva's *avatāras*. This can be seen from the time of the earliest textual references which portray Rudra-Śiva as a fierce deity who must be appeased. The *śata-rudrīya* litany of the *Kṛṣṇa-Yajurveda* expresses this in its opening line: "Salutations to you, Rudra, and to your wrath".[45] He appears as the fearsome Bhairava in order to cut off Brahmā's head as a punishment for his arrogance.[46] Similarly, Śiva's fury at being excluded from Dakṣa's sacrifice gives rise to Vīrabhadra who destroys the sacrifice.[47] Two important characters in the *Mahābhārata*, Aśvatthāman and Durvāsas, are also representative of Śiva's anger. Aśvatthāman is said to be born of portions from Mahādeva, death, desire and anger.[48] Although Durvāsas, who is born from Rudra, is assigned the role of testing people's adherence to *dharma*,[49] he is best known as the archetypal

---

43 Lorenzen cites the *Pāśupatasūtra*, dating from the Gupta period, which refers to Lakulīśa as an incarnation of Śiva, "Life of Śaṅkarācārya", p. 163.

44 See Chapter Two.

45 *namas te rudra manyave uto*, *Taittirīya-kṛṣṇa-yajurveda-saṃhitā*, 4.5.1.

46 *Śiva-purāṇa* 3.8.39ff.

47 *Kūrma-purāṇa* 1.14.

48 *mahādevāntakābhyāṃ ca kāmāt krodhāc ca...ekatvam upapannānāṃ jajne* , MBh 1.61.66-67.

49 *bhūtvā rudraś ca durvāsā...cakre dharma-parīkṣāñ ca bahūnām* , *Śiva-purāṇa* 3. 19. 28.

angry sage. In the Śaṅkara hagiographies it is his curse which causes Sarasvatī to be born as a mortal.

There are several other *avatāras* who, like Durvāsas, appear in order to test people's character. One significant episode in the epic (MBh 3.39-40) involves Śiva's manifestation as a tribal hunter (Kirāta). Arjuna performs *tapas* in the Himālayas in the hope of securing divine weapons from Śiva. The awesome power emanating from his *tapas* frightens the sages, who beg Śiva to stop it. He takes on the form of a Kirāta and challenges Arjuna in hunting and combat. Śiva is similarly requested to check the *tapas* of Upamanyu. He manifests himself as Indra and tests the devotion of the young sage. Ironically, in this episode it is Upamanyu who displays the anger characteristic to Śiva in threatening to destroy "Indra" with a mighty weapon.

The *avatāra* of Viṣṇu also engages in combat and is invariably called upon to destroy powerful demons. Nevertheless, he tends to be thought of primarily as a protector.[50] This aspect of Viṣṇu has been emphasized since the time of the epics. In the *Mahābhārata*'s version of the primeval battle between Indra and Vṛtra, the gods call upon Viṣṇu to save them from the assault of the Dānavas. They address him as "the world creator, protector, and keeper" and beseech him accordingly: "When of yore the earth was lost, lotus-eyed God, thou didst rescue it from the ocean assuming the form of a boar...we address thee for the good of the world:

---

[50] Gonda has aptly described the predominant conceptions of two great gods during the Vedic and Epic periods: Śiva is, "the power of the uncultivated and unconquered, dangerous and unreliable, unpredictable, hence much to be feared", while Viṣṇu represents "that pervasiveness which is essential to the establishment and maintenance of our cosmos....In short, Viṣṇu is, generally speaking, a friend nearer to man, Śiva a lord and master, ambivalent and many-sided", J. Gonda, *Viṣṇuism and Śivaism. A comparison*. ([1970], reprinted New delhi: Munshiram Manoharlal, 1976), pp. 5; 13.

protect the creatures and the Gods".[51] Krishna does, of course, reveal his destructive face to Arjuna: "I am Time, grown old, the destroyer of the world".[52] Moreover, as Alf Hiltebeitel has convincingly argued, Krishna seems to preside over the whole of the epic war as though it were a sacrificial ritual.[53] But Hiltebeitel also points out that Krishna intentionally absents himself from the battlefield in order to make way for the destruction to be wrought by Aśvatthāman.[54] As if to reinforce the portion of himself already present in Aśvatthāman, Rudra - Śiva gives him the power necessary to overcome the Pāṇḍavas: "the lord entered his body and gave him an excellent stainless sword".[55] Possessed by the great god, Aśvatthāman slaughters the entire camp of sleeping warriors. In the *Mahābhārata*, then, the role of bringing about the destruction which marks the end of the age is left to Śiva.[56]

The opposition of Śiva and Viṣṇu is reflected in the underlying tension between renouncer and householder in the Śaṅkara hagiographies. This is seen especially in the relationship between Śaṅkara, the epitome of the ascetic way, and his mother, a devotee of Viṣṇu, who seeks to keep him in

---

51 MBh 3.100.18ff., Van Buitenen's translation (*The Mahābhārata. Books 2 and 3*, Chicago, 1975) pp. 420-421.

52 *kālo 'smi loka-kṣaya-kṛta-pravṛddhaḥ, Bhagavavadgītā* 11.32.

53 *The ritual of battle: Krishna in the* Mahābhārata (Ithaca and London: Cornell University, 1976), esp. p. 356. Hiltebeitel argues that Aśvatthāman's massacre in the *Sauptika-parvan* follows the same pattern of Śiva's destruction of Dakṣa's sacrifice (pp. 299-335). Jacques Scheuer, in his *Śiva dans le Mahābhārata* (Paris: Presses Universitaires de France, 1982), raises some important objections to Hiltebeitel's thesis, but is sympathetic to it.

54 *Ibid*., pp. 314-316.

55 MBh 10.7.64.

56 The extent of Śiva's role in the epic is a contentious issue. In his *Visions of God. Narratives of theophany in the Mahābhārata* (Vienna: De Nobili Research Library, 1989, p. 229ff.), James W. Laine treats the arguments of Hiltebeitel and Scheuer with some caution (see note 44).

family life. Śaṅkara appeases his mother, according to all but one of our sources, with the promise to return home at the time of her death, even though this will be regarded as a breach of *saṃnyāsa-dharma*. Some of the inherent tension in the two modes of life is removed by this compromise. Four of the hagiographers describe a more direct encounter and *rapprochement* between the two opposing forces. No sooner does Śaṅkara leave home than he discovers that the nearby Krishna temple is threatened by the waters of the river he had previously moved nearer the house so that his aging mother could more easily perform her ablutions. Śaṅkara works a second miracle and reinstalls the deity on safer ground. In this way he obtains Krishna's blessing as he embarks on the path of the renouncer.

When Śaṅkara later returns home in fulfillment of his promise, the tension between Viṣṇu and Śiva is still in evidence. Another compromise must be reached. Because his dying mother is unable to comprehend his teachings on the formless Brahman, Śaṅkara invokes Śiva to ensure her passage to an auspicious realm. But the terrifying appearance of Śiva's attendants proves unbearable for her. In deference to her chosen ideal, Śaṅkara then calls upon Viṣṇu, whose more benign attendants arrive and convey her to Vaikuṇṭha.[57] Although Śaṅkara's renunciation has seriously threatened the order of the householder's life—as it almost undermined the Krishna statue—the support which Viṣṇu provides for the home is inevitably allowed to remain intact.

---

57 See CŚV 10.44, ŚDV 14.38. There are some significant variations in the narration of this episode. In GŚC 4.2, Śaṅkara asks his mother to choose between Śiva and Viṣṇu. In GVK 2.64, she hears his hymn to both gods. In VŚV 4.98, Śaṅkara calls directly on Nārāyaṇa when his mother is unable to grasp the formless Brahman.

Śaṅkara reveals the anger characteristic to Śiva's *avatāra*s when he curses the people of Kālaṭi who refuse to assist him with the arrangements for his mother's funeral. This important incident finds a place in nearly all the hagiographies.[58] Lakṣmaṇa-Śāstrī describes it quite concisely:

> He saw that the kinsfolk would not come to her home, that they would not provide [the necessary material for the cremation] fire and also that the [locals] were mean and abusive people. He sprinkled the corpse with water from his *kamaṇḍalu* which caused it to move [into position] and then, from his right hand [there emerged] a fire which covered the body and consumed it. Having performed the purification [rites] for his mother, the lord of wandering ascetics (*yati*), full of anger, cursed the residents of that place: "May there be no feeding of *yati*s in your homes. Let the burning of corpses take place in your homes. May there be no learning [in this place]. (GVK 2.65-66)

The uneasiness between householder and renouncer is certainly apparent here. This fundamental opposition is also manifest in one of Śaṅkara's only other notable displays of anger: his exchange of insults with Maṇḍanamiśra.[59]

The *dharma-śāstras* play an important role in mediating this conflict by defining and validating the respective spheres of the householder and renouncer. They enunciate a social code which clearly excludes the *saṃnyāsin* from the life cycle rituals of the householder. It is Śaṅkara's perceived breach of the social code to which the relatives and townspeople so strongly object. But

---

58 The episode is not found in the AŚV, which is the only text that does not include Śaṅkara's promise to return home. Because the TŚA does describe the promise, it is likely that the curse is also included in the text. But we cannot be certain since the latter third of the TŚA is no longer extant.

59 See Chapter Two, incident no. 21.

this episode may also reflect the inability of *śāstra* to successfully resolve the tensions between householder and renouncer. The *saṃnyāsin* threatens the social order with his renunciation, yet he poses an equal danger if he re-enters the sphere of the householder. It is only through the medium of the gift that the two may harmoniously interact. The householder provides alms to the renouncer who reciprocates with blessings or religious teachings.

Śaṅkara punishes the householders, whose refusal to assist in his mother's funeral ceremonies compels him to personally engage in activity he would otherwise have avoided. Thanks to his yogic power, he is able to escape the impurity incurred through physically disposing of a corpse. The householders, however, are not so fortunate. The effect of his curse ensures that their homes will be polluted by proximity to the funeral pyre. This threatens the sense of order the life cycle rituals strive to establish through maintaining the purity of the home. In an angry reaction reminiscent of Durvāsas, Śaṅkara denies his *pūrvāśrama* relatives and neighbours the opportunity to gain merit through the feeding of *saṃnyāsin*s. As a result, the special teaching promulgated by the renouncers will no longer enrich the community.

Although the hagiographers make some efforts to show that Śaṅkara transcends sectarian affiliations, the tradition which asserts he is the *avatāra* of Śiva is too well entrenched to be contradicted. It is indeed difficult to imagine how one born of Śiva could be fitted into another mythological context. For this reason, Viṣṇu can only play a limited supporting role. Even Govindanātha, the hagiographer who seems to have the strongest inclination towards Vaiṣṇavism, scarcely emphasizes Viṣṇu in his work. It is not until the closing scene of Śaṅkara's life that the author can indulge in his own predilections. After worshipping both Śiva and Viṣṇu, Śaṅkara sings a final hymn in praise of Viṣṇu. The last verse of the narrative describes Śaṅkara's attainment of identity with Viṣṇu. In sharp contrast to Govindanātha, Anantānandagiri, the most overtly Śaiva of the hagiographers, seeks to justify the supremacy of Śiva over Viṣṇu. This is on the authority of a *smṛti* verse:

> Following the succesive order of merit, the lowly are the servants of the honourable. According to the position of their family and caste, [men] have obtained the rank of one or another god. The deity of the brahmins is Śambhu, for *kṣatriya*s it is Mādhava. For *vaiśya*s it should be Brahmā, for *śūdras*, Gaṇanāyaka.[60]

The verse points to the significant link between the mythological and social orders which has been stressed in this chapter. The passage also reveals a feature typical of the Purāṇas: the manipulation of conceptual or narrative structures in order to demonstrate the superiority of a particular god.[61] Although some Vaiṣṇava elements may, for this reason, appear in a Śaiva context, the hagiographies retain a predominantly Śaiva perspective. This is in keeping with the Śaiva orientation which has been evident in the Śaṅkara tradition since at least the 14th century.

---

60 *pūjyeṣu sevakā nīcāḥ puṇya-mārga-kramānugāḥ / tattad-devapadaṃ prāpur yathā-jāti-kula-sthiti // viprāṇāṃ daivataṃ śambhuḥ kṣatriyāṇāṃ ca mādhavaḥ / vaiśyānāṃ tu bhaved brahmā śūdrāṇāṃ gaṇanāyakaḥ //* AŚV p. 2. Some of the AŚV manuscripts attribute the verse to Manu, but it is not found in Manu's *dharma-śastra.*

61 A similar approach is characteristic to the Advaita tradition: opposing viewpoints (with the exception of the *nāstika*) are not excluded but are instead subsumed in a hierarchy at whose summit stands Advaita Vedānta.

CHAPTER IV

Pilgrim and Conqueror: a Sacred Geography

The hagiographies devote much attention to Śaṅkara's all-India tour.[1] Indeed once he leaves home as a renouncer, his travels become the dominant theme of the narrative. The magnitude of his journey is underscored by the great distance he must travel to reach the very first of his destinations: the residence of his guru, Govinda. Each of the hagiographers seems to have a different idea of where this important meeting occurred. But even the shortest journey Śaṅkara is said to make in search of his teacher—from Kālaṭi to Cidambara, according to the AŚV — is in itself no mean feat for a boy. Vyāsācala's account avoids the confusion about its location by referring to the abode of Govinda simply as a far away place (*dūra-deśa*). All the hagiographers agree that Śaṅkara's travels extended as far north as Badarī, and right back down to the south.

While I have already made explicit my intention to refrain from treating the hagiographies as historical records, there is one point on which I am tempted to speculate, at the risk of self-contradiction. It seems quite likely to me that the all-India tour depicted in the texts—whatever its nature and true extent may have been—is based on a historical event. Such an assumption may, ironically, help to explain one of the reasons Śaṅkara remains so elusive to the historian. A wandering mendicant cannot easily be pinned down. I would suggest that the difficulty in determining the historical context of his life

---

1 The expression 'all-India' is, I am afraid, an anachronism. I use it mainly for the sake of convenience, but the term also highlights the nationalists' perception of Śaṅkara's journey.

stems in good part from the fact that Śaṅkara is not identified with a particular place. Moreover, there is no record of his association with a patron or king.[2]

Four of the hagiographers include an episode in which a king named Rājaśekhara, anxious to meet the celebrated child prodigy, arrives at Śaṅkara's home.[3] The king recites three plays he has writtten to the young sage, seeking his approval. Here the king must play the role of the supplicant, not of patron. Indeed the RŚA and ŚDV specify that Śaṅkara refuses to accept any money from the king. If Śaṅkara had led a truly peripatetic life from an early age, he may not have established any permanent residence. This would have reduced his access to material support, but it would also have left him free from the inevitable constraints of a relationship with a patron. We cannot, of course, determine whether this incident is a true reflection of the historical Śaṅkara. But it does reveal what is expected of the ideal *saṃnyāsin*. If he does not enter into a dependent relationship, the renouncer may stand above the king.

---

2 Connections between renouncer and king are not uncommon in the Śaṅkara tradition. The most well known example is Vidyāraṇya, who is believed to have been instrumental in the establishment of the Vijayanagara empire. Thanks to his efforts, the Śṛṅgerī Śaṅkara *maṭha* became very wealthy. For details, and a discussion of some long-standing misconceptions regarding Vidyāraṇya, see Hermann Kulke, "Mahārājas, mahants and historians. Reflections on the historiography of early Vijayanagara and Sringeri", in *Vijayanagara: city and empire. New currents of research*, ed. A. L. Dallapiccola (2 vols., Stuttgart: Steiner Verlag, 1985) vol. I, pp. 120-143.

3 See RŚA 1.39-40; TŚA 2.67-70; GVK 2.9-10; ŚDV 5.10-30. The texts appear to conflate the famous writer Rājaśekhara, who was not a king, with Kulaśekhara. The latter is identified with the Kerala king Rāmavarman Kulaśekhara who reigned c. 885-913 over the kingdom of Cochin. The village of Kālaṭi would almost certainly have been included in his domain. Rājaśekhara is the author of three *kāvya* works: two dramas and a no longer extant novel. For details see, A. K. Warder, *Indian kāvya literature*, vol. 5, (Delhi: Motilal Banarsidass, 1988), p. 321 ff.

According to the cultural code, the king bows before the *ṛṣi*, and not vice versa.[4] Thus a *saṃnyāsin* might be better off—at least in terms of social esteem—without a royal patron.[5]

The renouncer should cut the ties not only with his family and caste but with his native place as well. In order to insure that new attachments to place do not arise, the *śāstras* stipulate that the *saṃnyāsin* should not remain for long in any one spot, except during the rainy season.[6] That the homeland ties are not easily severed—at least in the eyes of the society at large—is apparent from the small number of religious leaders who have managed to transcend their regional identity. This is no mean achievement in India, where the native place is a key factor in the perception of personality. Because Śaṅkara was not encumbered by the limitations of a specific regional identity, it was probably much easier for him (and later, for the disciples) to successfully promulgate his teachings throughout the subcontinent.

There are two models for the hagiographers' representation of Śaṅkara's all-India journey. Both feature prominently in the *Mahābhārata*: the world conquest (*digvijaya-parvan*, 2.23-29)

---

4 See, for example, Manu's *Dharma-śāstra* 7.37ff.

5 An analogy can be drawn here with the status of Brahmin temple priests. Because they are perceived as servants of the deity, they are ranked lower in the social hierarchy than Brahmins who do not enter into service. For further discussion see Arjun Appadurai, "The puzzling status of Brahmin temple priests in Hindu India", *South Asian Anthropologist*, 4 (1983) 43-52, and C. J. Fuller *Servants of the goddess: the priests of a south Indian temple*, (Cambridge: Cambridge University Press, 1984). Phyllis Granoff has demonstrated the ambivalence towards the renouncer who enters the royal court in the Jain tradition, "Authority and innovation: a study of the use of similes in the biography of Hiravijaya to provide sanction for the monk at court", *Jinmanjari* 1 (1990), pp. 48-60.

6 See the citations in *Vāsudevāśrama Yatidharmaprakāśa: A treatise on world renunciation*, ed. and tr. Patrick Olivelle (2 vols., Vienna: Publications of the de Nobili Research Library, 1976/77), II p. 174.

and a great pilgrimage (*tīrthayātrā-parvan*, 3.80-93) which entails the circumambulation of the subcontinent. The *digvijaya* is, strictly speaking, appropriate only for a king. But the hagiographers transpose this ritual method of legitimising authority from the sphere of politics to the realm of metaphysics. The path to the highest good by way of the *tīrthayātrā* is open to all, or at least to the twice-born. Yet the renouncer has a special role to play here. The rewards of the pilgrimage only accrue to those who embody the ideals of the *saṃnyāsin*: "those whose hands, feet and especially whose minds are controlled; those who have knowledge, austerities and renown will obtain the reward of the sacred sites".[7] Even kings must emulate the qualities of the renouncer in order to obtain the benefits conferred by pilgrimage. In the *digvijaya* there is a special interplay of royal and ascetic values. This complementarity, which figures largely in the hagiographies, will be discussed separately below.

Because the all-India tour is so prominent in his life story, the nature of Śaṅkara's journey is in itself a source of considerable interest. Even if we cannot verify its historicity, the possibility of such a journey remains. While the enormous difficulties and risks entailed by long distance travel in the first millenium A.D. should not be underestimated, the travel records of the Chinese Buddhist pilgrims in India certainly demonstrate that people could and did undertake such journeys. Hsuan-tsang made his remarkable tour of the four quarters of India, including the no less arduous return journey to China, in the surprisingly short period of 16 years.[8] The more historical perspective of

---

7 *yasya hastau ca pādau ca manaś caiva susaṃyatam / vidyā tapaś ca kīrtiś ca sa tīrtha-phalam aśnute//* Mbh 3.80.30.

8 He began the journey from Ch'ang-an, present day Sian in Shensi province, in 629 A.D. and returned to the same city in 645. See Thomas Watters, *On Yuan Chwang's travels in India*, ed. T. W. Rhys Davids and S. W. Bushell, (2

the Chinese pilgrims' accounts stands in sharp contrast to the Śaṅkara hagiographies. The obvious variations in their description of Śaṅkara's peregrinations point to the futility of reading the hagiographies as history. Moreover, the texts reveal no attempts at verisimilitude in describing the journey. We read nothing concerning the everyday hardships a pilgrim must endure. But if their narratives are constructed without fixed temporal referents,[9] the hagiographers do create a spatial structure for the story. Indeed most of the major events of his life are intentionally situated in specific locations.[10] The sense of place is at once empirical and transcendental. Nearly all the sites mentioned in the texts are real places, yet there is a sacred geography which underpins the narrative and constitutes the setting for a cosmic drama.

The representation of empirical space will be considered first. The table on pages 142-143 sets out the places Śaṅkara is said to visit, in seven of the hagiographies, from the time he leaves home in search of his guru. The sequence of places listed follows the chronology of the narrative in each of the sources. The place names are given exactly as they appear in the texts. Asterisks are used to indicate unidentifiable places. To facilitate further comparison, I have indicated the locations of five important episodes in the life story. The TŚA is not included in the table because the sole extant text of this work breaks off at a point early on in the journey, while Śaṅkara is still at Śrīśaila. In the ŚDV, which describes Śaṅkara's travels in almost identical terms, this is only the seventh place he visits.

---

vols., London: Royal Asiatic Society 1904-1905), and especially the appendix by Vincent Smith, vol.2, pp. 329-344.

9 See Chapter Three for discussion.

10 Vyāsācala is an exception. He names only a few specific settings for the major episodes.

I will elaborate on some of the significant geographical details shown in the table for each of the hagiographies.[11]

AŚV. This text provides the most extensive account of Śaṅkara's *digvijaya*. Thirteen places are specifically mentioned as the venues for his debates against sectarian foes. In addition, there are numerous pilgrimage sites which figure prominently in the narrative. Yet of all texts, the AŚV mentions the greatest number of unidentifiable places. For these reasons the all-India tour of the AŚV will require special attention. After formal initiation from his guru, Śaṅkara sets out from Cidambara in a southerly direction. He already has with him a large entourage of disciples, including Hastāmalaka. Śaṅkara's first stop is at Madhyārjuna (Tiruviḍaimarudūr, Tamil Nadu) to worship at the Śiva temple. The great god comes forth from the *liṅga* to proclaim the truth of the Advaita doctrine. With this miraculous affirmation of his authority, Śaṅkara is fully prepared to embark on a *digvijaya*. This begins at Rāmeśvara, where he is confronted by various Śaiva opponents whom he defeats and converts to Advaita. Śaṅkara then travels to "the place where there is an image of the Lord known as Anantaśayana".[12] The reference is to the early temple of Padmanābhasvāmī in present-day Trivandram. The main shrine portrays Viṣṇu reclining on

---

11 I have relied on the following sources for geographical materials: *A historical atlas of South Asia*, ed. Joseph Schwartzberg (Chicago: University of Chicago, 1978); J. H. Dave, *Immortal India*, 4 vols.(Bombay: Bharatiya Vidya Bhavan, 1959-61); Nundo Lal Dey, *The geographical dictionary of ancient and medieval India*, (New Delhi: Oriental Books Reprint, 1971); P. V. Kane "List of *tīrthas*", in *History of Dharmaśāstra*, vol. 4 (rev. ed., Poona: Bhandarkar Oriental Research Institute, 1973), pp. 730-825; Bimal Churn Law, *Historical geography of ancient India*, (reprinted Delhi, Ess Ess Publications, 1976). In drawing up the maps which follow, I have used Schwartzberg and the state maps from the Survey of India (1:1 million series).

12 AŚV p. 43.

AŚV	CŚV	VŚV	GŚC
Cidambara	Badarī	*dūradeśa*	Kāśi
Madhyārjuna	Kālaṭi	Badarī[1]	Badarīka[1]
Rāmeśvara	Prayāga[4]	Kālaṭi	Kālaṭi
Anantaśayana	Gayā	Prayāga[2]	Badarīka
Subrahmaṇya	Vārāṇasī[1]	Magadha[3]	Prayāga[2]
Gaṇavara*	Ruddhanagara*[2]		Magadha[3]
Tulajābhavānī	Vijvaladvindura[3]	[Sanandana's	Gokarṇa
Ujjayinī	Amṛtapura*[5]	pilgrimage:	Śivavihāra[4]
Anumallapura*	Vijvaladvindura	Kālahasti	Haridvāra
Nirundha/Marundha*	Śṛṅgerī	Kāñcī	Kālahasti
Māgadhapura*	Kāñcī	Cidambara	Kāñcī
Indraprastha	Veṅkaṭeśvara	Śrīraṅga	Cidambara
Yamaprastha*	Cidambara	Agastyāśrama*	Śrīraṅga
Prayāga	Madhyārjuna	Rāmeśvara]	Rāmeśvara
Kāśī[1]	Rāmeśvara		Kāśmīra
Kailāsa/Amaranātha	Vakratuṇḍapurī*	Gokarṇa	Kāñcī[5]
Kedāra, Badarī	Madurai	Śrīvaligrāma[4]	Vṛṣācala
Kurukṣetra	Anantaśayana	Śāradā-*pīṭha*[5]	
Dvārakā, Nīlakaṇṭha	Vāsukikṣetra	*rucitadeśa*	
Ayodhyā, Gayā	Mṛdapurī*, Gokarṇa		
Jagannātha, Śrīśaila	Śrīśaila, Pāṇḍuraṅgeśa		
Rudranagara*[2]	Jagannāthapura		
Vidyālaya*[3]	Ujjayinī, Dvārakā		
Amṛtapura*[5]	Madhurā, Kurukṣetra		
Śṛṅgerī	Haridvāra, Badarī		
Ahobila, Veṅkaṭagiri	Dattātreya's cave		
Kāñcī	Kailāsa		

*unidentifiable places

[1]meets Vyāsa

[2]meets Kumārila-Bhaṭṭa

[3]meets Maṇḍana/Viśvarūpa

[4]meets his disciple, Hastāmalaka

[5]enters body of King Amaruka

RŚA	GVK	ŚDV
unspecified	unspecified	Indu-bhāva (Narmadā)
Badarī[1]	Badarikā[1]	Kāśī[1]
Prayāga[2]	Prayāga[2]	Prayāga[2]
Magadha[3]	Magadha[3]	Māhiṣmatī[3 and 5]
Narmadā (Magadha)	Revā (=Narmadā)	Narmadā (in Magadha)
Kālaṭi	Kālaṭi	Mahārāṣṭra
around Kerala	Subrahmaṇya	Śrīśaila
Mahāsurālayeśa *	around Taulava	Gokarṇa
Śivavalli *agrahāra*[4]	Madhyārjuna	Harihara
Gokarṇa	Anantaśayana	Mūkāmbikā
Harihara	Rāmeśvara	Śrībali *agrahāra*[4]
Mūkāmbikā[5]	Śrīraupya-*pīṭha*[4]	Śṛṅgerī
Anantaśayana	Gokarṇa	Kālaṭi
Madhurā (Madurai)	Sahya mountain	around Kerala
Rāmeśvara	Śṛṅgerī	Mahāsurālayeśa temple*
Śrīraṅga	Śrīśaila	Padmapāda's pilgrimage
Cidambara	Śeśācala (Tirupati)	Rāmeśvara
Śoṇagiri (Aruṇācala)	Narasiṃhagiri	Kāñcī, Veṅkaṭācala
Kāñcī	Jagannātha	Karṇāṭaka, Gokarṇa
	Kāśī	Dvārakā, Ujjayinī
	Śāradā-*pīṭha*[5]	Bāhlika-deśa, Naimiṣa
	Śṛṅgerī	Darada, Bharata
	Kāñcī	Śūrasena, Kurupāñcāla
	Badarī	Kāmarūpa
	Kāśī	Videha, Kośala,
	Nepāla	Aṅga, Vaṅga, Gauḍa
	Dattātreya's *āśrama**	Śāradā-*pīṭha* (Kāśmīra]
		Badarī, Kedāra

Places visited in:
- All 7 sources: Badarī, Prayāga, Kāñcī, Rāmeśvara
- Six sources: Magadha, Gokarṇa, Kālaṭi
- Five sources: Kāśmīra, Kāśī, Cidambara, Śrīvali/Śivavihāra
- Four sources: Śrīśaila, Śṛṅgerī, Tirupati, Anantaśayana

the primordial serpent (*ananta-śayana*).[13] Here Śaṅkara debates with the leaders of different Vaiṣṇava sects. The events which transpire in Rameśvara and Anantaśayana reflect the pattern the AŚV follows in describing the *digvijaya*. Each of the towns Śaṅkara visits is identified in terms of the predominant indigenous sect or sects.

From Anantaśayana, Śaṅkara travels to Subrahmaṇya in the South Kanara district of Karnataka. Although it retains its name, the present-day Subrahmaṇya may have lost some of its status as a site sacred to the god of the same name. Śaṅkara bathes in the Kumāradhārā river and worships the six-faced god who, in this place, has the form of the serpent Śeṣa.[14] Here he meets followers of sects devoted to Hiraṇyagarbha, Agni and Sūrya. Oddly enough, Anantānandagiri does not mention the presence of the votaries of Kumāra in this place, nor does Śaṅkara encounter them elsewhere in his tours of victory. Perhaps the sect of this deity had not yet attained the great popularity it enjoys nowadays in Tamil Nadu and elsewhere[15].

Śaṅkara then visits the town of Gaṇavaram on the Kaumudī river,[16] neither of which I am able to identify. But the place name is at least indicative of the cults of Gaṇapati which are said to be predominant here. In Tulajābhavānī, the modern Tuljapur in Maharashtra, Śaṅkara debates against the Śāktas. He

---

13 See K. R. Vaidyanathan, *Temples and legends of Kerala* (Bombay: Bharatiya Vidya, 1988), p. 28.

14 AŚV p. 65. See also P. Gururaja Bhatt, *Antiquities of South Kanara* (Udupi, 1969), p. 10.

15 F. Clothey observes that the Skanda-Murukaṉ cult was in decline between the 6th and 10th centuries and did not begin to return to prominence until the middle of the 10th century (Fred W. Clothey, *The many faces of Murukaṉ. The history and meaning of a South Indian god*. The Hague: Mouton Publishers, 1978, p. 73ff.).

16 AŚV p. 79.

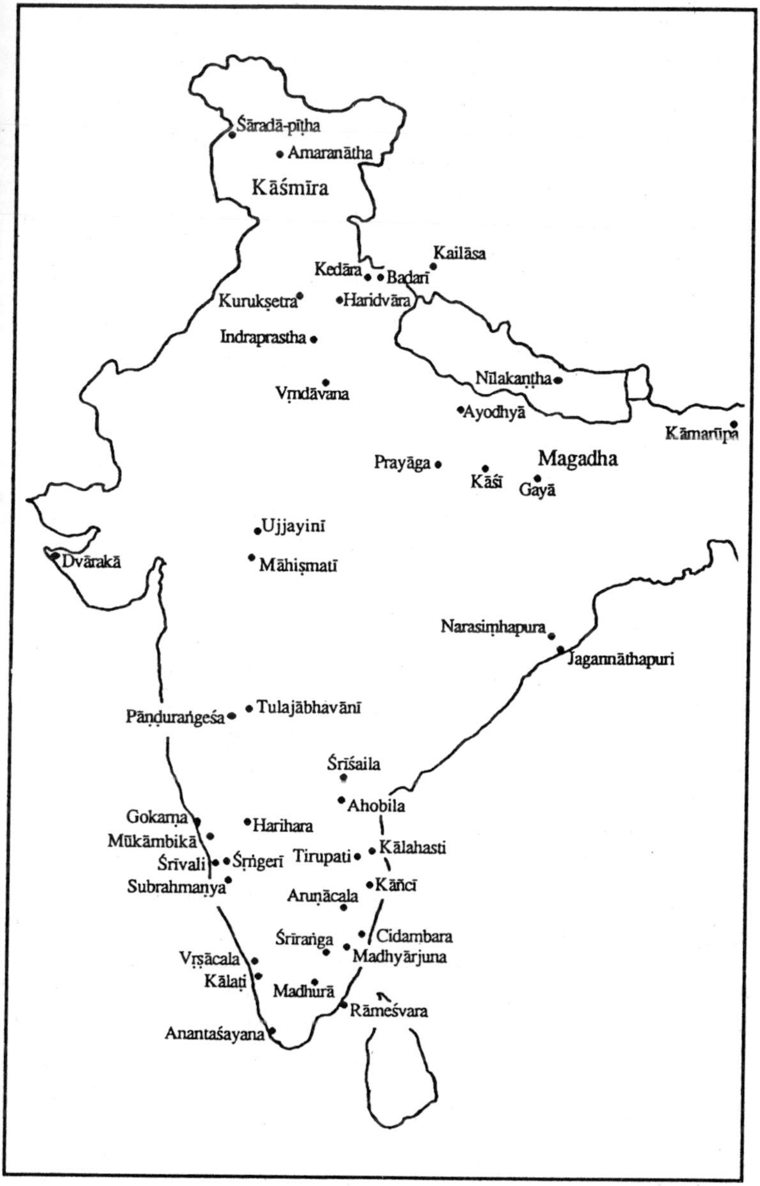
Śāradā-pīṭha
Amaranātha
Kāśmīra
Kailāsa
Kedāra
Badarī
Kurukṣetra
Haridvāra
Indraprastha
Vṛndāvana
Nīlakaṇṭha
Ayodhyā
Kāmarūpa
Prayāga
Magadha
Kāśī
Gayā
Ujjayinī
Dvārakā
Māhiṣmatī
Narasiṃhapura
Jagannāthapuri
Pāṇḍuraṅgeśa
Tulajābhavānī
Śrīśaila
Ahobila
Gokarṇa
Harihara
Mūkāmbikā
Śrīvali
Śṛṅgerī
Tirupati
Kālahasti
Subrahmaṇya
Kāñcī
Aruṇācala
Śrīraṅga
Cidambara
Madhyārjuna
Vṛṣācala
Kālaṭi
Madhurā
Rāmeśvara
Anantaśayana

then travels to Ujjayinī which is depicted in the AŚV as a stronghold of non-Vedic cults: Kāpālikas, Cārvākas, Jains and Buddhists. From here he sets out in a northwesterly direction and reaches the town of Anumalla.[17] In this unidentifiable place Śaṅkara defeats the followers of a manifestation of Rudra, who is worshipped as the lord of dogs and conqueror of the demon, Malla.[18]

The venues for the next two debates are also unidentifiable. First there is the town of Nirundha (or Marundha) which is further to the west.[19] Here Śaṅkara encounters the devotees of Viṣvaksena (a manifestation of Viṣṇu) and Manmatha (the god of love). Travelling to the north he reaches Māgadhapura, where there is a celebrated Yakṣa temple, and confronts the votaries of Kubera.[20] The identity of this place is especially puzzling. It is difficult to imagine how Māgadhapura could signify anything other than 'the city of the Magadhan(s)'.[21] But for some

---

17 AŚV p. 117.

18 G. D. Sontheimer has researched the folk traditions of Mallāri, known as Mailār in Karnataka and Mallaṇṇa in Andhra Pradesh. The cult was also widespread in Maharashtra. According to Sontheimer one of the most important cult centres is located in the town of Adimailar, near Hampi, in Bellari District, Karnataka (Günther D. Sontheimer, "Folk deities in the Vijayanagara empire: Narasiṃha and Mallaṇṇa/Mailār", in *Vijayanagara: city and empire. New currents of research*, ed. A. L. Dallipiccola [2 vols. Wiesbaden: Franz Steiner Verlag, 1985], vol I. 144-158, esp. pp. 148-49; see also his "God as the king for all: the Sanskrit *Mallāri Māhātmya* and its context", in *The history of sacred places in India as reflected in traditional literature*, ed. Hans Bakker [Leiden: E. J. Brill, 1990], pp. 103-130). It is difficult to say whether the Anumalla of the AŚV could be identified with Adimailār in Karnataka.

19 AŚV p. 119. The manuscripts vary as to the name of this place.

20 AŚV p. 123.

21 See George Grierson, "The Magadha pura of the Mahabharata", *Journal of the Bihar and Orissa Research Society*, 2 (1916), pp. 95-96. Even if we were to understand the name in a looser sense, 'a city [built/controlled] by a

reason, Anantānandagiri seems to be suggesting that the city is located in the northwest and not, as we would expect, in the east. Although he is far more conversant with the geography of south India, Anantānandagiri is not otherwise unreasonable in his description of north Indian sites.

Śaṅkara's next stop is the celebrated city of Indraprastha (now Delhi). He apparently finds the place bereft of its ancient and future glories. In the AŚV it is home only to a single sect: the followers of Indra. At this point Anantānandagiri may have indulged in some free association. He has Śaṅkara travel to Yamaprastha in order to defeat the devotees of Yama, the god of death. The subsequent series of debates take place in two important centres of religious life: Prayāga (present day Allahabad) and Kāśī (Benares). For Śaṅkara, these cities are very much alive. In each he encounters more than ten sects representing between them all manner of creeds. It is in Kāśī that the sixteen year old Śaṅkara also meets Vyāsa. He approves Śaṅkara's *Brahmasūtra* commentary and extends his span of life for another sixteen years. Vyāsa also directs him to continue his peripatetic teaching work.

Śaṅkara now sets off to the Himālayas. According to the Calcutta recension he follows a northern route and visits two famous *liṅgas*.[22] One is the *amara-liṅga*, presumably the pilgrimage site of Amaranātha in Kashmir, where a natural *liṅga* of ice is said to wax and wane in conjunction with the moon. The second is at Kedāra. In the Madras edition of the AŚV, Śaṅkara avails himself of his yogic power and travels from Kāśī by an aerial route to Kailāsa. Here he receives five crystal *liṅgas* from Śiva himself. Both recensions agree that he

Magadhan', we are still no closer to identifying the place. The kingdom of Magadha was located in what is now southern Bihar.

22 In the Bibliotheca Indica edition (1868) of the AŚV, p. 235.

next visits Badarī, where Nārāyaṇa grants him the boon of a hot spring to facilitate ritual bathing in this icy climate.

The AŚV is sketchy about the subsequent stage of the journey.[23] Śaṅkara travels to Kurukṣetra, or at least on the road to Kurukṣetra, and then makes a clockwise circumambulation of Dvārakā and other holy places. He next visits Nīlakaṇṭha, which probably refers to the great temple of that name near Kathmandu. From here he travels to Ayodhyā, Gayā, Jagannātha and Śrīśaila. At the latter place he worships the manifestation of Śiva known as Mallikārjuna and his consort Bhramarāmbā. He stays at Śrīśaila for a month or so, at which time he meets some brahmins from Rudrapura (Ruddhapura in the Calcutta edition). From them he learns of the great deeds of [Kumārila] Bhaṭṭācārya, who has defeated countless Buddhist and Jain opponents.

Thus far in the narrative, Śaṅkara has followed a clockwise path around the sub-continent, albeit with some irregularities. Having reached Śrīśaila (in the Kurnool district of Andhra Pradesh), he has completed more than 300° of his circumambulation. Now there is a disruption in the course of the journey. Anxious to meet Bhaṭṭācārya, Śaṅkara immediately proceeds to Rudra/Ruddhapura.[24] The text gives no indication whatsoever as to the location of this place. While Śaṅkara is denied the satisfaction of debating the great Mīmāṃsaka himself, Bhaṭṭācārya does offer him a contest with his nephew Maṇḍanamiśra, who lives "in a northern land"[25] Śaṅkara sets out to a place situated to the southeast of the ancient city of

---

23 AŚV p. 172.

24 AŚV p. 173.

25 *tathā ced udagdeśeṣu mad-bhaginī-bhartā...*, p. 174. The Calcutta edition has a different reading which is construed not with Maṇḍana but with Bhaṭṭācārya: *tathā dagdha-śeṣa-śarīra.*

Hastināpura.[26] The town he reaches is called Vidyālaya, a name indicative at least of the great scholarship of its leading citizen. We learn that the local inhabitants call the place Bijilabindu, but there are no more specific details of its location.[27] After the defeat of Maṇḍanamiśra, his wife Sarasavāṇī challenges Śaṅkara's expertise in the *śāstra*s. This leads to an adjournment of the debate and his quest for the understanding of the erotic arts. Dismissing all but four of his closest disciples, Śaṅkara travels to the western region. In a certain city he enters the body of a dying king, hence the appropriate name of the place, Amṛtapura. After mastering the *kāma-śāstra*, Śaṅkara returns to Vidyālaya to continue the debate with Sarasavāṇī. In this way, three of the crucial events in the life story unfold in some vague northern location.

Śaṅkara now resumes the final, southern leg of his tour. Utilising his yogic power, he travels immediately to Śṛṅgerī, by air. He concludes the episode with Sarasavāṇī by installing her as the supreme deity on the banks of the Tuṅgabhadrā river. Śaṅkara remains in Śṛṅgerī for twelve years, during which time he establishes a *maṭha*, a seat of learning, and the Bhāratī lineage of his ascetic successors. He then sets out on the road again to Ahobila (in the Kurnool district of Andhra Pradesh). At this sacred site of Narasiṃha, he is back in the vicinity of Śrīśaila where his grand *pradakṣina* was previously interrupted. From Ahobila (or Ahobala) he travels south to Veṅkaṭagiri (Tirupati), and worships the deity whose temple is probably the richest in India today. His journey comes full circle at Kāñcī where he spends the last of his days.

---

26 *hastināpurād āgneya-bhāga-sthalaṃ vidyālayam iti prasiddham*. Hastināpura was located some 90 kilometres northeast of Delhi.

27 *taddeśa-vāsinas bijilavindur iti vadanti*. The Calcutta edition reads Vijilavindu.

CŚV. Most of the places Śaṅkara visits in the AŚV also figure in the CŚV. However, the route of the journey in the CŚV is quite different. This is largely because Cidvilāsa does not use the same chronological sequence, nor the same setting, for the episodes which are common to both works. In contrast to Anantānandagiri, Cidvilāsa has Śaṅkara proceed directly to the north upon leaving home. This is also the case in the other six hagiographies. Yet Cidvilāsa makes him travel the furthest—all the way to Badarī—in order to meet his guru. He remains in the north during the first stage of his journey. However, there is one interruption right at the beginning, when he returns to Kālaṭi in order to attend to his dying mother. After this Śaṅkara quickly travels back north to Prayāga, where he gathers many disciples.

He meets Bhaṭṭācārya in a secluded forest on the outskirts of Ruddhanagara. As in the AŚV, there is no specific information concerning the location of this town, but the CŚV is more definite in situating it in the north. Śaṅkara arrives here from Vārāṇasī and will next travel to Kāśmīra. According to Cidvilāsa, Bhaṭṭācārya directs Śaṅkara to seek out Maṇḍanamiśra in Kāśmīra. His residence, known as Vidyālaya is in the town of Vijvaladvindura. After his victory in the debate and the subsequent defeat of Sarasvatī, complete with a soujourn in Amṛtapura to learn the *kāma-śāstra*, Śaṅkara commences the southern part of his tour

There are only two unidentifiable places in this section of the journey. Vakratuṇḍapuri, on the Gandhavatī, is the venue for debates with the followers of Gaṇapati (who is known by the epithet *vakratuṇḍa*).[28] This site may be analogous to the similarly unknown Gaṇavara mentioned in the AŚV. Another parallel occurs with Vāsukikṣetra, on the Kumāradhārā river. This place is clearly identical with Subrahmaṇya, a still extant

[28] CŚV 28.1.

pilgrim site of the six-faced deity, Kumāra, which was mentioned in the AŚV.[29] The second unidentified place is Mṛdapurī, which is unique to the CŚV. This town is presumably situated between Subrahmaṇya and Gokarṇa. Here Śaṅkara debates against Buddhist opponents.

VŚV. This is the only hagiography which contains very few details of Śaṅkara's tour. Nevertheless, Vyāsācala devotes nearly two chapters (7.98-9.34) exclusively to pilgrimage, though the journey is not Śaṅkara's but is made by his disciple Sanandana. Prior to this pilgrimage there is an important and revealing discussion between guru and disciple on the relative merits of wandering *vis à vis* remaining in one place and concentrating on Self-realisation. This episode will be considered in detail below as it is important for our understanding of the role of pilgrimage in the Śaṅkara tradition.

However scanty the details of Śaṅkara's journey here, they bear careful examination because the VŚV was so influential on the later hagiographers. When Śaṅkara sets out from the unspecified abode of his guru, Vyāsācala mentions only that he is desirous of visiting various pilgrim sites in the north. He eventually reaches Badarī, the northernmost.[30] From here, Śaṅkara travels by air, using his yogic power to make a quick return to his dying mother. After her death he wanders about, eventually reaching Prayāga, where he meets Bhaṭṭapāda. The Mīmāṃsaka directs Śaṅkara to debate his disciple Viśvarūpa, who lives in Magadha.[31] It is from here that Sanandana sets out for his pilgrimage. But we are not told anything of

29 CŚV 29.1ff.

30 VŚV 4.66. There is a significant variant in the manuscripts here. The editor has it that he reached Badarī in an instant (*kṣaṇena*), but two of the mss. read 'gradually' (*krameṇa*) which seems better.

31 VŚV 5.34.

Śaṅkara's movements during this time. In an unspecified place he is served by a Kāpālika, who is very keen to make a ritual offering of Śaṅkara's head. Meanwhile, Sanandana has just completed his pilgrimage and returns just in time to save the life of his guru.[32] Śaṅkara's life is again threatened, this time by a disease called *bhagandara.* The disciples go in various directions in search of medicines and doctors. One excursion is described in detail: a journey to the Sahya mountains, i.e., the Western Ghats.[33] Śaṅkara is finally cured, not by doctors or herbs but by the Aśvins.

At this point, Vyāsācala tells us that Śaṅkara wished to set out for Gokarṇa, although his visit to this coastal town is not described. South of Gokarṇa, he comes to the village of Śrīvali, an ancient centre of learning located just three kilometres south of Uḍipi, and now known as Shivalli.[34] Here he finds a new disciple whom he names Hastāmalaka. After this Śaṅkara meets some brahmins who tell him of the throne of omniscience (*sarvajña-pīṭha*) at the temple of Śāradā (i.e., Sarasvatī) in Kāśmīra.[35] He learns that while men from the north, east and west have gained entry there, none have yet come from the south. He decides to travel there in order to open the southern gate. His claim to the throne is tested by the goddess. As in the other hagiographies, he enters the body of a dead king, but there is no mention of the location where this occurs. After taking his seat on the throne, he departs to a land which is pleasing to him (*rucita-deśa*).

---

32 VŚV 9.49.

33 VŚV 10.18-130; 11.1-78.

34 VŚV 12.1ff. Shivalli formerly included Uḍipi ((Uḍupi), according to the *Karnataka State Gazetteer. South Kanara District* (Bangalore: Govt. of Karnataka, 1973), pp. 758-759.

35 VŚV 12.29ff.

Perhaps Vyāsācala was unable to focus on Śaṅkara's pilgrimage *per se* because the traditional stories he relied on provided him too few specific geographical details. Or it may have seemed out of keeping with the true spirit of Advaita to suggest that one of its foremost practitioners would emphasize the multiplicity of sacred space. But whatever his motivation may have been, Vyāsācala gives Sanandana's pilgrimage a prominent place in the narrative. The fact that his journey is confined to the southeast suggests that Vyāsācala is most intimately aquainted with this region. It should also be noted that Śaṅkara's first disciple, Sanandana whom he meets in Badarī, is identified as a native of the same region: *cola-deśa.*[36] Of the six places Sanandana visits, the longest descriptions are reserved for Kāñcī, and Rāmeśvara.[37] In view of the considerable attention Vyāsācala devotes to these two places, it is somewhat surprising that Śaṅkara himself is not said to visit these sacred sites. It may be that Sanandana's pilgrimage was in itself sufficient to connect Kāñcī and Rāmeśvara with the life story of Śaṅkara. Indeed in the GŚC, Śaṅkara is said to follow exactly the same route which Sanandana took in the VŚV.[38]

GŚC. Although Govindanātha does extend Śaṅkara's journey to include those sites which Sanandana visited in the VŚV, he virtually replicates the geographical details of Vyāsācala's text. The GŚC slightly varies the name of Hastāmalaka's native

---

[36] VŚV 4.90.

[37] Kāñcī in 7.102-146; 8.1-2 and Rāmeśvara in 8.94-141; 9.1-28. There is one uncertain place mentioned, the āśrama of Agastya (Phullamuni). Prior to reaching Rāmeśvara, Sanandana comes to this spot near the sea where Rāma is said to have lain on a bed of Kuśa grass, VŚV 8.77.

[38] For this reason I have considered the places Sanandana visits in effect a part of Śaṅkara's tour in drawing up the table of pilgrimage sites above.

village, Śivavihāra,[39] but it denotes the same place, adjacent to Uḍipi, which is mentioned in the VŚV. One addition is Śaṅkara's visit to Haridvāra which immediately precedes his pilgrimage in the southeast. With some diffidence, Govindanātha diverges from the VŚV in locating the *sarvajña-pīṭha* at Kāñcī. In this he highlights a contradiction which must have existed in the traditional stories of Śaṅkara's ascension to the throne of omniscience. The CŚV and the RŚA both locate the *sarvajña-pīṭha* at Kāñcī, while the VŚV, GVK and ŚDV state it is at the Śāradā temple in Kāśmīra.[40]

It appears that Govindanātha tried to at least partially reconcile the two versions of the story by mentioning both Kāñcī and Kāśmīra in conjunction with the *sarvajña-pīṭha*. But this results in a somewhat confusing description:

> Śaṅkara, the best of gurus, set out to the city of Kāñcī. Having quickly circumambulated the earth—[in which time] he was beautifying the section of Jambū-dvīpa [called] Bhārata and was greatly illuminating the celebrated land named Kāśmīra—he reached that city which is the place of the goddess of speech, who is named Kāmākṣī. The best of ascetics approached in order to ascend the throne of omniscience.[41]

---

39 GŚC 6.6.

40 See CŚV 25.46, RŚA 7.64., VŚV 12.30-31, GVK 3.24, ŚDV 16.55. The AŚV does not mention the *sarvajña-pīṭha*, but there appears to be some connection with the CŚV's description of the episode. In both texts Śaṅkara is tested at Kāñcī by learned people from the Tāmraparṇī region (Tirunelveli district, Tamil Nadu).

41 *...śaṅkaro deśikeśvaraḥ / bhūmiṃ pradakṣiṇīkṛtya javāt kāñcīpuraṃ gataḥ // jambūdvīpasya kurvāṇo śobhāṃ bhārata-khaṇḍake / śastaṃ kāśmīra-nāmānaṃ deśaṃ vidyotayan bhṛṣam // kāmākṣyā nāma vāg-devyāḥ sthānaṃ tat puram āptavān / sarvajña-pīṭham ārodhum iyeṣa yati-puṅgavaḥ //* GŚC 9.1-3.

There are two problems here. The first concerns the identity of the goddess. While it is well known that there is an important temple dedicated to Kāmākṣī in Kāñcīpuram, this goddess is not usually identified with Sarasvatī. The *Brahmāṇḍa-purāṇa*, which contains a *māhātmya* to Kāmākṣī, refers to her as Tripurasundarī, the consort of Śiva.[42] But on the other hand, the Purāṇa also describes her as Siṃhāsaneśvarī, the goddess of the throne.[43] The second difficulty arises because Govindanātha seems to intentionally leave the location of the temple in doubt. The confusion stems from what appears to be a reference to a verse of Vyāsācala's:

> In this world, Jambūdvīpa is [the continent which is] celebrated. The region therein which is celebrated is called Bhārata, and therein the region named Kāśmīra is celebrated. That is where Śāradā, the goddess of speech, is found...the abode of the Devī, in which there is a throne of omniscience (VŚV 12.30-31).[44]

Despite Govindanātha's acknowledgement of this text, he does make it clear elsewhere that he takes Kāñcī to be the site of the *sarvajña-pīṭha*. This is plainly stated in both the prefatory and concluding narrative summaries of the GŚC.[45] If the notion of a "quick circumambulation of the world" seems far-fetched, it must be remembered that Govindanātha, like the other

---

42 *The brahmāṇḍa-mahāpurāṇam*, (reprint of the Veṅkateśvara Press edition, Varanasi, Krishnadās Academy, 1983), chapter 39, p. 323b ff. In 39.66-67, there is an explanation of her name. She is known as Kāmākṣī because she has manifested Kā, who is Vāṇī (the goddess of speech) from one eye and Mā, i.e., Kamalā (Lakṣmī) from the other.

43 *Ibid*. 39.19.

44 *jambūdvīpaṃ śasyate'syāṃ pṛthivyāṃ tatrāpy etan maṇḍalaṃ bhāratākhyam / kāśmīrākhyaṃ maṇḍalaṃ tatra śastaṃ yatrāste śa śāradā vāg-adhīśā // ...devyā gehaṃ yatra sarvajñapīṭham*.

45 GŚC 1.40 and verse 9 of the concluding *stotra*.

hagiographers, is not averse to ascribing to Śaṅkara yogic powers which enable him to fly through the air. In this way Śaṅkara is presumably able to visit Kāśmīra in a roundabout journey from Rāmeśvara to Kāñcī.

RŚA. In describing twelve southern pilgrimage sites as opposed to only two specific places in the north, Rājacūdāmaṇi reveals the strongest regional bias of the hagiographers. As in the VŚV and GŚC, Śaṅkara meets Bhaṭṭa's disciple Viśvarūpa at an unspecified location in Magadha. After being instructed by Śaṅkara, the former Mīmāṃsaka and now new disciple, Sureśvara, is said to have made his residence on the Narmadā river in the land of Magadha, where he stays for some time.[46] This is strange because even the source of the Narmadā at Amarakaṇṭaka is quite a distance from the area usually designated Magadha, i.e., the southern part of present-day Bihar. It could be that Rājacūdāmaṇi is simply uninformed about the geography of north India. But the same verse also appears in the ŚDV, which has more extensive references to northern sites. According to the ŚDV (and the TŚA as well) Śaṅkara meets Maṇḍana/Viśvarūpa in Māhiṣmati, which definitely is situated on the Narmadā. It would not be surprising for the newly initiated Sureśvara to have left the city and sought a more secluded spot somewhere up river for his ascetic practice. In this light, it seems possible that the name Magadha might denote the greater political domain this ancient kingdom once encompassed. The RŚA contains a unique variation on the King Amaruka episode. In the other hagiographies this incident occurs in conjunction with the debate against Sarasvatī. According to Rājacūdāmaṇi, Śaṅkara decides to put himself to the test of gaining insight into worldly life. He enters the body of the dying king when he is at Mūkāmbikā, an important Devī

---

[46] *bahu-titham abhito'sau narmadāṃ narmadāṃ tāṃ magadha-bhuvi nivāsaṃ nirmame nirmamendraḥ*, RŚA 2.61.

temple in Kollūr, Karnataka.[47] The encounter with Sarasvatī is situated at Kāñcī towards the end of the narrative.

GVK. Lakṣmaṇa-Sāstrī follows along the lines of the RŚA in describing the early stage of Śaṅkara's journey. After debating Maṇḍana/Viśvarūpa in Magadha, he travels with his disciples as far south as Revā, i.e., the Narmadā river. Here he realizes his mother is dying and quickly goes to Kālaṭi by means of his yogic power. After performing his mother's funeral, he sets out for Subrahmaṇya and other places in the Taulava (South Kanara) region. Just prior to travelling to Gokarṇa, he visits Śrīraupya-pīṭha, an apparent variant of Rajatapīṭha, which is a former name of Uḍipi. This is where he gains a new disciple, Hastāmalaka. The *āśrama* of Dattātreya, in which Śaṅkara ends his days, is located in Māhurīpura according to the author's own commentary to the GVK. This is probably identical with the small present-day village of Māhūr in the Nānded district of Maharashtra. In the Dattātreya cult this is said to be where the divine sage sleeps and the site in which he instructed Paraśurāma.[48]

ŚDV. It is not surprising to find that this text, the most widely distributed of the hagiographies, reports the greatest number of places visited by Śaṅkara. The ŚDV follows the TŚA in locating the abode of Śaṅkara's guru on the Narmadā. He will return to this river when he debates Maṇḍana/Viśvarūpa in Māhiṣmatī, an ancient site on the Narmadā. The ŚDV also relates the details of the pilgrimage undertaken by Śaṅkara's first

47 RŚA 3.34-49. This temple gained prominence from the patronage of the Nāyakas of Ikkeri in the 16th century. See K. D. Swaminathan, *The Nāyakas of Ikkeri*, (Madras: P.Varadachary, 1957), p. 203.

48 See Hariprasad Shivprasad Joshi, *Origin and development of Dattātreya worship in India* (Baroda: University of Baroda, 1965), p. 199.

disciple, reproducing the relevant verses from the VŚV. Śaṅkara's *digvijaya* takes him to numerous old kingdoms in the north (Naimiṣa, Darada, Bharata, Sūrasena, Kuru, Pāñcāla) and east (Videha, Kośala, Aṅga, Vaṅga, Gauḍa). But these place names are simply listed without any elaboration at all. He travels to the western limits of the subcontinent at the Bāhlika country (western Punjab), where he defeats the Jains, and reaches the eastern frontier at Kāmarūpa in Assam, where he subdues the Śāktas.[49]

The Journey's End and Some Conclusions

The first and last stops of Śaṅkara's all-India tour were perhaps the most difficult for the hagiographers to locate. The only agreement as to where Śaṅkara meets his guru is found in the three texts which do not specify the site at all. About the place where he spends his last days, there seems to be even more room for speculation. In two of the texts Śaṅkara departs for his true abode on Mt. Kailāsa from a nearby site in the Himālayas. According to the CŚV he meets Dattātreya in Badarī, who takes him first to his cave and then to Kailāsa. In the ŚDV he travels from Badarī to Kedāra, from where he is escorted by the gods back to his home on the silvery peak. In the GVK Śaṅkara goes from Nepal to the *āśrama* of Dattātreya at Māhurī, which may be in Maharashtra. Three of the texts clearly situate Śaṅkara's passing in the south. For the AŚV and RŚA, Śaṅkara's last days are at Kāñcī. While in the GŚC, his life and death come full cycle at Vṛṣācala, present-day Trichūr in Kerala. This was the site of his parents' *tapas*. I cannot help but give Vyāsācala the last word on the end of Śaṅkara's journey: "he went to a land which was pleasing to him".[50]

---

49 ŚDV 15.142ff.; 15.158.

50 *rucita-deśam ayaṃ jagāma*, VŚV 12.82.

Places Visited by Śaṅkara in 4 or more sources

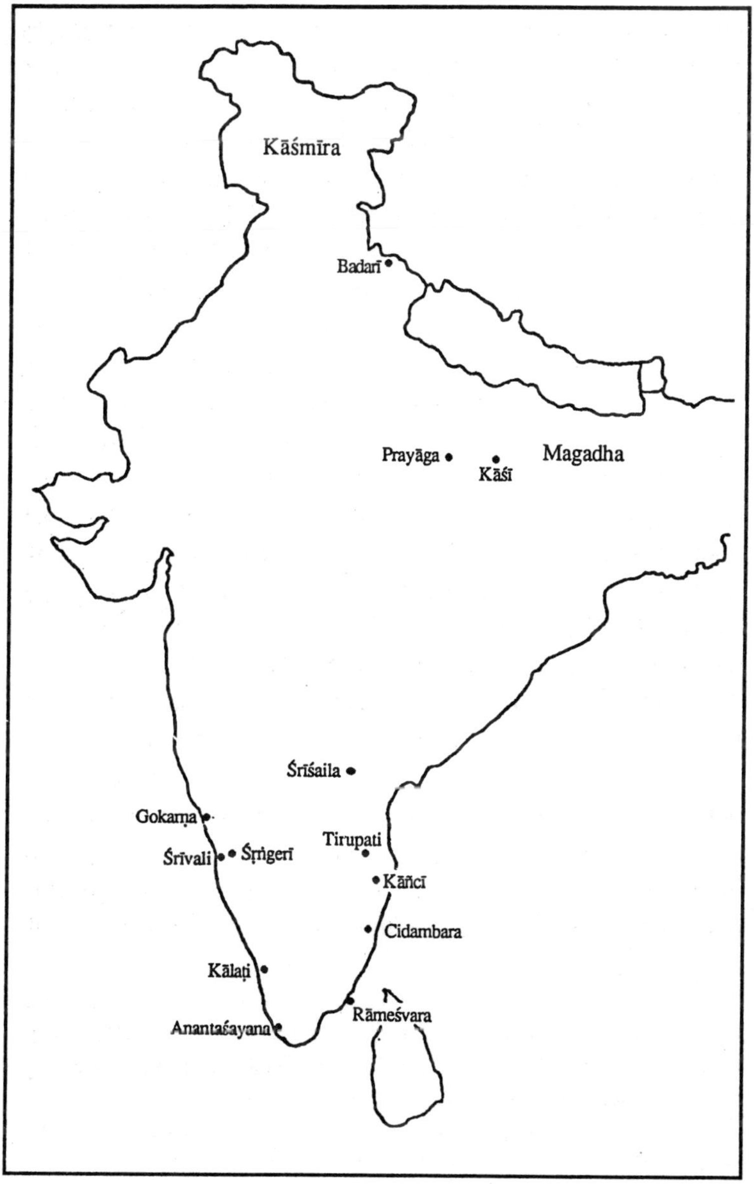

There are a few general conclusions which can be drawn concerning the geography of the Śaṅkara story. Four places figure prominently in all the Sanskrit sources shown in the table above: Badarī and Prayāga in the north and Kāñcī and Rāmeśvara in the south. Each of the hagiographers reveals an intimate acquaintance with several pilgrimage sites in the south, but on the whole they demonstrate little familiarity with northern India. This is in striking contrast to the medieval sources on pilgrimage which largely ignore the south.[51] Indeed one of the interesting sidelights of the hagiographies is in the glimpse they afford of a southern perspective of geography.[52] Nevertheless, six of our authors mention Magadha as the venue of important debates, and five include Kāśī and Kāśmīra. This reflects, above all, the imperative for Śaṅkara to establish his reputation in the north. In his day this was still the unquestioned centre of Sanskritic culture. But Śaṅkara is one of the first of an emerging group of religious leaders who were to claim a share of power for the south. Those texts which feature the *digvijaya*,[53] could hardly omit a northern tour of victory; those which treat the journey primarily as pilgrimage,[54] could lend it greater glory by including the far northern sites, so difficult of access. Surprisingly, there is not much stress on the notion of the *catur dhāma*, the sacred sites which adorn the four quarters of the subcontinent. Jagannāthapurī and Dvārakā, which mark the eastern and western quarters of the realm, figure in only three of the texts. More important for the construction of

---

51 See Richard Salomon, "*Tīrtha-pratyāmnāyāḥ* : ranking of Hindu pilgrimage sites in classical Sanskrit texts" *Zeitschrift der Deutschen Morgenländischen Gesellschaft*, 129 (1979) 102-128, for references to pilgrimage manuals and an important discussion on the relative merits of holy sites.

52 The north/south opposition is perhaps anachronistic, but I make the distinction because of its importance to current issues.

53 AŚV, CŚV, GVK and ŚDV.

54 VŚV, GŚC and RŚA.

the geography of the life story is the north-south axis of the subcontinent, whose poles are at Badarī and Rāmeśvara. Yet a popular tradition that Śaṅkara dispatched his four leading disciples to the cardinal points of the land is now firmly entrenched in India, although this is described in just two of the hagiographies, the CŚV and GVK.

I have dwelt at some length on the geographical particulars of the Śaṅkara story largely because it is in these details that our sources come closest to realism. Nevertheless, I do not want to suggest that the hagiographers were especially concerned with verisimilitude. Their emphasis on place reveals a different set of intentions altogether. While the focus of the narrative moves freely back and forth between the human and the divine mode, the events in the protagonist's life are, for the most part, firmly grounded in well known places on the Hindu pilgrim's trail. However remote the figure of Śaṅkara may be to the audience, the way is open to a direct experience of his life story: those who visit the sacred sites will walk in his footsteps. There is another dimension to the relationship between the hero and the setting of the narrative. On the one hand, Śaṅkara is invested with the sanctity of each site at which the various events in his life unfold, while on the other, he lends further glory to the place by virtue of his divine presence. In this way the hagiographies participate in the integration of geography and mythology. David Sopher's observations on the function of the Purāṇas are equally valid here: "The place-bound meanings of the chthonic religion, which lives on in folk belief and custom, is abstracted and refashioned in a corpus of mythology that is about place, but detached from it. Place is replaced by sacred nodes and geography itself becomes a cosmic geometry...a geometry that is given life by the institution of pilgrimage".[55]

Śaṅkara and the Pilgrimage Tradition

As the Āryans established themselves in the Indian subcontinent, the brahmanical culture must have gradually assimilated the sacred sites of the indigenous peoples. Even such prominent Āryan sites as Kurukṣetra may well have been pre-existing places of worship.[56] The lack of Vedic references to the subject does suggest the possibility that Hindu pilgrimage "essentially continues practices of non-*ārya*, sedentary peoples of India...[which] were incorporated in brahmanic tradition".[57] But the nomadic Āryans would scarcely have needed to be convinced of the virtues of a peripatetic life. The processional sacrificial rites (*yātsattra*), although not exactly a pilgrimage in the strict sense of the

---

55 David E. Sopher, "The message of place in Hindu pilgrimage", *The National Geographical Journal of India* 33 (1987), 1-17 [=*Homage to David E. Sopher*, ed. R. L. Singh and Rana P. B. Singh, Varanasi, 1987], p. 14. Some of the more important studies which deal with Hindu pilgrimage are: S. M. Bharadwaj, *Hindu places of pilgrimage in India* (Berkeley: Univ. of California, 1973); Agehananda Bharati, "Pilgrimage in the Indian tradition", *History of Religions*, 3 (1963), 135-167 and "Pilgrimage sites and Indian civilization", in *Chapters in Indian civilization*, ed. Joseph W. Elder (2nd ed., Dubuque Iowa: Kendall/Hunt, 1970), 83-126; J. Ensink, "Problems of the study of pilgrimage in India", *Indologica Taurinensia*, 2 (1974), 57-79; P. V. Kane, *History of Dharmaśāstra*, vol. 4 (2nd ed. Poona, 1973), pp. 552-584; Victor Turner, "The centre out there: pilgrim's goal", *History of Religions*, 12 (1973) 191-230.

56 J. Ensink observes that Kurukṣetra was guarded by four *yakṣas*, ("Study of pilgrimage", p. 73). He relies on the earlier work of Coomaraswamy which demonstrates that "Kuvera and other Yakṣas are indigenous non-Āryan deities or genii", A. K. Coomaraswamy, *Yakṣas* ([1928-31] reprinted New Delhi, 1980, vol. I, p. 36).

57 Ensink, "Study of pilgrimage", p. 74.

term, do point to the inclusion of wandering in Vedic ritual.[58] In this respect we might also understand pilgrimage to represent the nostalgia of the Āryans, once they found themselves confined in settlements, for their lost nomadic way of life. However we may choose to speculate on its origins, the fact remains that pilgrimage has held an important place for Hindus since at least the epic period. This is attested by the lengthy panegyric to pilgrimage, the *tīrthayātrā-parvan* of the *Mahābhārata* (3.80-93), which has been quoted by many later writers on the subject.[59]

In this section, the *Mahābhārata* marks one aspect of a major shift away from sacrificial rites. The epic has it that the pious visiting of sacred places excels even sacrifices.[60] Nevertheless, pilgrimage is not enjoined as a necessary duty. There is an analogy implied between *tīrthayātrā* and optional rites, although pilgrimage is clearly held to be superior: "in going to sacred places there are benefits which are not obtained

58 The *yātsattra*, as it is enacted on the Sarasvatī river, is concisely described by Ensink (*op. cit*., p. 69): "The ritual begins at Vinaśana, the point where the Sarasvatī disappears in the sands of the Indian desert...Every morning the *adhvaryu* takes his stand to the southeast of the *āhavanīya* fire in the *uttaravedi* of yesterday's sacrificial place and from there throws the *śamyā*, a stick about 90 centimetres in length, as far upstream as possible. If it falls down on even ground, it marks the place of the *gārhapatya* fire of the new sacrifical place. Should it fall on uneven ground, the *adhvaryu* has to throw again from that point. With a view to the daily removal a number of constructions in the sacrificial places are fitted out with wheels....The sacrificial post is dragged along to its new place. In their progress along the Sarasvatī, the sattrins come to a place where the Dṛṣadvatī meets the Sarasvatī". For textual references and a translation of an important source on the *yātsattra*, see W. Caland, *Pañcaviṃśa-Brāhmaṇa [Tāṇḍya-mahābrāhmaṇa]. The brāhmaṇa of twenty five chapters*, (Calcutta: Bibliotheca Indica, 1931), pp. 634 ff. (=25.10).

59 See the references in Ensink, "Study of pilgrimage", p. 59.

60 *tīrthābhigamanaṃ puṇyaṃ yajñair api viśiṣyate*, MBh 3.80.38.

by *agniṣṭoma* and other sacrifices".[61] Initially it is only the optional rites which are replaced. But eventually pilgrimage assumed still greater prominence, while the sacrificial cult continued to decline.

Unlike the man in the world, who may choose betweeen rites and pilgrimage, the *saṃnyāsin* has necessarily abandoned the way of sacrifice. He must give up all rites, both the obligatory and the optional.[62] Yet for the renouncer, wandering is a duty. He is by definition a *parivrājaka*, one who has gone forth from the home. Except during the two/four months of the rainy season, the *saṃnyāsin* (ideally) should not spend two nights in the same village.[63] It is difficult to gauge the extent to which this precept was actually lived in early times. As Olivelle has observed, the medieval texts give the impression that in practice most *saṃnyāsin*s lived in monastic centres.[64] While pilgrimage is not specifically prescribed for the renouncer, it is only natural that the course of his wandering will take him to a number of sacred sites. Moreover, there is (at least at the present time) the expectation that he *ought* to set out upon one or more long *tīrthayātrā*s. The accomplishment of such a journey, especially if he succeeds in reaching the more remote Himālayan sites, lends greater standing to the *saṃnyāsin* in the eyes of his peers and the community at large. The religious festivals held at major pilgrim sites, most notable of which are the *kumbha melā*s, are also an important factor in attracting *saṃnyāsin*s to visit these sacred places.

---

61 *agniṣṭomādibhir yajñair...na tat phalam avāpnoti tīrthābhigamanena yat*, MBh 3.80.40. The parallel with optional rites is pointed out by Ensink, *ibid*.

62 See *Vāsudevāśrama Yatidharmaprakāśa*. A treatise on world renunciation, ed. and tr. Patrick Olivelle (2 vols., Vienna, 1977), II. p. 175.

63 *Gautama-dharmasūtra*, 3.21.

64 *Yatidharmaprakāśa*, tr. Olivelle, II. p. 48.

The traditional stories of Śaṅkara's life which the hagiographies have preserved, albeit in a modified form, may comprise the earliest model for the all-India tour. Śaṅkara was not, of course, the first to make such a journey. He was preceded by the Chinese Buddhist pilgrims, whose records are so essential to our knowledge of Indian history, and there is no telling how many Hindu pilgrims may have also braved the rigours of road before his day. It is not so much the historicity of Śaṅkara's journey which is significant here, but rather the fact that his journey becomes paradigmatic. There is an analogy in the way the foundation of ten orders of *saṃnyāsin*s is traditionally attributed to Śaṅkara. The only available historical evidence for this monastic organisation is quite late.[65] What is more, our eight hagiographies have very little to say on the subject.[66] In fact, the recognition of Śaṅkara's authority in monastic matters need not derive from historical circumstances at all. Because he is construed as the restorer of the Vedic path and, at the same time, the ideal renouncer, it is only logical for tradition to make him the locus of spiritual authority for the ten orders of *saṃnyāsin*s. In the same way, Śaṅkara's *tīrthayātrā* sets the standard for the renouncer. Since this aspect of ascetic life is not restricted to the *saṃnyāsin*, the all-India tour is an ideal to which the pious householder may also aspire.

---

65 The ten orders are mentioned in the *Yatidharmasaṃgraha* of Viśveśvara (cited in *Yatidharmaprakāśa*, 66.13-16) which Olivelle places early in the 16th century, *op. cit.*, 1. p. 27. The ten orders are also refered to in the *Smṛtimuktāphala* of Vaidyanātha-Dīkṣita, cited by P.V. Kane, who dates the text c.1700 (*History of Dharmaśāstra*, Vol. I. part 2, p. 815). See also J. N. Farquhar, "The organization of the Sannyasis of the Vedanta", *Journal of the Royal Asiatic Society*, 1925, pp. 479-486.

66 The CŚV (24.36-37) is the only text which speaks of the ten orders. A reference to just one of the orders is found in the AŚV (p. 182) which mentions his founding of the Bhāratī lineage.

There is, nonetheless, some ambivalence towards pilgrimage in the Śaṅkara tradition. This comes to light in three of the hagiographies. In the VŚV and ŚDV (which reproduces Vyāsācala's verses on the subject), the problem is situated in a dialogue between Śaṅkara and his first disciple, Sanandana. The GŚC introduces an interesting variation, casting Śaṅkara and his guru Govinda in what is otherwise an almost identical scene. In Vyāsācala's version, Sanandana asks permission to go on pilgrimage. Śaṅkara initially tries to dissuade his disciple. He presents three basic arguments against pilgrimage. In the first place it is more important for the student to remain with his guru:

> Dwelling in proximity to the guru is the true dwelling at the sacred site (*kṣetra*), and the waters in which his feet [are washed] are the sacred waters (*tīrtha*). The seeing of the Self, by means of the guru's instruction, is indeed greater than seeing all the deities. Therefore one should remain near the guru, serving him, and not go to other places.[67]

Secondly, pilgrimage will lead one away from the pursuit of knowledge, which is proper to a *saṃnyāsin.* Life on the road is conducive only to the experience of fatigue, not to contemplation on the meaning of 'thou art that'. Finally, there are the more practical difficulties pilgrimage entails. The GŚC enumerates them most succinctly: "On the road there will be many impediments to the pilgrimage—sickness, hunger, thirst, lack of lodging, thieves, tigers, etc".[68] Sanandana's reply addresses only the first and last of the objections. By concentrating the mind on the guru, one remains near him even though in another place. As to the rigours of the road, the disciple looks forward towards proving his mettle: "is it

67 VŚV 7.73-74ab; ŚDV 14.2-3ab.

68 GŚC 3.36.

possible that merit can be easily obtained at the present time"?[69] He makes it quite clear that he feels compelled to undertake the journey.

It is significant that Sanandana ignores what is perhaps the most fundamental issue at stake: the compatibility of pilgrimage and Advaita. In the Advaita tradition the aspirant follows the way of knowledge. The doctrine of non-duality does not encourage the inclination to travel about. But it is also possible that the apparent contradiction was not seen to pose a serious problem. Pilgrimage may be reconciled with the Advaita path by analogy to other dualistic yet acceptable preliminary disciplines. In reply to Śaṅkara's warning that the ardours of travel will cause disturbance to the mind, Sanandana argues that resorting to holy places is purifying for the mind.[70] Now in his own works, Śaṅkara takes a strong stand against injunctions to ritual action. From the standpoint of Advaita, ritual action is clearly incompatible with the acquisition of knowledge. Nevertheless, he admits that mental purification is a necessary preliminary in the path of knowledge.[71] These considerations must remain purely hypothetical because Śaṅkara does not actually mention pilgrimage in this context. This episode is another instance of the fact that the hagiographers are not particularly concerned with Advaita doctrines. It is a popular audience which the texts address, and the readers will not be disappointed. The guru graciously gives his sanction, along with a healthy dose of advice, and sends the disciple off on his pilgrimage.

Pilgrimage does have a concrete social function insofar as it promotes greater integration in a land of pronounced

---

69 VŚV 7.80.

70 *sat-tīrtha-sevā manasaḥ prasādinī*, VŚV 7.87

71 For further elaboration, see J. Bader *Meditation in Śaṅkara's Vedānta* (Delhi: Aditya Prakashan, 1990), pp. 56-64.

geographical and ethnic diversity. It is in this respect that Śaṅkara's journey is especially important. While the hagiographies do not spell out their views on the physical dimensions of India, or rather Bhārata, it does seem that the subcontinent was perceived as a distinct geographical entity, though comprised of many different regions.[72] The AŚV states that Śaṅkara transformed "all the brahmins and the rest [of the twice-born] who inhabit the lands from Rāmeśvara to the Himālayas and in between".[73] Although it is not made as explicit in the other texts, the way in which the hagiographies describe Śaṅkara's journey suggests that it was seen to have a unifying effect on the land of Bhārata. In this light it is not surprising that many prominent leaders in the nationalist struggle would portray Śaṅkara as an apostle of Indian unity.[74]

The model of pilgrimage presented in the *tīrthayātrā* section of the *Mahābhārata* involves a circumabulation of the land (3.80.28). *Pradakṣiṇa*, the adoration of a holy object by walking reverently around it in a clockwise direction, is an ancient feature of Hindu ritual practice. The pilgrim circumambulates not only the shrine, but the entire temple complex and sometimes even the whole of the precincts of a sacred site.[75] By one further extrapolation, the land of Bhārata is itself perceived as a sacred sphere which the pilgrim can worship by means of *pradakṣiṇa*. Śaṅkara's all-India tour certainly fulfills this ideal. But there is yet another, greater way

---

72 See, for example, VŚV 12.30.

73 *setu-himācala-madhya-deśa-sthān aśeṣān brāhmaṇādīn...* , p. 194.

74 See Chapter Seven.

75 See Carl Gustav Diehl, *Instrument and Purpose. Studies on rites and rituals in south India* (Lund: C W K Gleerup, 1956), pp. 253-254. The circumabulation of the city of Varanasi is described by Diana L. Eck, *Banaras: city of light*, (London: Routledge and Kegan Paul, 1983), 350-57.

in which he is shown to encompass the whole of the country: as a world conqueror.

Digvijya: the conquest of the quarters

The *digvijaya* figures in five of the hagiographies. According to Anantānandagiri, Śaṅkara sets out from the abode of his guru "like a universal conqueror beginning his conquest of the proponents of the various doctrines which were current throughout the eight directions".[76] Cidvilāsa presents a similar picture:

> Circumambulating the land, he was extending his blessing to the land with every step of his lotus feet. Seeing, in due course on the roads, the various false signs [of religious life], Śaṅkara proceeded, with a desire to conquer the quarters.[77]

The TŚA, and following it the ŚDV, describe Śaṅkara as "the king of ascetics, who, in accordance with the command of his guru, resolved on a *digvijaya*".[78] The GVK says simply that he set out "desirous of conquering the worlds".[79] Although the *digvijaya* is clearly a royal ritual, the hagiographies make it appropriate to Śaṅkara by portraying a regal dimension of his personality. To this end, epithets designating him as the king or emperor of ascetics are commonly used. Moreover, all eight of our sources relate the episode in which he temporarily assumes the body of a king. In six of the texts, the royal phase

---

76 *viśva-jid iva*[sic]*aṣṭa-dig-vart[a]māna-nānā-mata-vādi-vijayam ārabhamāṇaḥ*, AŚV p. 17.

77 *tataḥ śrīśaṅkara...paśyan krameṇa mārgeṣu liṅgāni vividhāny api // bhuvaṃ pradakṣiṇī-kurvan pratasthe digjayecchayā / pāda-paṅkaja-vinyāsair dhanyāṃ tanvan bhuvasthalīm //* CŚV 31.1-2.

78 *yati-kṣitīśo'pi guror niyogān mano dadhe digvijaye...*, TŚA 4.16; ŚDV 7.60.

79 *jagatyāṃ vijayaṃ vidhitsuḥ*, GVK 3.6.

of Śaṅkara's career culminates in his ascension to the throne of omniscience.

The convention of entitling the Śaṅkara hagiographies *vijayas* is itself a strong indication that his life story was construed in terms of conquest. The word *vijaya* features in the titles of no less than twelve of the twenty works on Śaṅkara's life described by Antarkar.[80] V. S. Pathak considers the *vijaya* to be a genre of "historical epics...nearest to the heroic tradition of the *itihāsapurāṇa* literature".[81] Among the works in this category are: Ratnākara's *Haravijaya*, the story of Śiva's defeat of the demon Andhaka; Vāsudeva's *Yudhiṣṭhiravijaya*, a retelling of the main events of the *Mahābhārata*; and the *Pṛthvīrāja-vijaya*, which is according to Pathak, "not merely a *vijaya* epic dealing with the war and ultimate triumph of Pṛthvīrāja III. It also fully partakes of the nature of a *charita*, in treating the biography of the hero from his birth".[82] This latter work is particularly significant for us because it may have influenced the composition of Vyāsācala's *Śaṅkaravijaya* (and thus the GŚC, GVK and ŚDV as well). In a brief autobiographical statement, the Kashmiri author of the *Pṛthvīrāja-vijaya* tells the reader that "he was born in the line of the sage Upamanyu and that he was nourished with motherly solicitude by Śāradā, the name by which Sarasvatī the goddess of learning was known in Kashmir".[83] The VŚV devotes two entire chapters to recounting the story of Upamanyu and, along

---

80 W. R. Antarkar, "The Śaṅkara-Vijayas: a comparative and critical study" [unpublished Ph. D. thesis], University of Poona, 1960.

81 Vishwambhar Sharan Pathak, *Ancient historians of India. A study in historical biographies* (Bombay: Asia Publishing House, 1966), p. 101.

82 *Ibid*., p. 103. Pathak attributes the *Pṛthvīrāja-vijaya* to Jayānaka (12th century, Kashmir). A. K. Warder places both the *Haravijaya* and *Yudhiṣṭhiravijaya* in the 9th century (*Indian kāvya literature*, vol. 5, pp. 139ff.; 373ff).

83 Pathak, *Ancient historians*, p.99.

with three other hagiographies, situates the throne of omniscience at the Śāradā temple in Kashmir. More work needs to be done in order to determine the extent to which the *vijaya* does in fact constitute a separate genre in Sanskrit literature. But the theme of a heroic war against evil forces is certainly a conspicuous feature of the Śaṅkara hagiographies.

At first glance, a war-like expedition through the subcontinent may appear an unusual frame for the narrative of an ascetic whose primary role is the reinterpretation of metaphysical doctrines. Yet there are distinct patterns of ritual conquest embedded in the cultural code of traditional India which underpin Śaṅkara's *vijaya*. It is only fitting that the life story of a champion of tradition should embody some of these ritual models. The very real presence of warfare in ancient India is revealed by scattered references in the Ṛg Veda. The Āryans' opponents were not only the indigenous peoples (*dāsas*). Ṛg Veda 2.12 shows that the nomadic Āryan bands sometimes faced one another other on the battleground as well, each calling on the same god, Indra: "Whom the two battle-lines invoke as they meet each other, both groups of foes on this side and on that drawing to his self-same chariot".[84] In the *Mahābhārata* the battle lines are drawn within one and the same family. The story of Māthava Videgha in *Śatapaṭha-Brāhmaṇa* 1.4 describes the eastward expansion of the Āryans, whose victories are facilitated by the sacrificial fire. These texts suggest that there was a transition in the sacrificial cult from actual territorial conquest to a ritualisation of the battle. The sacrificial ground itself eventually came to represent the world, and all movement was contained within it. In this way the sacrifice became autonomous, cut off from the obvious dangers and risks of

---

84 Translated by Franklin Edgerton, *The beginnings of Indian philosophy* (Cambridge: Harvard University, 1970), p. 53.

armed conflict, and was safely circumscribed within the precise bounds of ritual rule.

In a number of influential studies, J. C. Heesterman has shown how remnants of the ancient Indo-Āryan warrior tradition persist in the *śrauta* ritual, which was as he describes it, "created out of the dismembered ruins of the warrior's sacrifice and therefore remained tied to its disembodied memory".[85] There are three large scale *śrauta* rites which clearly attest to this heritage. Two of these, the *rājasūya*, a royal consecration, and the *aśvamedha*, the horse sacrifice for the expansion of kingdom (or birth of a royal heir) may be performed only by a *kṣatriya*, while the *vājapeya* rite, the drink of strength, was open to either a *kṣatriya* or a brahmin desirous of overlordship.[86] The *rājasūya* has become well known to Indologists thanks to Heesterman's careful study,[87] and to van Buitenen's demonstration that this rite is the basis for the second book of the *Mahābhārata*, the *Sabhāparvan*.[88] Since the *rājasūya* has been enshrined in traditional Indian culture by both the *śrauta sūtra*s and the epic, it is not surprising that this ritual also finds a place in the Śaṅkara hagiographies.

There is, however, a problem in introducing the model of the *rājasūya* into the narrative. As a renouncer, Śaṅkara cannot

---

85 *The inner conflict of tradition. Essays in Indian ritual, kingship, and society* (Chicago: University of Chicago, 1985), p. 107. See also his other important articles on the subject collected here.

86 For a detailed description see P. V. Kane, *History of dharmaśāstra*, vol. 2, part 2, pp. 1206-1239. As Heesterman has also observed on several occasions, the *yātsattra* (see note 58 above) is another important remnant of earlier ritual practice.

87 Johannes Cornelis Heesterman, *The ancient Indian royal consecration* [thesis, Utrecht], (The Hague: Mouton, 1957).

88 J. A. B. van Buitenen,"On the structure of the sabhāparvan of the Mahābhārata", in *India Maior* (Festschrift for J. Gonda, Leiden, 1972), pp. 68-84, and also the introduction to his translation of book 2 of the Mbh.

undertake the ritual action. Moreover, because this rite is restricted to the *kṣastriya*, it can only be analogically associated with Śaṅkara. But this is precisely what the hagiographers set out to do. They cast some of the key events of the life story in the familiar image of the royal ritual. There are four specific elements of the *rājasūya* which are reflected in the narrative: the preparatory initiation (*dīkṣā*), the establishment of the four quarters (*digvyāsthāpana*), the chariot drive, and the enthronement.

In a detailed study on *dīkṣā*, J. Gonda has noted the close similarities between the various initiatory ceremonies: the *upanayana*, the consecration of the *yajamāna* in the *soma* sacrifice, the consecration of a king and the ordination of a monk.[89] In this respect, the parallel between the preparation of the royal sacrificer in the *rājasūya* and Śaṅkara's initiation as a *saṃnyāsin* is an obvious one. Perhaps it is because the rite is so well known that the hagiographies have little to say about the details of the ordination. But his self proclaimed renunciation at the time he is seized by the crocodile is clearly perceived to be inadequate. Śaṅkara must receive formal initiation from a recognised figure of authority. The CŚA spells out some of the instructions Govindapāda gives his new disciple. He must wear a loin cloth and waistband and carry a staff and water pot. To ward off heat and cold he may wear an ochre cloth or a bark garment. He must not dwell in any one town and should not beg alms in the same place.[90] While the heir apparent to the throne is given a bow and arrow along with his new garments, the renouncer sets forth with a more defensive weapon, the staff (*daṇḍa*), for "avoiding accidents with

89 J. Gonda, *Change and continuity in Indian religion* ([1965], reprinted New Delhi: Munshiram Manoharlal, 1985), p.317.
90 CŚA 9.25-26.

cattle, serpents and the like".[91] Śaṅkara is now fully consecrated to become the king of *saṃnyāsins*.

Although some of the texts do not refer to the *digvijaya* until later on in the narrative, it effectively begins the moment Śaṅkara sets forth from the abode of his guru. The journey is in itself an essential component of the *digvijaya*. Indeed this ritual conquest involves much more than simple combat. It represents, above all, a movement towards unity, in both the political and metaphysical spheres. In the first place, disparate kingdoms are always a potential source of conflict. The world conqueror brings together the warring states under the aegis of his superior authority. His emblematic white parasol signifies the protection and harmony he will afford them. Metaphysically, he becomes the sacred centre, the hub of the wheel, and restores the original unity which was lost in the demarcation of space. This is accomplished by establishing his presence in the four quarters of the land and yet at the same time remaining at the centre.

This is ritually enacted in *rājasūya* during the *digvyāsthāpana*, the establishment of the quarters of space. The royal sacrificer takes a single step in each of the four directions and a fifth at the centre, which is above.[92] In the *digvijaya-parvan* of the *Mahābhārata* (2.23-29), this sparse ritual is expanded to a full-scale conquest of the quarters. While Yudhiṣṭhira remains at the centre, the zenith, each of the quarters is secured by one of the other four Pāṇḍava brothers. Arjuna journeys triumphantly through the north. At the limits of the quarter, he reaches the city of the Gandharvas which no

---

91 *daṇḍena go-sarpādyupadrava-pariharaḥ*, *Jivanmukti-viveka* of Vidyāraṇya, ed. S. Subrahmanya Sastri and T. R. Srinivasa Ayyangar, (Madras: Adyar Library and Research Centre, 1978), p. 155.

92 According to some of the ritual texts, the king may carry out the rite by purely mental actions. See Heesterman, *Royal Consecration*, p. 104.

mortal can enter. Even here he succeeds. The gatekeepers graciously assent to providing tribute to Yudhiṣṭhira. Bhīma sets off to the east, establishing his presence in all the kingdoms up to the islands where the Gaṅgā empties into the sea. Sahadeva departs for the south. He crosses the Narmadā and makes his way to what is now the the Thāne district, just north of Bombay.[93] Once at the coast, he "subjugates" the Tamils, Keralas and Andhras, and even the lands of Antioch, Rome and Greece. But his conquest of these far-flung lands consists in no more than securing tribute, and even this is accomplished by proxy, i.e. through envoys. Nakula journeys to the west, winning tribute from kings and barbarians in the lands as far off as Persia.

A *digvijaya* also features prominently in Kālidāsa's *Raghuvaṃśa*. The legendary king Raghu undertakes a world conquest soon after succeeding his father Dilīpa to the throne. As the kingdom is already secure, it would appear that Raghu is motivated primarily by a desire to expand his realm: "He whose own territory and borders were protected...took a six-fold force and set out, desirous of conquering the quarters".[94] Raghu begins his march in the east and eventually arrives victorious at the mouths of the Gangā in the Bay of Bengal. He and his armies next travel south to the Kāverī River and defeat the Pāṇḍyas. Continuing his circumambulation of the subcontinent, he subdues the Keralas and travels up the southwestern coastline. His exploits in the western quarter culminate in his defeat of the Persians. Kālidāsa's description of this event gives further scope to the development of the analogy

---

93 He is said to reach Śūrpāraka which, according to N. L. Dey is the present day coastal town of Sopāra in the Thāne district (Geographical dictionary, s.v.).

94 *sa gupta-mūla-pratyantaḥ...ṣaḍ-vidhaṃ balam ādāya pratasthe digjigīṣayā, Raghuvaṃśa* 4.26.

between the royal and ascetic modes of life: "Then [Raghu] set out by an inland route in order to conquer the Persians, as an ascetic [sets out to conquer] his enemies, known as the senses, by means of knowledge".[95] He then travels north up to the Himālayas, and comes full circle in Assam where he defeats the Kāmarūpas. From there Raghu returns to his kingdom, resuming his place at the centre, and so completes the *digvijaya*.

With the notable exception of the AŚV, which depicts Śaṅkara's all-India journey as a circumambulation of the subcontinent, the route he follows in his conquest of the quarters is not so well delineated. Nevertheless, Śaṅkara's *digvijaya* fulfils the ritual expectations of the *rājasūya* and repeats the heroic behaviour exemplified in *Mahābhārata* and *Raghuvaṃśa*. First of all, he establishes his presence throughout the whole of India. In the course of his journey, he is victorious on the battleground of learned assemblies. Śaṅkara defeats his rivals, the leaders of numerous sectarian groups. The very existence of these sects indicates the chaos resultant from the fragmentation of the Vedic tradition. In restoring the authority and correct understanding of the essential sacred texts, he re-establishes the true centre of the Hindu tradition.

The ritual battle in the *rājasūya* takes place in the course of a chariot drive. At this point in the ceremony, the consecrated king must attack a peer. Heesterman has noted that this part of the rite suggests a new king challenging the old incumbent whom he seeks to replace.[96] In the Śaṅkara story, this pattern is repeated in his confrontation with Kumārila-Bhaṭṭa, whom the texts construe as the foremost authority of his day in the Vedic tradition. The old warrior is in no position to do battle with

---

95 *pārasīkāṃs tato jetuṃ pratasthe sthala-vartmanā / indriyākhyān iva ripūṃs tattva-jñānena saṃyamī//* (4.60).

96 *Ibid*., p. 138.

Śaṅkara in debate. But he passes the gauntlet on to his chief disciple, Maṇḍana/Viśvarūpa. Śaṅkara accordingly challenges him in what proves to be a contest which determines who will wear the mantle of traditional authority.

The enthronement is, of course, the highlight of the *rājasūya.* Although we might not expect this aspect of the rite to be so readily associated with Śaṅkara's life, six of the hagiographies describe his ascension to the seat of omniscience (*sarvajña-pīṭha*), which in this context can readily be construed as a throne. In four of the texts, his "enthronement" is the climax of the narrative.[97] The hagiographers are able to establish the necessary ground for this regal analogy on the basis of Śaṅkara's earlier experience of royal life. In response to Sarasvatī's challenge, he assumed the body of a dying king in order to master the *kāma-śāstra.* When the people see the king restored to life, he is ceremoniously returned to the throne:

> Then the king, who was renowned as Amaruka, lord of the earth, was anointed with abundant streams of cow's milk for the sake of prosperity. With special musical instruments—such as *ḍhakka* drums, cymbals and *mardala* drums, along with an uproar of conches and *bheri* drums—and with special hymns...recited by brahmins, and with special waving of lights which was performed by the hosts of townswomen, the citizens, who had obtained their greatest desire...seated the king on his throne.[98]

In this way, Śaṅkara undergoes a kind of coronation as a prelude to his sojourn in the king's body. Indeed he plays his royal role so well that, according to some of the texts, his disciples must

---

97 See VŚV 12.82, GŚC 9.16, RŚA 7.65ff., ŚDV 16.87.

98 AŚV p. 179.

come to the court and sing a hymn on the theme of the Advaita doctrine to "awaken" him.

Before Śaṅkara can ascend to the throne of omniscience, he must undergo a final test of his qualifications. The penultimate challenge is mounted by the "guardians" of the temple of wisdom, who are stationed at the four doors, aligned with the cardinal points of the compass.[99] It is Sarasvatī herself who casts the final judgement.[100] Just as Śaṅkara is about to ascend the throne, she stops him and puts the following question: "Although devoted to the renouncer's way of life, you were obtaining proficiency in the hidden arts, having enjoyed young women. How are you worthy to ascend to such a position? In this case the means are omniscience and also purity".[101] In addition to the obvious moral issue, this incident reveals the serious contradiction which arises when the boundaries between the ascetic and king are blurred. The hagiographers address the problem only in terms of the moral transgression. Śaṅkara replies, "from the time of birth I have not committed an offence in this body, mother".[102] This

---

99 This is the account presented in GVK 3.24-25. Two other texts describe the four doors to the Śāradā temple as well: VŚV 12.31ff and SDV 16.56ff. According to RŚA 7.63 he is challenged by Buddhists, Jains and others. In CŚV 25.50 he is confronted by learned men who dwell on the banks of the Tāmraparṇī River (Tirunelveli district, Tamil Nadu). Although the AŚV does not mention a *sarvajña-pīṭha*, Śaṅkara's final challenge comes in Kāñcīpuram (as in the CŚV) from people of the Tāmraparṇī. The arguments they raise are very similar in both the AŚV and CŚV.

100 In CŚV 25.47-48 it is an unidentified disembodied voice which calls out the challenge from the sky, stating that Śaṅkara must be tested in debate by learned men.

101 *tvañ cāṅganās samupabhujya kalā-rahasya-prāvīṇya-bhājanam abhūr yati-dharma-niṣṭhaḥ / āroḍhum īdṛśa-padaṃ katham arhasi tvaṃ sarvajñate'va vimalatvam apīha hetuḥ //* VŚV 12.80; ŚDV 16.85.

102 *nāsmin śarīre kṛta-kilbiṣo'ham janma prabhṛty amba [sic]*, VŚV 12. 81, ŚDV 16.86.

seems to satisfy Sarasvatī. But it is not clear whether this is really sufficient to resolve the contradiction. I suspect that some uncertainty may well remain on the part of the audience.

When Śaṅkara takes his proper place on the *sarvajña-pīṭha*, he is anointed with a shower of blossoms by the gods, as drums reverberate in the sky.[103] In the VŚV, RŚA, GŚC and ŚDV, this is the final episode of the drama. It now remains only for Śaṅkara to return to his divine abode on Mt. Kailāsa. In the GVK and CŚV, Śaṅkara's coronation is to be followed by a further establishment of his "kingdom". He dispatches his closest disciples to establish monastic centres in each of the four quarters: Padmapāda goes to Jagannāthapurī in the east, Hastāmalaka to Dvārakā in the west, Toṭaka to Badarī in the north, and Sureśvara (who was installed previously) is in the south at Śṛṅgerī. There is a parallel, although rather oblique, reference at the conclusion of the VŚV:

> The unique tree, whose flowers are knowledge and which yields the fruit of liberation, is named Śaṅkara. Together with his disciples who are the great trunks, and whose branches are their disciples, he served the fourfold realm for the alleviation of mens' misfortune.[104]

While the passage does not clearly testify to the foundation of the four *maṭhas*, we can read it as a metaphorical allusion to the expansion and continuity of Śaṅkara's reign. Moreover it reiterates the theme of the royal consecration in representing Śaṅkara, like the king, as the centre, the *axis mundi*, to which the four quarters are securely fixed.

---

103 RŚA 7.68-69; ŚDV 16.91-92 and CŚV 25.61, which mentions only the rain of flowers.

104 *ekaś śākhī śaṅkarākhyaś caturdhā sthānaṃ bheje pāpa-śāntyai janānām / śiṣyaiḥ skandhaiś śiṣya-śākhair mahadbhir jñānaṃ puṣpaṃ yatra mokṣa-prasūtiḥ //* VŚV 12. 83.

There is yet another model for the complementarity of king and renouncer which has probably influenced the Śaṅkara hagiographies. This motif figures prominently in the life story of the Buddha. At the time of his birth the learned brahmins foretell from his auspicious marks that he will become supreme, either as a universal monarch (*cakravartin*) or an enlightened seer:

> Should he desire earthly sovereignty, then by his might and law he will stand on earth at the head of all kings, as the light of the sun at the head of the constellations. Should he desire salvation and go to the forest, then by his knowledge and truth he will overcome all creeds and stand on earth, like Meru king of mountains among all the heights.[105]

The ancient legend of the *cakravartin* is elaborated in the *Cakkavatti-sīhanāda-suttanta (Dīgha-nikāya* 3.58ff.). Foremost among the seven emblems of the universal emperor is the celestial wheel, the embodiment of *dharma* by which he maintains the unity and prosperity of the realm. Upon the death of the emperor, his successor renews and reunites the kingdom by setting in motion the great wheel of *dharma*. He is, for this reason, literally a turner of the wheel, *cakravartin*. The wheel has a life of its own, as it were. The new king and his armies follow behind it as it moves through the four quarters, defeating rival kings. The victorious *cakravartin* returns, along with the wheel, to the central royal city. There is also a *cakravartin* who figures prominently in Hindu tradition: Bharata, a progenitor of the *Mahābhārata* heroes and common ancestor of the peoples of traditional India, the land of Bhārata.[106]

---

105 *The Buddhacarita or, Acts of the Buddha*, translated by E. H. Johnston, (New Delhi: Oriental Reprints, 1972), p. 8.
106 *Mahābhārata* 1.67.28-29.

Śaṅkara too is said to have auspicious marks at birth. According to the AŚV, "he was marked with the conch, wheel and the like on his hands, feet and waist; marked with the trident on the left side of the head and by the crescent moon on the right".[107] In a metaphor strikingly similar to the one Aśvaghoṣa employs for the Buddha, the young Śaṅkara is described as "the newly risen sun on the eastern mountains; like the pole star in the orb of the universe".[108] There is no question of him becoming a *cakravartin*. His destiny is instead to become king of ascetics. There is also an empirical basis for the analogy between Śaṅkara and the Buddha. The followers of Madhva's dualistic Vedānta sect accuse Śaṅkara of being a disguised Buddhist.[109] But even within the Śaṅkara tradition the resemblance between the two great teachers has not gone unnoticed. Anantānandagiri describes how Śaṅkara is at first mistaken for a Buddhist when he meets Kumārila-Bhaṭṭa.[110] Since we are not told the reason for his mistaken identity, we can asume that it was purely a matter of physical appearance. Perhaps Śaṅkara's shaven head was not typical of Hindu ascetics at the time. More significant still is the eventual establishment of Śaṅkarite monastic orders and institutions which are clearly in the Buddhist mould.[111]

Despite the obvious parallels with the Buddhist *saṅgha*, the Śaṅkara tradition is, above all, Śaiva in nature. As Śiva is the lord of yogis, it is only natural that when he manifests on earth in the form of Śaṅkara he should assert his claim as king of

---

107 *śaṅkha-cakrādi-cinhataḥ śirasi vāma-bhāge triśula-cihnaḥ dakṣiṇa-bhāge tvardha-candra-cihnaḥ*, AŚV p. 11.

108 *prāg-adrau bāla-bhānur iva brahmāṇḍa-golake dhruva iva* , AŚV p. 11.

109 In *Sumadhvavijaya* 1.51 he is said to be "renowned as a secret Buddhist", *pracchanna-bauddho ayam ataḥ prasiddhaḥ*, Nārāyaṇa-Paṇḍita, *Sumadhvavijaya* , ed. T. R. Kṛṣṇācārya (Bombay: Nirṇaya-sāgara Press 1912], p.11.

110 AŚV p. 173.

111 See Chapter Six.

ascetics. Nearly an entire chapter of the CŚV is devoted to an elaborate description of Śiva's domain on Mt. Kailāsa, which is presented in the image of a royal realm:

> In that place [Śiva-] Śaṅkara reigns forever, together with [his consort] Śivā. In certain parts [of the realm could be seen] Indra, Agni, Pāśin, Vitteśa, Marut and Nirṛti....It was auspicious with nine walls made of the nine gems. It had beautiful crystalline palaces, *gopuras* and towers....[Śiva was] sitting on a jewelled throne, adorned with divine ornaments, the heavenly river hidden in the semi-circular mound of his matted locks....His ornament was [like that of] the serpent king, shining with the lustre of the serpent hood gem. He was adorned with rings which bestowed undecaying boons every day, making [the petitioners] who were bowed down to him fearless.[112]

While the enumeration of these riches is certainly intended to mark the glory of his "kingdom", Cidvilāsa makes sure to remind the reader that neither Śiva nor the denizens of the realm have any interest in worldly goods: "the wealth of the lords of all the directions was treated as though worthless".[113] As a homeless wanderer, Śaṅkara accumulates no treasure, but he will conquer the four quarters and gain the throne of omniscience. In the process, he brings to an end the chaotic proliferation of sects and reunites the land under the banner of the true Vedic *dharma*.

---

112 *...rājate yatra satataṃ śivayā saha śaṅkaraḥ // indrāgni-pāśi-vitteśa-marun-nirṛtibhiḥ kvacit. ...nava-ratna-kṛtair eva prākārair navabhiḥ śubham // prāsāda - gopurāṭṭālaiḥ sphatikaiḥ suvicitritam....ratna-siṃhāsanāsīnaṃ divyābharaṇa -bhūṣitam / jaṭā-taṭa-kaṭāhāntarnilīna-svarga-nimnagam // ...phaṇa-ratna - prabhā-bhāsvat-phaṇirāja-vibhūṣaṇam...nirbhayān pra-ṇatān kartum akṣayyaṃ varam anvaham // dātuṃ ca teṣāṃ dadhatam ūrmikādi-pariṣkṛtaiḥ.* CŚV 3.3-22.

113 CŚV 3.12.

CHAPTER V

The Great Debates

In his own compositions, Śaṅkara provides ample demonstration of his consummate skill in philosphical argument. Given his place in a culture so reliant on oral tradition, there is every likelihood that his efforts were not confined to the written word. Indeed some of the controversies we find in Sanskrit philosophical texts may well have been debates which were recast in written form.[1] There is ample literary evidence that the kings of ancient India arranged large scale public debates.[2] These contests were undoubtedly festive occasions which were enjoyed by an audience of monks and laymen. For those who could not follow the philosophical discussion, the heated argument would have itself provided a good deal of entertainment. There was also the promise of a spectacle at the conclusion of the debate as the victor was lauded and the loser humiliated—even to the point of having to adopt the very doctrines against which he had unsuccessfully argued. It was perhaps through participation in such great debates that Śaṅkara established his reputation.

Public debate figures prominently in the narrative of the Śaṅkara hagiographies. Nevertheless most of the texts do not make a feature of philosophical argument. Details of the debates

---

1 See Patrick Olivelle, *Renunciation in Hinduism. A medieval debate*, (2 vols., Vienna: Institut für Indologie der Universität Wien, 1986-1987), vol. I, p. 17.

2 Esther A. Solomon documents the importance of debates in India in her study, *Indian dialectics: methods of philosophical discussion* (2 vols., Ahmedabad: B.J. Institute of Learning and Research, 1976-78), chapter 18, vol. II pp. 833-875.

are conspicuously absent from four of our sources: the VŚV, GŚC, RŚA and GVK.[3] Where the arguments are elaborated in the texts, the proceedings are often crude, in sharp contrast to the rigorous discussion we find in Śaṅkara's own work. This is probably because the hagiographies have been constructed so as to appeal to a general audience. As such, there is no need for them to treat the complex issues which are dealt with in Śaṅkara's own compositions. Philosophical argument must be relegated to a low priority, if it is to be included at all. Nevertheless, his participation in the debates remains a major concern. This can be seen in the hagiographers' efforts at verisimilitude—something we rarely encounter in the texts—when they describe the debates. The texts are more convincing in recreating the events which surround the debates, and in depicting the behaviour of the participants, than in representing the nature of the discussion itself.

Śaṅkara's debate with Maṇḍana/Viśvarūpa is the most important philosophical contest in the life story constructed by the hagiographers.[4] This episode, which features in all eight of our Sanskrit sources, marks more than a victory over a prominent opponent. In defeating the foremost ritualist of his day, Śaṅkara establishes the ascendancy of the renouncer's path. Śaṅkara's own works clearly reflect his preoccupation with demonstrating the superiority of the way of knowledge over the way of ritual action. Since his claim rests on the "true purport" of the *śāstras*, his compositions are filled with complex arguments concerning the interpretation of the sacred texts. The hagiographers represent the conflict between these opposing

---

3 The VŚV, GŚC and RŚA mention only the debates with Maṇḍana/Viśvarūpa and with Sarasvatī. The GVK cites, in addition to these, the debates with Vaiṣṇavas. Because the GVK deals somewhat briefly with Śaṅkara's life, Lakṣmaṇa-Śāstrī may have intentionally avoided elaborating on the debates.

4 See Chapter Two.

modes of interpretation in terms of a personal struggle between two contenders for the mantle of spiritual authority. Hence their attention is focussed on the fact of the debate rather than its substance.

There is no lack of detail about the circumstances of the meeting between the two great men. We read, first of all, about Maṇḍana/Viśvarūpa's impressive home, bustling with ritual activity:

> a *krośa* in breadth and the height of a palmyra palm. At its entrance he had made two altars, measuring a hundred hands, which were facing each other....his disciples numbered five hundred.[5]

His numerous parrots, who repeat snatches of erudite conversation, are further testimony to the extent of scholarship in his compound. The goddess of learning herself graces his home, having taken a human birth as Maṇḍana/Viśvarūpa's wife. What is more, the hagiographers elaborate fully on what transpires when the two opponents first meet face to face. We learn exactly how they address each other, both in terms of body language and direct speech.[6] Yet only three of our texts attempt to represent the actual content of the debate. The most extensive account appears in the TŚA and is repeated verbatim in the ŚDV.[7] Cidvilāsa also describes the contest, but more briefly and in simpler terms.[8]

The striking omission of the particulars of the debate in the other five hagiographies can be explained, in part, by the hypothesis that philosophical argument is unnecessary in texts which address a popular audience. By this I do not mean to

---

5 AŚV p. 174.

6 The hagiographers are evenly divided as to whether their initial encounter is cordial or hostile. See Chapter Two.

7 TŚA 4.50-51; 4.53-109; ŚDV 8.70-71; 8.74-130.

8 CŚV 18.6-37.

suggest that the Sanskrit hagiographies, some of which are written in very elaborate verse, were intended to communicate directly to a popular audience. Rather, the texts would have, I believe, been disseminated by learned teachers of the Śaṅkara tradition through narration to a general audience.

The presence of a popular audience is suggested by the treatment of the Śaṅkara-Maṇḍana encounter in the VŚV and GŚC. These works posit a purely supernatural measure for determining the outcome of the debate. Both participants are presented with a floral garland at the commencement of the contest. The loser is to be marked by the withering of his garland. During the first six days of the debate the vitality of the arguments—and the flowers—is sustained. The fading of Maṇḍana/ Viśvarūpa's garland on the seventh day bears witness to his defeat.[9] The supernatural milieu of the encounter is also suggested (in all of the texts) by the presence of the goddess Sarasvatī as the arbiter of the debate. Such details can only serve to please a popular audience. Surely they would much prefer to watch a spectacle in which divine forces manifest their approval or censure of the contestants, than to follow the intricacies of sophisticated argument.

Despite the long and rich tradition of philosophical debate in India there is, at least on a popular level, a distinct mistrust of intellectual prowess. In her seminal paper on Vedānta hagiographies, Phyllis Granoff has shown the extent of this suspicion:

> the overriding doubts that debate could determine truth were so widespread that even those debates seemingly conducted with all propriety and

---

9 This is made explicit in GŚC 5.57. The issuing of the garlands is described in VŚV 6.98, but the withering of Maṇḍana's is only obliquely referred to. We must presume that Sarasvatī perceives this as the deciding factor in VŚV 6.102. The spent garland is also described in ŚDV 8.132.

> according to all the correct rules required some form of divine sanction in order to convince onlookers that nothing untoward had occurred.[10]

If the discussion becomes too highly specialized, the public may, of course, lose track of the proceedings. But the gravest threat is posed by the debater who might successfully establish his position—even if it constitutes a wholly unacceptable view—simply on the basis of superior skills in argument. Only divine sanction can forestall such a possibility. Hence the intervention of divine forces, which is so prominent in the popular texts of the Hindu, Buddhist and Jain traditions, assumes even greater importance in the case of philosophical debate. Moreover, the miraculous serves to reinforce the truth of received doctrines, even among the faithful. Some of the hagiographies relate, for example, that Kumārila-Bhaṭṭa's final triumph over his Buddhist opponents, comes *after* he has defeated them in debate. He survives a great fall by invoking the saving power vested in the Vedas, and in this way tangibly demonstrates their ultimate authority. In a tradition which is based on the transcendent authority of the *śruti*, human reason cannot stand supreme. This too would tend to discourage an emphasis on the virtues of brilliant reasoning. In this light, we should expect our sources to focus on Śaṅkara's divine nature, and his heroic deeds in fulfilling his mission to restore the true Vedic tradition, rather than on his skill in argument.

Nevertheless, neither the question of popular appeal nor the ambivalent attitude towards the role of the intellect provide a wholly satisfactory account for the lack of details in the hagiographies concerning the Śaṅkara-Maṇḍana debate. Ironically, the most elaborate description of this debate is found

---

10 "Scholars and wonder-workers: some remarks on the role of the supernatural in philosophical con-tests in Vedānta hagiographies", *JAOS*, 105 (1985) 459-467, p. 460.

in the most widely distributed of our sources, the ŚDV.[11] The AŚV provides further evidence that a work aimed at a general audience can contain serious philosophical argument. This text, which is the second of the hagiographies in terms of the number of extant manuscripts, recapitulates Śaṅkara's debates against more than fifty different sects. In the case of the Śaṅkara hagiographies there is no need for any suspicion of the human intellect (although we must remember that the 'human' is mitigated by the fact that the Advaita guru is depicted as the *avatāra* of Śiva). Śaṅkara's adherence to the Vedic tradition is so well established that he may win debates without direct recourse to this sacred authority. This is emphasized in the description of his victory over Nīlakaṇṭha:

> With statements whose meaning was supported by hundreds of reasoned proofs, and which were like the guards of the inner apartments [of the tradition, namely,] the *śruti*, and which were severe towards hostile viewpoints, the ascetic demonstrated the *ātman* doctrine and defeated the Śaiva.[12]

The ŚDV describes in similar terms the conclusion of the contest between Śaṅkara and Bhāskara, "the alert one and foremost of the wise, whom he defeated by hundreds of reasoned proofs".[13] Moreover, Śaṅkara wins the great series of debates presented in the AŚV without any divine intercession, solely by virtue of more convincing arguments. It is Śaṅkara's skill in reasoning which enables him to logically demonstrate the

---

11 The ŚDV repeats the verses from the TŚA, see Chapter One.

12 *iti yukti-śatopabhṛṃhitārthair vacanaiḥ śrutyavarodha-sauvidallaiḥ / yatir ātma-mataṃ prasādhya śaivaṃ parakṛd-darśana-dāruṇair ajaiṣīt //* ŚDV 15.70. The Nīlakaṇṭha referred to here is probably the Śaiva-Viśiṣṭādvaitin, Śrīkaṇṭha who lived no earlier than the 12th century. See S. S. Suryanarayana Sastri, *The Śivādvaita of Śrīkaṇṭha*, ([1930] reprinted Madras: University of Madras, 1972) pp. 10ff.

13 *iti yukti-śatair...sumatīndraṃ tam atandritaṃ sa jitvā*, ŚDV 15.139.

authority of the Vedas, and to promulgate the "correct" mode of interpreting them. In this respect, our sources provide some exceptions to the typical ambivalence towards rational argument which Granoff has shown to be a prevalent feature of traditional religious biography.[14]

Now the AŚV is the one hagiography which, above all, focusses on Śaṅkara's debates. But it too is silent on the details of the crucial contest with Maṇḍanamiśra. I would suggest that there is a key issue which the AŚV—along with the VŚV, GŚC, RŚA and GVK—has sought to avoid, namely, Śaṅkara's denial of ritual action as a valid means of liberation. Throughout his own works Śaṅkara insistently argues that ritual action cannot be joined with the path of knowledge. It is knowledge alone which is the way of release. The most Śaṅkara will allow is that ritual action may constitute a remote means, or preliminary, to the pursuit of knowledge.[15]

The hagiographers, however, are loath to represent Śaṅkara as a critic of ritual action. The denial of the ritual practice which is integral to Vedic religion could easily appear contrary to the very tradition Śaṅkara is meant to restore. For this reason the hagiographies portray him as a saviour of the brahmins who have fallen from their proper path through ignoring the performance of the obligatory ritual actions, as delineated in the *śāstras*. This image of Śaṅkara is made most explicit in the AŚV. In this text the numerous debates follow a predictable pattern. Śaṅkara first refutes his opponents' sectarian doctrines and then counsels them, provided, of course, they are brahmins, to return to ritual practice. Here is a typical example of how

14 See her "Scholars and wonderworkers". For details on this and her other important articles on hagiography, see the Bibliography.

15 See J. Bader, *Meditation in Śaṅkara's Vedānta* (New Delhi: Aditya Prakashan, 1990), p. 57ff.

Śaṅkara presents the "true teachings" to a defeated opponent, in this case the Vaiṣṇava, Vipradeva:

> Having abandoned the branding of sectarian marks and the like, and carrying out the obligatory ritual action (*nitya-karman*) at the specified times, you should devote yourself always to [the formula] "I am Brahman". When [this] meditation is perfected, you will be liberated.[16]

While the observance of ritual action is just one component of the necessary practice here, there is certainly no suggestion that it should be dispensed with in order to attain liberation. But this is precisely the assertion that characterizes Śaṅkara's firm stand on renunciation which is reiterated throughout his own works. The portrayal of Śaṅkara as an adherent of ritual action, marks the hagiographies as being representative of a post-Śaṅkara Advaita tradition. After the time of his disciple Sureśvara, some of Śaṅkara's views—such as his uncompromising rejection of ritual action—were modified in various ways by other Advaitins.[17]

Had the hagiographers elaborated on the renouncer-householder debate, it would have been difficult for them to avoid raising the question of whether ritual action is a valid means to liberation. According to the VŚV, Maṇḍana does take such a stand, in the declaration of his position prior to the commencement of the actual debate: "Liberation is sought through ritual actions. In this case, the accomplishment [of ritual actions] should continue for the duration of men's lives".[18] But the VŚV, and the hagiographies which follow it,

---

16 *cihnāṅkanādikaṃ parityajya yathākālocitaṃ nitya-karma kurvan sadā ahaṃ brahmāsmīti bhāvaya / siddhāyāṃ bhāvanāyāṃ mukto bhavasi* , AŚV p. 49.

17 See Chapter Seven for further discussion.

18 *karmabhyo muktir iṣṭā tad iha tanu-bhṛtāṃ āyuṣaḥ syāt samāptiḥ* , VŚV 6.94; ŚDV 6.64.

do not tell us what transpires during the debate itself. Nor does the issue figure directly in the most substantial account we have of the argument, which is found in the TŚA and repeated by Mādhava in the ŚDV.

While it does not directly address the problem of defining the place of ritual action, the Śaṅkara-Maṇḍana debate in the TŚA/ŚDV stands out as one of the best examples of philosophical argument in the hagiographies.[19] This account of the debate has been summarized and analysed by Esther Solomon in her comprehensive study of Indian dialectics.[20] It will suffice to simply mention here the main topics which figure in the argument: the analysis of *tat tvam asi* and its function, the relationship of the senses, mind and *ātman*, and the question of whether the *śruti* asserts difference between the *jīva* and Īśvara. One of the most striking features of this version of the debate is the surprisingly fair treatment accorded to Maṇḍana/Viśvarūpa. Indeed he is permitted to end his argument with an especially forceful thrust: there are more *śruti* texts which assert difference than those which assert non-difference. But there is, as can be expected, a small flaw in his final point. He has claimed that there are other means of knowledge which give support to the statements in the *śruti* affirming difference. Śaṅkara catches him on this point, arguing

19 It is noteworthy that the ŚDV, the most widely distributed of the hagiographies, also provides elaborate details of arguments with Nīlakaṇṭha (15.39-71) and Bhāskara (15.90-140), along with briefer descriptions of the debates against the Pāśupatas (6.72-77) and the Jainas (15.142-153). The argument with the Jainas is repeated from TŚA 3.98-103. It is likely that the debates against Nīlakaṇṭha and Bhāskara are also drawn from the TŚA, but this cannot be verified as the latter part of the TŚA is no longer extant.

20 Esther A. Solomon, *Indian dialectics: methods of philosophical discussion* (2 vols., Ahmedabad: B. J. Institute of Learning and Research, 1976-78), vol. II. pp. 833-845. She also analyses the argument with Nīlakaṇṭha pp. 845-848.

that other means of knowledge can only weaken the *śruti* and render it devoid of meaning.

This is the final statement in the debate, according to the TŚA and Mādhava's ŚDV. Yet the two texts diverge on the conclusion of the episode. Tirumala-Dīkṣita ends the chapter, and the episode, with a single verse stating simply that Śaṅkara refuted Maṇḍana through superior argument:

> Having refuted each and every [*śruti* citation] by means of such stronger reasoned proofs and with greater skill in [meeting] difficult doubts, [Śaṅkara] whose fame is renowned, enumerated more than a hundred authorities concerning the non-difference between the supreme [Brahman] and the *jīva*.[21]

Although he has repeated the whole of the TŚA's version of the argument, some sixty verses in all, Mādhava chooses to omit this one verse. Instead he tells us that it was Sarasvatī who determined that the debate was over: "The strong logic of such statements, which was approved by the goddess of speech, shone forth".[22]

In contrast to the impressive account of the Śaṅkara-Maṇḍana debate in the TŚA/ŚDV, Cidvilāsa provides a briefer and simpler version. Yet it is he alone who makes explicit Śaṅkara's rejection of ritual action. Because this version of the debate is so little known, I include a full translation of the text.

---

21 *ityādyaiḥ prabalataraiḥ sa yukti-jātair duḥśaṅkā-nipuṇatarair nirasya tās tāḥ / ācakhyau paratara-jīvayor abhede mānaṃ prathita-yaśāḥ paraḥ-śatāni //* TŚA 4.110. There are some difficulties in the reading of this verse, hence the translation is tentative. I have followed the editor's suggestion, reading *yukti-jātair* instead of *yukti-jāte.*

22 *ityādyā dṛḍha-yuktir asya śuśubhe dattānumodā girāṃ devyā...* ŚDV 8. 131.

The Śaṅkara-Maṇḍana debate: Cidvilāsa's *Śaṅkara-vijayavilāsa*, ch. 18

5. Beginning with the first of the sciences [i.e., the Vedas], the learned Maṇḍanamiśra and the spiritual teacher, Śrī Śaṅkara, engaged in debate in stages.

6. Now [after some time] Maṇḍanamiśra said, "Let that be, oh best of ascetics. But renunciation is not possible in the *kali [-yuga]*. How is it that you have accepted it?

7-8. Listen to the authorities on this matter which are proclaimed in the *śruti* and *smṛti*. There are five things one should avoid in the *kali [-yuga]*: the sacrifice of horses, the sacrifice of cows, renunciation, offering meat to the ancestors and [arranging for] the birth of a son through the husband's brother. [In] all four stages of life, those who are without sacrifice and study of the Vedas,

9. Are excluded from brahminhood, even if they are undertaking severe *tapas* [i.e., in the fourth stage of life]. For all brahmins, the sacred thread is the means of liberation.

10. They who abandon it because of delusion go to hell. By getting rid of the tuft of hair and the sacred thread, how can one be a brahmin?

11. How can brahmins who do not perform the *saṃdhyā* worship be thought of as brahmins? A man who follows the dicta of the Vedas does not experience hell.

12. By means of ritual action heaven is attained [and also] empire and sons, oh ascetic. That is why the best of brahmins who are knowers of the Vedas carry out ritual action.

13. For the wise say that he who knows the proper time for ritual action and who carries out ritual action at the proper time is indeed a man of knowledge in this world.

14. But renunciation is prohibited on account of statements such as, "In the *kali-yuga* they know a man is wise and full of devotion who is intent on good works".

15. How is it that you have undertaken that very thing [which is prohibited, i.e., renunciation] and, what is more, as you were a *brahmacārin*"? Having heard his statement, the best of gurus [said]:

16. Listen, you fool, I will further explain the authority [in this matter] to you. As long as there are distinctions of social classes, and as long as the Veda continues [to exist],

17. The [paths of] renunciation and the sacrifical fire [will continue] in the *kali [-yuga]*. Whether one is in the first, second, or third stage of life,

18. When the mind becomes dispassionate, one should resort to the final stage of life. [As for] those faults which arise from one's family and those which may be born from one's karma,

19. Renunciation will burn all of them up, as a fire of grain husks [purifies] gold.[23] Even if he is dispassionate towards the ocean of worldly existence from the very first stage of life,

20. A brahmin who desires liberation should abandon his attachments and go forth as a renouncer. The stages of life are appointed by the *śruti*. For the brahmin, four [stages of life] are proclaimed.

21. For the *kṣatriya* it is stated there are three. For the *vaiśya* there are two, and for the *śūdra* one. Let one abandon the outer sacred thread (*sūtra*), cutting it off along with the tuft of hair.

22. It is Brahman that is called the *sūtra* [on which the world is strung], and that is what the wise should wear. It is said, that [Brahman] is the highest abode, in which the whole world[24] is manifest.

---

[23] Verse 18b-19a is found in *Saṃnyāsopaniṣad* 2.11.

[24] Following the alternate reading, *viśvaṃ*.

23. On this point it is said, the one who knows the *sūtra* to be such is the true knower of the *sūtra*. Let the yogi who is established in the state of *jīvan-mukti* abandon the outer *sūtra*.

24. It is those who understand the meaning as such who are invested with the sacred thread of knowledge, and it is knowledge which is the tuft of hair for men of knowledge. Being established in knowledge is described as *sat*.

25. The purified knowledge of those [knowers] is called a *śikhā*, as is the *śikhā* of the fire.[25] The supreme Brahman is indeed knowledge. The man who possesses that,

26. Is said to be one who [truly] has the tuft of hair. Not so the others who [just] wear [the tuft of] hair. Those who understand best say that the sacred thread is an accessory of ritual action,

27. Since it is not seen in the world prior to the end of studentship (*upakurvāṇaka*). It is worn so long as one engages in ritual action.

28. Therefore, the renouncing of that [sacred thread] is done in conjunction with [the renouncing of] ritual action. As in the case of the destruction of the sacred fire, one may abandon the sacrificial ladle, etc.;

29. As on account of the longing for [the beginning of] the householder stage of life [one may abandon] the waistband and the other things [worn during studentship]; as [one may abandon] the wife's waistband at the conclusion of the sacrifice,[26] and the sacrificial spoons (*graha*)[27] at the conclusion of the *soma* [rites];

---

[25] A play on two meanings of *śikhā*: 'tuft of hair' and 'flame'.

[26] According to P. V. Kane, the sacrificer's wife is made fit to participate in the *iṣṭi* rites by the wearing of a waistband (*yoktra*) made of *muñja* grass cord (*History of Dharmaśāstra* [2nd ed., Poona, 1974], vol. 2, part 2, p. 1040.

[27] This is following the alternate reading.

30. In the same way, the yogis seek to abandon the sacred thread. They should keep as their clothing [only] a couple of loin cloths, and a ragged cloth for warding off the cold.

31. They should keep a rosary and a sound bamboo staff. The *paramahaṃsa* [ascetic] should behave as a bee collecting various alms [from place to place].

32 The one whose senses are controlled, who is meditating always on the eternal, supreme Brahman, should abandon the tuft of hair, the sacred thread and obligatory ritual action".

33. As the revered teacher Śaṅkarācārya spoke in this way, stringing together the statements of the *śruti*, *smṛti*, *purāṇas*, etc.,

34. Maṇḍanamiśra, who was abashed, perplexed and confused within, stood there unable to give reply.

35. [Śaṅkara said], "What is it that you said previously, you fool? What do you have in mind now? How can something which is without consciousness, namely, ritual action, bring about the result of the supreme state?

36. It is considered by the *śruti* that the supreme Brahman is what brings about that [supreme state]. The performer of evil deeds who violates the traditional path will have misfortune.

37. Worse is he who would violate those in the supreme stage of life. Then, having heard the words of the guru who was angry, [Maṇḍana's] wife,

38. The virtuous Sarasavāṇī, came forth immediately [from her quarters]. She was [first] regularly summoning the ascetic to come for his alms, and afterwards [summoned] her husband to come for his meal.

39. [But] on the eighteenth day [of the debate] that wise woman, realising that her husband was defeated by the foremost of teachers,

40. Immediately summoned both of them to come for alms. Then Maṇḍanamiśra arose.
41. With great devotion he circumambulated [Śaṅkara] thrice and bowed to him a thousand times...

The question of the propriety of abandoning the sacred thread and tuft of hair is an issue which has long generated controversy in India. The debate appears at least since the time of the Jābāla Upaniṣad, in which Atri asks Yājñavalkya, "How can one be a brahmin without the sacred thread"?[28] Patrick Olivelle has demonstrated both the importance and the persistence of this controversy in the Hindu tradition.[29] One of the textual sources for the debates on renunciation Olivelle includes in his study, a portion of the *Pārāśara-mādhavīya*,[30] may well have been the model Cidvilāsa followed in composing his account of the Śaṅkara-Maṇḍana argument. Some of the same *smṛti* verses the objector in the *Pārāśara-mādhavīya* quotes to support his position are cited by Maṇḍana in the CŚV; Śaṅkara's rejoinder also contains some similar materials.[31]

---

28 *ayajñopavītī katham brāhmaṇa iti*, *Jābāla Upaniṣad* 5. Śaṅkara cites the authority of this Upaniṣad on several occasions in his own compositions.

29 Patrick Olivelle, *Renunciation in Hinduism. A medieval debate*, (2 vols.Vienna: Institut für Indologie der Universität Wien, 1986-1987), see esp. vol. I, pp. 26-36.

30 This work of Mādhava's is a commentary on the *Pārāśara-smṛti*. The text was published in the Bibliotheca Indica Series in 1893, under the title, *Parāśara-smṛti. Parāśara-mādhava*, (reprinted in 2 vols. Calcutta: Asiatic Society, 1973-74). Olivelle (*ibid.* 118-142) provides the text and a translation of an independent portion of this composition in which Mādhava discusses issues concerning renunciation that are not mentioned in the *Pārāśara-smṛti*.

31 In Maṇḍana's argument the following lines are equivalent to the citations found in the *Pārāśara-mādhavīya* on page 120 of the text reprinted in Olivelle (and on pp. 543-544 of the first volume of Bibliotheca Indica edition):

Although the debate on renunciation in the CŚV may rely more heavily on the work of Mādhava-Vidyāraṇya [32] than that of Śaṅkara, the substance of the discussion can be readily identified with Śaṅkara's own position. In the first place, the debate remains under the jurisdiction of the *śāstras* and hinges, accordingly, on the correct interpretation of the sacred texts. The views represented here are fully in keeping with the stand Śaṅkara takes on renunciation in his commentary to *Bṛhadāraṇyaka Upaniṣad* 3.5.1 and on *Brahmasūtra* 3.4.17-20. According to the CŚV, Śaṅkara's conclusion is unmistakable: ritual action—along with its accessories, the sacred thread and tuft of hair—must be abandoned in order to reach the supreme state.

CŚV 18.8b-9a = the citation of Hārīta

9b-10a = the citation from Atri

10b = the citation from *Padmapurāṇa*

11a = half of the citation from Baudhāyana.

Śaṅkara's reply contains the following material also found in *Pārāśara-mādhavīya* (Olivelle pp. 120-122; Bibliotheca Indica vol. I pp. 543-546):

CŚV 18.26b-30a = the citation from the *Vyāsa-smṛti*

30b-31b = the citation from the *Skāndapurāṇa* (minus the third *pāda*)

21b-26a - seems to be a summary of the citation from the Pippalāda- *śākhā [Brahmopaniṣad]*. While I have benefited from consulting Olivelle's rendering of the relevant verses, I have retained my own translations because of the different arrangement of materials in the CŚV.

32 While the identity has not so far been satisfactorily proven, it is significant that in his *Jīvanmuktiviveka*, Vidyāraṇya refers, in connection with the consideration of the renouncer, to the *Pārāśara-smṛti* commentary as being his own work: *...proktāḥ pārāśara-smṛtau vyākhyāne 'smābhir* (verse 11 of the introduction). For further discusssion see T. M. P. Mahadevan, *The philosophy of Advaita with special reference to Bhāratītīrtha-Vidyāraṇya* ([1938] 4th ed. New Delhi: Arnold-Heinemann, 1976), pp. 1-8, and Hermann Kulke "Mahārājas, Mahants and Historians. Reflections on the historiography of early Vijayanagara and Sringeri", in *Vijayanagara - city and empire. New Currents of Research*, ed. A.L. Dallipiccola (2 vols. Stuttgart: Steiner Verlag Wiesbaden, 1985) vol. I, 120-143, esp. pp.130-132.

However bold Cidvilāśa may seem in regard to the other hagiographers in focussing on the renunciation of ritual action, he too relies on Sarasvatī to decide the outcome of the debate. Cidvilāsa also shares with the others a determination to establish a realistic portrayal of the episode. Because the hagiographers generally show little inclination for verisimilitude, their efforts here are all the more conspicuous. To begin with, we learn precisely how long the debate continues: eighteen days, so far as Cidvilāsa is concerned.[33] We see that Sarasvatī only appears when the meals are served, although she clearly follows everything that transpires. The AŚV goes even further, specifying that she remains in the kitchen. Despite her exalted status as goddess and arbiter of the debate, she must appear as a proper brahmin wife until Śaṅkara frees her from the curse which binds her to a human form.

The hagiographers' efforts at verisimilitude are most apparent in their portrayal of how the contestants behave. Cidvilāsa has it that Śaṅkara insists on calling Maṇḍana a fool. Maṇḍana is equally abusive, and the terse exchange of insults which precedes the debate makes it clear that both parties share a mutual hostility.[34] Maṇḍana's acceptance of defeat is shown in his sudden attitude of humility towards his former enemy (verse 40). True to the terms of the debate, he must now adopt the garb of a *saṃnyāsin* and become a follower of Śaṅkara.

Most of the hagiographers are concerned with portraying Śaṅkara's behaviour in debate, but they are divided on how it should be represented. The VŚV, and following it the GŚC, do

---

33 The VŚV, GŚC, RŚA and GVK all agree it went on for seven days. According to the AŚV it was one hundred days. The TŚA/ŚDV account does not specify the duration of the debate.

34 The CŚV repeats the same heated dialogue as is found in AŚV p. 177. For a translation of the passage see Chapter Two, above. A similar but expanded account appears in ŚDV 8.16-31.

not give us any indication that he is inclined to anger. On the contrary, these texts stress that the Śaṅkara-Maṇḍana debate was conducted with great decorum:

> The two of them, who had assumed their seats, resolutely refuted each other's reply, the lotus of their faces blooming with a smile. They were distinguished by being neither hot-headed nor staring into space. There was no angry twisting of words. The debate went on between the two of them, neither of whom were [caught] without an answer.[35]

In its extensive account of the debate, the TŚA goes to still greater lengths in depicting the mutual respect between the two opponents. Here Śaṅkara repeatedly addresses Maṇḍana with honorific epithets such as 'wise one' (*prajña, manīṣin, vidvān*) and 'foremost of the wise' (*budhāgrayāyin*). Maṇḍana replies in kind, referring to Śaṅkara as 'king of ascetics' (*yati-kṣmādhipati*, *yatīśa*), 'noble one' (*arhat*) and 'yogi'. The AŚV and CŚV, on the other hand, are explicit in attributing to Śaṅkara anger, and perhaps even arrogance. In both these texts Śaṅkara invariably refers to his opponents as fools. Such behaviour may be intended to reflect the characteristic anger of Śiva, and hence, to suggest that Śaṅkara's similar behaviour marks him as an *avatāra* of the great god.[36] As well, this would help to establish Śaṅkara's reputation as a divine sage, akin to the irascible Durvāsa. It may also be that these texts wish to refer to the militant tradition among renouncers which was

---

35 *anyonyam uttaram akhaṇḍayatāṃ pragalbhau baddhāsanau smita-vikāsita-mukhāravindau / na sveda-vāri-gaganekṣaṇa-śālinau vā na krodha-vāk-chalam avādi niruttarābhyām //* VŚV 6.101. The last two *pādas* are somewhat freely rendered. The same verse appears, with minor variants, in ŚDV 8.73.

36 See Chapter Three.

eventually established among some of the orders tracing their lineage back to Śaṅkara.[37]

The ŚDV tries to combine both representations of Śaṅkara's personality. In this text the encounter with Maṇḍana begins with the angry exchange as described in the AŚV and CŚV, but the mood is then shifted radically to the respectful tones of the TŚA's version of the debate. The transition between these diametrically opposed modes of behaviour is facilitated by an episode from within the narrative. It is the intervention of Vyāsa, which brings to an end the tirade of insults between householder and renouncer. The ever-present sage reminds Maṇḍana that a *saṃnyāsin* must be offered proper hospitality. From this point on, The ŚDV describes only cordiality between the two contestants.[38]

It is ironic that the peacekeeper of this episode has himself experienced the anger of Śaṅkara, according to two of our sources. The AŚV and CŚV insist on portraying Śaṅkara's inclination for insulting his opponents, even in his meeting with Vyāsa. Anantānandagiri gives the following description of the incident:

> [One day] when the Paramaguru was absorbed in profound meditation on the bank of the Maṇikarṇika [-*ghaṭṭa*] at the time when the sun was at its meridian, Bhagavān Vyāsa, it is said, approaching in the guise of an old brahmin, and seeing [Śaṅkara] accompanied by six thousand disciples...threw down a challenge, saying "Who is he"? The disciples said this to [Vyāsa], who was

37 For details on militant *saṃnyāsin* s, see J. N. Farquhar, "The organisation of the Sannyasis of the Vedanta", *Journal of the Royal Asiatic Society*, 1925, 479-486, and Jadunath Sarkar, *A history of Dasnami Naga Sanyasis*, (Allahabad: Sri Panchayati Akhara Mahanirvani, n.d.).

38 The RŚA and GVK provide brief and matter of fact accounts of the debate. Neither hostility nor cordiality is reported.

> wearing a disguise: "Listen, old man, the guru who is supreme bliss [itself], whose name is Śaṅkara, is undertaking the destruction of [false] doctrines in the lands from [Rāma's] bridge up"....The old man, who was spoken to in this way, passing through the assembly of disciples, said this to Śaṅkarācārya, shaking his grey head: "Have you exerted yourself in the study of the *Brahmasūtra*"? The *ācārya*, who is the supreme guru, seeing him, said: "Oh brahmin, at whatever [point] is your choice of entry [into an examination of the text], I will address [myself] to that".[39]

Initially it is the disciples who accord minimal respect to the disguised Vyāsa, while Śaṅkara addresses him more politely as 'brahmin' (*vipra*). As the debate progresses, however, he calls Vyāsa a "very foolish old man" (*vṛddha mūḍhatara*). Their lengthy argument is drawn directly from Śaṅkara's *Brahmasūtra-bhāṣya* 3.1.1-3. The text concerns a complex exegesis of how the *prāṇas* depart from the body. Vyāsa, who is cast in the role of the *pūrva-pakṣin*, raises the opposing viewpoints put forth in the *bhāṣya*. As Śaṅkara brings his apparently successful argument to a close, Vyāsa is completely humiliated :

> Arguing (*jalp*) insistently, he caused the old man to slap his own cheeks [as a gesture of submision]. Then [Śaṅkara] said this to his disciple Padmapāda: "having made this old man, the best of opponents, to bow down, send him far away from my presence".[40] But although spoken to thus by the

---

39 AŚV p. 166 lines 15-20; p. 167 lines 4-7. See also CŚV 13.24ff., and ŚDV 7.1-12.

40 N. Veezhinathan, the editor of the Madras edition, adds an explanatory note (in Sanskrit): "In ancient times, this—i.e., slapping the cheeks and bowing down—was the retribution for one engaging in captious argument (*vitaṇḍa-vādin*)", p. 169. For further discussion see Chapter Six note 154.

> guru, [Padmapāda] kept silent. The old man, for his part, immediately departed upon hearing those words...".[41]

Śaṅkara's obvious disdain for the disguised Vyāsa is typical of the treatment his opponents receive throughout the AŚV and CŚV.

When he is informed by his disciple Padmapāda that the "old man" is in fact Vyāsa, Śaṅkara then does an about face. Fortunately Padmapāda has not carried out the guru's commands—to make the old man bow down and send him away—so it is still possible to make amends. Yet even here Śaṅkara's words reveal more cleverness than humility:

> If that one here is Vyāsa, whose understanding is incomparable, [then] he should protect me, even though [I have given] offence, [because I am one] for whom an opinion about *smṛti* is set aside by the direct experience of the meaning of Advaita. Like the sun whose rays are equally [shining] on such things as are [pure, i.e.] fit for sacrifice [and those that are not], and like the fire which is honoured [althought it] consumes all things, he should give up the unhappiness arising from [my] attack. If the doctrine whose purport is Advaita is strengthened by his *sūtras*, Vyāsa himself, who is dear to his students, should now approach. If that doctrine [of Advaita] is the highest truth, and if difference is false, Bādarāyaṇa should protect me, who is the composer of the Advaita commentary. I always take refuge in Vyāsa, the best of ascetics. He alone, who is gracious, should now remove all darkness.[42]

---

41 AŚV p. 169 lines 3-6.

42 AŚV p. 169 lines 11-20.

Once again Śaṅkara's argument is decisive. Vyāsa, who went off before being ordered out, now returns. At this point Śaṅkara at least makes the appropriate ritual gestures towards Vyāsa, "beginning with twelve circumambulations", and declares "I am [but] a fraction of you, I am your disciple".[43] Vyāsa, in turn, confirms the validity of his *Brahmasūtra* commentary, and the episode ends on a happy note.

In their zeal for showing Śaṅkara to be victorious in debate against all comers, the AŚV and CŚV are willing to include even Vyāsa in the long list of the defeated. He is certainly not spared from the abusive treatment Śaṅkara metes out to his opponents. The two hagiographies may also reflect the undercurrent of suspicion about Vyāsa which appears in the later Advaita tradition. Madhusūdana Sarasvatī, who was active in the 16th century, actually criticises Vyāsa in the conclusion of his *Siddhāntabindu*:

> I do not praise Vyāsa, who did not correctly bring together the entire purport [of the Upaniṣads] by means of the *sūtras*. I salute Śaṅkara and Sureśvara by whom the whole purport was tied together, even without the *sūtras*.[44]

Another hint of the ambivalence towards Vyāsa is found in the anonymous *Sarvasiddhāntasaṃgraha*,[45] which devotes a chapter to expounding his viewpoints. According to this compendium, the philosophical views expressed in the *Mahābhārata*, which Vyāsa is said to have compiled, are derived from the

---

43 AŚV p. 169 line 22.

44 *na staumi taṃ vyāsam aśeṣam arthaṃ samyaṅ na sūtrair api yo babandha / vināpi taiḥ saṃgrathitākhilārthaṃ taṃ śaṅkaraṃ naumi sureśvaraṃ ca // Siddhāntabindu by Madhusūdana Sarasvatī*, ed. Vasudev Shastri Abhyankar ([1928] reprinted Poona: Bhandarkar Oriental Research Institute, 1962), p. 153.

45 The work is sometimes ascribed, most improbably, to Śaṅkara.

Sāṅkhyas.[46] This suggests that Vyāsa may have been perceived as a dualist. As such, he would be a fitting opponent for a true Advaitin.

The pugnacious image of Śaṅkara, which is presented in the AŚV and CŚV, is undoubtedly connected with the emphasis on debate in these hagiographies. In the public forum such behaviour may well have been required of a successful debater. The audience would more easily recognise the stronger contestant from his confident manner, and from his ability to humiliate his opponent. According to the AŚV and CŚV, Śaṅkara's opponents—with the notable exception of Maṇḍanamiśra—are generally shown to treat him with some deference. They address him with respectful epithets, while he invariably refers to them as fools. This can only convey the impression of Śaṅkara's inherent superiority in debate. The audience is not left to doubt that Śaṅkara has the upper hand at all times.

The debate against Vyāsa also stands out as one of the few instances in which the hagiographies make direct use of Śaṅkara's own works. The AŚV incorporates the better part of his commentary to *Brahmasūtra-bhāṣya* 3.1.1-3 into the narrative: Śaṅkara repeats his own words while Vyāsa assumes the role of *pūrva-pakṣin*.[47] The only other direct reference to Śaṅkara's commentaries I have noticed is in the debate against the Ārhats (i.e., Jains) in ŚDV 15.142-153. These verses summarize some of the discussion in *Brahmasūtra-bhāṣya* 2.2.33-36. The hagiographies are, of course, suitable for narration to a popular audience, and as such may not be the

---

46 *vyāsokto bhārate...gṛhyate sāṅkhya-pakṣād hi, The Sarva-Siddhānta - Saṅgraha of Śaṅkarācārya*, ed. and tr. M. Raṅgācārya ([1909] reprinted, New Delhi: Ajay Book Service, 1983), p. 47 (text).

47 AŚV pp. 167-169. The CŚV and ŚDV agree that the debate concerns the interpretation of *Brahmasūtra* 3.1.1.

place for prolonged philosophical discussion. Nevertheless, it is surprising that the hagiographers have scarcely availed themselves of the abundant polemical materials in Śaṅkara's own compositions.

The lack of reference to Śaṅkara's *oeuvre* is all the more puzzling in the case of his debate against the Buddhists. Since all the hagiographies credit Kumārila-Bhaṭṭa with the defeat of Buddhists, they cannot represent a very serious challenge for Śaṅkara as far as our texts are concerned. Nonetheless, both the AŚV and CŚV include them among the opponents Śaṅkara must debate. Now whether Śaṅkara actually knew of Buddhist doctrines from primary sources or learned of them more indirectly, it is clear that he was reasonably well informed on the subject. In his *Brahmasūtra* commentary he presents arguments against three types of Buddhists: realists (Sarvāstivādins), idealists (Vijñānavādins) and nihilists (Śūnyavādins).[48] Yet his Buddhist opponents in the AŚV and CŚV represent neither of these three traditions. Indeed it is virtually impossible to recognise anything which is intrinsically Buddhist in their arguments. Because these debates comprise an unusual mixture of popular and learned perceptions, I will present them in their entirety.

Refutation of the Buddhist Doctrine:

Anantānandagiri's *Śaṅkaravijaya*, ch. 28

When he had thus refuted the Kāpālikas, Cārvākas, Saugatas, Kṣapaṇakas and Jainas, it is said a Buddhist named Śabala objected: "Oh *svāmin*, it seems you are the greatest of all. But what is the good of your knowledge? There is no benefit in

---

48 See 2.2.18-32. For a concise discussion see Daniel H. H. Ingalls, "Śaṃkara's arguments against the Buddhists", *Philosophy East and West* 3 (1954) 291-306.

Advaita because of the unreality of its conclusions. It is arguing [in effect, for the existence of] the horns of a hare. Why is it that you have abandoned visible results and are desiring unseen results? Even in the case of something unseen there will be no result for you who are opposed to the evidence of direct perception. Because what is unseen, being devoid of anything, is incapable of yielding results, and it is lifeless. But consciousness is what is predicated by the word *jīva*. That [*jīva*] is present in all the beings in the world. Although it is one, it bears many forms and is the impeller of such things as the mind. According to its desire, [the *jīva*] sports in various bodies, thinking, 'I am by nature eternally free; I am the agent, the enjoyer; I am non-dual and the highest bliss'. Having left the body, [the *jīva*] is liberated afterwards".

The Paramaguru said: "Oh Śabala, what is propounded by you is inadequate. Why? Because it is extremely contradictory. How can there be liberation for that [*jīva*] on the basis of the view that one goes to the other world immediately upon casting off the body? For in the Purāṇa [it is said]:

> He who is intent on truth and purity in honouring the gods and guests goes to the realm of Brahmā so long as fourteen Indras [reign].
>
> Let one perform the Agniṣṭoma, which gives joy to the gods. Because of that, one goes to the realm of Indra, called *satya*. Due to that *pauṇḍarīka* [rite] the worshippers of whatever god go to that god.

And in the *Bhagavadgītā* [7.21] there is the statement:

> Whatever form any devotee wishes to worship with faith, I grant him unwavering faith in that very form.

This god, who is pleased by my worship, will grant me residence in his realm when the body comes to an end. Because of the existence of hundreds of such scriptural authorities, it is established that, for the *jīva*, there is a passage to the other world immediately after the casting off of the body. It is well known that the *paramātman* has the nature of all the gods and grants [access] to all the worlds. It is established that the god who grants all of those worlds, desired by whatever [*jīva*], is the *ātman*, the one without a second. Hence it is even more incorrect to say that liberation simply follows immediately upon the casting off of the body, because one observes that there is no liberation without knowledge. In regard to the question of what the characteristic of knowledge is, it is well known that after having thought of all beings as being in himself, and himself in all beings, a man is liberated. As is said in the *śruti*:

> Seeing himself in all beings and all beings in himself, one goes to the highest Brahman—but not for any other reason [*Kaivalyopaniṣad* 10].

Therefore Śabala, abandoning your foolish ideas, abide in yourself". The Buddhist named Śabala bowed to the *paramaguru* and, intent on singing his praises, assumed the role of [all three kinds of bards:] *bandin, māgadha* and *sūta*.

Initially Śabala seems as though he may be enunciating the view of a Buddhist realist. But his insistence on the existence of the *jīva* is more suggestive of a Jain belief. Śabala's main argument, that the *jīva* is liberated simply with the death of the physical body, may be a misrepresentation of a Jain doctrine: liberation occurs only upon the complete cessation of all activities associated with embodiment.[49] Criticism of fasting to death (sallekhanā) as a means of liberation may also be

[49] See Padmanabh S. Jaini, *The Jaina path of purification* (Berkeley and Los Angeles: University of California, 1979), pp. 159; 268-273.

intended. Even if Anantānandagiri is in fact (mis)representing a Jain view here, there can be no doubt he takes it as Buddhist. In both the Calcutta and Madras editions of the AŚV, we read that the opponent is a Bauddha named Śabala/Śabara. The colophon in all three printed editions identifies the chapter as "The Refutation of the Buddhist Doctrine".

A similar confusion of Buddhists and Jains is found in the CŚV. When Śaṅkara travels to a place called Mṛdapurī he finds it is full of Saugatas,which term generally designates Buddhists. But the opponents are also described as Ārahatas which is more suggestive of Jains. Then at the conclusion of their argument, they are specifically referred to as Bauddhas. This is how Cidvilāsa presents the encounter, beginning with a description of the opponents' appearance:

Refutation of Buddhists/Jains:

Cidvilāsa's Śaṅkara-vijayavilāsa, 29.9-29

They had [whisks made from the] ornamented portions of peacock feathers and the clumps of their hair were pulled out.[50] They were arguing extensively that the highest *dharma* is *ahiṃsā*, and were saying clearly that everything is false other than the evidence of direct perception. [Although] never eating at night, their naked bodies were [quite] full. Having seen that the Ārhatas were of such a kind, the guru was completely amazed. The excellent Śaṅkarācārya, for his part, asked them [to explain] their customs.

Those who were following[51] the Saugata customs spoke of the customs of their sect: "The father and mother are

50 The text reads *viluṇṭhita-kacoccaya*. There may be a confusion of *viluṇṭhita* with *viluñcita*. The latter is the reading found in Mādhava's *Sarvadarśanasaṃgraha*, see note 54 below.

51 This is a tentative reading; *santamāḥ* seems very doubtful.

certainly the primary cause of the body. That which is to do with the body is the result of that [cause], but its dissolution in the earth is liberation. How is rebirth possible for a body which becomes ashes, and is like a drop of water which is dissolved in water, oh you who are devoid of understanding? Release from that [body] alone is liberation. The ignorant may speak of transmigration (*punar-bhava*). Men vainly perform *śrāddha* rites in honour of the deceased ancestors. Where does a deceased ancestor go? How does he consume the *śrāddha* [offering] in this world? Who has met an ancestor, or seen one on this earth? The experience of heaven is in this world, [in such things as] empire, [or] a young bride. The experience of hell is [also] in this world, [in such things as] calamity on account of tigers, enemies, etc. [The idea] that there is a world beyond this one is [based on] false appearance. If moving about is possible for the *jīva*, even though he is formless, then locomotion is possible even for the ether which is in a pot. The ignorant vainly argue that the unseen somehow exists. Therefore, you should resort to our wonderful doctrine, oh ascetic".

When the Buddhists had thus spoken, the teacher Śaṅkarācārya began his reply to the proponents of atheism. "Oh fool, how can there be liberation for you upon the casting off of the body? The *jīva*, having abandoned the dead [body] then enters the subtle body, as a leech (*jalūka*), having abandoned [one] blade of grass immediately [proceeds to] another blade of grass. Having performed ritual acts such as sacrifice, one attains heaven. The *śruti*, which is the weighty authority says, "heaven is attained by means of sacrifices such as the *jyotiṣṭoma*". Moreover, the *śrāddha* rite for the deceased should be performed, according to the precepts. This is ascertained from the purport of the *śruti*: "the ancestors are pleased by that". What was clearly stated by you—that the highest *dharma* is *ahiṃsā*—is incorrect, foolish one, because of the utterance of the *śruti*, "you should act as a sacrificer".[52] I will tell you of one authority in this matter and also of Gāyatrī, proclaimed by the *śruti*. [But] you pray with devotion to the goddess Tārā, oh lowest of the *kṣapaṇa* [-ascetics]. Those who are proponents of atheism and who are intent on reviling the Vedas will all go to hell, even if [their doctrine] originates from a Vedic seed". In this way, the Saugatas were admonished by the most excellent of gurus. Having bowed their heads to the ground, all of them who were alert, their pride destroyed, offered service to the chief of gurus. The guru, an ocean of compassion, entrusted all of them to [the task of] caretaking, beginning with taking care of the feet of the disciples, the first of whom is Padmapāda.

Despite the confusion about the identity of these opponents in the CŚV, the description of their appearance makes it clear they are Jains, not Buddhists. At the time of initiation, Jain monks are expected to remove their hair by pulling it out. As well, they are issued with a whisk made of peacock feathers for gently moving away insects.[53] It is clear that at least these two striking characteristics of Jain monks were familiar to Vedāntins. Mādhava mentions them in similar terms in his *Sarvadarśana-saṃgraha*.[54] The central argument propounded by the "Buddhists" in the CŚV is nearly identical to that found in the AŚV: liberation occurs when the body is cast off. Yet unlike the AŚV which devotes separate chapters to the refutations of Buddhists and Jains, the CŚV settles for a single

---

52 This is a tentative translation of *yāgīyāyāḥ*, which is itself a questionable reading (CŚV 29.25).

53 Padmanabh S. Jaini, *The Jaina path*, pp.244-245.

54 *luñcitāḥ picchikā-hastāḥ*, *Sarvadarśana Saṅgraha by Mādhavāchārya*, (Calcutta: Bibliotheca Indica 1858, reprinted Osnabrük: Biblio Verlag, 1981), p. 44, line 5.

encounter which manages to conflate these two groups of opponents to an even greater extent.

There are further similarities between the Saugata/Ārahata/Buddhist opponent in the CŚV and the Saugatas we meet in the twenty-sixth chapter of the AŚV. Anantānandagiri satirizes the Saugatas by twisting the meaning of the name. They are presented in such a way as to suggest that a Sugata is one who takes the easy path (a slight on the epithet of the Buddha, 'he who has walked the path well'). This is reflected in the physical appearance of their spokesman: a fat man with a tiny head. The Saugata in the AŚV argues that there is no need to perform ritual action. He crudely misinterprets the passage, "having taken on a debt, let one consume ghee", to support his claim that what is important is nourishing the body, not engaging in ritual. Indeed, "for those who eat everything, just obtaining happiness is the means to liberation".[55] He refers to the authority of the Sugata-*muni*,who teaches that *ahiṃsā* towards all creatures is the highest *dharma*. These arguments, minus the satire, can also be seen in the CŚV passage cited above. The parallel in the way the two hagiographies conclude the episode is particularly striking. In both accounts the Saugatas becomes attendants of Śaṅkara's disciples.[56] The AŚV has an added touch of irony. The Saugata's predilection for consuming everything is transformed into a more pious habit of eating the food left over by the disciples.

---

55 *samagra-bhakṣaṇa-śīlasya sukha-prāptir eva mokṣa-sādhanam* , AŚV p. 111

56 The AŚV (p. 112) has it that the Saugata, all of whose pride was destroyed, bowed to the supreme guru and became skilled in holding the office of attendant to the disciples of the guru, first of whom is Padmapāda: *saugataḥ paramagurum natvā nirasta-samastābhimānaḥ padmapādādiguru-śiṣyāṇāṃ pāda - rakṣā-dhāraṇādhikāra-kuśalaḥ ...abhavat.* The CŚV reads *nirasta-garvas te sarve pāda-sevā yayācire / padmapādādi-śiṣyāṇāṃ pāda-rakṣādi-rakṣaṇe / nyayūyujac* [following the alternate reading]*ca tān sarvān...guruḥ //* .

The AŚV also devotes a separate chapter to the refutation of the Śūnya doctrine. But it is not clear whether Anantānandagiri intends the reader to assume they are Buddhists. Just as there was nothing particularly suggestive of Buddhism in his description of the Saugata, the Śūnyavādin seems to be more of a nihilist and sceptic than a Mādhyamika. He is appropriately named Nirālamba, one who is without the support [of a religious belief]. On meeting Śaṅkara, he recites sarcastic verses, describing something he "saw on the way":

> The son of a barren woman, who had a bow made of the horns of a hare and a crown made of flowers from the sky, bathed in the waters of a mirage and went by. I saw him and bowed my head to him repeatedly, because of his being a god.[57]

However, he does put forth a more serious argument. He claims that because Brahman is equated with *ākāśa* it is void (*śūnya*). Since he defends his position with citations from the *Chāndogyopaniṣad* and the *Brahmasūtra*, we get the impression Nirālamba is a lapsed brahmin, rather than a Buddhist. This is confirmed by what transpires at the conclusion of the debate. Unlike the "Buddhist" and Saugata opponents who are relegated to the respective roles of bard and attendant when they are defeated, the Śūnyavādin asks to have Śaṅkara's teachings and is allowed to become a disciple.

Anantānandagiri's portrayal of the Jains (Chapter 27) stands in sharp contrast to his confused account of the Buddhists. He describes in no uncertain terms the outer trappings of two Jain opponents. The first is named Pūrṇasamaya. He wears "only a loincloth and carries a quadrant and an astronomical instrument in his hands".[58] His argument exaggerates the Jain concept of

---

57 AŚV, p.135.

58 *tataḥ kṣapaṇakaḥ kaupīna-mātra-dhārī gola-yantraṃ turīya-yantraṃ ca karābhyāṃ dhṛtvā*...AŚV chapter 27, p. 113.

time as an essential substance (*dravya*). He holds that everything depends on the knowledge of time. The supreme deity is in fact time. Hence he claims that even Īśvara is unable to disturb his thesis. Śaṅkara is surprisingly receptive to these statements and invites Pūrṇasamaya to come to him for refuge. The second opponent also wears the loincloth but looks like a ghost because his body is covered in [white] dust. He continually utters a *mantra* out loud, "*arhan arhan* ". In keeping with his frightening appearance, his position is more hostile than that of his predecessor. He argues that there is no need for ritual action. The *jīva* is naturally pure and is thus liberated when it escapes from the body. Ironically this is almost identical to the position of the so-called Buddhist who is described in Chapter 28 of the AŚV, which is translated above. When this second Jain opponent is defeated he becomes an attendant—or, more sarcastically, a merchant, according to the Calcutta edition—who is disposed to bringing goods such as rice to the guru each day. The well known mercantile propensities of the Jain community make them an easy target for satire.

Although they are cited among Śaṅkara's opponents, the Buddhists never really appear in the AŚV or CŚV. While there is every possibility that the two hagiographers had never encountered a Buddhist, it is difficult to explain why their doctrines—and moreover, Śaṅkara's own critiques of their views—are totally ignored. The Jains, on the other hand, are tangibly present in these hagiographies. They also figure in the ŚDV. Perhaps the intense rivalry between Jains and Śaivas in south India was not forgotten in the Śaṅkara tradition. The *Periyapurāṇa* describes some very grim events in the relations between Jains and Śaivas.[59] This may explain the peculiar

---

59 I have been able to consult only an abridged English rendering, *Periya Puranam: a Tamil classic on the great Saiva saints of south India*, by

account of Kumārila-Bhaṭṭa's victory over the Buddhists and Jains in the AŚV and CŚV. The contest was much more than a debate:

> He defeated countless Buddhists and Jains by means of different types of arguments in the various sciences. Having cut off their heads with axes, he threw them down into numerous wooden mortars and made a powder of them by whirling around a pestle. In this way he was fearlessly carrying out the destruction of those who held evil doctrines.[60]

Although both groups are lumped together in this passage, it was probably the Jains who were perceived as the real threat. Given that there may well have been no remnant of Buddhism in the milieu in which the hagiographies were composed, and because of the obvious similarities in some of the Buddhist and Jain doctrines, it is possible that our authors simply conflated the two. One thing is certain, however. The popular notion that Śaṅkara is responsible for the defeat of Buddhism cannot have come from the hagiographies.

Those who approach the hagiographies with the expectation of finding serious philosophical argument cannot but be disappointed. There is certainly nothing in our texts which approaches Mādhava's 14th century compendium, *Sarvadarśana*-

---

Sekkizhar, condensed English version by G.Vanmikanathan (Madras: Sri Ramakrishna Math, 1985), see esp. pp. 239-261, and 283-285. According to N. Mahalingam the work was composed in the 11th century (preface, p. v).

60 *bauddhān jainān asaṅkhyān aneka-vidyā-prasaṅga-prabhedhair nirjitya teṣāṃ śīrṣāṇi paraśubhiḥ chitvā bahuṣu ulūkhaleṣu nikṣipya kaṭa-bhramaṇaiś cūrṇīkṛtya, ity evaṃ duṣṭa-mata-dhvaṃsanam ācaran nirbhayo vartate iti*. AŚV p. 173. The CŚV has a similar but briefer description (16.20) : *vijitya saugatān sarvān...śirāṃsi chedayām āsa saugatānāṃ.*

saṃgraha.[61] If the hagiographers were aquainted with this work, they have not made use of it in their compositions. Neither have they chosen, except on two occasions, to reproduce or summarize the arguments which are readily available in Śaṅkara's own works. Clearly, the hagiographers did not aim to educate their audience in the variety of philosophical viewpoints which were prevalent in India.

Nevertheless, our texts are not without didactic intentions, and it is here that we can find much valuable material. The AŚV, which is the second most influential of the hagiographies in terms of the distribution of manuscripts, is primarily devoted to recounting Śaṅkara's debates. This text describes encounters with more than fifty opponents. The narrative is arranged in seventy-four brief chapters, which may have allowed for a daily reading. A deliberate episodic construction is also suggested by the recurrence of certain themes in almost each of the chapters. Since a translation of this work has yet to appear, I include here one of the more interesting chapters.

Refutation of Other Śaiva Doctrines: Anantānandagiri's *Śaṅkaravijaya*, ch. 5

[Page 31][62] When [Vidveṣavīra], the adherent of the Śiva sect which was instrumental [in promoting] the wearing of such things as the *liṅga* was refuted, [there arrived] some Ārādhyas, who were intent on worshipping at that sacred place (*pīṭha*). They were wearing the *prāṇa-liṅga*, and had the brand of the *liṅga* on the forehead. Their limbs were all adorned with shining

61 For a discussion of Sanskrit doxographies, see Wilhelm Halbfass, *India and Europe: an essay in understanding* (Albany: State University of New York, 1988), pp. 349-368.

62 The text is that of the Madras edition, edited by N. Veezhinathan (University of Madras, 1971).

ashes and *rudrākṣa-mālā* s numbering in the thousands were on their heads, necks and arms. They were people who ate indiscriminately [without regard for regulations concerning purity/impurity]. Having seen Śrī Śaṅkarācārya [the leaders of this group, i.e.], Pratipakṣacaṇḍabhairava, Vipakṣaśūla, Bhaktāgragaṇya, Paramatakālānala, and others said this: "Who are you, *saṃnyāsin* ? You have come here wearing a deceptive garb, as it were. Having [yourself] abandoned the sixfold Śaiva conduct which has all the Vedas as its authority, you caused Vidveṣavīra and others to fall away from their sect, and are [now] ready to depart."

[First opponent:] "Know me to be Pratipakṣacaṇḍabhairava, the leader of the excellent Ārādhya sect.[63] Do you think there is a deficiency in the Śaiva [doctrine]? The superiority of the Śaiva doctrine is shown by Brahmā's statement to Nārada: "The Vaiṣṇava is said to be better than the follower of Brahmā, oh best of *muni*s, and the Śaiva is greater than the Vaiṣṇava". The falling of a brahmin who has abandoned such a doctrine, which is the highest of the high, appears like the falling down of a man who has climbed to the top of a tree. For one who has gone to the top which is Śaiva—after taking hold of the branch, which is the Vaiṣṇava doctrine, from the base, which is the Brahmā [doctrine]—what is the point of falling from on high, as you have done?

If [your position is] that there is no superiority for Rudra, who is the presiding deity of our sect, [we reply that] his superiority is stated in the *śatarudra-mantra*s: "Salutations to you, Rudra, salutations to your wrath. Salutations to your arrows. Let there be salutations to your bow and to your arms".[64] [The poet-seer] began with the aim of eulogising

---

63 Literally, the sun for the lotus of the Ārādhya sect (*ārādhya-mata-padma - bhāskara*).

64 *Kṛṣṇa-yajurveda* 4.5.1.

Rudra, even though he is the personification of the Vedas. Because of his exceedingly terrifying form and because he is the highest of all, [the poet-seer] whose body was trembling, remained silent for a long time. For annulling his transgressions, he composed the eulogy, in which every quarter [of every stanza] is preceded with a salutation".

[The opponent continues with an analysis of this and another Vedic text:] "Oh Rudra, salutations to your wrath", i.e. anger, which is the cause of the dissolution of the fourteen worlds. [Page 32] Immediately after that [he says] "salutations to your arrow", which is the cause of dissolution: "oh Rudra, let there be salutations to your bow, and salutations to your arms", which bear the Pāśupata weapon. Having repeatedly saluted the god in each quarter [of each stanza], [the poet-seer] became one whose transgressions were annulled. "And he is the lord of immortality".[65] Rudra is the agent, its lord because of his being the highest of all. This [superiority] is because of the superiority of that aim of man known as liberation among the fourfold aims of man—*dharma, artha, kāma* and *mokṣa*—[which is stated] by the excellent *mantra* in the *Puruṣasūkta*. Moreover, in the case of the *Puruṣasūkta*, Nārāyaṇa is the poet-seer, and the Puruṣa is the deity. The Puruṣa is Rudra himself. It is established by numerous *śruti* [texts] such as, "Salutations to the thousand-eyed one, to the one who has a thousand bows",[66] that his is the state of possessing a thousand heads, a thousand eyes and a thousand feet. And [it is established] also by the *śruti*, "He who has eyes on all sides, mouths on all sides, arms on all sides and feet on all sides...."[67]

Now there is this consideration. [It may be argued that] the Vedic statement has Nārāyaṇa as its object because of his

65 *Taittirīyāraṇyaka* 3.12.

66 *Kṛṣṇa-yajurveda* 4.5.5.

67 *Śvetāśvatara Upaniṣad* 3.3.

identity with the one who has a thousand heads, on account of such texts as, "The god who has a thousand heads, whose eyes are everywhere, who is beneficent to all, is the universal Nārāyaṇa, the imperishable god, the highest abode".[68] But it is not so because it would be inconsistent with the conclusion. This is because when the introduction [of a topic] is weak, proceeding with the introduction in accordance with a [predetermined] conclusion has no validity in Mīmāṃsā. In the *Śvetāśvatara Upaniṣad*, the conclusion is made in this way after [first] mentioning the Puruṣa [in 3.8-9]:

> That which is beyond this world is without form and without ill. They who know thus, become immortal. But others experience only suffering. Therefore, the one who is the face, head and neck of all, who dwells in the heart of all beings, who is all-pervading, he is the Lord, the omnipresent, the auspicious one (*śiva*). (3.10-11)

[Page 33] In this way, because there is a unity of the introduction [of the topic] and the conclusion, there will be syntactical connection. This is because of the conformity in what has been explained in the text "the Puruṣa has a thousand heads" with the meaning of the text "he who is the face, head and neck of all". [Furthermore] it is Śiva alone who is explained by both these statements: "Hṛī and Lakṣmī are his wives, day and night are his sides".[69] Hṛī means Gaṅgā and Lakṣmī is Pārvatī. The state of being their husband is possible for Śiva. It is said in the *Skanda [-yāmala?]:*

---

68 *Mahānārāyaṇa Upaniṣad* 235-237 in the edition of Jean Varenne, *La Mahā Nārāyaṇa Upaniṣad* (2 vols., Publications de l'Institut de Civilisation Indienne, Paris: Éditions E. de Boccard, 1960) I, p. 62.

69 *Taittirīyāraṇyaka* 3.13.

> The Gaṅgā descended impetuously from the Himālayas onto Śiva's head. Sadā-Śiva, who was agitated by its burden, said to her:
>
> 'Having attained me, the highest Puruṣa,[70] who is the source of Brahmā, Viṣṇu and the rest, you should be modest. Do not be excessively loud'.
>
> She bowed to that great God out of devotion. Ever since then, she who is intertwined in his matted locks is said to be Hrī by the wise, on account of her modesty.

And it is said in the *Rudrayāmala*:

> Maheśvarī, the supreme *śakti*, is mounted on the platform of his lap. She who is all-enchanting, the dark one, is called Mahālakṣmī.
>
> In former times, crores of Lakṣmīs and Vāks [i.e., Sarasvatīs] were born from a spark of her *tejas*. Crores of Haris and Brahmās and other [gods] were born from the *tejas* of Śiva.
>
> They disappear again into their [respective] places following the dissolution.

[Page 34] Thus it is established that being the husband of Gaṅgā and Lakṣmī is the special property of Śiva. In the previous statement,"day and night", the neuter gender is a Vedic usage. The state of having day and night as his sides applies to Rudra alone. Because his right side has the appearance of pure crystal, it has the nature of day. The state of having a side which has the nature of night is also the special property of Rudra alone because of the dark colour of his left side, on account of its being shared by [his wife], the goddess [Pārvatī]. Thus, because the Vedic passage has Śiva as its focus and

---

70 This is a tentative translation of *puruṣa-śreṣṭha*.

because Śiva alone is the cause of the world, the superiority of that doctrine *vis à vis* all the others is established".

[Pratipakṣacaṇḍabhairava continues his argument, citing the *Atharvaśiropaniṣad* and the *Śivarahasya*. Now he presents his final points:] [Page 35] "On account of the authority of such texts, the state of being the universal Self and the creator of Hari, Brahmā and the other [gods] is possible [only] for Śiva. Because of wearing such things as ashes, *rudrākṣas* and the brand of the *liṅga*, by worshipping at the sacred site (*pīṭha*), and by recitation of the *Rudrādhyāya*, one is freed from all wrongdoing and attains union with Śiva. Thus it is excellent. And it is said in the *Śivagītā*:

> [Even] one who has committed theft, who has gone to the wife of his guru, who has consumed liquor, or who has committed the murder of a brahmin—[if] he is covered in ashes, residing in the cremation ground,[71] and reciting the *Rudrādhyāya*, he is freed from all wrongdoing.
>
> On account of the merit obtained from crores of births, devotion to Śiva arises. What is the use of many words about this for those whose devotion to Śiva is firm.
>
> Even he who is devoured by crores of great crimes, minor offences and the like, is freed..."

[The second opponent, Vipakṣaśūla now comes forward. He cites passages from the *Mahānārāyaṇa Upaniṣad* and the *Kaivalya Upaniṣad* which extol the greatness of Śiva. He then recites a long passage from the *Kālāgnirudra Upaniṣad* on the wearing of the triple lines of ashes (*tripuṇḍra*). He concludes his argument as follows:]

---

71 Lit., lying on a couch of ashes, (*bhasma-śayyāśayāna*).

[Page 38] "In the whole of the Upaniṣad it is explained that the *tripuṇḍra* has the nature of all the gods, the Vedas and time, and that it bestows liberation. Hence, no one is capable of describing the greatness of wearing ashes. Therefore, the wearing of the *tripuṇḍra* is to be done by men in all stages of life, beginning with studentship. In the same way, there are indeed authorities for the wearing of *rudrākṣas*, and the *liṅga*. It is said in the *Agastyasaṃhitā* that, 'From the wearing of *rudrākṣas* on the head, neck, ears and arms, a man becomes Nīlakaṇṭha [i.e., Śiva]. If he is a brahmin, he becomes higher than the highest'. Because of hearing that the benefit is only for one whose body is heated (*tapta-tanūḥ*), on the authority of texts such as, 'One whose body is not heated, who is raw, does not attain this',[72] the branding of the *liṅga* should certainly be done".

At that point, Śrī Śaṅkara said this: "the twice-born should not wear such things as the branded *liṅga* because there is no authority for it. Now the purport of the Vedic text, *atapta-tanūḥ*, should be described in this way. The 'heating' (*tāpa*) is not by means of fire, but is by way of austerity (*tapas*) alone. For the brahmin, austerity consists in such things as fasting in accordance with the phases of the moon (*kṛcchra-cāndrāyaṇa*). The term 'heating' is defined by this kind of *tapas* because it is stated he is emaciated by *kṛcchra-cāndrāyaṇa* s.[73] Moreover, [your interpretation] is contrary to the words of the *ṛṣis*. It is said in the *Bṛhannāradīya [Purāṇa]*:

---

72 *atapta-tanūr na tad āmo āsnute*, Rg Veda 9.83.1. Louis Renou translates this *pāda*, "Celui dont le corps n'a pas été échauffé, (l'être) cru, n'atteint pas à cet (effet du breuvage sômique), (Études Védiques et Pāṇinéennes [Paris: Éditions E. de Boccard, 1961], vol. 9, p. 29).

73 This follows Sāyaṇa's gloss of *atapta-tanūḥ*: "one whose body is not made to endure penance by means of such things as the vow to subsist only on water", *payo-vratādinā asaṃtapta-gātraḥ*.

> After seeing, oh king, one whose body is branded with the *liṅga* and one who is branded with the wheel (*cakra*), a bath must always be taken. Or else one should gaze at the sun.
>
> Let one not honour, even by merely speaking to, a degraded one who is endowed with the branded *liṅga*, or branded with the *cakra*, or devoted to heretical practice.
>
> [Page 39] He has the same aspect as a corpse and should be forsaken, like a *śūdra*. Even the offering to the wise (*kavya*) or sacrificial gift (*havya*) given to him would be useless.

On account of seeing him, even food which is consecrated by *mantra*s should be rejected. [Nevertheless] one may eat despite the presence[74] of a *śūdra*, [provided] he is without the brand of the *liṅga* or *cakra*.

> Even if one is intent on the prescriptions of the Vedas and devoted to the Vedānta, he would be immediately degraded merely because of [the presence of] the brand of the *liṅga* or *cakra*.

In the *Mārkaṇḍeya-purāṇa* [it is said:]

> And of old, there was a great discussion between Gāyatrī and the brahmins. From that time, the heretics and those who had Īśa as their deity were cursed by her.
>
> She said to them angrily: "In the *kali* [-*yuga*], you will thus become [people] who abandon the duty prescribed in the Vedas and who are who are totally devoted to *tāntrika* precepts.
>
> Hence when the *kali-yuga* comes, the vilest of the twice-born will become heretics, marked with such

74 Literally, 'the sight', *īkṣaṇa*.

> things as the *liṅga* and *cakra*, who have lost the purport of the Vedas.
>
> Deserving to be cursed [they will be] fallen away from the paths of *jñāna* and *karman*, afflicted by anger, lust and the rest; evil-natured, without truth and *dharma*.
>
> After thirty thousand years have elapsed in the *kali* [*-yuga*], they will perish and be completely destroyed. There is no doubt that afterwards [people] will again recall the purport of Advaita, and will be intent on truth and *dharma*.

Therefore, branding is not proper.

[You claim that] the purport of the Upaniṣad you cited is that liberation arises even from the worship of Rudra alone—who is endowed with properties such as being united with Umā—because [Brahman] is difficult to propitiate, on account of verses such as, "Brahman is *satyam, jñānam anantam*" and "[Brahman is] that from which words turns away, and which is not reached by the mind".[75] [Page 40] [You also claim that] because of his being the *avatāra* of the supreme Brahman, one should by all means wear ashes and *rudrākṣas* in order to gratify him. But our conclusion is that the carrying of the *liṅga*, trident and drum cannot be agreed to because it is without basis".

[Now a third opponent, Bhaktāgragaṇya, comes forward. He puts further arguments for the supremacy of Śiva based on the Vedic story of Rudra's destruction of the triple cities of the demons.[76] He emphasizes that through this deed, Rudra became the lord of the animals (*paśu-pati*), and then tries to connect his supremacy among the gods with this lordship. In relation to Śiva, the gods are seen as though *they* are domestic

---

75 *Taittirīya Upaniṣad* 2.1.1 and 2.4.5.

76 The story of the destruction of Tripura discussed here is from *Kṛṣṇa-yajurveda* 6.2.3.

animals:] [Page 41, line 14] "Therefore the marks of the *liṅga*, etc., of the destroyer of the cities are borne by the gods too. Because they are principally devotees of Śiva and because of being *paśus*, their wearing of the marks of Paśupati is indeed correct. Moreover, in this world it is seen that the worshippers and the one who is to be worshipped are such. Thus the wearing of his brands is certainly agreed to by us, as devotees of Śiva".

Śaṅkara replied: "The branding of such things as the *liṅga* on the part of the gods, who are devotees of Rudra, the one who brought about the destruction of the triple cities is not proven. Why? Because there is no authority for such a thing. There was certainly no branding of the *liṅga* on *munis* such as Nārada, even though they wore ashes, *rudrakṣas* and crystals. Hence the mark of the branded trident, *liṅga*, etc., is never found on the gods, *munis* and the like.

[Page 42] According to the statement of the *Kaivalya Upaniṣad*, "know it to be from faith, devotion, meditation and yoga", the branding of the *liṅga* is not a subsidiary of knowledge. It is proven that liberation is only to be brought about by knowledge on account of *śruti* texts such as,"there is no other path for going" and "it is to be obtained only by means of the mind".[77] Because the external branding is of no use for liberation which can be obtained [only] by a pure mind, and because of the [previously] mentioned censure of such things as the branded *liṅga*, it is established that the branding of the *liṅga* is certainly not correct.

Even in your sect, according to which there is the state of the part and the state of the whole [i.e., a relationship between the worshipper and the worshipped as in the case of the devotee], Bhaktāgragaṇya, and Śiva, even there the branding of the *liṅga* is meaningless because there is no difference between

---

77 *Śvetāśvatara Upaniṣad* 3.8 and *Kaṭha Upaniṣad* 4.11.

the two. Also, what was stated [regarding] the servant having the branding of the king is improper and untrue. The king has the mark of such things as the one [royal] umbrella. It is not for the servant. God bears special weapons such as the trident. You said that even the devotees should carry those weapons. If that is so, then for those who are carrying such things as the trident made of iron, there will only be a [heavy] burden. There is no other purpose [served], and they do not have the capacity to bring about an effect such as that [which the gods are capable of]. Moreover, the god [Śiva] has such marks as a blue throat and the ornament of serpents. You should wear those as well. For a mortal who dies simply because of the venom of the scorpion and the like, there is no capacity for consuming the *kālakūṭa* [poison, which Śiva drank]. How can one who runs away because of seeing a rope, which is mistaken for a serpent, be adorned with serpents? Therefore, give up your vile ideas, renounce the branding of the *liṅga* , offer your ritual actions, which are prescribed in the Vedas, to Bhagavat, [while] enquiring (*anusandhāna*) into the oneness of *jīva* and Īśa. When that knowledge is firm, the cessation of the primary ignorance which is the cause of the cycle of birth and death is engendered and you will be liberated upon the destruction of the subtle body. Thus instructed, Bhaktāgragaṇya and his followers, Paramatakālānala and the rest, bowed to Śrī Śaṅkarācārya, the ascetic and supreme guru. Together with their relatives, sons and friends, they abandoned the branding of the *liṅga*. Properly instructed, they became followers of pure Advaita.

In this chapter, Anantānandagiri strives for the verisimilitude which is typical of the accounts of debate in the hagiographies. The appearance of the Śaivas is depicted in detail, and they are assigned appropriately colourful names. Because the central issue here is sectarianism, the opponents' dress is all the more significant. The ashes on their bodies, the numerous strings of *rudrākṣa* beads, the *liṅga* which they carry, and above all, the brand of the *liṅga* on their foreheads are unmistakable indications of their sectarian affiliations. Śaṅkara's dress, on the other hand, is not explicitly described. Anantānandagiri does suggest, however, that his appearance is at least nominally Śaiva, by way of the opponents' criticism that he is wearing a deceptive garb (*māyā-veṣa-dhārin*). The implication is that he looks like a Śaiva yet does not behave accordingly. Śaṅkara's tacit approval of wearing ashes and *rudrākṣa* beads, in his statement "*munis* such as Nārada...wore ashes, *rudrākṣas* and crystals", is a further suggestion that he himself dresses in this way. It is only natural that Śaṅkara, whom the hagiogaphers construe as a manifestation of Śiva, should reflect an image appropriate to the deity. But Anantānandagiri's emphasis on dress lends a special sense of urgency to the debate between the followers of Śiva and his *avatāra*.

The Śaivas' fundamental premise is that Rudra-Śiva is the supreme deity. On this basis, they argue that union with the deity is achieved by worshipping him and through a process of identification which entails wearing the signs which are characteristic to Śiva. Unlike many of the other opponents in the AŚV, the Śaivas justify their position by appeal to the *śāstras*. Their acceptance of the authority of the *śāstras* marks them as brahmins, albeit fallen ones. For this reason, Anantānandagiri takes their argument seriously. Indeed he seems particularly partial to the Śaivas, and represents them in a most favourable light. Hence the debate consists primarily in the exegesis of sacred texts, ranging from the Vedas and Upaniṣads to the Purāṇas and (Tantric) Yāmalas.

Śaṅkara's reply focusses on a single issue: the propriety of wearing external insignia, in particular those which are branded into the flesh of the devotees. It is likely that such practice became widespread in India with the rise of devotional cults. Even Rāmānuja is said to have been branded on the shoulders with the emblems of the conch and wheel at the time of his initiation.[78] Śaṅkara's argument against branding is twofold. In the first place, he maintains that there is no valid scriptural authority for this. He makes the point with citations of some interesting passages which censure the practice of branding. Secondly, he claims that external trappings are no substitute for inner accomplishment. It is knowledge alone which brings about liberation, and to this end the mind should be purified. The argument is completed with a sarcastic and humorous touch. If the devotees wish to emulate Śiva they should try adorning themselves with serpents and consume the deadly poison he drank when the ocean was churned by the gods and demons.

In defeating the various sects, Śaṅkara aims not so much at their elimination as at the reformation of their doctrines. While the Śaivas are warned to give up their extreme practices, they are allowed to continue their devotional ways. Śaṅkara suggests they adopt a method which is, in fact, advocated in the *Bhagavadgītā*: carrying out one's duties as an offering of service to the Lord. But further justification is needed for the approval of the devotional, hence dualistic, cults. Anantānandagiri relies upon a common explanation for irregularities in the Hindu tradition: the exigencies of the *kali-yuga*. Men's capabilities have reached such a low ebb in this evil age that few are really capable of pure Advaita. Śaṅkara realises a compromise is necessary. In order to protect the traditional social order, he decides to allow a reorganization of the devotional sects. He

---

78 *Guruparamparāprabhāvam* [Teṉkaḷai version], cited in John Braisted Carman, *The theology of Rāmānuja. An essay in interreligious understanding* (New Haven: Yale University, 1974), p. 31.

dispatches Paramatakālānala, one of the defeated Śaivas who is by now a good disciple, to preach a reformed version of his personal creed. The Śaivas are the first of the six sects which are re-established under Śaṅkara's authority.[79] The disparate sects are thus united under the umbrella of the Vedic tradition, which is upheld by Advaita Vedānta. This is one of several legacies of Śaṅkara which are examined in the following chapter.

---

79 See AŚV chapters 67-72, CŚV 31.15-21 and GVK 3.36. The six sects comprise: Śaivas, Vaiṣṇavas, Sauras, Śāktas, Gāṇapatīyas and Kāpālikas. See Chapter Six for further discussion.

CHAPTER VI

Śaṅkara's legacy: the Advaita tradition, the *maṭhas* and the establishment of the sects

Śaṅkara's commentaries are undoubtedly his best known legacy, both to those within and outside of the Advaita tradition. For the followers of Advaita these works represent *the* authoritative exegesis of the fundamental Vedānta texts. So influential were his commentaries that even his opponents could scarcely afford to ignore them. It is not surprising, then, that the composition of these works figures largely in the hagiographies. Our sources tell us that the very first task to which Śaṅkara is entrusted by his guru, Govinda, is to write a commentary on the *Brahmasūtra*. The completed work is inspected and approved by Vyāsa himself, traditionally regarded as the author of the *Brahmasūtra*. The importance of this particular work is also underscored by the hagiographers in their portrayal of Śaṅkara's great concern with commissioning a disciple to compose a sub-commentary on his *Brahmasūtra-bhāṣya.*[1]

Of course, if Śaṅkara were just an author of texts, there would not be much of a story to tell. For the hagiographers, his

---

1 This sets the scene for an additional episode in four of our sources. Śaṅkara's first choice for the job, the learned Sureśvara, caused considerable jealousy among the other close disciples who resented the favour shown to this new-comer and former adversary. They prevailed upon Śaṅkara to reconsider his decision. Eventually he relented and asked Sanandana/Padmapāda to compose the *vārtikā* instead. Angered at being stripped of his appointment by the others' prevarications, Sureśvara uttered a curse to prevent the furtherance of the *vārtikā*. Later on in the narrative Sanandana/Padmapāda's manuscript is destroyed in a fire. See VŚV 7.28-71; RŚA 2.53-60; ŚDV chapter 13; GVK 2.57-60.

legacy goes well beyond the bundle of manuscripts he left behind. The hagiographies emphasize that Śaṅkara's primary mission is the restoration of the Vedic tradition, which will effect a corresponding renewal of harmony in the social sphere. In keeping with the nature of the great god of whom he is an *avatāra*, the work entails both destruction and regeneration. To begin with, he undertakes the composition of the commentaries which will re-establish the correct understanding of the *śāstra*s which underpin the tradition. From the firm ground of these expositions he must confront and defeat the prevailing forces hostile to Advaita Vedānta. His opponents are not simply vanquished, but are reformed so that they return to the Vedic path (if they are brahmins) and embrace Śaṅkara's teachings, or (if they are not), they can at least perform useful service to him and to his disciples. The successful culmination of his mission is marked by his ascension to the throne of omniscience. The enthronement, like his birth, is accompanied by auspicious celestial omens and signs of the earth's regeneration. In this way his life bears witness to the manifestation of the divine in the world of men. It is the promise of the continuity of this hierophany which constitutes his greatest legacy. However, the hagiographies also reveal a more tangible heritage. There are ample descriptions of Śaṅkara's efforts in training the disciples who will continue his teaching work and perpetuate his name.

The use of royal imagery in presenting Śaṅkara as the reigning authority on sacred tradition makes the question of his succession seem almost inevitable. One would expect this to have been an important issue for the hagiographers. Yet only three of our texts, the AŚV, CŚV and GVK, are explicit in stating Śaṅkara's intentions about perpetuating his lineage. According to these sources, he founded monastic institutions (*maṭha*s) in which his principal disciples were installed as leaders. The VŚV, which so influenced later hagiographers, contains what is at best an oblique reference to the dissemination of Śaṅkara's teachings and the continuity of his lineage. Vyāsācala metaphorically describes Śaṅkara as a great banyan tree with his disciples as four main trunks and their disciples as the branches.[2] The GŚC, RŚA and TŚA do not mention the issue of succession, nor do they speak of the establishment of monastic centres.[3]

The Founding of the *Maṭhas*

The widely distributed ŚDV by Mādhava also has surprisingly little to say on this subject. In the first place we learn simply that Śaṅkara set up temples in Sringerī (i.e., Ṛṣyaśṛṅga; Śṛṅgerī) and elsewhere. After defeating Sarasvatī in debate, he requests that she, "abide in sacred sites such as Ṛṣyaśṛṅga, where she will be worshipped as [the goddess] Śāradā, in places which have been established by us".[4] He obtains Sarasvatī's assent and eventually,

> Set up a temple there in which all the arts and crafts were manifest and which equalled the palace of Indra. He initiated the worship of the deity who bears the name of Śāradā and is worshipped even by Brahmā and the other [gods]. She is maintaining the

---

2 VŚV 12.83.

3 The available portion of the TŚA is similarly silent about the question of succession and the foundation of *maṭhas*. These details would, of course, be expected in the latter part of the work, if at all, and this is no longer extant. However, in this instance I am inclined to speculate that Tirumala-Dīkṣita probably said little, if anything, about the *maṭhas*. The fact that Mādhava has relied so heavily on the TŚA in composing the ŚDV (and assuming that he had the entire MS. before him), suggests that the TŚA is very unlikely to contain more on the subject than what we find in the ŚDV.

4 *tasmād asmat-kalpiteṣvarcyamānā sthāneṣu tvaṃ śāradākhyā diśantī iṣṭān arthān ṛṣyaśṛṅgādikeṣu kṣetreṣvāssva*...ŚDV 10.71.

> promise she made. Even today she is radiant, dwelling in the town of Śṛṅgerī and granting the boons which [men] desire.[5]

The establishment of temples is certainly indicative of Śaṅkara's efforts in regenerating sacred sites, and the promise he secures from the goddess of learning will be a boon to the continuity of traditional knowledge. But the ŚDV provides us with just a single hint that Śaṅkara founded monastic institutions which would continue his work:

> He installed certain [of his disciples] in *āśrama*s such as the one at Ṛṣyaśṛṅga, for [ensuring] the greatness of his creed, but this was not [done] out of pride.[6]

While this does suggest that some disciples were expected to carry on the Advaita Vedānta tradition of their teacher, there is no indication of how they will do this, nor is it clear which disciples will be in a position of authority. It is also doubtful how the term *āśrama* in this passage should be understood.[7] *Āśrama* here may be synonymous with *maṭha*, especially if we construe the latter in its narrow sense, i.e., the residence of an ascetic. In its wider sense, and the way in which it is generally understood at present, the term *maṭha* designates a teaching and residential institution in which a religious leader trains his students.[8] This definition could, by extension, also

---

[5] *prakalpya tatrendra-vimāna-kalpaṃ prāsādam āviṣkṛta-sarva-śilpam / pravartayām āsa sa devatāyāḥ pūjām ajādyair api pūjitāyāḥ // yā śāradety abhidhāṃ vahantī kṛtāṃ pratijñāṃ pratipālayantī / adyāpi śṛṅgerī-pure vasantī pradyotate 'bhīṣṭa-varān diśantī //* ŚDV 12.68-69.

[6] *nija-mata-gurutāyai no punar māna-hetoḥ katicana viniveṣyātharṣyaśṛṅgāśramādau* , ŚDV 16.93.

[7] Neither of the two commentators on the AŚV discuss this term, nor do they specify where the other centres are.

[8] For discussion see P. V. Kane *History of Dharmaśāstra* (2nd ed., Poona, 1974), vol 2, part 2, pp. 906-907. Kane makes the important observation that

be applied to the term *āśrama*. But the fact that the hagiographers who do speak with certainty about the foundation of monastic centres invariably use the term *maṭha*, makes me hesitant to read too much into Mādhava's statement.

The most obvious explanation for the silence in five of our texts about the *maṭhas* is that during the period in which they were composed the Śaṅkara institutions did not have the prominence they now enjoy.[9] As for the question of succession, this may not have seemed an essential topic to the hagiographers because the strong presence of the disciples in the narrative was itself sufficient to suggest that the continuity of the lineage was ensured. It may also be that the hagiographers did not wish to set Śaṅkara apart from the illustrious lineage with which he was identified. While his place in an ancient line of teachers—going back to Vyāsa or even to Śiva[10]—could only serve to underscore his legitimacy as a claimant to the mantle of spiritual authority, the notion of a separate Śaṅkara lineage might have had precisely the opposite effect. It is very likely that the dissemination of the hagiographies coincided with the rise of the *maṭhas*. Unfortunately the precise chronology of this relationship will have to remain largely undefined since the dates of some of our texts are uncertain and so little is known of the early history of the *maṭhas*. Nevertheless there are some conclusions which can be drawn from the three texts that refer directly to the *maṭhas*.

---

introduction of *maṭhas* in the Hindu tradition was probably inspired by Buddhist *vihāras*.

9 There is no mention of the *maṭhas* in the VŚV, RŚA, GŚC, TŚA and ŚDV. For a discussion on the dates of these texts see Chapter One.

10 See Chapter Three.

The oldest of these works is the AŚV.[11] Anantānandagiri tells us that after installing Sarasvatī in Sringerī, Śaṅkara founded a monastic institution there:

> In that place he established his own *maṭha*. He established a seat of learning and established the Bhāratī tradition among his disciples....The Paramaguru remained there in that seat of learning for twelve years, and imparted the true teaching on the knowledge of pure non-duality to many students. Then he made a particular disciple, named Padmapāda [or Sureśvara, according to the Calcutta editions], the superintendent of the seat...and departed.[12]

After leaving Sringerī, Śaṅkara visits various pilgrim sites and then travels to Kānchipuram (i.e., Kāñcīpura). Here he constructs two sister cities, consecrates a temple to the goddess Kāmākṣī, instals a *śrī-cakra* and continues to impart teachings on the way of liberation. In summing up his achievements, Anantānandagiri again refers to Śaṅkara's direct legacy. Although the substance of the text is the same in both recensions of the AŚV, there is a significant variant in the particulars. The Calcutta editions leave us in some doubt as to whether any other centres were established in addition to the one at Sringerī:

> He established the lineage of his disciples, which would last until the end of the eon, in the locality

---

11 See Chapter One.

12 *nija-maṭhaṃ kṛtvā tatra vidyā-pīṭha-nirmāṇam kṛtvā bhāratī-saṃpradāyaṃ nija-śiṣyeṣu cakāra...tatraiva paramaguruḥ dvādaśābda-kālaṃ vidyā-pīṭhe sthitvā bahu-śiṣyebhyaḥ śuddhādvaita-vidyāyāḥ samyag-upadeśaṃ krtvā tad anantaraṃ padmapādākhyaṃ kañcicchiṣyaṃ pīṭhādhyakṣaṃ krtvā...niścakrāma*, AŚV pp. 182-184.

> of Śṛṅgagiri. He also gave the teaching on the path of liberation to all his disciples.[13]

But the Madras edition clearly states that Śaṅkara founded institutions in several places, of which Kānchipuram is singled out for special mention:

> He established the lineage of his disciples, which would last until the end of the eon, in various cities, the first of which was the seat of learning (*vidyā-pīṭha*) at Kāñcī...[14]

This discrepancy is one of the many bones of contention in the conflict which has arisen between the Śaṅkara *maṭhas*. The history of the present-day dispute surrounding Śaṅkara's legacy is a complex problem which will be discussed separately below.

The CŚV is still more elaborate in its portayal of the founding of the monastic institutions. Indeed Cidvilāsa is probably the first hagiographer to describe the establishment of four *maṭhas*.[15] As in the AŚV, the centre at Sringerī is set up in conjunction with the installation of Sarasvatī. But where Anantānandagiri reserves his attention for the glorification of Kānchipuram, the CŚV devotes three chapters to an excursus on

---

13 *...nija-śiṣya-paramparāṃ ākalpaṃ śṛṅgagiri-sthāna-sthāṃ krtvā sakala-śiṣyebhyo mokṣa-mārgopadeśaṃ ca kalpayitvā*, Bibliotheca Indica edition (1868) p. 264; 1881 Calcutta edition, p. 203. I have omitted the compound qualifying the lineage, *tadīya-virodhāṅgīkāra-samarthāṃ*, because of the difficulty in the reading. As it stands the compound may be understood as 'who were capable of agreeing to contradict the [bad tendencies] of those [brahmins whom he had converted to Advaita]. The term *tadīya* probably refers back to the brahmins mentioned in the preceding passage: *śuddhādvaita-vidyā-niṣṭhān...brāhmaṇādīn kṛtvā* . In the Madras edition there is a different reading: (*śuddhādvaita-niṣṭhā-gariṣṭhān...brāhmaṇādīn kṛtvā*) *...tadīya-sevāṅgīkāra-samarthāṃ*, i.e., who were fit to accept the service of those [brahmins whom he had converted to Advaita].

14 *...nija-śiṣya-paramparāṃ ākalpaṃ kāñcī-pīṭhādi-tat-tat-paṭṭaṇa-sthāyinīṃ kṛtvā*, AŚV (Madras ed.), pp. 194-195.

15 See Chapter One.

the beauty and sanctity of Sringerī. This lyrical prelude sets the mood for Cidvilāsa's account of the first *maṭha* Śaṅkara is to found:

> There, in the proximity of the goddess of speech, the best of preceptors constructed the Śrī *maṭha*, beautified with heavenly *gopuras* and towers, and he established a seat of learning. He installed on that seat the one who was foremost among his four [disciples], the eloquent Sureśācārya, best in the knowledge of Brahman.[16]

In his account of the other monastic centres, Cidvilāsa emphasizes their connection with the four quarters, Purī in the east, Dwārkā (i.e., Dvārakā) in the west and Badarī in the north:

> In the eastern quarter...in the proximity of the Jagannātha [temple] he established a *maṭha* and made the excellent Padmapādācārya the head of the *maṭha*.[17] In the western quarter he constructed a *maṭha* and made [his disciple] Hastāmalaka its superintendent.[18] ....There in the northern quarter he had a heavenly *maṭha* built. He forcibly made the excellent Toṭakācārya, who followed him like a shadow, the superintendent of the *maṭha* [although the disciple] did not desire it. With his head bowed down out of humility [Toṭaka] bore the burden of

---

16 *...śrīmān deśika-puṅgavaḥ / vāgdevyāḥ savidhe divyaṃ gopurāṭṭāla-śobhitam // śrī-maṭhaṃ tatra nirmāya vidyā-pīṭham acīkḷpat / caturṣvekaṃ vāvadūkaṃ sureśācāryam agrimam // brahma-vidyā-variṣṭhaṃ taṃ tat-pīṭhe viniveśya saḥ /* CŚV 24.31-33a.

17 *aindryāṃ kakubhi...jagannāthasya cābhyarṇaṃ maṭham ekam acīkḷpat / padmapādācārya-varyaṃ tan-maṭhādhīśam ācarat //*CŚV 30.10-11.

18 *paścimasyāṃ* [sic] *harityeṣa maṭham ekaṃ vinirmame / hastāmalaka-nāmānaṃ tad adhyakṣaṃ tatāna saḥ/* CŚV 31.5b-6a.

> duties—other than that [of service to the guru]—the first of which was to the *maṭha*.[19]

While Sringerī is presented as the most important of the four centres, it does not fit quite as neatly into the geographical schema as do the other three.[20] Nevertheless the linking of the four cardinal points of the subcontinent with the four principal disciples makes for a powerful image of the perpetuation of Śaṅkara's reign.

The GVK is the only one of the eight hagiographies known to be composed at the behest of an incumbent of a Śaṅkara institution. Hence it can be reasonably assumed that Lakṣmaṇa-Śāstrī's version of the life story (c. 1740) represents the traditions which were current in the Sringerī *maṭha* where his services were engaged.[21] In his description of the founding of the monastic centres, we find the same geographical frame of reference as in the CŚV. Lakṣmaṇa-Śāstrī's account of the succession to Śaṅkara's spiritual domain makes the royal analogy even more transparent:

> ...The respected Śaṅkara said to the *muni* Padmapāda, "You will be the one who sets in motion our tradition in the eastern quarter and the guru of all the people [who live there]". Because of that command, the respected yogi Padmapāda made his abode in the Jagannātha *maṭha*. The ascetic Sureśvarācārya was previously [established] in Śṛṅgapurī by order [of Śaṅkara]. The guru appointed the excellent ascetic Hastāmalaka to the western quarter. Having established a beautiful *maṭha*, that excellent ascetic dwelt in Dvārakā in accordance

---

19 *kauberyāṃ diśi tatraikaṃ maṭhaṃ divyaṃ akārayat / tan-maṭhe toṭakācārya - varyaṃ chāyānuvartinam// anicchantaṃ maṭhādyanyat-pāda-sevā-dhuran-dharaṃ / balāt kṛtvā maṭhādhyakṣaṃ praśrayāvanatānanam//* CŚV 31.28-29.

20 Refer to the map on p. 145.

21 See Chapter One.

> with the dictate of his guru. Having commanded Toṭakācārya [to establish himself] in the northern quarter, [Śaṅkara] the yogi was delighted. In accordance with his words [Toṭaka] dwelt in the Jyotir *maṭha* in proximity to the forest of Badarī.[22]

The fact that virtually identical versions of this episode appear in the two texts suggests that Lakṣmaṇa-Śāstrī probably relied on the CŚV. In any case, it is certain that both texts reflect the oral tradition at Sringerī. For it is only in these two texts that we find the episode in which Śaṅkara perceives an auspicious omen—a serpent shielding a frog from the hot sun on the river bank—which convinces him that Sringerī is an ideal place to establish a centre of learning.

Although the existence of a *maṭha* at Sringerī is first described in the AŚV, the notion that there were four monastic centres was obviously not current when this text was composed. Now the monastic centre at Sringerī is known from inscriptions to date (at least) from 1346 A.D.[23] Since there is no real basis on which to date the VŚV, we must allow for the possibility that this text could predate the Sringerī *maṭha*. But chronology alone will not explain the absence of the *maṭhas* from the other hagiographies. The RŚA and GŚC were both

---

22 *...śaṅkarāryaḥ śrī padmapādam munim anvabhāṇīt / aindryāṃ diśi tvaṃ nija-saṃpradāya-pravartako loka-gurur bhaveti // tad-ājñayā padmapādārya-yogī cakre jagannātha-maṭhe nivāsam / sureśvarācārya-yatiḥ puraiva tacchāsanād asti sa śṛṅgapuryāṃ // guruḥ sa hastāmalakaṃ yatīndraṃ nyayūyujat paścima-dig - vibhāge / sa dvārakāyāṃ nyavasad yatīndro guror girā cāru maṭhaṃ vidhāpya // taṃ toṭakācāryam athottarasyām ājñāpya diśyāpa mudaṃ sa yogī / sa copakaṇṭhaṃ badarī-vanasya jyotir-maṭhe tad vacanād avātsīt //* GVK 3.59-62.

23 See the important discussion on the epigraphy of Vijayanagara and Sringerī in Hermann Kulke, "Mahārājas, mahants and historians: reflections on the historiography of early Vijayanagara and Sringeri, in *Vijayanagara—city and empire. New currents of research*, ed. A. L. Dallipiccola (2 vols., Wiesbaden: Franz Steiner Verlag, 1985), vol I, pp. 120-143.

composed in about 1650, some three hundred years *after* the establishment of the Sringerī *maṭha.* While it is possible that the reputation of Sringerī was not very extensive in 1650, it does seem unlikely that the great Vidyāraṇya, so intimately associated with this centre of learning, remained unknown to Vedāntins in Tamil Nadu and Kerala at this time . What seems far more likely is that Sringerī was known then, but not as a centre founded by Śaṅkara himself.

Here I must inject a note of caution. First of all, in the absence of adequate historical records my discussion of the *maṭhas* remains necessarily conjectural. Secondly, I must state that it is not my intention to denigrate the Śaṅkara *maṭhas* in any way.[24] However, I would suggest that on the basis of the hagiographies—and only on the evidence of these texts—the assumption that Śaṅkara founded monastic centres seems questionable. While I admit the notion that they were established by Śaṅkara would certainly lend further prestige to the *maṭhas*, I do not believe that a contrary claim need lessen their authority. The monastic centres are in any case an integral part of the Śaṅkara tradition and were founded in the spirit of that tradition. The *maṭhas* have provided the stong institutional base which is largely responsible for the successful preservation and propagation of the Advaita *sampradāya.* Finally, I would add that the historical evidence for the connection between Śaṅkara and the *maṭhas* (or the lack of it) is probably far less significant than what is firmly believed in the tradition.

---

[24] I have the utmost respect for the *maṭhas* and for their lineage of *ācārya* s. It was my great privilege to have met three of the incumbent Śaṅkarācāryas, all of whom impressed me as eminently worthy representatives of their tradition. It is my hope that these revered leaders and their followers will not see my discussion as being disrespectful. See the interviews with the Śaṅkarācāryas in Appendix A.

Initially, the Sringerī *maṭha* was perhaps best known as the residence of Vidyāraṇya and of his guru, Vidyātīrtha/Vidyāśaṅkara, who may well have established this seat of learning.[25] The impressive memorial to him which dominates the complex at Sringerī, the Vidyāśaṅkara temple dating from 1357 A.D.,[26] bears witness to the esteem in which the great guru was held. In the opening verse of the ŚDV, Mādhava makes his obeisance to this same Vidyātīrtha.[27] The fame of his pupil Vidyāraṇya would have itself been sufficient to establish the reputation of Sringerī as a centre of learning, even if Śaṅkara had not visited the town. The only certain conclusion we can draw from the fact that the VŚV, GŚC and RŚA make no mention of Sringerī is that the authors of these three works did not count this religious centre in their preferred list of pilgrimage sites. However it would also seem that while at least one Advaita *maṭha* had long been flourishing, the idea that Śaṅkara himself had founded monastic centres was not very widespread prior to 1650.[28] Up until this time, the Advaita institutions were probably identified not with Śaṅkara but with their respective founders or with a very prominent incumbent of the particular *maṭha*.

---

25 Hermann Kulke argues persuasively that Vidyātīrtha was, in fact, the founder of the Sringerī *maṭha*, "Mahārājas Mahants and historians", pp. 134 - 136. See Chapter Seven for further discussion.

26 *Gazetteer of India. Karnataka State Gazetteer. Chikmagalur District* (Bangalore, 1981), p. 625.

27 This should not be understood as a salutation to the author's own guru, as the commentators on the ŚDV wrongly suggest, since the ŚDV cannot be the composition of Mādhava-Vidyāraṇya (see Chapter One). It is more likely to be a tribute to the guru of the most prominent Advaitin of his day, Vidyāraṇya, in the company of whose successors the author of the ŚDV probably moved.

28 The first inscription which, to my knowledge, specifically identifies Śaṅkara as the founder of a *maṭha* is dated 1652. It records a grant to the Śṛṅgerī *"dharma-pīṭha"* established by Śaṅkarācārya; *Epigrapha Carnatica*, vol. VI, no. 11, cited in P. V. Kane, *History of Dharmaśāstra*, II. 2. p. 907.

The striking disparity in what our sources say concerning the *maṭhas* reflects the existence of different textual traditions. It appears that the hagiographies were composed within two entirely distinct groups, as is shown in the following diagram:

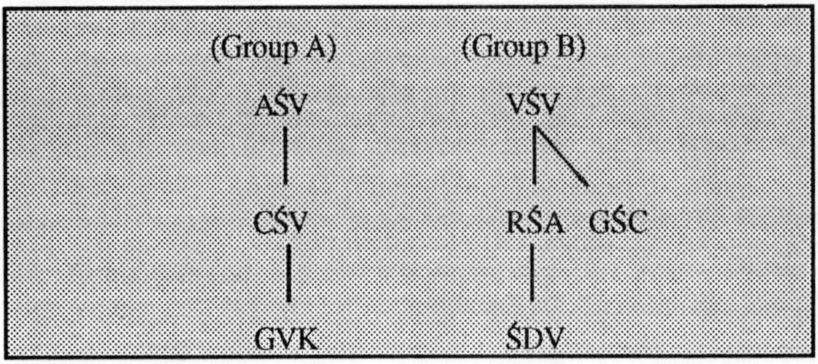

For the sake of clarity, the relationships within each group have been simplified here.[29] All the works in group A describe the foundation of a *maṭha* at Sringerī. The CŚV and GVK elaborate on the establishment of four centres in the four quarters of the subcontinent. In group B there is no mention of *maṭhas*, and it is only in the ŚDV that Śaṅkara is said to visit Sringerī. The ŚDV describes the temple he set up there but is unclear as to whether he actually established monastic institutions or simply dispatched some of his disciples to existing religious centres.[30]

---

29 For details see the table on page 24 The TŚA has been omitted from this simplified table. The work seems to stand by itself, except for its profound influence on the ŚDV. See Chapter One.

30 Dhanapatisūri's commentary on ŚDV 16.93 does not elaborate on the nature or location of the *āśramas* which Śaṅkara is said to have set up. However, in his comment on ŚDV 12.68, which describes the building of a temple at Sringerī, he adds the following: "There he established a *maṭha*, a seat of learning, and the Bhāratī tradition among his disciples...He made a particular disciple named Sureśvara the superintendent of the seat". Although he does not identify his source, it is clear that these are the exact words found

The writers in group B appear to be unaware of the group A texts. The ŚDV alone seems to be familiar with a few of the episodes unique to the group A texts, but these may have been learned from oral tradition.[31]

It is certain that two of the group A texts, the CŚV and GVK, were composed on the basis of traditions current in the Sringerī *maṭha*. As for the AŚV, Anantānandagiri speaks at such length about the institutions Śaṅkara set up at Kānchipuram that it is likely he was affiliated with one of these organizations. The emphasis on institution building in the group A texts stands in strong contrast to the group B texts, which reveal no institutional affiliations on the part of their authors. Hence the division in the two groups of texts probably reflects the differing perspectives of those within an official organization from those who were independent of any institution. We certainly find evidence of such a division today. Among those who count themselves as followers of Śaṅkara, there are many who are not associated with any of the flourishing Śaṅkara organizations. It should also be mentioned that the institutionally oriented hagiographers appear to have had direct experience only with the centres at Sringerī and

---

in the AŚV (The the fact that Sureśvara is named tallies with the Calcutta edition). However it is possible that Dhanapatisūri may have been using the no longer extant PrŚV, which is a summary of the AŚV. He quotes this work elsewhere on several occasions. For a detailed discussion of the PrŚV see Appendix B.

31 See the table of incidents in Chapter Two. The table shows clearly that the ŚDV lacks several incidents found in the group A texts. Mādhava includes only three incidents (nos. 24, 36 and 40) which occur in the Group A texts. The ŚDV also features the initial angry exchange between Śaṅkara and Maṇḍana/Viśvarūpa as in the AŚV and CŚV, but Mādhava may have learned of this through oral tradition as well. Of the Group A texts, it is only the GVK which knows of the group B texts, i.e., the VŚV and RŚA. However this does not affect the GVK's description of the *maṭha*s.

Kānchipuram. The reference to the other *maṭhas* in the north, east and west (at Badarī, Purī and Dwārkā, respectively), which we find in the CŚV and GVK, merely acknowledge the existence of these centres. These three *maṭhas*, along with whatever other Śaṅkara institutions may have existed during the period in which our sources were composed, must have lacked the services of a hagiographer.

However it would be misleading to imply that the hagiographers had exclusive rights to the Śaṅkara life story. Even though it fails to appear in the most widely distributed of the hagiographies, the ŚDV, the story of Śaṅkara's founding four *maṭhas* has gained currency throughout the subcontinent and has been accepted even in courts of law.[32] The limited distribution of CŚV and GVK manuscripts, the only texts which mention the establishment of the four *maṭhas*, suggests that oral tradition was responsible for popularizing this belief.[33] But it is difficult to say much more about this. Unlike our texts which are amenable to various kinds of scrutiny, such oral tradition often proves an elusive object of study, especially when the field of research extends throughout the whole of India.

The Bequest of a Śiva *Liṅga*

Popular tradition attributes two further legacies to Śaṅkara. As in the case of the *maṭhas*, these are described only in the group

---

32 In *Madhusudan Parvat v. Shree Madhav Teerth* (Indian Law Reports, 1909, Bom. 278), the High Court at Bombay stated in its ruling, "It is not disputed that the religious reformer Shankar, about the 8th century A.D., established four Maths or monasteries for Sanyasis...in the North, South, East and West of India". See also, Jogendra Chunder Ghosh, *The principles of Hindu law* (3d ed., 2 vols. Calcutta: S. C. Audy, 1917), I. 910.

33 See the details in the table on p. 24.

A texts. The first of these concerns a bequest from Śaṅkara to his immediate successor. The second is rather more complex as it involves an apparent contradiction: the establishment of six devotional sects under the aegis of Advaita Vedānta, the bastion of non-duality. Śaṅkara's appointment to this task of six disciples—previously renowned as his leading sectarian opponents—will require special consideration.

There are two separate versions of the episode in which Śaṅkara makes a material bequest to his successor, Sureśvara. These reflect the same relationship within the group A texts which is seen in the accounts of the *maṭhas*. The CŚV and GVK agree with each other but differ from the AŚV. More specifically, the AŚV speaks of five crystal *liṅgas* which Śaṅkara receives from Śiva. While the CŚV and GVK tell of a jewel encrusted Gaṇeśa figure (*ratna-garbha-gaṇapati*) and a special Śiva *liṅga*, the *candramaulīśvara*. The account of the incident in the AŚV is problematical in that only the Madras edition of the text mentions the bestowing of the five *liṅgas*.[34] The setting of the episode is Kailāsa:

> "Parameśvara manifested five crystal *liṅgas* right before the Paramaguru....[Śaṅkara] established the one known as the *mukti-liṅga* at Kedāra and enjoined the worshippers in that place to worship it....He reached Nīlakaṇṭha [in Nepal] and there established the one known as the *vara-liṅga*.[35]

---

[34] From the information supplied in the preface by N. Veezhinathan, the editor of the Madras edition, it appears that he accepted this reading on the basis of the six MSS. which include the episode, as opposed to ten MSS. and the Calcutta edition which say nothing about the *liṅgas*. He argues that his preferred reading is substantiated by two other texts, the *Mārkaṇḍeyasaṃhitā* and the *Śivarahasya*, both of which mention the incident in their brief accounts of Śaṅkara's life.

[35] *paramaguror agrataḥ parameśvaraḥ pañca sphāṭika-liṅgāni prakāśayām āsa....kedāra-kṣetre ekaṃ mukti-liṅgākhyaṃ pratiṣṭhāpya tat-kṣetra-pūjakān*

He installs the third one, the *bhoga-liṅga*, at Sringerī.[36] It is the fourth, the *yoga-liṅga*, which he gives to Sureśvara at Kānchipuram, admonishing him to worship it, and the fifth one, the *mokṣa-liṅga*, is also entrusted to him, on the understanding that he must send it to Chidambaram.[37] The question of whether this episode represents an interpolation in the text is no doubt crucial to the dispute between the *maṭhas*, which is discussed separately below. But I will leave this problem to the disputants. What strikes me as a more significant issue is that a material bequest from Śaṅkara came to be seen, at some stage, as essential to the authority of his successors.

The connection between the bequest and the continuity of the lineage is made quite explicit in the CŚV:

> [Śaṅkara's] teacher gave him the *candramaulīśa [liṅga]* and a jewel encrusted Gaṇeśa which had come from Śiva [and was passed on through the lineage] here, in succession.[38]....He gave [Sureśvara] the supreme *candramaulīśvara* and the jewel encrusted Gaṇeśa which had come, in succession, from Śiva, saying, "You must worship them".[39]

---

pūjārthaṃ niyojayām āsa....nīlakaṇṭha-kṣetraṃ prāpya...paramaguruḥ vara-nāmakaṃ liṅgaṃ pratiṣṭhāpya ... AŚV p. 172. The Calcutta edition says he went to the *amara-liṅga* (i.e. Amaranātha in Kāshmīr), not to Kailāsa, and makes no mention of his receiving any *liṅgas* from Śiva.

36 AŚV (Madras ed. only) p. 184.

37 AŚV (Madras ed. only), pp. 189; 208. According to the anonymous booklet sold at the Chidambaram temple, the crystal *liṅga*, known as the *candramaulīśvara*, which is worshipped in the *sanctum sanctorum* was given to the hereditary priests of the temple, the Dīkṣitars, by Naṭarāja-Śiva.

38 *....candra-maulīśaṃ ratna-garbhaṃ gaṇādhipaṃ / śivāt kramād ihāyātaṃ dadau tasmai sa deśikaḥ*, CŚV 9.53.

39 *śivāt kramāt samāyātaṃ candra-maulīśvaraṃ paraṃ / ratna-garbhaṃ gaṇapatiṃ pūjayeti dadau...*, CŚV 24.37b-38a.

Here the authority of the lineage is concretized in both a spiritual and a material form. The ultimate source of authority must remain supramundane, if it is to endure the vicissitudes of worldly life. But the tangibility of the sacred insignia of the lineage makes it possible for the incumbent (and his successor) to demonstrate the validity of his claim to the mantle of authority. This concern is especially relevant within the context of a monastic centre, where the question of the right to succession is imperative to the continuity and the unity of the institution. In this light it is not surprising that Śaṅkara's material legacy should feature only in those hagiographies which are closely linked to an official organization. The GVK presents essentially the same episode as is found in the CŚV, with the exception that Śiva is not the original benefactor:

> [Śaṅkara] who had been given the eminent *candramaulīśvara liṅga* and a Gaṇeśa encrusted with genuine jewels by a great *siddha*, gave them to Viśvarūpa [=Sureśvara] and told him to worship them for a long time.[40]

The similarity in the accounts of Śaṅkara's bequest in the two hagiographies composed along the lines of Sringerī traditions, highlights the importance of this material legacy for the *maṭha*. Even today the worship of the *candramaulīśvara liṅga* is a conspicuous part of the ritual life in the Sringerī *maṭha*. The heads of Dwārkā and Kānchipuram *maṭha*s also possess a *candramaulīśvara liṅga* which they worship daily.[41]

---

40 *śrī-candra-maulīśvara-liṅgaṃ asmai sad-ratna-garbhaṃ gaṇanāyakaṃ ca / sa viśvarūpāya susiddha-dattaṃ dattvā nyagādīc ciram arcayeti //* GVK 3.33.

41 The Sringerī, Kānchipuram and Dwārkā *maṭha*s all claim that Sureśvara presided over their centres. This accounts for the presence of a *candramaulīśvara liṅga* in each of the three. The conflicting claims about Sureśvara are another contributing factor in the dispute between the *maṭhas*, discussed below.

It is difficult to draw any definite conclusions about Lakṣmaṇa-Śāstrī's intentions in identifying a *siddha* as the donor of the *liṅga* and the Gaṇeśa figure. However, it will be worthwhile to make a small digression here in order to consider the significance of the appearance of a *siddha* in the Śaṅkara tradition. While the *siddha* cults remain something of a mystery to scholars, it is clear that they are not a part of mainstream brahmin culture, which defines itself in terms of its links with the Vedas. Hence they are rather unlikely company for such an orthodox figure as Śaṅkara. Along with the relatively well known cult of the Nāthas who count Gorakhnātha as the foremost of 84 *siddhas*,[42] there is also a strong tradition of Tamil *siddhas*.[43] But the *siddha* who gives the *liṅga* and Gaṇeśa to Śaṅkara comes from yet another cult.

In his own commentary to the GVK, Lakṣmaṇa-Śāstrī explains that the *siddha* mentioned in the text is in fact Revaṇasiddha, a great yogi, but there is no further elaboration. Now Revaṇasiddha is renowned as one of the five founding *ācāryas* of the Vīraśaiva or Liṅgāyata tradition. Yet very little is known of Revaṇasiddha,[44] or the other legendary *ācāryas*. Each of the five is said to have been born from a *liṅga*, and what is more, each is believed to have founded a *maṭha* in different parts

---

42 See George W. Briggs, *Gorakhnāth and the Kānphaṭa Yogīs* (Calcutta: YMCA Publishing House, 1938), and Mircea Eliade, *Yoga: immortality and freedom* (Princeton: Princeton University Press, 1969), pp. 301-321.

43 See Kamil V. Zvelebil, *The poets of the powers* (London: Rider and Co., 1973).

44 If he is identical to Reṇukācārya, as is asserted by the Vīraśaivas themselves, then he was probably more or less a contemporary of Basava, i.e., 13th century, and was the author of the *Siddhānta-śikhāmaṇi*. See the introduction by R. N. Nandi to the revised edition of S. C. Nandimath, *A handbook of Vīraśaivism* ([1942] 2nd ed., Delhi: Motilal Banarsidass, 1979), p. xxvi.

of the subcontinent.[45] These five *maṭhas* are located in Kedāra, Kāśī, Śrīśaila, Ujjayinī and Rambhāpurī (present-day Bālehonnūr, Chikmagulūr District, Karnataka).[46] It is the *maṭha* at Rambhāpurī in the Kannada country, the locus of the popular Vīraśaiva sect, that Revaṇasiddha himself is said to have founded. Given that Sringerī is also situated in very same district of (present-day) Karnataka, it is likely that this Vīraśaiva *siddha* would have been known to the author of the GVK.[47]

Lakṣmaṇa-Śāstrī also casts Revaṇasiddha in a later incident in the narrative of the Sringerī lineage. He appears in a dream to Harihara who is lamenting his defeat at the hands of Ballāla. Revaṇasiddha tells Harihara that by the grace of Vidyāraṇya, he will obtain the royal power of the throne (of what will be the kingdom of Vijayanagara). Revaṇasiddha equates Vidyāraṇya with the insignia of his office, the *candramaulīśvara liṅga*, in telling Harihara that he must see this *liṅga*, i.e., he must go to the Sringerī *maṭha* whose incumbent is Vidyāraṇya.[48] These two episodes in the GVK were probably framed on the basis of earlier stories about Revaṇasiddha. Such tales of his magical

---

45 See Nandimath, *Handbook of Vīraśaivism*, pp. 8 ff., and H. M. Sadasivaiah, *A comparative study of two Vīraśaiva monasteries* (Mysore: Prasaranga Manasa Gangotri, 1967), pp. 87-88.

46 All but the last of these are places Śaṅkara is said to have visited. See the table in Chapter Four.

47 In his notes to the second edition of the GVK (Srirangam: Vani Vilas Press, 1966, p. 32 verso), K. R. Venkataraman offers the rather implausible explanation that the name Revaṇa refers not to Revaṇasiddha but to the one who dwells on the Revā (=Narmadā) river, i.e., Śaṅkara's guru Govinda. But Venkataraman admits that the next mention of Revaṇasiddha in the text (GVK 5.59) does refer to the Vīraśaiva *ācārya*. (p. 51). The note is probably occasioned by the attacks on this text which have arisen in connection with the dispute between the *maṭhas*, discussed below.

48 GVK 5.59-6.1.

powers would have contributed greatly to making him a popular figure of legend in the Kannada country.

The appearance of Revaṇasiddha in the GVK is doubly significant for our study of the life of Śaṅkara. In the first place it affords us a glimpse of the way in which certain elements of popular, non-brahmin, cults have been incorporated into the Śaṅkara tradition. Secondly, we get some insight into the formative period of the Śaṅkara *maṭhas*, for which we have so few historical details. David Lorenzen provides much important information about the monastic centres developed by the Vīraśaivas and an earlier sect, the Kālāmukhas, in the Kannada region during the 10th-13th centuries A.D.[49] From the evidence of inscriptions it is clear that the Vīraśaivas took over several pre-existing Kālāmukha *maṭhas*, and probably adopted some of their beliefs as well. One of the most important of these centres was the Kōḍiya *maṭha*, attached to the Kedāreśvara temple in Belagāve (Shimoga District). This *maṭha*, in the site believed to be the "Kedāra of the south", was already well established as a Kālāmukha centre in 1162, as is attested by a lengthy inscription which describes its activities in great detail.[50] Such inscriptions are, of course, primarily a record of the financial bequests by royal patrons and wealthy benefactors, without which monastic centres could not survive. These early financial records also point to the fact that the various religious institutions in a given region must have been in competition for funding.

---

49 David N. Lorenzen, *The Kāpālikas and Kālāmukhas: two lost Śaiva sects* (New Delhi: Thompson Press, 1972), pp. 141-172.

50 *Ibid.* pp. 99-104; 170-172. Belagāve is situated 21 kms. northwest of Shikaripur. For further details see *Gazetteer of India. Karnataka State Gazetteer. Shimoga Distict* (Bangalore: Govt. of Karnataka, 1975), pp. 629-630.

The Advaita *maṭha* at Sringerī would certainly have had several rival Vīraśaiva institutions to contend with.[51] The nearest and most important of these, the Rambhāpurī *maṭha*, said to have been founded by Revaṇasiddha, is located only 25 kilometres to the southeast of Sringerī.[52] An inscription dated 1369 records a donation to the Vīrabhadra temple, attached to the *maṭha*, by the Vijayanagara king Bukka I,[53] who was also an important patron of Sringerī. There is every possibility that the competition for funding may have led the Sringerī *maṭha* and the neighbouring Vīraśaiva *maṭha* to make parallel claims, lest they be outdone by their rival in the eyes of their patrons. The similarity in the notion of the five original *ācāryas* founding the five Vīraśaiva monastic centres to the idea of four *maṭhas* founded by the four principal disciples of Śaṅkara is probably more than just coincidence. This shared tradition may well have been inspired by still earlier Tāntrika texts which describe four seats (*pīṭhas*) of the goddess in different parts of the subcontinent.[54]

Another interesting parallel in the Viraśaiva and Śaṅkara orders is in the importance they place on connecting their

51 Evidence of this rivalry in the last century is attested by a court case heard in Bombay in 1843: *Sri Sunkur Bharti Swami v. Sidha Lingayah Charanti*, Moore's Indian Appeals, vol. 3 (1841-46) 199-219 [pp. 125-37 in the reprint, Allahabad: Law Publishers, 1989]. The Sringerī *maṭha* claimed that it was the sole right of their *ācārya* to have his palanquin carried sideways in procession.

52 See *Gazetteer of India. Karnataka State Gazetteer. Chikmagalur District* (Bangalore: Govt. of Karnataka, 1981), pp. 564-565.

53 *Ibid.*

54 See D. C. Sircar, *The Śākta pīṭhas* (2nd ed., Delhi: Motilal Banarsidass, 1973), pp. 11-17. Nandimath, suggests that the Vīraśaiva idea of five centres comes from the Kubjikāmata Tāntrika tradition (*Handbook of Vīraśaivism*, p. 143, n.22). This may be by way of analogy with the symbolism of the five faces of Śiva, corresponding to the four directions and a fifth, above. The possibility of a Tāntrika origin of the notion of four *maṭhas* is more transparent in the Śaṅkara tradition which refers to its centres as *pīṭhas*.

traditions with a Himālayan centre: Kedāra for the former and the nearby Badarī for the latter. There are, of course, some different reasons why each of the two traditions are closely linked with a Himālayan site. In the case of the Vīraśaivas, the notion that Kedāra was a pre-eminent sacred place may have been inherited from the Kālāmukhas.[55] For the Śaṅkara order, the connections with this ancient pilgrimage site would have been useful in establishing their legitimacy as southern claimants to the Vedic orthodoxy, whose centre of power had been firmly entrenched in the north. Nevertheless, both traditions shared a common urge to found their own Himālayan institutions. It is very difficult to find information on the date of their establishment, but the British colonial administrators at the turn of the century were convinced that, "The *rāwal*, or chief priest of Kedārnāth is always a Jangama [i.e., Viraśaiva] from Mysore" and that at the Badarī temple, "The chief priest, known as the *rāwal*, is always a Brāhman of the Nambūdri class",[56] i.e., the caste, unique to Kerala, in which Śaṅkara is said to have been born. The Badarī institution must have been established prior to 1740 since it is mentioned in the GVK. According to Lakṣmaṇa-Śāstrī, Śaṅkara "ordained that the worship of the god [Badarī-Nārāyaṇa] should be conducted only by people from Kerala".[57]

The take-over of the Kālāmukha *maṭha*s by the Vīraśaivas suggests that monastic centres can continue to flourish despite (or perhaps in some cases because of) changing their affiliations. Such transformations would also account for the

---

55 According to Lorenzen, the Kālāmukhas, like the still earlier Pāśupatas, regarded pilgrimage to Kedāra in the Himālayas as an extremly important practice (*Kāpālikas and Kālāmukhas*, p. 174).

56 *Imperial Gazetteer of India. Provincial Series: United Provinces of Agra and Oudh*, vol. II ([1908] reprinted New Delhi: Usha, 1984), pp. 287-288.

57 *devaṃ tvimaṃ kerala-loka eva saṃpūjayatvity api so 'nvajānāt*, GVK 3.56.

existence of certain shared traditions among *maṭhas* of different persuasions. I have no specific evidence that any of the existing Śaṅkara institutions were previously of another denomination. But the hagiographies themselves reveal the possibility that rival centres could be won over. The texts which describe the *digvijaya* relate how most of Śaṅkara's opponents became followers of Advaita. In the AŚV the numerous debates often conclude with a set formula which varies only slightly: "He made all the people in that place devoted to Advaita". Since the venue for the debates in the hagiographies is usually within temple complexes, it can be inferred that the residential compound—whether it was actually a *maṭha* or simply a pilgrims' quarters—would have itself become in some way affiliated to the Śaṅkara tradition. In such situations it was likely that certain previously established practices would persist within the institution, even though they were not really appropriate to Advaita Vedānta. This would also explain, at least in part, the hagiographers' account of Śaṅkara's third institutional legacy: the organization of devotional sects.

Ṣaṇmata-sthāpana: Establishing the Six Devotional Sects

It is only the three hagiographies which reveal affiliations with an official institution that represent Śaṅkara as the founder of devotional sects. Nevertheless all of our sources tell of his visits to temples and describe his worship of their presiding deities. In this respect the texts have helped to establish the popular image of Śaṅkara as both non-dualist and devotee. This portrayal would certainly appear to contradict the metaphysical viewpoint of his own work. Leaving aside for the time being a more detailed consideration of this contradiction,[58] I will restrict myself here to examining the way the hagiographers address the question. For them, I suspect, the answer was very simple. By the time our sources were composed, devotional practice had so pervaded Hindu religious life that it could be accommodated within almost any tradition. Moreover, the hagiographers could scarcely afford to isolate Śaṅkara from the popular *bhakti* cults if they wished to succeed in presenting him to a wider audience as the foremost of religious leaders.

Of the three texts that depict the *ṣaṇmata-sthāpana*, the most elaborate account is found in the AŚV, which devotes a separate chapter to the establishment of each of the six sects. The first and longest of these chapters is allocated to the Śaivas, in keeping with Anantānandagiri's apparent personal preferences. He first addresses the problem of justifying Śaṅkara's approval of the devotional cults. The widespread belief in the inevitability of imperfection during the *kali-yuga* proves to be a convenient explanation. Despite the successful completion of Śaṅkara's *digvijaya*, the establishment of the *maṭha*(s) and the instruction of his disciples, the darkest age was prevailing. Even Śaṅkara must acknowledge this harsh reality:

> In this *kali-yuga*, men, in whom the shoots of wisdom are destroyed by various evils, are not qualified for the knowledge of pure non-duality. Moreover, moral conduct is unrestrained and is [just] according to one's own desires.[59]

The evils of the age require that some compromise be made to the integrity of the Advaita position. In order to make the most of the limited opportunities to protect what remains of the

---

58 For further discussion see Chapter Seven.

59 *kalāv asmin yuge nānā-pāpa-vidhvasta-jñānāṅkureṣu martyeṣu śuddhādvaita-vidyāyām anadhikāriṣu vṛttiḥ punar api yathecchaṃ viśṛṅkhalaṃ bhavatīti samyag vicārya*, AŚV p. 195.

dharma in the *kali-yuga*, Śaṅkara decides to allow the continuity of dualistic beliefs: "For the sake of protecting the world and for protecting the *varṇāśrama-dharma*, he contrived to carry out the formulation of sects which have for their basis the [notion of] difference between the *jīva* and Īśa".[60]

Just as these deliberations are in progress, the disciple Paramatakālānala makes an opportune appearance on the scene. Śaṅkara calls him and says, "Tell me succinctly what favour [you wish]. Depending on whether it is appropriate to the work to be done in the future, I will carry out your wish".[61] The disciple's reply is not so brief, but it is to the point. He assures his guru that he accepts and follows his teachings, yet he still retains his Śaiva orientation:

> ...Although my mind remains concentrated, thinking only [of the teaching] 'I am that', my inclination is fixed in this way: as a spark of fire arises from the contact of fire and wood, the whole world, which arises from the supreme Śiva, is pervaded by *jīva*s [in the form of] gods, men and animals. Therefore, in accordance with the saying that the *jīva*s are a portion of Īśa, it is a traditional doctrine that Śiva should be worshipped by all. Hence, we cherish the Śaiva point of view...[62]

Śaṅkara's initial reaction reveals his distaste for this position: such a path is possible, but it can only be suited to the unlearned who are incapable of following the way of Advaita. Nevertheless he realizes that Gāyatrī's curse upon the brahmins—which he cited in his argument against the Śaivas during his *digvijaya*—had now come to pass. The brahmins of

---

60 *loka-rakṣārthaṃ ca varṇāśrama-paripālanārthaṃ ca mata-kalpanāṃ jīveśa-bhedāspadāṃ racayitum upakramya...* (*ibid.*).

61 *bho śiṣya tava yat prītiḥ tad vadasva samāsataḥ / bhāvi-kāryocita-vaśāt tat karomi mataṃ tava //* (*ibid.*).

62 AŚV p. 195.

old who had argued with the goddess had indeed been born again in the *kali-yuga* with such limited capacities that they were attached to one deity or another. With some resignation, Śaṅkara agrees to his disciple's wishes. He acknowledges that Paramatakālānala is (true to his name) capable of undertaking a *digvijaya* himself. Śaṅkara directs him to "establish the Śaiva sect, which has six subdivisions of its own, on a long term basis which is of benefit to the world".[63] While it is clear that the responsibility for the decision ultimately rests with Śaṅkara, Anantānandagiri conveys the impression that his actions are also undertaken in response to the wishes of his disciples. This is further evidence that Śaṅkara is constrained by circumstances to allow the foundation of the sects.

It is striking that unlike Sureśvara, who gives himself over completely to the Advaita doctrine after being defeated in debate, Paramatakālānala never really severs his cult affiliations. This could perhaps have been read as a failure on Śaṅkara's part, despite the ill effects of the *kali-yuga* and the power of Gāyatrī's curse. Accordingly, Anantānandagiri provides further justification for the persistence of the Śaiva tendencies in the disciple:

> Paramatakālānala, who was born from a portion of Lord Śiva's trident, had renounced all ritual action. Bearing a single staff and holding in his hands a spear, water pot and *ḍamaru* drum, he was like Śiva made manifest to those who saw him.[64]

Since he is a manifestation of Śiva, albeit a minor one, the disciple cannot be expected to alter his predisposition. What is more he is a true ascetic, and he is successful in his mission:

---

63 *bahu-kālaṃ śaiva-mataṃ svāvāntara-ṣaḍ-bhedānvitaṃ lokopakāra-rūpaṃ kalpaya*, AŚV p. 196.

64 *Ibid.*

> Seeing him, some became his disciples, as followers of the Śaiva path, thinking, 'the Advaita proclaimed by Śaṅkara is hard to understand but the Śaivism this guru has explained is to our liking. Being taught by this guru we experience Kailāsa'.[65]

Paramatakālānala, and the others who are chosen to establish the devotional sects, follow directly in the footsteps of their guru in conducting their own *digvijayas*. Anantānandagiri is content to repeat for them the formula with which he described Śaṅkara's conquest of the quarters. There is only one small modification needed. Each of his emissaries makes some of "the brahmins and the rest, who inhabit the lands from Rāmeśvara to the Himālayas and in between, adherents of his *sect*". Anantānandagiri usually limits the application of the term *mata*, i.e., 'sect' or 'doctrine', to that which is outside of the Advaita viewpoint. This sets Advaita apart as the one true tradition, in contrast to the multiplicity of sects and doctrines. Hence the emissaries who carry out the founding of the *mata*-s seem to be restricted to the second tier of disciples. Their dualistic inclinations exclude them from the inner circle.

Anantānandagiri's presentation of the establishment of the Śaiva sect sets the pattern for the five other doctrines which are described in the subsequent chapters. In this context it is apparent that the word *mata* comprehends both 'sect' and 'doctrine'. As for the term *sthāpana*, literally 'establishment', we need to understand 're-establishment' or 'reorganization'. The fact that the sects were already in existence is obvious from Śaṅkara's earlier defeat of the leading exponents of the six doctrines. For this reason Śaṅkara's act of *sthāpana* must constitute primarily a reorganization. In the first place, the

---

65 *tam īkṣya ke cid advaitaṃ gahanaṃ śaṅkaroditam / guruṇā tena samproktaṃ śaivaṃ ruci-karaṃ hi naḥ // śikṣitā guruṇā tena vayaṃ kailāsa - bhāginaḥ / bhavāma iti tacchiṣyā babhūvuḥ śaiva-mārga-gāḥ//.*

overwhelming multiplicity of sects Śaṅkara encountered during his *digvijaya* are reduced to a fixed and manageable number. The choice of the number six is probably intended to reflect the six *darśanas*, the traditional category in which the orthodox metaphysical viewpoints are grouped. This parallel would lend more legitimacy to the six devotional doctrines. The individual sects are also internally restructured so that each has six subdivisions which form a mirror image of the outer framework. The six sects are further unified in being brought under the aegis of Advaita Vedānta. Indeed they remain wholly subservient to Śaṅkara. Upon the completion of their respective *digvijayas*, the emissaries Śaṅkara has chosen return, "possessed of many disciples, and bow to the feet of their supreme guru".[66]

There are a number of significant and problematic details in connection with the six sects which should be considered here. To begin with, it is difficult to account for the only variation in the pattern which is fundamental to this portion of the narrative. In the case of every sect except the Vaiṣṇavas, it is a single disciple, formerly a sectarian opponent, who is chosen to serve as Śaṅkara's emissary. Yet neither of the two disciples who are selected to reorganize the second sect, namely the Vaiṣṇavas, have previously appeared as opponents. The first of these is Lakṣmaṇa, who has not figured at all in the narrative up until this point. The second is Hastāmalaka whom we otherwise know as one of the four principal disciples. Now the AŚV stands out from the other hagiographies in that it does not distinguish four close disciples. Nevertheless Anantānandagiri assigns Hastāmalaka a prominent place by including him in an original group of twelve disciples who are said to accompany

---

66 *bahu-śiṣyasametaḥ punar āgatya paramaguru-caraṇaṃ natvā...* AŚV p. 197.

Śaṅkara right from when he first sets out from the abode of his guru.[67]

While it is surprising that Lakṣmaṇa, who is presumably someone of importance, was not singled out for mention previously, it is possible that the reader is meant to count him as one of the Vaiṣṇavas whom Śaṅkara debated during his *digvijaya*. What is far more puzzling is why Hastāmalaka, a long standing disciple, should be included in the company of former opponents. The problem is further complicated by the revelation of the divine origins of the two disciples. They are said to be "born from a portion of Vāyu and the serpent Śeṣa".[68] This may well be an intentional allusion, albeit anachronistic, to the two chief rivals of the Advaita lineage, namely Rāmānuja and Madhva. Rāmānuja, whose name was originally Lakṣmaṇa, is sometimes identified as an incarnation of Śeṣa,[69] while Madhva is invariably said to be a manifestation of Vāyu.[70] Both were initially students of

---

67 The twelve are Padmapāda, Hastāmalaka, Samitpāṇi, Cidvilāsa, Jñānakanda, Viṣṇugupta, Śuddha-kīrti, Bhānumarīci, Kṛṣṇadarśana, Buddhivṛddhi, Viriñcipāda, and Śuddhānantānandagiri, AŚV p. 17. The absence of Toṭaka in the AŚV is conspicuous.

68 *...śeṣa-sarpa-vāyvaṃśa-jatau*, AŚV (Madras ed.) p. 197. The Calcutta editions similarly read, *...śeṣa-vāyu-satya-jātau.*

69 *Prapannāmṛta* 46.57 relates, eg., *tadā phaṇīśvaro bhūtvā sahasra-phaṇa-maṇḍitah...*, *Prapannāmṛta by Anantācārya* , ed. Śrīnivāsa Nṛsiṃhācārya (Bombay: Veṅkateśvara Steam Press, śaka 1829 [=1907]). See the discussion in Phyllis Granoff's, "Scholars and wonderworkers: some remarks on the role of the supernatural in philosophical contests in Vedānta hagiographies", *JAOS* 105 (1985), p. 463.

70 This is made explicit in the hagiographies of Madhva, eg. *Sumadhvavijaya* 2.26: *vāyur ayam āvir abhūt pṛthivyāṃ*, see also 2.24, Nārāyaṇapaṇḍitācārya, *Sumadhvavijaya*, ed. T. R. Kṛṣṇācārya (Bombay: Nirṇayasāgara, śaka 1834 [1912]) p. 19. Hastāmalaka is also identified as an incarnation of Vāyu in ŚDV 3.3 (=TŚA 2.3), *pavano 'py ajani...*

Advaita gurus but, of course, the two of them later repudiated these teachers.

The parallel between the great Viśiṣṭādvaitin, Lakṣmaṇa/Rāmānuja, and the Lakṣmaṇa of the AŚV becomes even more striking in the description of Lakṣmaṇa's return from his *digvijaya*. Not only is he accompanied by numerous disciples, but he has with him a "collection of works beginning with the *bhāṣya* which effected the expansion of his sect".[71] It is difficult to avoid thinking of Rāmānuja's rival commentary on the *Brahmasūtra* here. However, the editor of the Madras edition, wishing to deny this association, adds a note asserting that the two Lakṣmaṇas should not be confused. He argues that the Viśiṣṭādvaita guru became a *saṃnyāsin* after being a married man, while the Lakṣmaṇa of the AŚV renounced directly from the state of *brahmacarya*.[72] Although his point is certainly valid, I am inclined to think that this discrepancy does not rule out the possibility that Anantānandagiri is making an allusion to Rāmānuja. The question of the Vaiṣṇava's renunciation strikes me as a separate issue, to which I will return. In the case of the second emissary, Hastāmalaka, the apparent connections with the rival Vedāntin, Madhva, are far more tenuous. There are certainly no similarities in their names. But if we take into account the other hagiographies, another link between the two emerges. Five of the hagiographers tell us that Hastāmalaka was born just outside of present-day Uḍipi, the birthplace of Madhva and the centre of his sect.[73] While the AŚV does not

---

71 *mata-vijṛmbhaṇa-hetukaṃ bhāṣyādi grantha-cayaṃ*, AŚV p. 197.

72 It would appear that Prof. Veezhinathan is anxious to show that the AŚV was composed soon after the time of Śaṅkara, in which case the anachronism is not possible (p. 197n.). His arguments are probably aimed at defending the text from the criticism generated by the dispute between the maṭhas, discussed below.

73 The hagiographers say Hastāmalaka was born in Śrīvali or Śivavihāra, the present-day Shivalli, situated three kilometres south of Uḍipi. Madhva was

mention his native place, the text does tell us that Hastāmalaka consecrated statues of deities such as Krishna in Rajatapīṭha (i.e., Uḍipi) and other places.[74]

It would surely have been foolish for Anantānandagiri to suggest that Rāmānuja and Madhva were actually Śaṅkara's disciples, and this was probably not his intention. However, there are good reasons why Anantānandagiri might have wished to *allude* to the two rival Vedāntins. The fact that both of them first studied under Advaita teachers—even if they were eventually repudiated—reinforces Śaṅkara's primacy among the Vedānta gurus. Moreover by fitting Rāmānuja and Madhva into this episode in the narrative, Anantānandagiri could also suggest that the Viśiṣṭādvaita and Dvaita doctrines were fundamentally Vaiṣṇava, and as such were actually under the aegis of Advaita. By the time in which the AŚV was composed, the Madhva doctrine, like that of Rāmānuja, was already a substantial threat to the Śaṅkara tradition. While our hagiographers would not go so far as to include Rāmānuja or Madhva in the narrative, they may well have wished to respond to this threat.[75] It was perhaps with this in mind that Anantānandagiri composed his account of Śaṅkara's Vaiṣṇava disciples in such a way as to suggest that Rāmānuja and Madhva were actually under Śaṅkara's jurisdiction.

---

born in the town now known as Belle, nine kilometres southeast of Uḍipi. According to the *Sumadhvavijaya* (2.24), his conception occurred in the course of his parents' penance for a child at Rūpyapīṭha, i.e., Uḍipi. It is striking that GVK 3.10 specifically mentions Śrīraupyapīṭha as the birthplace of Hastāmalaka. For descriptions of Belle, Shivalli and Uḍipi, see *Karnataka State Gazetteer. South Kanara Distict* (Bangalore: Govt. of Karnataka, 1973).

74 *rajatapīṭha-sthaleṣu kṛṣṇādi-deva-pratiṣṭhāṃ kṛtvā*, p. 198.

75 While there are a few anachronisms in our sources, notably in the ŚDV (discussed in Chapter One), I doubt that Anantānandagiri would have made such a gross mistake as to directly include Rāmānuja and Madhva in the Śaṅkara life story.

It is also possible that this episode in the AŚV is in response to the two hagiographies of Madhva, *Maṇimañjarī* and *Sumadhvavijaya*, which mount a vitriolic attack on Śaṅkara. These were both written by Nārāyaṇapaṇḍita, the son of Madhva's direct disciple, Trivikramapaṇḍita.[76] Since Madhva flourished in the 13th century, it is likely that his hagiographer was active by the early part of the 14th century. Hence the two texts may well predate the AŚV. If Anantānandagiri had in fact known of Nārāyaṇapaṇḍita's works, a reply would have been in order. Some of the later Śaṅkara hagiographies were even more likely to have been composed to counter Nārāyaṇapaṇḍita's defamatory attacks.

Returning now to the narrative, we find that Śaṅkara asks his two Vaiṣṇava disciples about their inner inclinations. They reply:

> Although by virtue of your teachings, *svāmin*, we are established in the knowledge that I am that alone which is the cause of all—i.e., Brahman, who is unthinkable, unmanifest, and of endless forms, who is truth, knowledge and infinite—our consciousness is always pervaded by the lotus feet of Nārāyaṇa. Our settled opinion, which arises from thousands of [scriptural] authorities, is that he alone is Brahman.[77]

Śaṅkara responds to their statement with unqualified approval, "It is true" (*samīcīnam*). But he insists on one precondition before he will grant their wish. Lakṣmaṇa and Hastāmalaka are still *brahmacārin*s. They must become renouncers in order to establish the Vaiṣṇava sect. The disciples willingly agree to this demand and set off on their *digvijaya*. The same pattern repeats in the chapters on the Saura, Śākta and Gāṇapatīya sects.

---

76 See Bibliography for details.

77 AŚV p. 197.

Each of the chosen emissaries explains how he identifies his own preferrred deity with Brahman. Each becomes a *saṃnyāsin* and embarks on a *digvijaya*.

Given Śaṅkara's insistence on the need for renunciation—both in his own works and from the vantage point of the hagiographers—it is striking that he chooses disciples who are not yet *saṃnyāsin*s to establish the devotional sects. I can only assume that Anantānandagiri's intention is to show these disciples to be immature. This would account for their inability to fully surrender the dualistic doctrines to which they previously adhered. The mature disciple, best represented by Sureśvara, is presumably capable of wholly embracing the principles of Advaita. It is only the Śaiva, Paramatakālānala, who was a *saṃnyāsin* prior to his nomination as an emissary. This is in keeping with his image as a minor manifestation of Śiva, the lord of ascetics. The special treatment reserved for Paramatakālānala also reflects Anantānandagiri's own Śaiva orientation. By the end of the AŚV we find that Paramatakālānala has in fact been promoted into the first rank of disiciples. In the penultimate chapter he is one of three whose individual hymns to the guru are recorded.[78] The Śaiva is again singled out for special mention in the final chapter of the AŚV. Just prior to Śaṅkara's departure from the earth, we learn that he dispatched his disciples, "Paramatakālānala and the other ascetics", to various places.[79]

The inclusion of the Kāpālikas as the sixth dualistic doctrine is probably the most peculiar feature of the *ṣaṇmata-sthāpana*. Not only are they wholly unorthodox, but according to the hagiographers the Kāpālikas went so far as to threaten

---

[78] The first hymn is recited by Padmapāda and the third by Bhānumarīci. The remaining disiciples recite a communal hymn of praise to Śaṅkara.

[79] *tataḥ paraṃ sarva-loka-gurur ācāryaḥ sva-śiṣyān paramatakālānalādi-yatīn tad-anyāṃś ca tatra tatra viṣayeṣu preṣayitvā.*

Śaṅkara's life. It was only the timely intervention of his faithful disciple, Padmapāda, that saved his skull from becoming a ritual vessel. Yet all three of our sources which describe the *ṣaṇmata-sthāpana* agree that the Kāpālikas, despite their gruesome ritual practice, are the sixth sect established by Śaṅkara. This raises the question of why there should be six sects in the first place, and how the Kāpālikas came to be counted among these.

The AŚV and CŚV both speak of *pañca-pūja*, the worship of five deities. The five are usually identified as Śiva, Viṣṇu, Śakti, Gaṇeśa and Sūrya.[80] In the *pañca-pūjā* ritual, or *pañcāyatana-pūja*, as it is sometimes called, the image of one's preferred deity takes the central place, with the four other gods arranged around it in the four directions.[81] The AŚV frequently mentions this as one of the brahmin practices that Śaṅkara's reformed opponents return to. This is what happens when the Kāpālikas are defeated:

> [Śaṅkara] the ascetic ordered his disciples to carry out their purifi-cation. The disciples, chief of whom is Padmapāda, made them follow the path of the brahmins. They were made to be always intent upon an early morning ritual bath, to have the firm

---

80 The deities are sometimes represented iconographically by a Śiva *liṅga* which has four faces. The five deities enumerated reflects the perception only of the Smārta tradition. There are also different schemes of the five deities such as those envisioned by the Lākulīśa-Pāśupata cult and the Śaiva Siddhāntas. See V. S. Pathak, *History of Śaiva cults in northern India from inscriptions* (Varanasi, 1960), p. 56. Pathak mentions, for example, the establishment of Śiva, Śakti, Kārttikeya, Sarasvatī and Gaṇeśa in a Śaiva Śiddhānta temple.

81 See Polagam Sri Rama Sastrigal, "The six orthodox ways of worship", in *Sankara and Shanmata. Souvenir of the conference on Sankara and Shanmata*, Madras, June 1-9, 1969 (Madras: Sankara and Shanmata conference committee [no details on the editor of the volume, unpaginated]).

> vow of practising the *sandhyā* ritual, to be intent on the five *pūjās* and the five *yajñas*.[82]

The enumeration of five sacrifices (*pañca-yajñas* or *mahāyajñas*), a prominent feature of religious life in traditional India, goes back to the *Śatapatha Brāhmaṇa*. These sacrifices are in effect daily observances, by way of offerings, which are to be made to animals, men, the ancestors, the gods and the Vedas.[83] The practice of the five *pūjas*, on the other hand, does not appear to be so old. V. S Pathak, rejects the claim that Śaṅkara established this custom, and argues that it became popular in the 11th century A.D.[84] The linking together of the five *pūjas* and five *yajñas* in the AŚV suggests that the former may be modelled on the latter. *Pūjā*, of course, came to be regarded as (a latter-day) equivalent to *yajña*.[85] Since one of the five sacrifices is the *deva-yajña*, it is quite possible that the notion of the *pūjā* to the five *devas* developed as a microcosmic reflection of the *pañca-yajñas*.

Despite the eventual popularity of the *pañca-pūjā*, it was not the sects of five deities that gained special recognition, but six. The origins of this category are more obvious. The idea of six devotional sects, as was mentioned earlier, is most probably derived from the concept of the six *darśanas*. Mādhava-

---

82 *ājñāpayām āsa yatiḥ śiṣyāṃś teṣāṃ viśodhane / padmapāda-mukhāḥ śiṣyāś cakrus tān brāhmaṇādhva-gān / prātaḥ snāna-ratān nityaṃ sandhyā-karma-dṛḍha-vratān / pañca-pūjā-pañca-yajña-parān...* AŚV p. 105. Cf. CŚV 30.53, although in the CSV it is only the Śākta opponent who is specifically said to become *pañca-pūjā-parāyaṇa*. It is conspicuous that the second set of Kāpālikas Śaṅkara encounters (chapter 24) are not brahmins but *śūdras*. There is no question of them following orthodox practices. Instead Śaṅkara simply tells them to go away, preferably far away.

83 See P. V. Kane, *History of Dharmaśāstra* (rev. ed. Poona: 1974) vol. 2, part 2, pp. 696-704.

84 *History of Śaiva cults*, p. 56.

85 P. V. Kane, *op. cit.*, pp. 714-717.

Vidyāraṇya's commentary on the *Pārāśara-smṛti* is perhaps the earliest available authority for the notion of six devotional sects.[86] He cites a single verse which testifies to this and links the sects to the six *darśana*s:

> The path of devotion has six standpoints: the Śaiva, the Vaiṣṇava, the Śākta, the Saura, the Gāṇapatīya and the Skānda.[87]

Given the powerful influence of Mādhava-Vidyāraṇya on the Advaita tradition, it is surprising that the hagiographers chose to name the Kāpālikas rather than the cult of Skanda/Kumāra as the sixth sect. Perhaps this incident in the Śaṅkara story does go back to much older oral traditions. According to Fred Clothey, the cult of Skanda was in relative eclipse from the sixth to the tenth centuries.[88] Hence the historical Śaṅkara may not have met with any of the votaries of this sect. The Kāpālikas, on the other hand, were flourishing in Śaṅkara's day. The fact of their presence, or perhaps even an actual encounter, is reflected by the appearance of the Kāpālikas in all but one of the hagiographies.[89]

---

86 The work is most commonly referred to as the *Pārāśara-mādhavīya*. I have used the Bibliotheca Indica edition, *Parāśara-smṛti with the gloss by Mādhavācāryya*, ed. Candrakānta Tarkālaṅkāra ([1893] reprinted in 2 vols. Calcutta: Asiatic Society, 1973-74). It is conspicuous that Mādhava-Vidyāraṇya enumerates not 6 but 16 *darśanas* in his *Sarvadarśanasaṃgraha.* Nevertheless, many other doxographers did emphasize that there were 6 darśanas. See Wilhelm Halbfass, *India and Europe: An essay in Understanding*. (Albany: State University of New York, 1988), pp. 352-354.

87 *śaivañ ca vaiṣṇavaṃ śāktaṃ sauraṃ vaināyakan tathā / skāndañ ca bhakti - mārgasya darśanāni ṣaḍ eva hi //.* Ibid. vol. 1, p. 327 (Ācārakāṇḍa). Mādhava-Vidyāraṇya attributes the verse to a *Purāṇa-sāra*, which is apparently no longer extant. See Ludo Rocher, *The Purāṇas* (*A history of Indian literature,* ed. Jan Gonda, vol. II, fasc. 3, Wiesbaden: Harrassowitz, 1986), p. 216.

88 Fred W. Clothey, *The many faces of Murukan̲: the history and meaning of a south Indian god* (The Hague: Mouton, 1978), pp. 73ff.

89 See the table of incidents (nos. 28 and 37) in Chapter Two.

Śaṅkara's meetings with the Kāpālikas, as described in the ŚDV and AŚV, have been carefully examined by David Lorenzen.[90] There is no need to restate the findings of his thorough investigation, but I would like to draw attention to his observations on the hagiographers' apparent confusion of the Kāpālikas and Kālāmukhas. Lorenzen has shown that the Kāpālikas tended to be solitary ascetics, in contrast to the Kālāmukhas who founded large monastic centres, chiefly in Karnataka.[91] It is difficult to imagine how a solitary group of ascetics could have been established on an institutional basis, as in the case of the other five sects. But given that the hagiographers did conflate the Kāpālikas with the Kālāmukhas, the monastic establishments of the latter may have suggested good possibilities for reorganization. It should also be noted that the Kālāmukhas were far less unorthodox than the Kāpālikas. Lorenzen cites some Kālāmukha inscriptions which reveal an attitude compatible with brahmin culture.[92]

The wide distibution of Kāpālika ascetics and the presence of large Kālāmukha monasteries,[93] if taken together, would have made a formidable impression on our hagiographers. However, I can suggest no reason other than the existence of a strong oral tradition—somehow connecting Śaṅkara with the Kāpālikas—for motivating the hagiographers to enumerate

---

90 *The Kāpālikas and the Kālāmukhas: two lost Śaivite sects* (New Delhi: Thompson Press, 1972), pp. 31-48. According to Lorenzen, the Kāpālikas flourished from the 6th to the 14th centuries (p. 53).

91 *Ibid.*, pp. 43-44. The Kālāmukhas were active primarily during the 11th - 13th centuries (p. 97).

92 *Ibid*., pp. 103-107; 149-150.

93 By the time the Śaṅkara hagiographies were written, the Kālāmukha monasteries had probably been taken over by the Vīraśaivas (and perhaps by other sects as well). It is not clear how the hagiographers would have defined the affiliations of these centres, but the perception that they were, at least in some way, still Kālāmukha *maṭhas* may well have persisted.

them as the sixth sect. Anantānandagiri's account certainly reveals an ambivalence towards this unorthodox cult. Although he obviously feels they cannot be excluded from the *ṣaṇmata-sthāpana*, he does his utmost to ensure that the Kāpālikas are marginalized:

> When the five sects that were capable of worship which is according to the Brāhmaṇas were thus established, the renowned Kāpālika, Vaṭukanātha, approached the Paramaguru and saluted him profusely. With his palms folded together out of modesty, he said, "Svāmin, you destroyed all the different sects, along with mine...You are intent on establishing in this mortal world five sects, beginning with the Śaivas, which follow the practice of pure Advaita. You should consider allowing some place for my sect [as well]...The revered Paramaguru said, "Disciple, set up your sect with the function of being a prima facie view for the Śaivas, Vaiṣṇavas, Sauras, Śāktas and Gāṇapatyas, which attain their aim through the Vedas. Without that [prima facie view] it will not be possible for them to have a fully established argument.[94]

In this way the Kāpālikas are admitted to the select group, but must remain very much junior partners to the five more orthodox sects. Vaṭukanātha is, like the others, allowed to set off on his own *digvijaya*. He carries this out quickly and returns to his guru, informing him that he has "spread the Kāpālika sect everywhere, in all directions, among numerous devotees". Nevertheless Vaṭukanātha is, in the end, relegated to the role of a servant, living near, but not with, the five principal disciples.[95] This provides us with another interesting

---

94 AŚV, p. 202.

95 *mukhya-śiṣya-pañca-yati-samīpe tad-dāsa iva samavartata,* AŚV p. 203.

perspective on the way in which disparate elements are included in the Śaṅkara tradition and, on a broader scale, reflects the operation of "inclusivism" in the Hinduism tradition as a whole.[96]

The account of the *ṣaṇmata-sthāpana* in the CŚV is much simpler than that of the AŚV. Cidvilāsa stresses, above all, the role of the disciples in persuading Śaṅkara to allow the establishment of the devotional sects:

> Tripurāmbākumāra, Paravādidavānala, the wise Baṭukanātha, Mahādhuṇḍigajeśvara, Divākarācārya and Bindumādhavapaṇḍita bowed to the great teacher, Śaṅkarācārya...and petitioned him. The six excellent disciples said: ...You have perfected the wonderful Advaita doctrine, which is in harmony with the Vedas and Vedānta, since the other [doctrines] in this world are worthless. Oh revered one, in your doctrine the overlord is the supreme Brahman, who is eternal.
>
> [But] in this *kali [-yuga]* how is access to something without attributes, without dependence, without modification and without interval possible, for the understanding of those whose minds are impure? In this case, oh storehouse of fame, you should proclaim the six doctrines: Śaiva, Śākta, Vaiṣṇava, Saura, Gāṇapata and Kāpāla.
>
> Petitioned in this way by his disciples, Śaṅkara, the illustrious teacher [said], "Whatever may be the doctrine with regard to which your desire is strongly manifest, abandon such things as the [sectarian] marking and that which is done with a hot iron in contradiction of *śruti* and *smṛti*, and you may

---

96 The term 'inclusivism', coined by Paul Hacker, is not without its difficulties but remains nonetheless most useful. For an extensive discussion on "inclusivism" see Wilhelm Halbfass, *India and Europe*, pp. 403-418.

> proclaim it as authorized (*sammatī*)". [Thus] the guru gave his permission to the disciples who had repeatedly requested it. They saluted their excellent teacher and set off for a *digvijaya.*[97]

By agreeing to his disciples earnest requests, Śaṅkara can, to at least some extent, be absolved from the charge of self-contradiction in encouraging the development of dualistic doctrines.

Unlike his description of Śaṅkara's other legacies, Cidvilāsa does not seem to want to elaborate upon the earlier account of the *ṣaṇmata-sthāpana* in the AŚV. Instead the CŚV largely follows Anantānandagiri's narrative.[98] The parallels in names of the emissaries mentioned in the two texts are particularly striking. The Śākta whom Cidvilāsa calls Tripurāmbākumāra is known as Tripurakumāra in the AŚV. Similarly, the name of the Śaiva in the CŚV, Paravādidavānala, is only a slight variant of Paramatakālānala. In both texts the Kāpālika is the same, Baṭukanātha, the only difference being in the orthography of the initial 'B'/'V'. But it is conspicuous that Cidvilāsa does not seek to justify the inclusion of the Kāpālikas in the six sects. In the case of the Gāṇapatīya, Mahādhuṇḍirājagajeśvara, the CŚV departs from the AŚV's choice of Girijāputra. However, Anantānandagiri does refer to a Duṇḍhirāja-gaṇapatikumāra among the Gāṇapatīya opponents Śaṅkara confronted in his own *digvijaya.*[99] The Saura is identical in both sources, Divākarācārya. The most obvious disparity in our two sources is in regard to the Vaiṣṇavas. Cidvilāsa appears to ignore the two emissaries described in the AŚV in mentioning a single representative, Bindumādhava. This name may refer to the

97 CŚV 31.15b-24.

98 For a discusion of the relationship between the two works see Chapter One.

99 AŚV p. 85.

opponent, Mādhava, whom Śaṅkara debated at Anantaśayana, according to the AŚV.[100]

The GVK condenses its narration of the *ṣaṇmata-sthāpana* into a single verse:

> Those who were faithful to the six [doctrines], the Śaivas and the rest, petitioned the lord of ascetics [to permit] the development of each of their own doctrines. Each of them, who were skilled in their own doctrines, obtained the favour of the world-guru and set out.[101]

In his own commentary to the GVK, Lakṣmaṇa-Śāstrī identifies the six sects and their emissaries. This provides us with what is perhaps the strongest evidence of his reliance on Anantānandagiri. The details are exactly the same as are found in the AŚV, with a single exception: the GVK commentary names just one of the two Vaiṣṇava representatives cited in the AŚV—Lakṣmaṇa.[102] Yet in the absence of further comment it is not possible to determine what the author of the GVK thought about this Vaiṣṇava emissary *vis à vis* Anantānandagiri's allusions to Rāmānuja.

I have devoted much attention to the *ṣaṇmata-sthāpana* because I feel it best represents the kind of inclusivism that has enabled the Śaṅkara tradition to expand its sphere of operations from the small circle of solitary ascetics and the elite realm of scholarly exegesis to the mainstream of popular religious life. The image of Śaṅkara as the reformer of the devotional sects,

---

100 AŚV p. 56.

101 *śaivādayaḥ ṣaḍ-yamino yatīśaṃ samprārthya taṃ sva-sva-matodayāya // anugrahaṃ prāpya jagad-guroś ca te prasthitāḥ sva-sva-mata-pravīṇāḥ //* GVK 3.36.

102 The so called *Prācīna-Śaṅkaravijaya* (PrŚV) cited in the commentary to the ŚDV, which seems to be a summary of the AŚV, similarly mentions only Lakṣmaṇa as the Vaiṣṇava emissary (Ānandāśrama ed. of the ŚDV, p. 600). For a discussion on the PrŚV see Appendix B.

together with the pan-regional perspective he is shown to embrace in the hagiographies, have helped to secure for him a position of leadership as a pre-eminent spokesman of the Hindu tradition. Yet the extent to which his successors in the Śaṅkara institutions are entitled to inherit this mantle of spiritual authority is not as certain, despite the efforts of the hagiographers who have sought to popularize the legacies of the great guru.

Asceticism and Institutionalism

It may seem surprising that my examination of institutional legacies has ignored the establishment of the ten ascetic lineages, which is nowadays invariably attributed to Śaṅkara. I have reserved comment about this legacy simply because the hagiographers have so little to say about it. To begin with, the five sources in which we find no mention of the foundation of the *maṭhas*, the bequest of the *liṅga* or the *ṣaṇmata-sthāpana*, are similarly silent about the organization of ascetics. Of the three hagiographies which focus on Śaṅkara's institution building, it is only the CŚV which refers to the establishment of ten lineages. This is said to occur while Śaṅkara is residing at Sringerī, but we learn nothing more than their names.[103] The AŚV mentions the founding of just one ascetic line in Sringerī, named Bhāratī.[104] While the GVK neglects the subject altogether.

---

103 *sampradāyān daśaivaitān śiṣyeṣv āracaya svataḥ / tīrthāśrama-vanāraṇya - giri-parvata-sāgarāḥ // sarasvatī bhāratī ca purīty ete daśaiva hi /* CŚV 24. 36-37a.

104 *bhāratī-saṃpradāyaṃ nija-śiṣyeṣu cakāra,* AŚV p. 182. The final chapter in the Madras edition of the text refers to the founding of the Indra-sarasvatī order at Kānchipuram, but the editor's decision to include this reading on the basis of only two MSS., seems very questionable (p. 208).

A definitive statement on the origins of the tenfold classification of ascetics will have to await the further study of the numerous extant manuscripts dealing with renunciation. But thanks to the work of Patrick Olivelle, who has made substantial contributions in this area,[105] it is possible to make some tentative observations. To begin with, we can infer from the names of two famous *saṃnyāsins* of the 13th century that at least two ascetic lines, Tīrtha and Giri, existed at this time. The Dvaitin Madhvācārya was given the monastic name Ānandatīrtha by the Advaita guru he would later repudiate. While Ānandagiri, the scholar who commented on many of Śaṅkara's works, probably belonged to the Giri lineage. Textual evidence for the ten categories of renouncers goes back at least to the beginning of the 16th century. Viśveśvara Sarasvatī, who was active about this time (and was the teacher of the famous Advaitin, Madhusūdana Sarasvatī), states in his *Yatidharma-saṃgraha* that ascetics should receive one of the ten approved names from their gurus.[106] This reference certainly establishes

---

105 He follows the pioneering work of P. V. Kane, who must have examined many of the eighty odd compositions exclusively devoted to renunciation he listed in his *History of Dharmaśāstra*, (vol. 1, part 2, pp. 989-1158). Some of Olivelle's important publications include: an edition and translation of *Vāśudevāśrama Yatidharmaprakāśa. A treatise on world renunciation* (2 vols. Vienna: Institut für Indologie der Universität Wien, 1976-77), and an edition with notes of the *Saṃnyāsapaddhati of Rudradeva* (Madras: Adyar Library, 1986). Critical editions of two more texts, along with selections from other works are included in his *Renunciation in Hinduism: a medieval debate* (2 vols. Vienna: Institut für Indologie der Universität Wien, 1986-87).

106 *tato nāma prakartavyaṃ guruṇā sarva-saṃmatam / tīrthāśrama-vanāraṇya - giri-parvata-sāgarāḥ // sarasvatī bhāratī ca purī nāma yater daśa /* Viśveśvara Sarasvatī, *Yatidharmasaṃgrahaḥ*, ed. V. S. R. Gokhale (Ānandāśrama Sanskrit Series no. 60, 2nd ed., Poona: Ānandāśrama, 1928), p. 103. The passage is quoted in *Vāsudevāśrama Yatidharmaprakāśa* (Olivelle's edition) vol. 1, p. 99 (66.13-15), see also vol. 2, pp. 26-28 for further discussion.

the existence of ten proper names for renouncers, hence the concept *daśanāmi-saṃnyāsin*s. Yet whether the notion of *daśanāmins* originally entailed the existence of discrete lineages is not certain. Perhaps initially the accepted practice was for the guru to select the name which best suited the temperament of his disciple, and eventually the custom arose whereby the pupil took on the monastic "surname" of his teacher as a kind of patronym.

In any case, the fact that a tradition of ten names was well established by the early 16th century suggests that the classification of *daśanāmi-saṃnyāsin*s was known to most of our hagiographers. There are two possible reasons why our sources scarcely elaborate on Śaṅkara's organization of monastic lineages. This notion may simply not have been very widespread until some time after the composition of our texts, i.e., post-1750. But perhaps it was only those hagiographers who were themselves (apparently) *samnyāsin*s, namely Cidvilāsa and Anantānandagiri, who saw a special need to broach the subject. In this respect, it is all the more conspicuous that Anantānandagiri mentions just the Bhāratī lineage. It should also be noted that even the CŚV does not speak of the connection between the *daśanāmin*s and the four *maṭha*s, a relationship which is now accepted as an integral part of ascetic tradition.

As we have seen, those texts which focus on Śaṅkara's legacies—the AŚV, CŚV and GVK—all reveal institutional links, in contrast to the other five hagiographies which show no sign of affiliation to any particular Śaṅkara organization. While it cannot be denied that the *maṭha*s have played a major role in propagating the teachings and the life story of Śaṅkara, the division in our sources points to the fact that these institutions did not have a monopoly on the Śaṅkara tradition. Indeed the most influential of the hagiographies, the ŚDV, is one of the five "independent" texts which make no mention of the *maṭhas* or the other legacies. Nonetheless, the incumbents of the monastic centres which claim to be the very *maṭhas* Śaṅkara established in the four quarters of the subcontinent, declare the ŚDV to be the most authoritative source for his life story.[107]

Just as the Śaṅkara *maṭhas* have taken up an independent text and given it official status, it seems that they may have appropriated what was previously a separate organization: the *daśanāmi-saṃnyāsins*. Although it cannot be proved that the *daśanāmins* were originally independent of the four *maṭhas*, there is certainly very little in the hagiographies which suggests an association between the two. Moreover, there is a dearth of evidence to indicate exactly how the establishment of the ten ascetic lineages came to be attributed to Śaṅkara in the first place. The few available studies which deal with the history of the *daśanāmi-saṃnyāsin* s simply assume Śaṅkara to be their founder without offering any justification for the claim.[108] Jadunath Sarkar admits the paucity of written records concerning

---

107 I was able to ascertain this through interviews with the Śaṅkarācārya of Sringerī, H. H. Śrī Abhinava Vidyātīrtha (who reigned until his death on 21 September 1989) and H. H. Svāmī Svarūpānanda who holds the seats of both the Dwārkā and Jyotir *maṭhas*. I did not have the opportunity to meet the incumbent of the Purī *maṭha*. The Paramācārya of the Kānchipuram *maṭha* (the authenticity of which the other four monastic centres call into question) recognized the AŚV as the foremost authority. See Appendix A for details of the interviews.

108 See for example, J. N. Farquhar, "The organization of the sannyasis of the Vedanta", *Journal of the Royal Asiatic Society*, (1925) pp. 479-486; Jadunath Sarkar, *A history of dasnami naga sanyasis* (Allahabad: Sri Panchayati Akhara Mahanirvani, n.d), p. 54 ff.; G. S. Ghurye, *Indian sadhus* (Bombay: Popular Book Depot, 1953), p. 92 ff.; Haripada Chakraborti, *Asceticism in ancient India* (Calcutta: Punthi Pustak, 1973), p. 178 ff.; Swāmi Sadānanda Giri, Society and sannyāsin. *A history of the daśnāmī sannyāsins* (Varanasi: Swāmi Sadānanda Giri, 1976), p. 16 ff.

the *daśanāmins* prior to 1750,[109] while Swāmi Sadānanda Giri states that he is constrained in his study to rely largely on interviews of fellow *saṃnyāsin*s.[110] It is, of course, dangerous to draw conclusions from the absence of records alone. Yet I would suggest that the lack of documentation concerning *daśanāmin* monks is an indication that they were, prior to c. 1750, probably a very loosely organized body which was independent of a central institution. There is certainly no requirement for a *saṃnyāsin* to spend time in one of the four Śaṅkara *maṭha*s, and I would venture to say that many monks have never done so, even though they may trace their lineage back to Śaṅkara.

As might be expected, the textual evidence for the connection between the monastic centres and the *daśanāmin*s derives only from the former. There are several compositions known as *maṭhāmnāya*s which describe this relationship. Baldev Upādhyāy has prepared an edition of one of these works, entitled *Maṭhāmnāyasetu*, on the basis of several manuscripts and two early publications.[111] A prose version was published under the curious title *Maṭhāmnāyopaniṣad.*[112] Little is known about the origins of these texts, whose ascription to Śaṅkara seems most unlikely to be authentic. The *maṭhāmnāya*s describe, in very similar terms, the special characteristics of four traditions

---

109 *A history of dasnami naga sanyasis*, p. 82.

110 *Society and sannyāsin*, p. 17.

111 This appears as an appendix to his Hindi translation of the ŚDV: Mādhavācārya, *Śri Śaṅkara-digvijaya* ([1943] 3d ed., Hardwar: Śrī Śravaṇanātha Jñāna Mandir), pp. 601-611. There is a brief introduction describing the various sources and their discrepancies, but no variant readings are given. The text consists of 39 verses in the *śloka* metre.

112 In *Unpublished Upanishads*, ed. Pandits of the Adyar Library under C. Kunhan Raja (Madras: Adyar Library, 1938), pp. 48-49. The edition is based on a single defective manuscript.

(*āmnāyas*) in the cardinal points of the subcontinent.[113] For each of the *āmnāyas*, the texts specify the names of its *maṭha* and its own lineage, the ascetic lines affiliated to it, the sacred site with which it is associated, the presiding god and goddess, the direct disciple of Śaṅkara who first occupied the seat, the sacred body of water associated with it, the name to be given to *brahmacārins*, along with the particular Veda and *mahāvākya* which are to be recited there. Most important for our discussion is the following relationship between the *daśanāmins* and the *maṭhas* indicated in the text.

āmnāya	site of *maṭha*	ascetic lineage
West	Dwārkā	Tīrtha, Āśrama
East	Purī	Vana, Āraṇya
North	Badarī	Giri, Parvata, Sāgara
South	Sringerī	Sarasvatī, Bhāratī, Purī

The scheme clearly suggests that the *maṭhas* exercise some sort of jurisdiction over the *daśanāmi-saṃnyāsins*. But in practice the authority of the monastic centres may well be merely honorary.

This can be determined from the lists of the lineage (*guru-paramparā*) in each of the four *maṭhas*.[114] While these records

113 The texts also refer to three supramundane traditions: one above, the *ūrdhvāmnāya*, and two within, the *ātmāmnāya* and *niṣkalāmnāya*. The latter name does not appear in the *Maṭhāmnāyopaniṣad*, which seems to be incomplete in its final section. The *Maṭhāmnāyasetu* also specifies the regions which are under the jurisdiction of each *āmnāya*. The chief discrepancy in the two versions concerns the identity of the disciples who first occupied the seat in the *maṭhas*.

114 The guru-paramparās of the four monastic centres, along with that of the Kānchipuram *maṭha*, are given in Baldev Upādhyāy, *Śrī Śaṅkarācārya: Śrī*

may not be reliable as historical documents, they are revealing about the relationship of the monastic centres and *daśanāmin*s. The Purī *guru-paramparā* shows that the vast majority of the presiding *ācārya*s of that *maṭha*, including the present incumbent Śrī Nirañjanadeva Tīrtha, belong to the Tīrtha order. Yet according to the *maṭhāmnāya*s, this order is based in Dwārkā, not Purī. The Sringerī *guru-paramparā*, on the other hand, indicates that from the thirteenth to the thirty-fourth *ācārya*, Chandrasekhara Bhāratī (reigned 1912-1954), the incumbent was always of the Bhāratī order, in keeping with the scheme of the *maṭhāmnāya* s. However, the young student and future *ācārya* whom Chandraśekhara Bhāratī himself initiated was given the monastic name Śrī Abhinava Vidyātīrtha. His successor, in turn, is Śrī Bhāratītīrtha the thirty-sixth and present *ācārya*. The names of the two latter incumbents are most appropriate in so far as they commemorate two of the most famous *ācārya*s in the lineage of this *maṭha*. Nevertheless the *maṭhāmnāya* s do not link the Tīrtha order with Sringerī. The unquestioned orthodoxy of the mode of succession at Sringerī in this century[115] highlights the fact that in defining the relationship between the *matha*s and *daśanāmin*s, the *maṭhāmnāya* s have established a harmonious theoretical model, and not a set of inviolable rules.

The Rāmakrishna order provides another intreresting case in point. Since Śrī Rāmakrishna received an Advaita initiation from Totapurī, a *saṃnyāsin* belonging to the Purī order, the Rāmakrishna monks trace their affiliation to the Sringerī *maṭha*. Yet, as far as I know, the Rāmakrishna order has no significant

---

Śaṅkarācārya ke jīvancarit tathā upadeśoṃ kā prāmāṇik vivaraṇ (Allahabad: Hindustani Academy, 1950), pp. 169-194.

115 The thirty-fifth and thirty-sixth incumbents at Sringerī exemplify the ideals of the Śaṅkara order. Both were initiated into *saṃnyāsa* directly from *brahmacarya* at an early age, in imitation of Śaṅkara. Both were clearly designated as heir-apparents to the *pīṭha* long before the death of their gurus whom they were to succeed.

connections with Sringerī. The sacred site with which they have a far more real link is the city of Purī, both from a regional point of view and because it was the abode of Caitanya with whom Śrī Rāmakrishna came to be identified. Nevertheless the association with Sringerī provides the necessary legitimacy for the Rāmakrishna order.[116] The Sringerī *maṭha*, in turn, stands to gain in prestige from being perceived as the spiritual authority for an organization which has been held in great esteem throughout India.[117] In this way, both older and newer orders of *daśanāmin*s may have found it worth their while to accept the *maṭha*s' claim of authority, as set out in the *maṭhāmnāya* s. So long as the four monastic centres do not make unwanted intrusions into their affairs, the *daśanāmin*s can

---

116 There were two problems the Rāmakrishna order faced in legitimating its monastic order. Firstly, although Śrī Rāmakrishna maintained life-long celibacy, he was nonetheless married. Secondly, it has been questioned whether the real founder of the order, Swāmī Vivekānanda a non-brahmin, had the right to become a *saṃnyāsin*. There is a long-standing dispute, which goes back to before the time of Śaṅkara, as to whether a non-brahmin can become a monk. It is very doubtful that the orthodox Sringerī maṭha would itself permit the monastic initiation of a non-brahmin. See Farquhar's "Organization of the sannyasis" for further discussion on this issue. Furthermore, Swāmī Vivekānanda had to argue for *kṣatriya* status in order to defend himself from an even more serious charge that as a *śūdra* he was definitely excluded from becoming a *saṃnyāsin*. He spoke out publicly on this issue during an address he delivered in Madras soon after returning from his first overseas journey (*The complete works of Swami Vivekananda* [6th ed., 7 vols. Mayavati: Advaita Ashrama, 1948] III, p. 211).

117 A new complication in the relationship has been recently introduced with the Rāmakrishna Mission's plea before the Calcutta High Court in 1980 that it be granted minority status as a non-Hindu organization, representing the "religion of Shri Ramakrishna". This and other statements from their writ are cited in a booklet by Ram Swarup, *Ramakrishna Mission in search of a new identity* (New Delhi: Voice of India, 1986, p. 2) which attacks the mission for forsaking its Hindu heritage.

remain effectively independent of the *maṭhas*, while enjoying the legitimacy the relationship confers on them.

From a historical perspective there is little which justifies the attribution of the *maṭhāmnāya*s to Śaṅkara. But the mythological image of Śaṅkara which is established in the hagiographies provides a sound basis for ascribing the texts to this incarnation of Śiva, the lord of ascetics. The symmetrical integration of the *daśanāmin*s into the Advaita tradition, described in the *maṭhāmnāya*s, is a logical extension of one of the dominant motifs of the Śaṅkara story. The hagiographies' representation of his efforts in restoring harmony to the land becomes an even grander scheme of unification, linking the monastic centres and the ascetic lineages with the transcendent authority of the four Vedas and the sacred geography of the subcontinent.

While the monastic centres appear to have been successful in incorporating the *daśanāmin*s within their own institutional framework, there are limits as to how far the *maṭha*s can extend their jurisdiction. If they are perceived to overstep their proper bounds, the monastic centres put at risk the whole of their sphere of authority. There is at present an undercurrent of dissatisfaction with the Śaṅkarācāryas among some sectors of the Hindu population. This is more than mere anti-brahmin sentiment.[118] One prominent brahmin spokesman who articulates his disapproval is P. V. Kane. In his magisterial work, *History of Dharmaśāstra*, he strongly criticizes the Śaṅkara *maṭhas* for assuming the right to make pronouncements in "matters such as prescribing penances for lapses, settling

---

118 The anti-brahmin movement in Tamil Nadu is extremely antagonistic to the Śaṅkarācāryas and to Śaṅkara himself. See, for example, the Dravidar Kazhagam tract: K. Veeramani, *Kanchi Sankaracharíar: saint or sectarian?* ([first published in Tamil, 1985], English ed., Madras: Dravidar Kazhagam, 1988).

disputes between castes and deciding questions of outcasting".[119] According to Kane, it was only since the time of British rule that the Śaṅkarācāryas began to claim virtually exclusive jurisdiction in questions of religious practice. He argues that they have usurped the role of the councils of learned brahmins who had previously arbitrated in disputes requiring expertise in *dharma-śāstra*. Kane pleads that rightful authority be restored to the paṇḍit councils.[120] More recently, the Śaṅkarācārya of Purī has gained much opprobrium from all sectors of the population for his defence of *sati*.[121] Similarly the *ācārya* who holds the seat in both the Dwārkā and Jyotir *maṭhas* has met with censure, and detention, for his attempts to lay a foundation stone for the Rāmjanmabhūmi temple in Ayodhyā.[122] Such forays into the sphere of politics tend to erode the standing of the Śaṅkara *maṭhas* as a whole.

The high profile which the *maṭhas* enjoy nowadays is likely to obscure the fact that there are many followers of Śaṅkara who have not been members of an institution. In distinguishing an unaffiliated grouping in the Śaṅkara tradition, however, I must emphasize that I do not wish to suggest it is independent. The notion of an independent status would contradict one of the most essential beliefs in the Śaṅkara

---

119 *History of Dharmaśāstra: ancient and mediaeval religious and civil law* (5 vols. Poona : Bhandarkar Oriental Institute, Poona), 1962-75, vol. 2, part 2, p. 966 ff. Another eminent jurist critical of the Śaṅkarācāryas is Jogendra Chunder Ghosh, *The principles of Hindu law* (3d ed., two vols., Calcutta: S. C. Audy and Co., 1917), vol. I p. 922.

120 Op. cit., p. 974.

121 The Week, October 22, 1989, reported a womens' anti-Śaṅkarācārya rally in Purī. More general disapproval is revealed in India Today, 30 April 1988, p. 71. See also, Jürgen Lütt, "The Śaṅkarācārya of Puri", in *The cult of Jannath and the regional tradition of Orissa*, ed. A. Eschmann, H. Kulke, G. C. Tripathi (Delhi: Manohar, 1978), pp. 411-419.

122 *India Today*, May 31, 1990, p. 29.

tradition. The centrality of one's own guru and the recognition of a still greater relationship which locates the teacher within an honoured lineage, are so integral to the tradition that they hardly need mention. Every *daśanāmin* who has undergone formal initiation takes his place within a *guru-paramparā* which is firmly linked, whether directly or indirectly, to the lineage of the ideal renouncer in the person of Śaṅkara. The same applies, by analogy, to a lay disciple of a *daśanāmin.* The fact that the *maṭhas* trace their lineages right back to Śaṅkara (and therefore by implication still further, to Vyāsa or even Śiva), does not negate in any way the validity of a less extensive *guru-paramparā.*

At present there are undoubtedly far fewer prominent spokesmen for the Śaṅkara tradition who are not affiliated with the *maṭhas* than there were in the past. Some of the reasons for this are readily apparent. Since the advent of British rule there has been a steady erosion of traditional values. This decline has been further accelerated by the effects of urbanization. The Mahārājas' loss of power meant that individual paṇḍits were much less likely to find patrons. Similarly, councils of learned brahmins were rarely convened to adjudicate in problems concerning the interpretation of *dharma-śāstra.*[123] The limited resources now allocated to Sanskrit studies are hardly an incentive for the pursuit of this "profession".[124] Although the

---

123 For a discussion of paṇḍit *pariṣads* held since the advent of the British, see J. T. F. Jordens, "Orthodoxy and heresy: reflections of the 1881 Calcutta pandit council", in *World perspectives on Swami Dayananda Saraswati,* [ed.] Ganga Ram Garg (New Delhi: Concept Publishing, 1984), 239-252. See also Richard W. Lariviere , "Justices and *Paṇḍitas*: some ironies in contemporary readings of the Hindu legal past", *The Journal of Asian Studies* 48 (1989) 757-769, for an examination of the role of the paṇḍit in the colonial courts.

124 See Edwin Gerow, "Some thoughts on Indian government policy as it affects Sanskrit education" in *Studies in the language and culture of South*

options available to individuals were severely limited during the British rāj, religious institutions could, with efficient and imaginative management, reorient themselves and seek alternative sources of funding.[125] As the paṇḍit councils and other traditional authorities began to disappear, there were new opportunities for the survivors. Not only did some of the Śaṅkara *maṭhas* consolidate their position, they were able to expand their sphere of authority, especially in the south. They also had the good fortune of receiving an unexpected boost from the colonial administration. The favourable reception of Śaṅkara's work by scholars such as F. Max Müller meant that the spokesmen for this relatively acceptable native tradition were likely to receive greater recognition, both from Hindus who had adapted to the realities of British rule and from the colonial masters themselves.

While I would not attempt to characterize the nature of the unaffiliated stream or streams in the Śaṅkara tradition, I do think the designation of such a grouping is warranted. Despite the fact that the *maṭhas* have claimed Śaṅkara's principal disciples for their own, there is no indication that the likes of Vācaspatimiśra, Vimuktātman, Śrī Harṣa, Madhusūdana Sarasvatī or Appaya-Dīkṣita, to name just a few prominent Advaitins, were ever members of a Śaṅkara institution. Such luminaries of the Śaṅkara tradition hold a no less prestigious place than Vidyāraṇya, who is perhaps the most famous incumbent of a monastic centre. There are no doubt many other important Advaitins, along with countless *daśanāmin*s, who

---

Asia, ed. E. Gerow and M. D. Lang (Seattle and London: University of Washington, 1973), pp. 111-124.

125 For an analysis of how the present incumbent of the Kānchipuram *maṭha* has broadened its power base, see Mattison Mines and Vijayalakshmi Gourishankar, "Leadership and individuality in south Asia: the case of the south Indian big-man", *Journal of Asian Studies* 49 (1990), 761-786.

have remained independent of the Śaṅkara *maṭhas*. To this list of the "unattached" we must also add five of our eight hagiographers.

The existence of two streams in the Śaṅkara tradition ultimately derives from a more fundamental dichotomy. From a conceptual point of view this is probably best expressed in terms of *pravṛtti* and *nivṛtti*. An examination of this opposition is reserved for Chapter VII. On an empirical level, the two perspectives on Śaṅkara may be understood in terms of the distictinction between the ascetics who bear the staff, the *daṇḍins*, and those who reject it. This emblem of renunciation has figured in various controversies. Once the legitimacy of renunciation itself was established,[126] the remaining doubts about orthodoxy centred on the insignia of the *saṃnyāsin*. One particular topic of debate was whether the renouncer should have a triple *daṇḍa* or a single one.[127] Perhaps the most difficult problem of all was occasioned by the outright rejection of the *daṇḍa*. Śaṅkara himself refers to this matter in the *Chāndogyopaniṣad-bhāṣya* (2.23.1):

> What is stated in the Veda about the condition of the wandering mendicant is not the taking up of the sacred thread, the triple *daṇḍa*, the water pot and the like. The *śruti* says it is "being shaven-headed, without possessions and not attached"...and the *smṛti* says such things as, "therefore the knower of

---

126 The arguments concerning the legitimacy of *saṃnyāsa* are reflected in our hagiographies by the Śaṅkara-Maṇḍana debate, which is so central to the narrative. Śaṅkara's victory marks the ascendancy of the renouncer. See Chapter Five.

127 See Olivelle, *Renunciation in Hinduism*, vol. I, pp. 26-56.

> *dharma* is without insignia, his insignia are not apparent".[128]

For Advaitins, the renouncer's abandonment of the sacred thread is accepted without question.[129] But the *daṇḍa* and waterpot (*kamaṇḍalu*) are, along with the ochre cloth, the most characteristic emblems of the *saṃnyāsin*. Without these the renouncer's status becomes problematic.

Even though the *samnyāsin* has renounced the ritual practice associated with the first three stages of life (*āśrama*), the *dharma-śāstras* make it clear that he is expected to follow certain prescriptions. Since there is an inseparable link between *āśrama* and *dharma*, those who enter the fourth stage must still be subject to a *saṃnyāsa-dharma*. However, Śaṅkara's statements on the renouncer describe him as beyond the *āśramas* altogether:

> The expression "established in Brahman", should be understood solely with reference to the wandering mendicant, who has given up all ritual action along with its accessories. He is beyond the *āśramas*. It is he who is called a Paramahaṃsa.[130]

Śaṅkara's comments appear to be wholly reliant on the authority of the *Jābāla Upaniṣad*. This text describes the Paramahaṃsa ascetics as those "whose insignia are not apparent, whose way of life is not apparent, who go about like

---

128 *vedoktam pārivrājyam / na yajñopavīta-tridaṇḍa-kamaṇḍalvādi-parigraha iti / muṇḍo 'parigraho 'saṅga iti śruti...tasmād aliṅgo dharma-jño 'vyakta-liṅga ity ādi-smṛtibhyaś ca /.*

129 The argument over the renunciation of the sacred thread appears in Cidvilāsa's version of the Śaṅkara-Maṇḍana debate. This is discussed above in Chapter Five.

130 *brahma-saṃstha-śabdo nivṛtta-sarva-karma-tat-sādhana-parivrāḍ-eka-viṣaye 'tyāśramiṇi parama-haṃsākhye vṛtta iha bhavitum arhasi* (*Chāndogyopaniṣad-bhāṣya* 2.23.1).

madmen but are not mad".[131] The existence of the *atyāśramin*, the ascetic who goes beyond the four stages of life, calls into question the validity of the rules set out for the renouncer, and by extension, the whole concept of *āśrama-dharma*. Śaṅkara offers what may be a partial solution to this dilemma in conjunction with a somewhat different issue in *Brahmasūtra-bhāṣya* 2.3.48. Here he admits that obligations can only apply to those who see the body as distinct from the Self. The one who truly knows, for whom there is no difference, has no obligations. Yet, Śaṅkara says, it cannot be assumed that he acts as he pleases, for he has no desires which would impel him to action in the first place.

Vidyāraṇya picks up this line of thought and tries to develop it both as a principle and as a practical solution to the confusion surrounding the status of the *atyāśramin*. In his *Jīvanmuktiviveka* he posits the existence of two types of Paramahaṃsas: those renouncers who are knowers (*vidvat-saṃnyāsin*) and those who are seeking to know (*vividiṣā-saṃnyāsin*). He states that the latter are characterized by such things as the *daṇḍa*, while the former have no possessions whatsoever, as described in the *Jābāla Upaniṣad*. If this distinction is accepted, then there is scope for both the ascetic who follows *saṃnyāsa-dharma* and for the *atyāśramin*. Vidyāraṇya also strives to protect the diginity of the emblems of renunciation in the face of their rejection by the highest grade of Paramahaṃsa. He suggests that the *vidvat-saṃnyāsin* is never truly without the *daṇḍa*: "the Paramahaṃsa who bears the staff [consisting] of knowledge is said to be the pre-eminent holder of the single *daṇḍa*".[132]

---

131 *avyakta-liṅgāḥ avyaktācārāḥ anunmattā unmattavad ācarantas* (*Jābālopaniṣad* 6).

132 *ayaṃ jñāna-daṇḍo yena paramahaṃsena dhṛtaḥ sa eva mukhya eka-daṇḍīty ucyate* (Vidyāraṇya, *Jīvanmuktiviveka: liberation in life*, ed. and tr. S.

I will leave aside the question of whether or not Vidyāraṇya has successfully resolved the dilemma posed by the *atyāśramin*. This brief examination of the problem should, however, be sufficient to indicate that there are two distict possibilities for the representation of Śaṅkara: either he is seen as a *daṇḍin* or as an *atyāśramin*. As far as the present-day Śaṅkarācāryas are concerned, the *daṇḍa* constitutes the essential emblem of their authority. When the incumbent of the Kānchipuram *maṭha* was reported recently to have left aside his *daṇḍa* and gone to an undisclosed place of retreat, the Śaṅkarācārya of the Dwārkā/Jyotir *maṭhas* stated publicly that his actions "constituted a breach of *śāstra*".[133] This was in contrast to his subsequent statement concerning the water pot: "not much importance could be attached to the carrying or leaving behind of the *kamaṇḍalu*".[134]

With the exception of the GVK, the hagiographies do not make a special point of emphasizing that Śaṅkara is a *daṇḍin*. Nevertheless, the portrait of Śaṅkara they paint conforms to the stereotype of the renouncer—attired in orange cloth, carrying both the staff and water pot—and not the *atyāśramin*. Some of the texts make this explicit, while in others his ascetic regalia are only implicit. The ŚDV, for example, describes how he arrives at the abode of his guru, wearing fresh ochre-coloured clothes and bearing a *daṇḍa*.[135] After his formal initiation, the text is more indirect in referring to his insignia. When Śiva appears in the guise of an untouchable to put Śaṅkara's non-duality to the test, he criticizes the way in which renouncers are

---

Subrahmanya Sastri and T. R. Srinivasa Ayyangar [1935] revised ed. Madras: Adyar Library, 1978), p. 165 (text).

133 *The Hindu*, 26 August 1987, p. 9. He also took the opportunity to add that the Kānchipuram *maṭha* was not one of the centres established by Śaṅkara and could only be considered a branch of the Sringerī *maṭha*.

134 *Ibid*.

135 *daṇḍānvitena dhṛta-rāga-navāmbareṇa*, ŚDV 5.90 (=*Patañjali-carita* 8.19).

able to "fool the householders with their *daṇḍa*, water pot, orange clothes and clever speech, even though they are without a trace of real knowledge".[136] Lakṣmaṇa-Śāstrī, on the other hand, sees to it that the *daṇḍa* and *kamaṇḍalu* feature directly in the narrative. He makes Śaṅkara hesitate for a moment, before departing the mundane sphere, wondering what to do about his ascetic accoutrements:

> 'I have relinquished all my disciples and all my books, yet the staff and the water pot remain'. [Then] the yogi abandoned those two things as well. The *daṇḍa* was transformed into a tree and the water in the *kamaṇḍalu* became a *tīrtha*... (GVK 3.69-70).

Lakṣmaṇa-Śāstrī is quite perceptive in linking the emblems of renunciation to the work of teaching and writing which Śaṅkara is obliged to undertake. It is precisely these ties, the magic power of his *daṇḍa* and *kamaṇḍalu* notwithstanding, which fix him within the bounds of *saṃnyāsa-dharma*. In the hagiographies the nature of Śaṅkara's mission does not allow him to be an *atyāśramin*. It is even more compelling for the monastic centres to represent Śaṅkara as a *daṇḍin* in support of their claims to the inheritance of his spiritual authority.

The Disputes Between the *Maṭhas*

There is no evidence of antagonism between the institutional and unaffiliated streams in the Śaṅkara tradition. Since his hermeneutics were restricted within the context of an already defined Mīmāṃsā orthodoxy (which eventually coalesced into Smārta orthopraxy), Śaṅkara's *modus operandi* was far less likely to generate major schisms than that of an independent

---

136 ŚDV 6. 27 (=TŚA 3.67).

religious leader like the Buddha. The rift between the two opposing schools in the Śaṇkara tradition, the Bhāmatī and Vivaraṇa, did not result in a parting of the ways. So long as the centrality of the *guru-paramparā* is accepted, doctrinal disputes are not very likely to disrupt the continuity of the Advaita tradition. A perhaps more serious threat to its integrity is posed by the disputes arising between and within the various Śaṅkara institutions.

In the absence of empirical evidence for the particulars of his life story, we may never know how Śaṅkara put his own teaching into practice. For this reason there is probably little to be gained in speculating on the extent to which the incumbents of the Śaṅkara *maṭhas* actually emulate the life-style of the man in whose name the institutions were established, or re-established as the case may be. One thing is certain, however. Once a religious teacher is enshrined within a formal organization, powerful politico-economic interests come into play. Like any other institution, the Śaṅkara *maṭhas* have experienced internal power struggles and conflicts with rival centres over jurisdictional boundaries. Such disputes shift the focus of attention away from the pristine sphere of the metaphysical to the turmoil of every day life. More specifically, organizational conflict has the potential to weaken the ascetic foundations on which the Śaṅkara tradition is established. The concerns of institutional wrangling sit uncomfortably with the spirit of renunciation.

Given the popular tradition of the four monastic centres in the quarters of the subcontinent, it was probably inevitable that the coexistence of two powerful *maṭhas* in the south would give rise to controversy. The rivalry between Sringerī and Kānchipuram has erupted into what is perhaps the most serious dispute between the Śaṅkara institutions in the past 150 years. The conflict hinges on the status of the Kānchipuram *maṭha*.

The Sringerī argument is essentially that Śaṅkara founded only four monastic centres, of which they are the official *maṭha* of the southern *āmnāya.* As such, they have jurisdiction over the whole of south India. They refer to the centre at Kānchipuram as the "Kumbakonam *maṭha*" because it was, they claim, first established in the 18th or 19th century in Kumbakonam (Thanjāvūr District, Tamil Nadu). They hold that if the Kumbakonam *maṭha* is indeed a Śaṅkara institution, it is necessarily subject to Sringerī, the sole legitimate southern *maṭha.* The Kānchipuram side admits that Śaṅkara did found four *maṭhas* in the cardinal points of India, in which his principal disciples were installed. But they argue that his own *maṭha*, was established at Kānchipuram, where Śaṅkara spent the last of his days. Hence they maintain that theirs is the fifth and central *maṭha.* They also explain that their centre was relocated in Kumbakonam during the middle of the 18th century because of the "fear of Muslim atrocities".[137] Some of the spokesmen for Kānchipuram have gone so far as to counter-attack with the claim that the Sringerī lineage has been interrupted or that the present site of the *maṭha* is not its original location.

In order to appreciate the magnitude of this dispute one must bear in mind that since the turn of the century the monastic centres at Sringerī and Kānchipuram have been by far the most powerful of the Śaṅkara *maṭhas*. The various administrators of the two *maṭhas* have tried every avenue in the pursuance of their respective claims. The matter was brought before the courts in 1844, but this settled just one contested point concerning the jurisdiction of the *maṭhas*.[138] A more

---

137 *The Voice of Śaṅkara: Śaṅkara Bhāratī*, 4 (1979), pp. 87-90. It was not until 1977 that their headquarters were finally shifted back to Kānchipuram.

138 An adherent of Sringerī filed a suit against the Kānchipuram *ācāryas* who had assumed the rights to maintain the image of the deity in the Jambukeśvara temple at Tiruvanaikovil (Tiruchirapalli district, Tamil Nadu). The courts

traditional resolution was sought in 1934. Each party convened large paṇḍit councils in Benares to pass judgement on the disputed claims.[139] For the past fifty years the partisans have produced a steady stream of newspaper articles, pamphlets and books in various languages.[140] These publications generally

---

reportedly ruled in favour of the Kānchipuram *maṭha*. The Sringerī adherent filed two subsequent appeals to higher courts but both were rejected. Extracts from the court proceedings are given in a booklet by N. Krishnaswami Reddiar, *Some judicial references and administrative records regarding Sankaracharya Mutts* (Madras: D. Ramanathan Chettiar, 1987). It must be noted, however, that the booklet is itself party to the dispute. The author, a retired judge at the High Court of Madras, provides only such information as supports the claims of the Kānchipuram *maṭha*.

139 I have seen several references to a booklet published in Benares in 1934, entitled *Śrī Jagadguruśaṅkaramaṭhavimarśa*, which reportedly found in favour of Sringerī, but I have not been able to obtain a copy. Neither have I sighted the document supporting the Kānchipuram claims, entitled *Śrī Śaṅkarapīṭhatattvadarśanam* (Benares, 1934). Both publications are briefly described by W. R. Antarkar, in his unpublished thesis, "Śaṅkara-vijayas: a comparative and a critical study" (University of Poona, 1960), pp. 494-495.

140 Some of the books written on behalf of the Sringerī claims are: J. V. Rāj Gopal Śarmā, *Śrīmad jagadguru śaṅkaramaṭha vimarśa* [in Hindi] (Varanasi, 1963); R. Krishnaswamy Aiyar and K. R. Venkatraman, *The truth about the Kumbhakonam mutt* ([publisher and place not identified], 1965); V. Raj Gopal Sharma, *Kanchi Kamakoti math: a myth* (Varanasi: Ganga-tunga Prakashan, 1987); Mudigonda Venkatarama Sastry, *Kāmakoṭi Śatakoṭi: one hundred proofs exposing the spurious and concocted books depended by* [sic] *the Kanchi Mutt as its authorities* [first published in Sanskrit, 1963], tr. T. Ramalingeswara Rao (Varanasi-Bangalore: Ganga-Tunga Prakashan, 1990). Some of the publications in support of the Kānchipuram *maṭha* claims are: A. Nataraja Aiyer and S. Lakshminarasimha Sastri, *The traditional age of Sri Sankaracharya and the maths* ([1962] reprinted Madras: Rajan and Co., 1988); Polagam Sri Rama Sastrigal, *The mutts founded by Sri Sankara Bhagavatpada* ([originally published in Tamil, but no details supplied in the English edition] Madras: B. G. Paul, 1973); Anantaanendra Sarasvati, *Sri Sankaracharya and Sankarite institutions* (Tiruchirapalli: Theni Printers, 1982). Anantaanendra Sarasvati's book mentions still more publications generated by the dispute

contain a wealth of fragmentary information, much of which is taken out of context, woven together with unsubstantiated allegations. They do reveal, however, that the conflict is a deep-seated one which, to date, remains completely unresolved.[141] It seems most ironic that this dispute has persisted at a time when the *ācāryas* of both the Sringerī and Kānchipuram *maṭhas* have been men of great integrity and true *saṃnyāsins*. They may well have remained unattached in the face of the power struggles which religious institutions seem invariably to generate. But I am not so sure that the same can be said of those who have participated actively in the fray.

I have done my best to avoid being drawn into the conflict, all the more so because I do not wish this work to serve as further fuel for the dispute.[142] Yet I cannot dispense with the issue altogether because the hagiographies, the very heart of this study, are themselves a focal point in the controversy. What is more, allegations abound that the texts have been tampered with. For the most part, however, the hagiographies are embroiled in the conflict only in so far as their authenticity is concerned. This means, in effect, that the texts are approved or rejected on the basis of whether they contain the particular

---

(pp. 133 ff). There is also a booklet written on behalf of the Dvārakā *maṭha* attacking the Kānchipuram *maṭha*: Manjulal Sevaklal Dave ([1963] reprinted Mysore: Sri Sharada Mudrana Prakashanalaya, 1976).

141 An unsigned article which called into question the authenticity of the Sringerī *guruparamparā*, (undoubtedly written on behalf of Kānchipuram) appeared in the *Indian Express* (Madras edition) on 25 June 1989. This resulted in a spate of letters to the editor. A series of letters were published in four instalments on 12 August 1989, 26 August, 2 September and 7 October. The two earlier instalments were allocated a half page each and the two latter ones a full page in this large format newsapaper. Another smaller series of letters on the authenticity of the Kānchipuram *maṭha* appeared in *The Illustrated Weekly*, 11 October 1987, p. 4.

142 The work of foreign scholars is often cited as evidence for various conflicting claims in the polemical literature.

details of Śaṅkara's life which one *maṭha* or the other holds to be true. Perhaps the single most important issue in this regard is the question of where Śaṅkara spent his final days.[143] The Kānchipuram side endeavours to prove that Śaṅkara ended his days in their city. This is instrumental in putting their claim that Śaṅkara's "own" *maṭha* was in Kānchipuram. The Sringerī partisans argue that the authorities on which the Kānchipuram *maṭha* relies are wholly unreliable. The mode of attack here, one adopted by both parties in the dispute, involves demonstrating the "inauthenticity" of the opponents' textual sources, usually by reference to the inconsistencies or idiosyncracies in the work. The long-standing tradition of corroborating or debunking a text by reference to supporting *ārṣa* sources is also employed.[144] Sometimes there is even recourse to historical analysis.

It is not only the rival spokesmen of the *maṭhas* who have dragged the hagiographies into the dispute. Some of the editors of the texts are themselves aligned with one or the other *maṭhas*. This casts some doubt on the authenticity of the readings they have chosen and on the composition as a whole, especially in the eyes of the partisans. The VŚV is an interesting case in point. The text itself stands more or less neutral in the controversy. While there is a lengthy *māhātmya*

---

143 The significance of this particular controversy is emphasized in the Government of India's *Report of the Hindu Religious Endowments Commission* (1960-62). In its discussion of the Kedāra temple the report states: "There are 20 Sankara digvijays, but it is not known whether Sankara attained moksha in Kedar or Kumbakonam. A proper and authentic guide book should be published by the Committee for the benefit of the public" (p. 157). The obvious slip in referring to Kumbakonam instead of Kānchipuram is further evidence of the prominence of the dispute between the Sringerī and Kumbakonam/Kānchipuram *maṭha*s.

144 The Kānchipuram side claims the support of the *Śivarahasya* and the *Mārkaṇḍeya-saṃhitā*, the authority of which are disputed by Sringerī.

in praise of Kānchipuram, there is no mention of a *maṭha*, nor is it specified that Śaṅkara ever went there in the first place. It was his disciple Sanandana's[145] visit to the city which occasioned the tribute to its glories. The fact that Sringerī is not mentioned at all in the VŚV would not, of course, endear the work to the adherents of that *maṭha*. But the real cause of Sringerī's rejection of this work is the belief that the text has been tampered with.[146]

I have found nothing in the text constituted in the published edition of the VŚV which suggests interference on the part of the editor. However, the editor's introduction contains materials which would justifiably cause alarm in Sringerī. To begin with, his summary of the life of Śaṅkara is drawn not from the VŚV itself, as one would expect, but from the AŚV. This hagiography is the favourite of the Kānchipuram *maṭha* and anathema to Sringerī. Even more alarming is the page the editor appends to the introduction. Here he states that after the printing of the work was completed, he received a copy of the *Jagadgururatnamālā*, whose commentary cites five verses purportedly from the last chapter of the VŚV. The man who brought the *Jagadgururatnamālā* to the editor's attention was a reputed traditional scholar, but he is also known as a spokeman for the Kānchipuram *maṭha*.[147] This alone would make the Sringerī adherents suspicious. The contents of the five verses make matters still worse. They describe how Śaṅkara ends his days at the Kāmakoṭi *maṭha* in Kānchipuram.

---

145 The VŚV does not speak of the transformation of Sanandana into Padmapāda which is described in five other hagiographies. See the table of incidents in Chapter Two.

146 This was expressed during a personal interview with H. H. Śrī Abhinava Vidyātīrtha in Sringerī. See Appendix A for further details.

147 Namely, Polagam Śrī Rāma Śāstrigal, author of *The mutts founded by Sri Sankara* (see note 140).

Although the editor admits that only one of these verses is found in the manuscripts he used in preparing the edition, he has nevertheless gone ahead and put this questionable material into print. His only justification for this is that, "it will be of great interest to scholars". Moreover, the one verse from the *Jagadgururatnamālā* commentary the editor states is justified by the available manuscripts is, in fact, substantially different. The verse in question marks the culmination of the narrative. Śaṅkara has gone to Kāshmīr hoping to gain the throne of omniscience. He passes the tests set by the learned scholars who guard the doors to the temple and, once inside, successfully meets the final challenge posed by Sarasvatī herself:

> In this way [Śaṅkara] who was fit to be in the assembly, rendered the goddess speechless, ascended the throne of omniscience and rejoiced. He was honoured by the [divine] mother of speech and also by the men who were fit to be in the assembly. [Then] he went off to a place which was pleasing [to him].[148]

The verse which appears in the commentary to the *Jagadgururatnamālā* reads:

> In this way [Śaṅkara] rendered the goddess speechless and ascended the throne of omniscience in the *maṭha* which he himself had established. He was honoured by the [divine] mother of speech and by the respected people who had come to challenge him, and he dwelt for some time in Kāñcī.[149]

---

148 *evaṃ niruttara-padāṃ sa vidhāya devīṃ sarvajña-pīṭham adhiruhya nananda sabhyaḥ / mātrā girām api tathā puruṣaiś ca sabhyaiś saṃbhāvito rucita-deśam ayam jagāma* // VŚV 12.82.

149 *evaṃ niruttara-padāṃ sa vidhāya devīṃ sarvajña-pīṭham adhiruhya maṭhe sva-kḷpte / mātrā girām api tathopagataiś ca miśraiḥ sambhāvitaḥ kam api kālam uvāsa kāñcyām* //.

Some of the hagiographers do, of course, locate the throne of omniscience in Kānchipuram. But the author of the latter verse does little justice to the integrity of the narrative by abruptly shifting the setting from Kāshmīr to Kānchipuram. The suggestion that the throne of omniscience is inside Śaṅkara's "own" *maṭha* is even more out of step with the narrative. It is the author of this verse, and not the editor, who appears to have been tampering with the text. Had the Sringerī adherents examined the published edition of the VŚV more closely, they would have noted that two of the six manuscripts the editor used belong to the Kānchipuram *maṭha*. Even these manuscripts do not support the alterations to the text. Yet in the heat of argument the VŚV has been cast into disrepute.

In what is perhaps the earliest work in English in support of the Kānchipuram claims, T. S. Narayana Sastry makes a concerted effort to discredit the most influential of the hagiographies, the ŚDV.[150] His main argument centres on Mādhava's "plagiarism" of the VŚV and RŚA.[151] But Narayana Sastry also cites anecdotal evidence that the ŚDV was composed during the 19th century at the behest of the Sringerī *maṭha* in order to further their case against Kānchipuram. The joint "authors" are said to have collaborated in a scheme which involved the extraction of verses from various sources and the devious attribution of the compilation to Mādhava (i.e., Mādhava-Vidyāraṇya).[152] While it is true that the Sringerī *maṭha* now takes the ŚDV to be the most authoritative account of Śaṅkara's life, the text provides no support for the claims

---

150 *The age of Śaṅkara* ([1916] 2nd ed., Madras: B. G. Paul and Co, 1971). It is interesting to note that the author was a colleague of M. Krishnamachariar, who espouses similar historical arguments in the introduction to his *History of classical Sanskrit literature* ([1937] reprinted, Delhi: Motilal Banarsidass, 1974), p. cx.

151 See the discussion on "plagiarism" and the ŚDV in Chapter One.

152 *Op. cit.*, pp. 158-167; 247-248.

regarding their sphere of jurisdiction. Indeed the ŚDV makes no mention of the Sringerī *maṭha* at all. If Sringerī adherents had sought to construct a text in support of their claims, I trust they would have done a better job.

Ironically, one of the few hagiographies which do refer to Śaṅkara's foundation of a monastic centre at Sringerī is the AŚV, which is rejected by this same *maṭha*. This text stands at the very centre of the dispute between Sringerī and Kānchipuram. The main thrust of the argument against the authenticity of the AŚV is that the text has been so greatly altered it is no longer possible to determine the nature of the original. Hence the work as we know it stands discredited. In this instance the accusations cannot be so lightly dismissed. The editor of the 1868 Calcutta edition of the AŚV was not party to the dispute, but most scholars who have examined the work have commented on its deficiencies. A new edition was prepared by N. Veezhinathan at the University of Madras in 1972. However, this would provide little comfort to Sringerī. Like most of his distinguished colleagues at Madras, the editor has personal links with Kānchipuram. The introduction by the late Professor T. M. P. Mahadevan clearly reveals these affiliations.

In his preface the editor describes two distinct groups of manuscripts. Now for the most part, the differences between what he defines as the A and B groups are actually quite insignificant. Both agree on the issue which is central to the Kānchipuram argument: it was in Kānchi that Śaṅkara attained liberation. Yet there are several very striking disparities between the A and B manuscripts. One obvious instance is in recounting the circumstances of Śaṅkara's birth. I have provided translations of the two different versions of this event in Chapter I. The most questionable divergence, as far as our dispute is concerned, appears in connection with the discussion of the *maṭhas*. The group B manuscripts and the Calcutta editions refer to the founding of only one *maṭha*. This occurred at Sringerī. The A manuscripts state that a monastic centre was also established at Kānchipuram. Since I have not examined the 16 manuscripts the editor used in preparing the Madras edition, I cannot make a definitive statement about the very real possibility that alterations may have been carried out by interested parties.[153]

To further complicate matters, there are counter accusations that Sringerī partisans have tampered with the text. Here I must add a personal anecdote. I had been seeking opinions about a problematic reading in the AŚV episode in which Śaṅkara humiliates Vyāsa. This, incidentally, is one of the idiosyncracies in the text which has earned it considerable disapproval.[154] One of the people I questioned was an eminent

---

153 There is one point about which I cannot help but be suspicious. In the final chapter of the AŚV, we read that Śaṅkara wishes to return to his own divine realm. He sends forth his disciples to various lands and begins the process of dissolving his body in a manner befitting a great yogi. In conjunction with the dispatching of his disciples, the editor incorporates in the text a reference to the fact that Sureśvara belonged to the Indra-Sarasvatī lineage. This reading appears to be justified by only two of the sixteen available manuscripts (p. 208n.). Now it is to the Indra-Sarasvatī lineage which the Kānchipuram *ācārya* s belong. The validity of this lineage has long been challenged by Sringerī on the grounds that it was not one of the ten originally founded by Śaṅkara.

154 In this episode Vyāsa, disguised as an old brahmin, challenges Śaṅkara's exposition of the *Brahmasūtra*. A debate ensues between the two. After Śaṅkara has made the final point in his argument, Anantānandagiri writes: *āgraheṇa jalpan vṛddhasya kapola-tāḍanam ācakāra*. From a strictly grammatical point of view, one would read, "[Śaṅkara] who was arguing insistently, slapped the cheeks of the old man". This is how the particular scholar I questioned understood the passage. One could, with some latitude, see a causative implication in the text. This would permit a less precise but more logical reading: "[Śaṅkara] who was arguing tenaciously, brought about [a gesture of submission, namely] the slapping of the cheeks on the part of

traditional scholar in Vārāṇasī, who happens to have had a long association with Kānchipuram. After reading the passage, he made a gesture of disapproval and said, "Oh, this is silly. Someone must have added it to the text". I have been fortunate that the variant readings in the AŚV have had little impact on the issues with which I have been primarily concerned in studying the hagiographies. But I have certainly had to tread warily in discussing difficulties in the texts with both traditional scholars and academics. Those who are most interested in the texts are likely to have affiliations with one or the other *maṭhas*.

There are many more arguments concerning the hagiographies in the substantial body of polemical literature generated by the dispute between the *maṭhas*. But the debates in this literature are just a preliminary to greater battles which are fought in courts of law. What is undoubtedly the most significant legal case involving the jurisdiction of the Śaṅkara *maṭhas* came before the High Court at Bombay in 1908.[155] It is worth examining this in some detail, especially since it foreshadowed a more recent case brought against the Kānchipuram *maṭha*. At the turn of the century, the Śaṅkarācārya of Dwārkā succeeded in obtaining a court injunction which prevented a local rival from calling himself 'Śaṅkarācārya' and from soliciting offerings under that name. The defendant was the head of a *maṭha* at Dholka in Gujarat which, he claimed, was a branch of the Jyotir *maṭha* at Badarīnāth. He described how long ago disputes arose between the incumbent of the Jyotir *matha* and the local authorities. As

---

the old man". See Chapter Five for more discussion on the Śaṅkara-Vyāsa debate.

155 *Madhusudan Parvat v. Shree Madhav Teerth*, The Indian Law Reports, Bombay Series, 33 (1909), pp. 278-293; The Bombay Law Reporter, 11 (1909), pp. 58-68.

a result the Śaṅkarācārya left the *maṭha* for good, along with his disciples, and set up centres in Gujarat and elsewhere. Although the Dwārkā incumbent won the case, the court did not go so far as to allow his claim for an account and the recovery of the funds received by the self-styled Śaṅkarācārya.

The Dholka *maṭha* was not content to let the matter rest. They brought their appeal to the High Court, and ironically, before a British judge. The counsel for the Śaṅkarācārya of Dwārkā based most of his arguments for the exclusive jurisdiction of that *maṭha* on the authority of the *Maṭhāmnāya*. However in concluding his statement he raised one very curious point to reinforce the special privilege due to the incumbents of the four *āmnāya maṭhas*. He cited a "rule of ascetic life" according to which, "no *saṃnyāsin* is entitled to accept pecuniary gifts unless he is a Shankaracharya".[156] I have never seen another reference to such a "rule". Indeed I suspect that it remains an implicit assumption about the office of Śaṅkarācārya primarily because it is a practical necessity, yet is not supported in the *dharma-śāstras* or later compendiums. The counsel for the appellant maintained that the *Maṭhāmnāya* was not written by Śaṅkara. He appealed instead to the work of [Anant]ānandagiri and Mādhava. These "authoritative biographers", he continued, prove that Śaṅkara did not confer rights of jurisdiction to his successors. The counsel reiterated that the appellant was a Śaṅkarācārya of the Jyotir *maṭha*, whose branch was in Dholka. He argued that those who followed the religion propounded by Śaṅkara had the right to choose for themselves a guru, a right which could not be challenged in a court of law.

In his ruling, Chief Justice Scott accepted the claim that Śaṅkara established four *maṭhas* in the four quarters of India. He also observed that in the course of time new *maṭhas* were established, while the original centres did not always maintain

156 *Ibid.*, p. 287.

their prestige. This was on the evidence of a letter dated 1852, which the incumbent at Dwārkā had received from the Sringerī Śaṅkarācārya. The letter submitted to the court reveals some very interesting information on the state of affairs in the *maṭhas* at the time. The Chief Justice gave the following summary of what the Sringerī *ācārya* had written:

> He relates how the Acharyas of the Govardhan [i.e., Purī] and Jyotir Maths degraded themselves to the position of Gosains and thus these two Maths remained without any Acharya although the Govardhan Math was subsequently revived by a Sanyasi from Gougak Nakhal. He describes how Sanyasis of the Sringeri Math have established Maths and set themselves up falsely as independent Acharyas and he combats the doctrine that any branch maths can exist. He then proposes that certain areas should again be recognized as territories of the respective Maths.[157]

The term 'Gosains' here presumably refers to religious teachers who engaged in commercial activities.[158] Such gurus could not, of course, legitimately occupy the seat in a Śaṅkara *maṭha*, which is reserved only for true *saṃnyāsin*s. Although no names are mentioned, there is every possibility that the Sringerī *ācārya* had the Kumbakonam/Kānchipuram institution (among others) in mind when he disallowed the existence of branch *maṭhas*. Justice Scott took issue with the latter comment. He noted that the jurisdiction of the Sringerī *maṭha* was reported to have been divided into five or six branches in 1835.[159]

---

157 *Ibid.*, p. 289.

158 See Bernard B. Cohen, "The role of the Gosains in the economy of eighteenth and nineteenth century upper India", *Indian Economic and Social History Review*, 4 (1964), pp. 175-182.

159 This was on the basis of *Sri Sunkur Bharti Swami v. Sidha Lingayah Charanti*. See note 51 for further details.

On the question of the *maṭhāmnāya* s, the Chief Justice stated that there is no one authoritative version of the text. The defendant had shown the court several versions, all of which differed from the text cited by the Dwārkā *ācārya.*[160] Justice Scott also accepted the defendant's evidence that the Śaṅkarācāryas of Sringerī, Dwārkā and Purī received offerings when they were on tour in districts outside their alleged jurisdiction. Ultimately however, the failure of the plaintiff to satisfy the court of his right to exclusive privileges was not the real basis on which the ruling was made. The Chief Justice found that it was not the business of the civil courts to settle disputes between religious leaders. Accordingly, he allowed the appeal and set aside the ruling of the lower court.

In 1984 a very similar case was brought before the High Court at Madras.[161] This time the Kānchipuram Śaṅkarācāryas were the defendants. One K. Rajendran, whose affiliations were unstated, filed a petition demanding that the Government of Tamil Nadu declares that the incumbents of the Kānchipuram *maṭha* were not Jagadguru-Śaṅkarācāryas. It was argued that the preceptors of the current *ācāryas* "fraudulently assumed the title of Sankaracharya of Kumbakonam, which was later rechristened as Kanchi Kamakoti Peetam in 1942". This, the petition claimed, was to the "derogation of the status, style and dignity" of the Śaṅkarācārya of Sringerī. The *maṭhāmnāya* s were cited as evidence of Sringerī's jurisdiction over the whole of south India. The existence of three of its branch *maṭhas* in Tamil Nadu was

160 However, the *maṭhāmnāyas* have found some official support. The *Report of the Hindu Religious and Charitable Endowments Commission. United Provinces* (Allahabad: Government Press, United Provinces, 1931) recommends relying on the authority of the *Maṭhāmnāyasetu* in placing the Badarī and Kedāra temples under the control of the Śaṅkarācārya of Jyotir *maṭha* (p. 29a).

161 *Rajendran v. Govt. of Tamil Nadu*, Madras Law Journal (vol.169), 1985, pp. 337-342; All Indian Reporter, Madras, (vol. 72), 1985, pp. 44-49.

said to be further proof of Sringerī's authority in that state. As well the petition sought redress from the court against the Tamil Nadu government's support for the "pseudo and bogus" Kānchipuram *maṭha*. The alleged support was twofold. Firstly, the government had appointed the Kānchipuram *ācārya* as sole trustee for the Kāmākṣī-amman temple. Secondly, both the Chief Minister and the Minister for Hindu Religious and Charitable Endowments had participated in a conference organized (at least in part) by the Kānchipuram *maṭha*.

In its ruling, the court did not respond to any of the specific allegations. The judge restricted himself to citing various precedents, chief of which was *Madhusudan Parvat v. Shree Madhav Theerth*. The court rejected the suit in a manner much like the ruling of the Bombay High Court in 1908. It found that it is not the duty of the government to declare that a particular person is, or is not, a Śaṅkarācārya. It remains to be seen whether there will be further legal challenges to the authority of the Kānchipuram *maṭha*. But the appearance of two opposing analyses of the 1984 case in *The Madras Law Journal*—reverting yet again to the hagiographies—suggests that the battle between Sringerī and Kānchipuram is far from over.[162]

Some final considerations on the Śaṅkara *maṭhas*

At present, no definitive statement can be made about the founding of the *maṭhas* or their early history. It is not until the 19th century that a clearer picture of the *maṭhas* begins to emerge. There is little doubt that the Śaṅkara tradition is now at

---

162 S. Balasubramaniam, "Adi Sankara and courts: Sri Kamakoti Peetam and Sri Sringeri Peetam as respondents in one case", *MLJ* [vol. 170, nos. 13-14, 10 April], 1986, pp. 9-11; M. Mariappan, "Adi Sankara and courts: a reply", *MLJ* [vol. 173, nos. 5-8, 26 February] 1987, pp. 32-34.

its zenith in the south. However, it remains to be seen whether the legacy of Śaṅkara's spiritual authority will reside in a single southern institution or whether it will be shared by the two leading seats of power. In surveying the nature of the polemics in the Sringerī-Kānchipuram dispute, the overwhelming impression is that the former occupies the place of an incumbent, while the latter appears as a challenger. The 14th century Vidyāśaṅkara temple at Sringerī stands as a reminder of its illustrious past. The current *ācārya* and his honoured predecessor, whose names hark back to the days in which the temple was constructed, bear witness to the determination of the Sringerī *maṭha* to perpetuate its distinguished lineage. If the Kānchipuram *maṭha* lacks the focal point of a historical monument, they possessed a living treasure in the person of the nonagenarian *ācārya*, Śrī Candraśekharendra-Sarasvatī. He had been one of the most revered religious leaders in Tamil Nadu, and had an all-India reputation as both a learned scholar and strict ascetic.

The extensive report compiled by the Hindu Religious Endowments Commission in 1960-62, serves as a barometer by which we can measure the degree of official recognition accorded to the *maṭha*s during the first two decades of Indian independence.[163] The Śaṅkara *maṭha*s as a whole were singled out for special mention because they were seen to be among the few Hindu institutions which have remained true to the aims with which they were established. A closer examination, however, reveals that the report is completely silent about the Purī and Jyotir *maṭha*s. This is probably due in large part to the

---

163 *Report of the Hindu Religious Endowments Commission*, C., P., Ramaswami Aiyer, chairman (Government of India: Ministry of Law, 1960-1962), p. 22.

disputed line of succession in these two centres.[164] The activities of the Dwārkā Śaṅkarācārya and the affairs of that *maṭha* received the unqualified approval of the commission. But far more attention is paid to the Sringerī and Kānchipuram *maṭhas* and several comments from their *ācāryas* are included in the report. The fact that Kānchipuram figures prominently in the document testifies to the success of the *maṭha* in establishing its reputation.[165] This achievement is all the more significant given that all four *āmnāya maṭhas* have consistently refused to recognize the legitimacy of the Kānchipuram centre.

Perhaps an even better indicator of the status of the *maṭhas* is in their capacity to attract the attention of political leaders. During the short-lived Chandra Shekhar government, each of the two key partners in the uneasy coalition took the opportunity to visit a Śaṅkara *maṭha*. In what was to prove a run-up to the election campaign, Rajiv Gandhi visited Sringerī on 2 November 1990,[166] while Chandra Shekhar met the

---

164 From 1960-64, the succession at Purī remained very uncertain. For an account of this and earlier problems in the *maṭha* see, Jürgen Lütt, "The Śaṅkarācārya of Purī", pp. 415-417. The Jyotir *maṭha* was defunct for a long period of time and was only reestablished in 1941 (William Cenker, *A tradition of teachers: Śaṅkara and the Jagadgurus today* [Delhi: Motilal Banarsidass, 1983], p. 124). Although Swāmī Svarūpānandajī is secure in his position as the incumbent of the Jyotir *maṭha*, I observed the encampment of another claimant to this seat at the Allahabad Kumbha Melā in January 1989.

165 In their proposal for establishing a religious tribunal, the commission expressed great interest in making use of an organization comprising the heads of various different monastic centres which was founded by the Kānchipuram *maṭha* (*Report* p. 127). The commission included the whole of the memorandum submitted by Kānchipuram as an appendix to the report (pp. 499-510).

166 *Tattvāloka* [a bi-monthly published by the Sri Abhinava Vidyatheertha Mahaswamigal Educational Trust, Sringerī], 13 (Dec./Jan 1991), p. 81.

Kānchipuram *ācāryas* soon after on 25 December.[167] Many other prominent politicians visit the *maṭhas* ostensibly seeking advice and blessings, but with at least one eye on the vote banks. Because of his large following in Tamil Nadu, the senior *ācārya* of Kānchipuram has for many years been a force to be reckoned with in state politics as well, however anti-brahmin its tenor.[168] His successor, Śrī Jayendra-Sarasvatī probably wields even more influence in the power structures of Tamil Nadu today.[169] Yet despite receiving visits from political leaders, the two *maṭhas* have not compromised their ascetic traditions. Neither has so far actively entered the political arena.[170] In keeping with what is expected of the guru in the social code, the *ācāryas* bestow their blessings without condition, receiving in return the honour accorded them and the *maṭha* by their V.I.P. visitors.

---

167 *The Hindu* , International edition, 5 January 1991, p. 2.

168 See Franklin A. Presler, *Religion under bureaucracy: policy and administration for Hindu temples in south India* (Cambridge: Cambridge University, 1987), pp. 119; 131.

169 See Mines and Gourishankar, "The south Indian big-man", pp. 775-778.

170 The present and previous Sringerī *ācāryas* have eschewed the political arena. After Śrī Bhāratī Tīrtha succeeded Srī Abhinava Vidyātīrtha in October 1989, he stated in an interview with the press that the decision on the volatile Ayodhyā dispute should be left to the courts (*India Today*, 15 November 1989, p. 48). The retired senior *ācārya* of Kānchipuram has always remained above politics. However, his successor Śrī Jayendra-Sarasvatī has made some statements to the press which suggest he does not wish to remain aloof from contentious issues. There was speculation that his growing interest in social and political matters prompted a rift with the senior *ācārya*, which precipitated Jayendra-Sarasvatī's temporary resignation of his position. See K. P. Sunil, "The curious case of the missing monk", *The Illustrated Weekly*, 13 September 1987, pp. 9-17. The story also appeared in *India Today*, 30 September 1987, pp. 96-97. *The Hindu* (New Delhi edition), gave daily (usually front page) coverage to the disappearance and eventual reappearance of the *ācārya* from 24-28 August 1987 with follow-ups on 10 September, p. 9 and 4 October 1987, p. 4.

Whether or not Śaṅkara himself ever envisaged the foundation of monastic centres, it cannot be doubted that the Śaṅkara *maṭhas* maintain a high profile in contemporary Hinduism. In the great gatherings of the faithful at the Kumbha Melās, the Śaṅkarācāryas stand at the forefront of the innumerable ascetics and gurus who congregate at these religious festivals. As Sanskritic culture has declined in modern India, the Śaṅkarācāryas have assumed perhaps even greater significance as custodians of ancient traditions. Because of their very real integration in the social fabric of India, the Śaṅkara *maṭhas* are not exempt from the conflicts which are prevalent on the local, regional and national levels. Indeed the disputes testify to the vitality of the Śaṅkara tradition today.

CHAPTER VII

Reflections on Representing Śaṅkara

In this study I have primarily focussed on the ways in which Śaṅkara is portrayed in eight Sanskrit hagiographies. These are the primary sources for a life of Śaṅkara that became popular throughout the whole of India. The hagiographers construct their story as a demonstration, and in celebration of Śaṅkara's divinity. The protagonist is cast firmly in the mould of an *avatāra*, as an incarnation of the great god whose name he bears. Accordingly, the narrative assumes the proportions of a mythic drama. The divine hero-sage must rescue the earth and her denizens from the dark forces of chaos. The disorder which occasions Śiva to take a human birth stems from the decline of the Vedic tradition. More specifically, it is the rise of sects which misinterpret, ignore or even reject the transcendent authority of the Vedas, that has threatened the stability of the social order. Only the perpetuation of the true Vedic tradition, the hagiographers insist, will ensure the continuity of *dharma*.

The dynamics of the Śaṅkara story evolve from the interplay of divine and human forces. However, there is no suggestion that these opposing forces deserve equal attention. The mundane realm functions primarily as a sign of the greater order that lies beyond. The human mode in the narrative is remarkably and intentionally undeveloped. The hagiographers have little interest in defining the personality of the protagonist, except in so far as it will demonstrate his connection with Śiva. The tension between the mundane and supramundane realms is epitomized by the opposition of the householder and renouncer. The householder stands for concerns of this world, in contrast to the transcendental aims of the renouncer. The dénouement of the conflict comes in the Śaṅkara-Maṇḍana encounter. Their debate represents the struggle for supremacy in the interpretation of the *śruti* and *smṛti* texts which are the ultimate source of authority in the Vedic tradition. Śaṅkara's victory over the householder, who follows the path of ritual action, marks the ascendancy of the renouncer and the transcendent way of knowledge.

There is little scope for temporal concerns in the narrative. Although the events in the story unfold in a linear sequence, suggesting the presence of chronology, there is no external referent to fix the time of the events. The birth of Śaṅkara, for example, occurs not at a particular point in time but in accordance with a mythological paradigm or, to use Eliade's expression, in the "Great Time".[1] This is in keeping with the Śaiva Purāṇas which maintain that Īśvara appears on earth in every age, accompanied by four disciples. Another perhaps more familiar expression of this notion is found in the *Bhagavadgītā*: the hierophany occurs *whenever* there is a decline of *dharma*. Given this conceptual framework, the divine hero cannot be subject to the constraints of time. It is only during the scenes of Śaṅkara's childhood that temporal referents are conspicuous in the narrative. This is the period when he is most vulnerable to the pull of the worldly forces which he will overcome at the moment of his renunciation. Yet, here too mythical models take precedence over chronology. In the Krishna legends much prominence is given to the child god, so adorable and easy of access. These resonances would undoubtedly register with the readers of the Śaṅkara story. The *Mahābhārata* and the Śaiva Purāṇas provide a more specifically Śaiva mythological context for the hagiographers. Śaṅkara's renunciation is set within the

---

1 Mircea Eliade, *The myth of the eternal return or, cosmos and history*, tr. Willard R. Trask (reprinted, Bollingen Series XLVI, Princeton: Princeton University, 1971), p. 112.

frame story of Upamanyu. At the age of five this child-sage left his home, and a tearful mother, to perform austerities which would win the grace of Śiva.

The lack of historical referentiality in the Śaṅkara story is another instance of the tendency in some Hindu traditions to deny a favoured place to the fixing of dates. Chronology is of course a constituent factor in the *guru-paramparā* (and the royal lineages). Yet it is the sense of continuity and transmission which remain uppermost, not the dating of its individual members. A lineage assumes greater validity if it can be traced back to a great atemporal being, namely a god or legendary sage. Similarly, in all the orthodox *guru-paramparās* the teachings which are transmitted ultimately owe their authority to the Vedas. This sacred corpus allows little place for temporal detail. Whatever trace of historical reference does appear in the Vedas was assiduously reinterpreted by the Mīmāṃsakas, the most influential of exegetes. In this and many other respects, the Advaita tradition owes much to Mīmāṃsā. Is it any wonder, then, that the life of Śaṅkara should itself be represented as an existence virtually bereft of historical particulars? Within the Advaita tradition, Śaṅkara can be designated simply as the *bhāṣyakāra*, i.e., *the* commentator on the *Brahmasūtra*. Like the legendary Vyāsa, traditionally believed to be the author of this text, the person of Śaṅkara merges with the transcendent scriptures on which he has commented.

In contrast to the de-emphasis of time in the Śaṅkara story, the hagiographers have a great deal to say about place. The episodes in the life story are almost invariably linked with specific sites on the Hindu pilgrim's trail, and the places named are many. The sacred sites in which the narrative unfolds are fit for the visits of gods, immortal sages and pilgrims of various persuasions. In permitting the free interaction of divine and human forces, such locations comprise an ideal setting for a drama of cosmic dimensions. In the hagiographies Śaṅkara appears as the quintessential wanderer. If he did in fact resist settling down, in keeping with the highest ascetic precepts, this might help to explain why Śaṅkara did not come to be identified with a particular region of the subcontinent. The extensive journeys he makes are defined in terms of patterns established long before his day. The most conspicuous paradigm is the *digvijaya*. Sanskrit literature is replete with evidence that traditional India aspired for a great leader who would conquer the four quarters and reunite a divided land under a single banner. The strong presence of these aspirations in the portrayal of Śaṅkara is reflected both in the generic title for his life story, *Śaṅkara-vijaya*, and in the recurrence of imagery relating to conquest in the narrative. What is more, Śaṅkara's all-India pilgrimage itself became a potent image which nationalist leaders and latter-day politicians would emulate as proof of their capability to lead a united India.

Śaṅkara's combative engagements in the course of his *digvijaya* are largely confined to public debate. Nevertheless, the stakes were not insignificant. Maṇḍana/Viśvarūpa, Śaṅkara's most powerful adversary, had to abandon family and home, not to mention his cherished doctrines, upon losing the debate. Śaṅkara's triumph is more than a personal affair. His is a victory for the *saṃnyāsin* who henceforth would serve as the pre-eminent spokesman for the Vedic tradition. Yet despite the defeat of the leading exponent of ritual action, the hagiographers made considerable efforts to show that this path was not discredited but was subsumed within the Advaita tradition. They portray Śaṅkara's concern with ensuring that his brahmin opponents resume the ritual duties they had abandoned. The distinct emphasis Śaṅkara places in his own works on the denial of ritual action as a means of liberation is conspicuous only by its absence in the hagiographies. In this respect, the life story reflects the milieu of the post-Sureśvara Advaita tradition which had moved away from some of the positions enunciated in Śaṅkara's own compositions.

The legacies attributed to the hero-sage by the hagiographers underscore the discrepancy between the image they have constructed of Śaṅkara and the views expressed by the author of the *prasthānatrayī* commentaries and the *Upadeśasāhasrī*. In the life story, not only does Śaṅkara insist that his opponents return to ritual practice, he is instrumental in bringing *bhakti* within the fold of orthodoxy. This raises a question crucial to the representation of Śaṅkara. Can he be at once a non-dualist and a supporter of devotionalism? The account of Śaṅkara's establishment of monastic centres entails a second and perhaps more profound problem. Is it a necessary contradiction to claim that Śaṅkara was both a man of action and one who renounced worldly life? I will turn shortly to an examination of these issues. But let me first conclude my comments on the hagiographies.

The representation of Śaṅkara as an *avatāra* was probably the most effective means for facilitating his glorification in traditional India. It was the norm, not the exception, to deify saints, sages, and even kings, in order to secure for them a permanent place in popular culture. Naturally the hagiographers were also eager, as Tirumala-Dīkṣita admits, to "publicize the Advaita lineage".[2] By the time the Śaṅkara story began to take its present shape, virtually the entire Hindu tradition was permeated by the spirit of *bhakti*. The hagiographers would have been compelled, both by their personal beliefs and in order to popularize Advaita, to integrate Śaṅkara with the prevailing forces of devotionalism. All of our texts elaborate on Śaṅkara as a devotee. They recount his visits to numerous temples and provide details of the hymns he sings in praise of the presiding

---

2 TŚA 1.5.

deities. His acts of worship embrace all the Hindu deities (that are appropriate to the ritually pure castes), despite the distinctly Śaiva framework of the Śaṅkara story.

The very nature of Śaṅkara's mission entailed the reform of the devotional sects. According to the hagiographies, the dark forces of the *kali-yuga* were responsible for the proliferation of cults throughout the subcontinent. Their disruptive influence was manifest in their rejection of the authority of *śruti* and *smṛti*. The focus on a single deity and the consequent exclusion of all others generated conflict which posed a serious threat to the social order. One sign above all marked their disregard for ritual purity and the mutual hostility characteristic to the cults: the branding of sectarian emblems. The *avatāra* cannot of course fail to achieve his object. Śaṅkara defeats the sects and puts an end to their impure practices. Three of the hagiographers envisaged a far greater kind of restoration. They describe how Śaṅkara went about achieving a formal reconstitution of six devotional sects. However uneasily this sits with the views of his own compositions, the image of Śaṅkara as the *ṣaṇmata-sthāpaka* is very much in keeping with the spirit of the narrative.

The same three hagiographies portray Śaṅkara as the founder of monastic centres. This episode, however, is not so clearly prefigured in the narrative. Even more striking is the absence of any reference whatsoever to the *maṭha*s in five of our sources. The only logical explanation for this is that the establishment of monastic centres was not very widely attributed to Śaṅkara until some time after the composition of our Sanskrit sources. The hagiographers who do speak of the *maṭha*s were strongly influenced by their own institutional affiliations. This points to the existence of two streams in the Śaṅkara tradition. One remained without affiliations to a formal organization, and is for that reason difficult to define. The second stream has a more concrete presence derived from the institutions, in particular the *maṭhas*, which have given it shape. The *maṭhas* have successfully promoted the notion that Śaṅkara is the archetypal renouncer and is therefore the logical founder of the *daśanāmi-saṃnyāsins*. In forging links (even if they are in principle only) with the *daśanāmi-saṃnyāsins*, the monastic centres have considerably enhanced their own stature. As traditional structures are disappearing in the face of an increasingly modern India, the Śaṅkara *maṭhas* have managed not only to survive but have prospered. The Śaṅkarācāryas are at the very forefront of contemporary Hinduism. The public controversies and rivalries in which they have been embroiled, whatever view one may take of them, are further evidence for the vitality of the tradition the Śaṅkarācāryas represent.

I set out in my study of the hagiographies determined to eschew a historical perspective, at least where Śaṅkara himself was concerned. For the most part, I have not deviated from this intention. Nevertheless, my reading of the texts has brought to light some of the ways in which the Advaita tradition has developed, particularly in regard to the role of the legacies attributed to Śaṅkara. Yet it strikes me that the real value of the hagiographies lies in what they tell us about the ways in which Śaṅkara has been received in India. Their representation of Śaṅkara reveals an image that is fluid and dynamic, as are the conceptual models on which the life story is constructed. What is especially appealing about hagiographies is that they lie at the juncture of what is thought and what is lived. As such they afford us glimpses of the interactions between popular culture and the learned elite.

There was perhaps no better way for the Śaṅkara tradition to gain entry into the mainstream of Indian culture than through the currents of *bhakti*. Since the time of Śaṅkara, the *bhakti* movement has stood out most prominently in the interface between popular and elite expressions of Hinduism. Even if his authorship of devotional hymns is very doubtful,[3] there is no good reason to rule out the possibility that *bhakti* may have figured in Śaṅkara's personal life. Given that temple worship was already prevalent in his day, it is more likely than not that he did visit some of the shrines which are the focal point of devotional experience. In our own day, we have clear evidence that *bhakti* and non-dualism are not necessarily incompatible in the person of Ramaṇa Maharṣi (1879-1950). Although it was with some reluctance, Śrī Ramaṇa composed several devotional hymns. In conversation, he revealed how he was in fact "compelled" to do so:

> The opening words of the *Eleven Verses [Aruṇācala-padikam]* suddenly came to me one morning, and even if I tried to suppress them, saying: "What have I to do with these words?" they would not be suppressed until I had composed a song beginning with them, and all the words flowed easily without any effort. In the same way the second stanza was composed the next day and the succeeding ones the following days, one each day...[4]

It would be difficult, if not impossible, to mark the point at which *bhakti* came to dominate almost every aspect of Hinduism. For this reason there seems little to be gained in arguing whether the image of Śaṅkara as a devotee is a deliberate construction or a natural consequence of the *bhakti*

---

3 See Robert E. Gussner, "A stylometric study of the authorship of seventeeen Sanskrit hymns attributed to Śaṅkara'", *Journal of the American Oriental Society*, 96 (1976), pp. 259-267.

4 A. Devaraja Mudaliar, *Day by day with Bhagavan. From a diary [dated] March 16, 1945 to January 4, 1947* (2nd ed., Tiruvannamalai: Sri Ramanasramam, 1977), p. 194. See also T. M. P. Mahadevan, *Ramana Maharshi: the sage of Aruṇācala* (London: Allen & Unwin, 1977).

movement. But this issue raises a more fuṇdamental epistemological problem in the study of Hinduism.

The historian is inclined, if not constrained, to search for disjunctions and tensions which will define the object of study. Such a project normally involves the drawing of intellectual boundaries within a chronological framework. As a result of this approach Śaṅkara is usually placed before, and apart, from the ascendancy of devotionalism. Yet in traditional Indian scholarship and especially in Advaita, the focus tends to be on (re)discovering continuities and finding ways to integrate disparate conceptions.[5] From this perspective it makes no sense to emphasize the distinctions between non-duality and *bhakti*. The idea is to harmonize the (apparently) contradictory views. However tempting it may be to separate Advaita and *bhakti* into discrete categories, we must at least acknowledge the validity of an approach which has precisely the opposite aim. Now that the imperialistic underpinnings of Oriental Studies stand exposed, we can no longer afford to simply dismiss hermeneutics which do not conform to European models.

Unlike the tension between *bhakti* and Advaita, which is perceived largely from without, the opposition of *pravṛtti* and *nivṛtti* is one that is embedded in the religious life of India.[6]

---

5 As Halbfass has pointed out, Śaṅkara's own works reveal a concern with the harmonization, or rather concordance (*samanvaya)*, only of the differing metaphysical articulations in the śruti. The attempts to establish a concordance of opposing doctrines is conspicuous in some of his followers, notably Mādhava-Vidyāraṇya, after whom this trend became increasingly strong (*India and Europe: an essay in understanding* [Albany: State University of New York, 1988], p. 356.

6 This opposition also features prominently in Jainism and Buddhism. But in these traditions the monk occupies a much more privileged place than in Hinduism. For the Jain or Buddhist the householder is virtually excluded from the pursuit of liberation itself. Many Indologists have discussed the tension

Perhaps the best known attempt at a resolution of the tension between the urge to engage in the activities of the world and the impulse to turn away from it is that of the *Bhagavadgītā*. In his commentary to this popular scripture, Śaṅkara gives the following explanation of the two key terms:

> The word *pravṛtti*, activity, means the path of ritual action, whose objects are set out in the *śāstras*. It is the cause of bondage. *Nivṛtti* means the path of renunciation, which is the cause of liberation.[7]

One need not read between the lines to discover Śaṅkara's preference for *nivṛtti* over *pravṛtti*. While these terms themselves are not the usual focus of his discussion, Śaṅkara's insistence on the renunciation of ritual action is clearly one of the dominant themes in his work. Most European and American Indologists would, I think, agree that Śaṅkara stands solely on the side of *nivṛtti*. This position has been clearly and persuasively articulated in a piece by Karl Potter published in 1982.[8] Nevertheless this view is not so widely shared by Indian scholars. M. Hiriyanna comments, for example, that Śaṅkara "does not necessarily give up all activity as is abundantly illustrated by the strenuous life which [he] himself

---

betweeen *pravṛtti* and *nivṛtti*. J. C. Heesterman, for example, traces it back to the formulation of the ritual *sūtras* but sees it also as a continuing presence in Hindu traditions (See his essays in *The inner conflict of tradition: essays in Indian ritual, kingship, and society* [Chicago: University of Chicago, 1985]. Greg Bailey has devoted an entire monograph to the concepts of *pravṛtti* and *nivṛtti*, in which he argues for a hermeneutical approach to Indian religions based on this opposition: *Materials for the study of ancient Indian ideologies; pravṛtti and nivṛtti* (Pubblicazioni di Indologica Taurinensia no. 19, Torino: Istituto di Indologia, 1985).

7 *pravṛttiḥ pravartanaṃ bandha-hetuḥ karma-mārgaḥ śāstra-vihita-viṣayaḥ, nivṛttiṃ ca nivṛttir mokṣa-hetuḥ saṃnyāsa-mārgaḥ*, comment on 18.30.

8 "Śaṃkarācārya: the myth and the man", *Journal of the American Academy of Religion. Thematic Studies*, XLVIII (1982), pp. 111-125.

led".[9] These antithetic hermeneutical perspectives add yet another dimension to the *pravṛtti/nivṛtti* opposition.

In the first place I would like to examine very briefly Śaṅkara's own statements on the subject. It is generally recognized that when he speaks of the renunciation of all action (*sarva-karma-saṃnyāsa*),[10] Śaṅkara is referring specifically to ritual action. However, by 'ritual action' (*karman*) we must understand the entire sphere of religious activities, including such things as meditation. For Śaṅkara denies that any action can lead to liberation. The problem with action is that it presumes an agent,[11] and the presence of an agent entails duality. Liberation is attained only through knowledge, culminating in the realization of the non-difference of the Self and Brahman. Nevertheless, ritual action is not entirely excluded from Śaṅkara's program. It has a place as a preliminary discipline which facilitates the arising of knowledge through the purification of the mind (*sattva-śuddhi*).[12] In fact, Śaṅkara admits that religious injunctions do apply so long as one perceives the body to be distinct from the Self.[13] What is more, the erroneous conception of difference actually impels one to act.[14] Ultimately Śaṅkara's analysis of religious duties rests on the distinction of two types of individuals: those who know and those who do not. It is only the latter category who must engage in religious activities. So long as Arjuna believes

---

9 *Outlines of Indian philosophy* ([1932] reprinted London: George Allen & Unwin, 1968), p. 381.

10 For example, *Bhagavadgītā-bhāṣya* 5.26.

11 *ahaṃ kartā mamedaṃ syād iti karma pravartate, Upadeśasāhasrī (padyabandha)*, 1.13.

12 *Bhagavadgītā-bhāṣya* 5.26.

13 *satyaṃ vyatireka-darśino niyojyatvaṃ, Brahmasūtra-bhāṣya* 2.3.48

14 *sarvatrābhimānasyaiva pravartakatvād abhimānābhāvāc ca samyag - darśinaḥ, ibid.*

himself to be different from Brahman he must carry out his duties as a warrior.[15]

Śaṅkara does not directly address the question of religious activity in regard to the practices advocated in his own Advaita tradition. Yet it is clear that certain activities are expected of the student, either implicitly or explicitly. The most notable of these is resorting to a guru in order to hear the teachings of the *śruti*. This has led some writers to assume that Śaṅkara's position on renunciation is self-contradictory.[16] The key issue, I would suggest, is not so much renunciation *per se* but the concept of agency. Indeed, Śaṅkara maintains that both *pravṛtti* and *nivṛtti* depend on an agent.[17] What must be abandoned is the idea that one is a doer. Śaṅkara gives some indication of this line of thought in Chapter 13 of the *Upadeśasāhasrī*. He first negates the notion of agency and then goes on to speak of concentration on the Self:

> So long as there was ignorance, there were duties for me. I am eternally free, pure and ever awake. How can there be meditation, non-meditation, or some other duty for me"?....Thus, [with the mind] concentrated, one should always know that the Self is everything.[18]

The concentration mentioned here is, strictly speaking, no longer an activity because there is no sense of agency. This, I believe, is how Śaṅkara would explain the way a *saṃnyāsin* can

---

15 See the introduction to chapter 5 in Śaṅkara's *Bhagavadgītā-bhāṣya*.

16 See the discussion in Sengaku Mayeda's introduction to his translation, *A thousand teachings: the Upadeśasāhasrī of Śaṅkara* (Tokyo: Unversity of Tokyo, 1979), pp. 88-94.

17 *kartṛ-tantratvāt pravṛtti-nivṛttyoḥ, Gītā-bhāṣya* 4.18.

18 *ity etad yāvad ajñānaṃ tāvat kāryaṃ mamābhavat / nitya-muktasya śuddhasya buddhasya ca sadā mama // samādhir vāsamādhir vā kāryaṃ cānyat kuto bhavet* / (13.16-17a)....*ity evaṃ sarvadātmānaṃ vidyāt sarvaṃ samāhitaḥ*/ (13.25).

continue to function—wandering, begging and preaching—and yet remain true to his resolution of renouncing all actions. There may be activities but they do not belong to the *saṃnyāsin*, who should identify only with the Self. Thus the notion "I am acting" does not arise.[19]

Leaving aside the question of whether this position is logically coherent, I would suggest that without understanding renunciation in terms of the negation of agency, it does not seem possible to justify the considerable activities that Śaṅkara himself must have engaged in. Even if all the episodes in the hagiographies are discounted, the fact remains that Śaṅkara was a prolific writer. He was also involved in the training of students.[20] If he could engage in these activities without contradicting his principles of renunciation, then there were sufficient grounds for the development of stories which expanded his sphere of action. But just how far could the hagiographers go in representing Śaṅkara as a man of action? According to Karl Potter, they went too far:

> the very purpose of the hagiographies is to blunt Śaṃkara's own sharp dichotomy between *pravṛtti* and *nivṛtti*....The hagiographies remake Śaṃkara. The philosopher acquires a charisma by virtue of adulation based on a completely erroneous assessment of his philosophy.[21]

Given that there was scope in Śaṅkara's life for considerable activity, some caution is needed in characterizing him solely in terms of *nivṛtti*. I would agree, however, that the life stories

---

19 For a more extensive discussion of the problem see my *Meditation in Śaṅkara's Vedānta* (New Delhi: Aditya Prakashan, 1990), Chapter 3, especially pp. 56-62.

20 This is attested to by Sureśvara in his *Naiṣkarmyasiddhi,* especially 4.74 and 4.77.

21 "The myth and the man", p. 121.

intentionally underplay the strong stand on renunciation which is so conspicuous in Śaṅkara's own work. This is not surprising since, as Potter has observed, the hagiographers were intent on using the Śaṅkara story as a means for resolving the tensions between *pravṛtti* and *nivṛtti*. The forces which impelled the man of pure heart to turn away from the world and those which demanded that he interact were absorbed and reconciled in the person of Śaṅkara. In this sense the hagiographers have indeed remade Śaṅkara, portraying him in a way which is conducive to social harmony. However, the recasting of Śaṅkara's image entails still more fundamental issues to which I will return after considering the allegation that Śaṅkara has been misrepresented by the hagiographers.

Now Vidyāraṇya stands out in the Advaita lineage both as a leading *saṃnyāsin* and as a theorist who sought to extend the boundaries of the tradition to include elements which Śaṅkara himself may not have admitted. As Potter has rightly argued,[22] in allowing the *saṃnyāsin* to observe ritual prescriptions, Vidyāraṇya is adopting the very position Śaṅkara had sought to refute in his commentary on *Bṛhadāraṇyakopaniṣad* 3.5.1 and *Chāndogyopaniṣad* 2.23.1. Moreover, in the light of Vidyāraṇya's organizational activities, particularly in regard to his position as pontiff of the Sringerī *maṭha*, he bears a striking resemblance to the protagonist of the Śaṅkara hagiographies. But Potter does not pursue the possibility that the hero of the hagiographies is modelled on Vidyāraṇya. His hypothesis instead is that the protagonist is a fictional character based on the conflation of two entirely different people:

---

22 Ibid., pp.113-117. Another pertinent point, but one I will not directly address here, is Potter's observation that the Advaita tradition eventually turned away from Śaṅkara in adopting the position of his opponent Maṇḍana Miśra (the author of the *Brahmasiddhi)*, who advocated the need for prescribed meditation, p. 122.

> Perhaps there was a man, possibly named Śaṃkara, who was a social entrepreneur, an organizer. Advaita tradition also celebrates an outstanding philosopher, Śaṃkarācārya....The followers of the entrepreneur find it advantageous to take advantage of the accidental identity of names. Since the general public doesn't understand philosophy very well...the conflation of the two Śaṃkaras is not difficult...The result is a mythological creation, the philosopher-entrepreneur. But no such person ever existed.[23]

The result of this myth-making is, in Potter's view, that the actual philosopher is eclipsed by a social reformer and institution builder whose activities contradict the principles enunciated in Śaṅkara's own work.

Potter attributes the "co-opting" of Śaṅkara to a difference in cultural values: "In another society this wholesale aggrandizement of a person might be resisted or resented, the sense of a historical personality's unique character being deemed worthy of salvage".[24] Now it is true that Sanskrit poetics are characterized by a sense of impersonality which contrasts sharply with the emphasis on the individual in European literature. This has been eloquently elaborated by Daniel Ingalls.[25] Yet all cultures bear witness to major shifts over time in the perception of public figures. Is this not all the more apparent in the case of religious leaders? As for the project of demythologizing saints and cultural heroes, there are epistemological problems which cast doubt on the whole

---

23 *Ibid.*, pp.121-122

24 *Ibid.*

25 However, as Ingalls reminds us, Prākrit and vernacular works are concerned with individuals and their circumstances: *An anthology of Sanskrit court poetry: Vidyākara's "Subhāṣitaratnakośa"* (Harvard Oriental Series, vol 44, Cambridge, Mass.: Harvard University, 1965), pp. 23-29.

enterprise. The axiological issues are perhaps an even larger stumbling block. Is it necessarily better to focus on what is empirically verifiable rather than on what is believed? Here I must admit that my own discussion of the *maṭhas* and the *daśanāmins* came closer than I would like to the program of the demythologizers. But ultimately does it really matter whether we can prove or disprove that Śaṅkara was directly responsible for the establishment of a great monastic order? To whom will this be of value? What is clear, however, is that Śaṅkara came to be identified as an ideal renouncer. As such, his image could meaningfully link the *saṃnyāsin* tradition with the divine prototype of the ascetic.

While Potter has recognized the resemblances between Vidyāraṇya and the Śaṅkara of the hagiographies on a conceptual level, Hermann Kulke has focussed on the political and historical connections between the two individuals.[26] Kulke's hypothesis is that the Śaṅkara tradition at Sringerī derives primarily from the three famous *ācārya* s, Vidyātīrtha, Bhāratītīrtha and Vidyāraṇya, who won substantial patronage from the founders of the Vijayanagara empire. He points out that the inscriptions which praise the three pontiffs make no mention of Śaṅkara whatsoever. On the other hand, the Sringerī *ācāryas*, and in particular Vidyāraṇya, are lauded for deeds which are among those attributed to Śaṅkara in the hagiographies.[27] This leads Kulke to conclude that the Sringerī *ācāryas* concretized a Śaṅkara tradition in order to establish their *maṭha*

---

26 "Mahārājas, mahants and historians: reflections on the historiography of early Vijayanagara and Sringeri", in *Vijayanagara-city and empire: new currents of research*, ed. Anna Libera Dallipiccola (2 vols. Stuttgart: Steiner Verlag Wiesbaden, 1985), vol. 1, pp. 120-143.

27 *Ibid.*, pp. 134-136. Kulke cites as evidence for this the epithet, "establisher of the Vedic path", the references to extensive compositions, the defeat of Buddhists and Jainas, victory over Kumārila-Bhaṭṭa and a *yātrā/digvijaya* to Vārāṇasī (p. 136).

as the centre of a unified Hindu orthodoxy. The *maṭha*, in turn, served the purposes of their patrons, the Vijayanagara kings, by legitimating their claims to the rulership of a realm whose boundaries stretched as far as the *dharma*.

Although it certainly challenges some long-standing beliefs, Kulke's hypothesis corroborates the traditional view that Vidyāraṇya occupies a pre-eminent place in the Śaṅkara order. The differences in Vidyāraṇya's exposition of Advaita do not jeopardize his authority in the eyes of the tradition, nor is a disjunction with Śaṅkara perceived.[28] This suggests that doctrines alone do not reveal the workings of the Advaita tradition. It is here that the hagiographies find their place, in allowing us glimpses of some of the structures which shape the context of the Śaṅkara order. The link between Śaṅkara and Vidyāraṇya may be understood in terms of an image which appears again and again in the hagiographies: at the very centre of the tradition there is a lineage, stretching back to Patañjali, Vyāsa and ultimately Śiva. It is from this *guru-paramparā* that Śaṅkara's spiritual authority is seen to derive, and from him it is transmitted to his legitimate successors. The claimant to this lineage must demonstrate to his peers that he has received the authority of the guru.[29] The presence of an unbroken *paramparā* pervades the tradition, like the continual hum of the tamboura. Yet the guru, as the soloist, may introduce fresh interpretations in expressing the age-old themes. It is precisely

---

28 There is, at least at present, a critical stream within the Advaita tradition. Its most prominent representative is Svāmī Saccidānandendra Sarasvatī. He insists that since the Pañcapādikā Śaṅkara's views have often been misrepresented by subcommentators (Swamy Satchidanandendra Saraswati, *Misconceptions about Śaṅkara* [Holenarsipur: Adhyatma Prakasha Karyalaya, 1973], p. 9).

29 This isue is discussed by the present-day Śaṅkarācāryas in the interviews which appear in the Appendix.

because the Śaṅkara lineage is a living order that it can and does adapt itself to changes in circumstance.

The concrete edifices of the Śaṅkara institutions are not the only places where the image of the *guru-paramparā* reverberates. Mines and Gourishankar have shown that this traditional power structure operates in some south Indian political organizations as well.[30] They describe the way in which these institutions are organized around the charismatic personality of a single leader. The central leader, assisted by his appointed lieutenants, is linked by direct ties to all members of the organization, which functions wholly on the basis of this relationship. Upon his death a splintering of the organization may occur, each faction headed by a claimant to the authority of the central leader. This is amply illustrated by the evolution of the DMK Party in Tamil Nadu. When its founder Annadurai died in 1969, the DMK split into three parties, each led by a former lieutenant. Eventually the AIADMK Party of M.G. Ramachandran gained the ascendancy. Although the new "guru" asserted that he was the heir of Annadurai, M.G.R. was very much his own man and took the party in new directions. After his death in 1987, the party split into two factions, one ruled by his widow, the other by his former mistress.[31]

The Śaṅkara *maṭhas* have certainly witnessed their share of power struggles, resulting from disputed claims of succession. In the middle of the 19th century the Śaṅkarācārya of Sringerī himself admitted that some *saṃnyāsins* had set themselves up in unauthorized *maṭhas*.[32] But even when the succession is

---

30 Mattison Mines and Vijayalakshmi Gourishankar, "Leadership and individuality in south Asia: the case of the south Indian big-man", *Journal of Asian Studies*, 49 (1990), pp. 761-786.

31 *Ibid*., p. 764. For further details on the political front, see *India Today*, January 15, 1988, pp. 6-15 and January 15, 1989, pp. 24-26.

32 See Chapter VI, p. 301 for details.

orderly, as Mines and Gourishankar have pointed out, [33] the institution will take on a different face in keeping with the unique charisma of the new leader. Vidyāraṇya is perhaps the best example of this phenomenon within the Śaṅkara tradition. While paying all due respect to his illustrious predecessors in the Advaita lineage, Vidyāraṇya put the stamp of his own personality on the Sringerī *maṭha*. Whatever policies a new incumbent undertakes must, of course, be shown to be compatible with the intentions of his predecessor. One of the most effective means for accomplishing this is by assimilating the personality of the previous guru. There is every possibility that this is what happened at Sringerī in the 14th century. What is more, Vidyāraṇya may have reached further back in the lineage in order to recast the *bhāṣya-kāra* himself in his own image. But if this was one of the earliest reappropriations of Śaṅkara, there were many more to follow.

Some of the most significant reinterpretations of Śaṅkara occurred during the nationalist period. Rāmmohan Roy set the stage for what was to come by proclaiming Vedānta to be the true and original Hinduism. Vivekānanda identified Śaṅkara as the embodiment of Vedānta. It was Śaṅkara, he explained, who first sought to restore the real Hindu tradition, and who "wanted to bring the Indian world back to its pristine purity".[34] Vivekānanda painted the picture of an India degraded by foreign elements. For him the task at hand was a "reconquest of this...degradation".[35] The work had been started by the

---

[33] *Op. cit.*, p. 764.

[34] *The complete works of Swami Vivekananda* (6th ed., 7 vols. Mayavati, Almora: Advaita Ashrama, 1946-48), III, p. 265.

[35] *Ibid.* Vivekananda provides the most curious explanation for this. He identifies Buddhism (which he says was itself degraded from the real teachings of the Buddha) as the culprit: "All these horrors that you are trying to reform are the outcome of that reign of degradation. The Tartars and the Baluchis and all the hideous races of mankind came to India and became Buddhists, and

Vedānta, in the person of Śaṅkara. But, Vivekānanda insisted, it was still going on, and he himself was obviously carrying the torch. While the struggle for independence was reaching its peak, Nehru was rediscovering his Indian roots. He found in Śaṅkara the prototype of the nationalist leader, who was marked by

> a continual insistence on self-sacrifice and detachment....He was evidently a man who was intensely conscious of his mission, a man who looked upon the whole of India from Cape Cormorin to the Himalayas as his field of action and as something that held together culturally and was infused by the same spirit, though this might take many external forms. He strove hard to synthesize the diverse currents that were troubling the mind of India of his day, and to build a unity of outlook out of that diversity....It would seem that Shankara wanted to add to this sense of national unity and common consciousness....By locating his four great monasteries in the north, south, east and west, he evidently wanted to encourage the conception of a culturally united India.[36]

These were the ideals on which a unified secular India could be established. The reinterpretation of Śaṅkara has continued unabated since independence. Swāmī Chinmayānanda, the well known Vedānta preacher who has expounded the *Bhagavadgītā*

---

assimilated with us, and brought their national customs, and the whole of our national life became a huge page of the most horrible and the most bestial customs" (*ibid.*).

36 Jawaharlal Nehru, *The discovery of India* ([1946] reprinted London: Meridian Books, 1956), pp.182-183.

throughout India and abroad, gives the following reappraisal in a piece entitled "Sankara, the spiritual general":[37]

> But pen alone would not have won the war of culture for our country. He showed himself to be a great organizer, a far sighted diplomat, a courageous hero and a tireless servant of the country. Selfless and unassuming, this mighty angel strode up and down the length and breadth of the country serving his motherland and teaching his countrymen to live up to the glory and dignity of Bharat.[38]

This passage could as easily be read as a tribute to Swami Chinmayānanda himself. But what is more striking is his image of a "spiritual general" which recasts Śaṅkara firmly in the present day milieu of militant Hinduism.

Implicit in these re-presentations of Śaṅkara are the images which were first given shape in the hagiographies. The rich symbolic potential of the Śaṅkara story is inherent in the diverse materials these Sanskrit sources comprise. As the hagiographies began to proliferate so too did the contradictions in their portrayal of Śaṅkara. Mādhava was largely successful in harmonizing some of the disparate elements in his *Śaṅkaradigvijaya*. By weaving together many of the episodes popular in his day, he also created the most comprehensive of the hagiographies. The countless renderings of the text—in various languages, and more recently, in the mass media—have assured almost universal recognition for this version of the life story. Although the particulars now seem fixed, the image is by no means frozen. The modern period has seen continual reworkings of his figure, many more than I have briefly sketched above. For political and religious leaders as well as the

---

37 This was the introductory essay to *Sankara the missionary* (Central Chinmaya Mission Trust: Bombay, 1978), pp. 3-7

38 Ibid., p. 5.

educated public, the Śaṅkara story strikes a chord deep within which resonates with the sound, 'self-sacrifice'. So long as this message is heard, Śaṅkara remains a dynamic symbol of the ascetic values which are at the very heart of Indian culture.

APPENDIX A

Interviews with the Śaṅkarācāryas

The Śaṅkarācāryas are the living face of the Advaita tradition. They have a high profile in contemporary India, primarily in the religious sphere, but increasingly so in the political sphere as well. I had the privilege of meeting three of the four most prominent Śaṅkarācāryas during a field trip to India in 1988-89. It also happened that my visit coincided with the year-long festival proclaimed by the Government of India in commemoration of the twelve hundredth anniversary of Śaṅkara's birth. This was a time when the name Śaṅkara was very much in the air.

I prepared in advance a list of questions, in Sanskrit—along with a description of my research—which I hoped to put to the *ācāryas*. This proved to be fortuitous for two reasons. Firstly, my use of the language which is so strongly fostered in the *maṭhas* encouraged the officials to open all doors and extend a cordial reception. Secondly, I soon found that my abilities to converse in Sanskrit were severely limited. What I had written helped smooth the way. I had also hoped that I would be able to tape record the interviews, but this was not permitted except on one occasion. Fortunately the aural comprehension did not prove to be as trying as my efforts in speaking. I have arranged the interviews chronologically, following the order in which they occurred. My own questions have been abbreviated here, but the answers appear in full.

With H. H. Jagadguru Śrī Candraśekharendra-Sarasvatī

Kānchipuram, 18 December 1988.

I was taken by an old devotee to meet the senior *ācārya*, usually referred to as the Paramācārya, or by the Tamil honorific, Periyavar. It was late afternoon. We entered the sparsely appointed compound of the *maṭha* just as the public *darśana* had ended. The crowd was predominantly comprised of orthodox brahmins, the women wearing their "nine yard" sārīs, the men without an upper garment, as is the protocol (in south India) in the presence of the sacred. The Paramācārya, then aged 95, was seated cross-legged on the ground in the inner courtyard. True to his reputation for great austerity, he had only a single piece of cloth to cushion him from the bare concrete floor. Because of his advanced age, the duration of his audiences was being limited, and visitors were kept at some distance, behind a barrier. Yet despite his age, his health seemed remarkably good. With the exception of his hearing, he was fully alert. I was asked to address my questions to him, which were then repeated by an attendant, to whose voice he was obviously well accustomed. The Paramācārya's replies were in Sanskrit, brief but clear. However, in the time allotted I was not able to put all of my questions to him.

Q: There are numerous accounts of Śaṅkara's life. Which of these is best?

A: It is as Monier-Williams has stated. [In the *Sanskṛit-English Dictionary*, Monier-Williams describes the *Śaṅkara-vijaya* (i.e., AŚV) as "Ānanda-giri's biography of Śaṃkarācārya recording his controversial victories, as a Vedāntin, over numerous heretics". This is in contrast to Monier-Williams' reference to the *Śaṅkara-digvijaya* of Mādhava as, "a fanciful account of the controversial exploits of Śaṃkarācārya", pp. 1054-1055.]

Q: What authority do the Śaṅkara-*vijayas* have?

A: The merits or demerits of a biography (*carita*) should be judged by a thorough and analytical study of the biography, and by what erudite scholars of former times have said about the concerned *carita*. None of the Śaṅkara *caritas* can be dismissed as not having a historical (*aitihāsika*) value. *Caritas* are *aitihāsika* accounts of great men.

Q: Is Śaṅkara an *avatāra*?

A: Śaṅkara is a partial (*aṃśa*) *avatāra* of Śiva.

Q: What are the primary duties of the present-day Śaṅkarācāryas?

A:. What Ādi-Śaṅkara has done should not be forgotten. The present *pīṭhādhipatis* should continually remind the people of what Śaṅkara has accomplished. The routine of the *maṭhas* is to spread the teachings of Śaṅkara, and the ancient Vedic *dharma* among the people.

Q: By what rules is the succession in the Śaṅkara *pīṭhas* determined? Is there a *śāstra* which is the authority for this?

A: There is no *śāstra* which governs the succession of the *pīṭhādhipatis* in the *maṭhas*. Rather, it is tradition which should always be followed in this matter. All the *maṭhas* follow only the traditional ways which are obtaining from ancient days.

With H. H. Jagadguru Śrī Abhinava-Vidyātīrtha

Sringerī, 4 January 1989.

The Sringerī *maṭha* is situated in the picturesque country of the Western Ghats on the banks of the Tuṅgā river. This is an area which has, fortunately, so far escaped environmental devastation. On the one side of the river is the town and the temple complex, dominated by the beautiful 14th century Vidyāśaṅkara temple. Adjacent to this temple, which is built in a combination of the Hoysala and Dravidian styles, is a more recent structure within which is an old shrine to the goddess Śāradā. The temple compound is dotted with smaller shrines, the *samādhis* of previous Śaṅkarācāryas. The residence of the *ācārya* is on the other side of the Tuṅgā. When I came to the river, I found that the old wooden bridge had been demolished, and a new one was under construction. A small boat ferried me across. Upon entering the lush green environs of the Śaṅkarācārya's compound, I was greeted by signs in Kannada, Hindi and English warning of the danger of snakes. I was taken to meet the *ācārya* by his personal secretary, a brilliant young engineer, fluent in numerous languages, including Sanskrit and English. It was he who saved the day when my Sanskrit conversation failed me. His Holiness came out of the residence, took his seat on a low wooden stool, and beckoned me to sit just in front of him. He was then 72 years old and quite radiant, despite the heart condition which proved to be fatal eight months later. While he would not permit me to tape record the conversation, I was allowed to counter question him at length. He was most kindly disposed to me, and seemed genuinely concerned that I receive all the information I was seeking.

Q: Which of the numerous accounts of Śaṅkara's life is the best?

A: The Mādhavīya *Śaṅkara-digvijaya* is the best. No one who lived with Śaṅkara has written about him. If any such claim is made it can only be a concoction. All that has been written about his life is on the basis of tradition, and none of these texts can be construed as the work of a contemporary of Śaṅkara. The Mādhavīya has been accepted by the tradition for a long time. The Vyāsācalīya *Śaṅkara-vijaya* is not so reliable because there are various different versions of the text. It can be accepted that Śaṅkara was born twelve or so centuries ago. He was a historical entity, unlike Rāma and Krishna, for whom there is no historical evidence. The Purāṇas are not to be taken as representing historical facts, but are meant to help the people to follow the correct path.

Q: What authority do the Śaṅkara-*vijaya*s have?

A: These *vijaya*s are of the nature of *kāvya* not history [the English term 'history' is used here]. Although it is based on actual history, in *kāvya*, the author has the freedom to embellish his work. For example, in enumerating the various opponents encountered by Śaṅkara, additional adversaries [who may not have been contemporaries of Śaṅkara] might be cited by the author. These *vijaya*s are not intended to be authoritative (*pramāṇa*).

Q: Is Śaṅkara an *avatāra*?

A: Śiva does not become manifest as an *avatāra* in the sense of being born of a mother. He makes his appearance in various different forms. We say that Śaṅkara is an *avatāra*, he never made such a claim. We deduce this from his deeds and achievements. Bhū-Devī implored Śiva to vanquish the evil forces which were prevalent. In answer to that plea he descended as Ādi-Śaṅkara. Whether Śaṅkara is an *aṃśa* or a *pūrṇa-avatāra*, is not of concern to Vedāntins. This is a matter for Paurāṇikas. In the *Skānda Purāṇa* it is stated that Śiva will appear in a form such as that of Ādi-Śaṅkara.

Q: What is the significance of Śaṅkara's performing the funeral rites for his mother, though he was a *saṃnyāsin*?

A: The *saṃnyāsin* has great respect for the mother. In the instance of Śaṅkara's carrying out the cremation of his mother, it must be said that if Śaṅkara's *pūrvāśrama* relatives had been present, he would not have had to perform this task. Yet in this matter there was a human to human relationship. Śaṅkara had given his word to his mother that he would come to her in time of need. Because there was no one else to help him, he had to dispose of his mother's body himself. He simply burned the body, but did not perform any of the rituals in this connection. He was only disposing of the mortal coil. In so far as the present-day *ācāryas* are concerned, even now, in time of calamity one may have to dispose of a corpse.

Q: What are the primary duties of the present-day Śaṅkarācāryas?

A: They are: ritual bathing, meditation on the *Om*, ritual worship of the Lord (*īśvara-pūjā*) and the practice of the four attainments (*sādhanā-catuṣṭi-sampatti*), i.e., discrimination, dispassion, tranquillity, control etc., and the intense desire for liberation (*viveka, vairāgya, śamadamādi* and *mumukṣutva*). The *saṃnyāsin* is not bound to worship. He performs *pūjā* so that others will follow his example, as is stated in the Gītā [3.23], *yadi hy ahaṃ na varteyaṃ*... ["were I not to act..."]. The *saṃnyāsin* may take part in such activities, but there is no obligation for him to do so. For him, the main imperatives are *śravaṇa-manana-nididhyāsana*. He may join in all activities meant for the peace of the world, but such actions are not binding for him.

Q: What is the relationship between Devī worship and Advaita, as taught by Śaṅkara?

A: What is ultimately prescribed is meditation on Brahman without qualities (*nirguṇopāsanā*). Meditation based on qualities (*saguṇopāsanā*) is also prescribed—in the form of worship. But this is merely a stepping stone. It is only a means and not the ultimate goal. Although there are different forms of *saguṇopāsanā*, there are no real differences between them. In the *Lalitā Sahasranāma* , it is said: *"śrī śivā śiva-śaktyaikya-rūpiṇī lalitāmbikā"* [Lalitā is Śivā, she whose form represents the identity of Śiva and Śakti] This is very close to the standpoint of *nirguṇopāsanā*. Any form of *saguṇopāsanā* can be prescribed. The varieties of *saguṇopāsanā*s which are prescribed are only different insofar as they are meant to suit the differences in individual temperaments. The special significance of Śāradā-Devī for the Sringerī *maṭha* is that she is the goddess of learning, which holds the highest place for us.

Q: By what rules is the succession in the Śaṅkara *pīṭha*s determined?

A: The procedure for choosing the successor to the *pīṭhādhipati* of the *maṭha* is as follows. Many young people are studying in the *maṭha*. They are watched over for a period of ten years or so. The one who is chosen should be someone who can remain a *brahmacārin*, who can become a paṇḍit, who is detached but can take up the considerable responsibilities of the *maṭha*. The recognition of all of these qualities is dependent on the perception of the guru. After the choice is made, prayers are offered to Īśvara that it be successful.

With H. H. Jagadguru Śvāmī Svarūpānanda

(of Dwārkā and Jyotir *maṭhas*)

Kumbha Melā grounds, Allahabad, 25 January 1989.

I was advised that Svāmījī would be camping at the festival grounds for the duration of the Kumbha Melā. Luckily, I arrived at the vast tent city which had sprung up at the confluence of the Gaṅgā and Yamunā when there was a lull in the crowds. Since there was not a special day for ritual bathing at the time, the crowd was perhaps only a couple of million strong. It would soon swell to more than ten million. The government had spent huge sums of money on preparing the festival grounds. Although this was widely criticised, the result was that all was kept orderly, and immaculately clean. When I found Svāmījī's encampment, there were already several thousand people awaiting his *darśana* in an enormous *paṇḍāl*. The expectations of the crowd were whipped up by lively preliminary speeches. There was a surge of excitement when Svāmījī finally entered the *paṇḍāl*. He spoke in Hindi for about forty-five minutes, exhorting the audience to follow the path of *bhakti*. At the close of his discourse, he sang a Rāma *bhajan*, to which the audience responded with much enthusiasm. After the crowd departed, I was ushered into an adjoining tent in which Svāmījī held court before a select gathering. I had some doubts that I would be able to put my questions, as he would only be giving a short audience and there were a dozen or more people ahead of me, all anxious to speak with him. An attendant announced me, telling Svāmījī that I was the person from Australia who had previously sent him a letter with questions in Sanskrit. He immediately turned to me and asked me if I had any further questions. I was permitted to tape record his answers, which were in Hindi,[1] presumably so that all could follow him.

Q: Which of the numerous accounts of Śaṅkara's life is the best?

A: We follow the Mādhavīya *Saṅkaradigvijaya* in our place. Other *carita*s are acceptable, but if there is anything in them opposed to the Mādhavīya, one should accept [the version in] Mādhava above all the others.[2]

Q: What authority do the Śaṅkara-*vijaya*s have?

A: That which is a *pramāṇa* is a *pramāṇa* in its own right. Whatever the *carita* of Śankara, it has the nature of *śabda* [-*pramāṇa*], that is to say it is history (*itihāsa*). Therefore, it is a *pramāṇa.* If there is any trouble [in interpretation which suggests inauthenticity], and there is authoritative evidence for this, then one can dispute its authenticity. But as long as there is no such evidence available to show, that the incidents recorded in the *carita* of Śaṅkara are untrue, we should take it as authoritative. Such is the rule:

utprekṣeta hi yo mohāt ajātam api bādhanam
sa sarva-vyavahāreṣu saṃśayātmā kṣayaṃ bhaje.

If on account of delusion one imagines some trouble, even though it has not arisen, that sceptic experiences ruin in all his activities. If there is a fly or some such thing in one's food, then it is proper to leave it. But if we become prejudiced and start imagining, 'what if there is a fly in it', 'what if there is poison in it?', then it will be difficult to

[1] I am grateful to Yogendra Yadav and Sudha Joshi for their help in going through the tape recordings of the interview with me. I am also grateful to Michael Mavro who arranged for me to meet Svāmījī.

[2] This question was answered in a previous personal communication, August 1988.

have the meal. Therefore, we should follow that which is *itihāsa* as our *pramāṇa.*

Q: Is Śaṅkara an *avatāra*?

A: It has been said that, *"caturbhiḥ saha śiṣyais tu śaṅkaro 'vatariṣyati"*, i.e., Śaṅkara will descend along with four disciples. This is written in the *Bhaviṣya-Purāṇa*. This proves he is the *avatāra* of Śiva. This is also described in the Veda: *namaḥ kapardine ca vyupta-keśāya ca*.[3] There is also the verse, *"kapardine vyupta-keśāya jaṭā-maṇḍala-dhāriṇe namaḥ"*. The meaning is, "I bow to the one who is adorned with coils of matted hair, and I also bow to the one whose hair is shaven". That shaven-headed form of Śiva also applies to Śaṅkara, who is therefore an *avatāra*.

Q: What is the significance of Śaṅkara's performing the funeral rites for his mother, though he was a *saṃnyāsin*?

A:. He was a *saṃnyāsin*, and for a *saṃnyāsin*, [it is said], "He should give up contact with the ritual fire" (*agneḥ sparśaṃ varjayet*). Well, he gave a promise to his mother before taking *saṃnyāsa:* "I will perform your funeral rites". In order to keep this pledge, he broke the rules and performed his mother's last rites. He is Īśvara, and he is an *avatāra*, therefore he can do this. All others should not follow this. [It is said] *īśvarāṇāṃ vacaḥ satyaṃ tathaivācaritaṃ kaccit*. Īśvara's words are true, and his deeds are also true. But some [actions] should not be followed by the pupils. Therefore, it is said, "Do whatever the guru says, but do not do what he does". It is not proper to follow everything. When Śaṅkara became a *paramahaṃsa-parivrājaka*, all his actions were then suited to one in that state. Apart from this he never broke the rules.

3 *Kṛṣṇa-yajurveda*, *Taittirīya Saṃhitā*, 4.5.5.

Q: What are the primary duties of the present-day Śaṅkarācāryas?

A: Those activities of Ādi-Śaṅkara which are established (*niṣṭhā*) in Advaita should be followed by the *ācāryas* of the Śaṅkara *pīṭhas*. All of the *ācāryas* follow these activities: the study (*adhyayana*) of, and the *manana*, and *nididhyāsana*, on Śaṅkara's [*Brahmasūtra*] commentary, as well as teaching and promulgating it. This was also the work of Śaṅkarācārya.

Q: What is the relationship between Devī worship and Advaita, as taught by Śaṅkara?

A: Bhagavān Śaṅkara's [way] is Kevalādvaita. It is believed:

> *īśvarānugrahād eva kiṃ canādvaita-vāsanā*
> *mahad-bhaya-paritrāṇād viprāṇām upajāyate.*[4]

It is only by the grace of Īśvara that a disposition for Advaita is produced in wise men, which delivers one from great fear. Īśvara has five forms: Śiva, Viṣṇu, Gaṇeśa, Sūrya and Jagadambā. Whichever of these one worships, it is made fruitful when the worship is employed for becoming established in Advaita, i.e., in the knowledge of the true principles (*tattva-jñāna*). Uninterrupted *sādhanā* certainly follows from that. In the four *pīṭhas* of Bhagavān Śaṅkara, the worship of the *yantra* of Tripurasundarī, i.e., Śrī Vidyā-Rāja-Rājeśvarī-Mātā, is traditionally followed. That worship is, in a way, *nididhyāsana*. What is done in this *pūjā* involves [first] taking Jagadambā as one's own Self, then summoning that very Self into the *yantra*, and becoming the devotee of the concealed deity, worshipping her as the Self, [gradually] merging everything in that *bindu*, making oneself identical with that [deity]. In the same way, *saṃsāra* is created out of Brahman by wrong

---

4 This citation corresponds to the first verse of the *Avadhūtagītā* ascribed to Dattātreya, which differs slightly in reading *...puṃsām advaita-vāsanā* .

attribution (*adhyāropa*). By a process of elimination (*apavāda*), the *saṃsāra* merges back into Brahman. This is the nature of *upāsanā* and *nididhyāsana*. In the Śaṅkara *sampradāya*, this is practised with devotion.

Q: By what rules is the succession in the Śaṅkara *pīṭhas* determined?

A: The description of all this and of all the *pīṭhas* is in the *Maṭhāmnāyopaniṣad.* There is also a description of the *ācāryas* in that Upaniṣad.[5] In our place, the first important thing is that there are qualifications prescribed:

śucir jitendriyo veda-vedāṅgādi viśāradaḥ//yoga-jñaḥ sarva-śāstrāṇāṃ sa mad-āsthānam āpnuyāt.[6]

[These are] purity, control of the senses, being learned in Vedas and Vedāṅgas, and knowing how to establish the concordance (*samanvaya*) between all the *śāstras*. Such a one occupies our *pīṭha*. Sometimes the guru appoints the successor directly to the *pīṭha*. Sometimes he first tells the disciples, who later instal the successor. If the guru does not designate a successor, then the learned and just disciples of the *sampradāya* appoint him. There is only one *ācārya* in one *pīṭha*, not many.

---

5 The first portion of the response is from a previous personal communication, August 1988.

6 The quote is from a work entitled *Mahānuśāsana*, which is attributed to Śaṅkara. A version of the text is published as an appendix to Baldev Upādhāy's edition and Hindi translation of the ŚDV, Mādhavācārya, *Śrī Śaṅkaradigvijaya* (3d ed., Hardwar: Śrī Śravaṇanātha Jñānamandir, 1985), pp. 612-616. The composition comprises 26 verses in the *śloka* metre. It gives various rules to be followed in the four *āmnāya maṭhas*. It is the 10th verse in Upādyāy's edition which is cited here.

APPENDIX B

Two Lost Works

Prācīna-Śaṅkaravijaya

The authenticity of fragments from two no longer extant works on Śaṅkara's life has been accepted by several scholars in India.[1] There is an apparent reference to the first of these texts in the influential *Śaṅkaradigvijaya*. In the opening verse of the ŚDV, Mādhava tells us that he has clearly abridged/collected the essential matter in the old (*prācīna*) work on Śaṅkara's life.[2] He gives no further indication as to the nature of this text. Dhanapatisūri, the earlier of the two commentators on the ŚDV, quotes some 800 verses which he implies are taken from this work but does not identify its author.[3] Acyuta, the second

---

1 One of the first to call attention to these two texts was T. S. Narayana Sastry, *The age of Śaṅkara* ([1916], 2nd ed. Madras: B. G. Paul and Co., 1972). See also, W. R. Antarkar, "Bṛhat-Śaṅkara-Vijaya of Citsukhācārya and Prācīna-Śaṅkara-Vijaya of Ānandagiri A/S Ānanda-Jñāna", *JUB*, 29 (1960), 113-121. Antarkar argues here for the authenticity of both texts. In his unpublished thesis he has emphasized the place of the BṛŚV as the earliest and most authoritative source on Śaṅkara's life.

2 *prācīna-śaṅkara-jaye sāraḥ saṃgṛhyate sphuṭam*. The reference to the *prācīna-śaṅkara-jaya* is problematical. It is quite possible that the commentators totally misconstrued Mādhava's citation. Mādhava was probably referring to the VŚV as the old work on Śaṅkara.

3 Dhanapatisūri's commentary on the ŚDV, entitled *Ḍiṇḍima*, is dated 1798, and a second commentary, *Advaita-rājyalakṣmī*, by Acyuta is dated 1824. Both are included in the Ānandāśrama edition of the ŚDV (1891). For Dhanapatisūrin's citations of the PrŚV, see his comment on ŚDV 1.28 (p. 25), on 15.1 (p. 529), on 15.2, where 58 verses are quoted (pp.530-532), on 15.4, in which 403 verses are cited (pp. 533-550), on 15.5 (p. 550), and on

commentator on the ŚDV, attributes the composition to Ānandagiri.[4] For the sake of convenience, I will refer to this no longer extant text as the "Prācīna-Śaṅkaravijaya" (PrŚV). The 800 odd verses Dhanapatisūri cites from the PrŚV correspond very closely with the material in chapters 4-51 of the AŚV.[5] These chapters are exclusively concerned with the debates between Śaṅkara and his sectarian opponents. Now the AŚV is a mixture of prose and verse, in which the prose is predominant. From the blocks of continuous passages cited by Dhanapatisūri, it would appear that the PrŚV was composed wholly in verse, and that its contents—at least in regard to the debates they describe—are briefer than those of the AŚV. In many, but not all cases, the verses found in the AŚV are identical to those of the PrŚV. It is difficult to say with complete certainty whether the AŚV is an elaboration of the briefer account of Śaṅkara's life in the PrŚV, or vice versa. Surely Dhanapatisūri and Acyuta are not much help here for they appear to conflate the PrŚV with AŚV.[6] But my feeling is

---

15.28 in which 351 verses are quoted (pp. 554-569). It must be noted, however, that in the Ānandāśrama edition of the ŚDV, there is only one place in which Dhanapatisūri actually specifies the PrŚV as the source of his citations, in his comment on ŚDV 1.28 (p.15). Acyuta also attributes only a single citation specifically to the PrŚV, i.e., in his comment on 1. 85 (p. 26). In both instances the quotes are very brief. The longer citations, although apparently from the same work, are not specifically identified.

4 See his comment on ŚDV 1.2 (Ānandāśrama ed. p. 3). But later on, in his comment on ŚDV 16.103 (p. 624), Acyuta refers us to "a collection of stories which should be seen in the 'Bṛhacchaṅkaravijaya', by Ānandajñāna, i.e., Ānandagiri".

5 N. Veezhinathan has conveniently collected the 800 odd verses of this work, cited in the commentary of the ŚDV. These are included as an appendix to the Madras edition of the AŚV and are rearranged according to the corresponding chapters of the AŚV.

6 Just prior to Dhanapatisūri's comment on ŚDV 15.2, which is where he gives the first portion of the 800 odd verses that appear to comprise the PrŚV,

that the stanzas of PrŚV were composed as a summary of the AŚV.

To begin with, the influence of the PrŚV on the Śaṅkara tradition seems negligible. No manuscript of this text is preserved, in contrast to the twenty or so extant manuscripts of the AŚV. Nor do we find many references in other works to the PrŚV. I am aware of only two places where the PrŚV is cited, both of which are post-18th century: (1) Ātmabodha's *Suṣamā*, a commentary to the *Gururatnamālikā*, attributed to Sadāśiva Brahmendra,[7] and (2) in the commentaries to the ŚDV, dated 1798 and 1824. Moreover, in the substantial portion of the text preserved in the ŚDV commentaries, the PrŚV seems to contain no more information—and in some cases even less—than the corresponding passages in the AŚV. In the absence of clear evidence for the priority of the PrŚV, I prefer to assume that the text is a later recasting in verse of the AŚV.

---

he quotes a substantial passage of mixed prose and verse. He does not identify the source of either passage. But their subject is one and the same—Śaṅkara's debates against proponents of the major Hindu sects. Then, immediately after citing 400 continuous verses, presumably from the PrŚV, Dhanapatisūri quotes a prose passage which, although corresponding closely to chapter 63 of the AŚV, is actually only in part direct quotation, and in part a paraphrase of what is found in the AŚV. The source of these two prose passages Dhanapatisūri cites is uncertain. But there is no doubt that the two prose passages summarize the corresponding text in the AŚV. This may suggest that the PrŚV verses are also summaries of the material in the AŚV.

[7] T.M.P. Mahadevan questions the ascription of this text to Sadāśiva Brahmendra (16th c.?), *Gauḍapāda: a study in early Advaita*, Madras: University of Madras, 1975, p. 12. In the commentary, *Suṣamā*, Ātmabodhendra cites the *Patañjali-carita* of Rāmabhadra-Dīkṣita, a work composed c.1700. See T. S. Kuppuswami Sastri, "Rāmabhadra-Dīkṣita and the southern poets of his time", in *The Indian Antiquary*, 33 (1904), pp. 126-142; [continued on] pp. 176-196. Refer especially to p.179.

One additional factor which has led me to this tentative assumption is that Cidvilāsa, the author of the CŚV, does not seem to know of the PrŚV. While this evidence alone cannot be very conclusive, we would expect Cidvilāsa to have referred to the PrŚV, had it been available to him. It is clear that he did seek a source for further information on Śaṅkara's debates, for nearly all the verses common to the CŚV and AŚV are concerned with this very topic. Most of the verses common to the AŚV and CŚV can be also found in the PrŚV. The table on the following page illustrates this connection, enabling us to compare how the three texts relate the names of Śaṅkara's opponents from six major Hindu sects and the places where the debates with them were held. The table highlights the complete correspondence between the AŚV and the PrŚV, both in terms of the opponents' names and the places where the debates are said to have occurred. While the CŚV repeats many of the same names, it differs in locating the venue of the debates, in all but one instance. Indeed, I am unable to find a single instance in which Cidvilāsa has quoted a verse directly from the PrŚV. Rather, what he has done is to borrow verses from the AŚV as well as to summarize some of its prose portions on the subject of the debates.

It is likely that Cidvilāsa had before him another source, which he saw as more authoritative, and it was perhaps from this that he drew the information on the sites of the debates. For he also differs from the AŚV in specifying the locations of some of the major incidents in Śaṅkara's life.[8] Because the AŚV devotes considerable attention to the debates themselves, Cidvilāsa may have found it a convenient supplementary source. In any case, it should now be clear that the extant

---

8 Both works speak of Śaṅkara's visit to Madhyārjuna, for example. According to the AŚV this is where Śiva comes out of the *liṅga* to declare the supremacy of Advaita. But in the CŚV it is in Kāśī.

	PrŚV	AŚV	CŚV
Śaiva place opponents	Rameśvara Vidveṣavīra Vipakṣaśula, and others Bhaktāgragaṇya	Rameśvara Vidveṣavīra Pratipakṣacaṇḍabhairava Vipakṣaśūla Bhaktāgragaṇya Paramatakālānala	Kāśī Vīravidveṣa Paravādadavānala
Vaiṣṇava place opponents	Anantaśayana Viṣnuśarman Brahmagupta, and others Vipradeva Śārṅgapāṇi Mādhava Vyāsadāsa, Nāmatīrtha	Anantaśayana Viṣṇuśarman Brahmagupta,Kṛṣṇadāsa Kamalābhakta Vipradeva Śārṅgapāṇi Mādhava Vyāsadāsa, Nāmatīrtha	Anantaśayana Viṣṇuśarman Padmanābha Kṛṣṇadvaipāyana Varāhācārya Vyāsadāsa Bindumādhava
Saura place opponents	Subrahmaṇya Divākara	Subrahmaṇya Divākara	Cidambara Māṭhara Divākarācārya
Gāṇapatīya place opponents	Gaṇavara Gaṇakumāra Herambasuta Virabhadra, and others	Gaṇavara Girijāputra Vighnaduṇḍhirājagaṇa- pati-kumāra, Heramba- suta, Vīrabhadra, Skanda	Vakratuṇḍapuri Dhuṇḍirāja- vīravighneśa
Śākta place opponents	unspecified not named	Tulajābhavānīpura Tripurakumāra Bindubhakta Pūrṇānanda Śaktivīlāsa Cidānanda	Ujjayinī Tripurāmbākumāra Bindubhuk Pūrṇānanda Vīraśākta Śuddhavidyā
Kāpālika place opponents	unspecified Vaṭuka	Ujjayinī Vaṭuka	Rāmeśvara Baṭukanātha

portion of the PrŚV is substantially the same as the AŚV. Although we find some verses in the CŚV to be identical to verses in the PrŚV, these same verses can also be seen in the AŚV, which is most probably their source. Therefore, the extant fragment of the PrŚV will not have much bearing on our reading of either the AŚV or CŚV.

Bṛhat-Saṅkaravijaya

It is not possible for me to speculate further on the nature of the work which Cidvilāsa appears to have considered more authoritative than the AŚV. However, I would reject the claim of T. S. Narayana Sastry that the CŚV is modelled on the so-called *Bṛhat-Śaṅkaravijaya* (BṛŚV).[9] Narayana Sastry apparently possessed an incomplete manuscript of the BṛŚV. He states that the text was composed by Citsukha, who was acqainted with Śaṅkara while both were still boys, and that the author was an eye witness to the lives of both Śaṅkara and Sureśvara.[10] Needless to say, the existence of such a manuscript would stimulate a great deal of interest. Unfortunately, he never managed to publish the manuscript, nor has another copy since come to light. Aside from a few brief quotations and the Sanskrit text of one short chapter, he has provided only an English summary of the work.

It is possible to make some assessment of the BṛŚV on the basis of the single complete chapter which Narayana Sastry has

---

9 *The age of Śaṅkara* ([1916], 2nd ed. Madras: B. G. Paul and Co., 1972), p. 271n.

10 *Ibid.*, pp. 39n-40n. He maintains that the work was in three parts, concerning, (1) the earlier Advaita *ācārya* -s, (2) the life of Śaṅkara and (3) his successors. His copy of the MS. apparently contained only the second part. W. R. Antarkar has informed me that he met the author's son but was unable to trace this sole MS. of the work.

reproduced in his book.[11] This chapter describes the birth of Śaṅkara in 32 verses in the *śloka* metre. Verses 1, 2ab and 4 in the BṛŚV are virtually identical to the first three verses on p. 8 of the AŚV (Madras ed.). Twenty four of the remaining 29 verses, are very similar—and indeed in most cases identical—to verses found in the CŚV between 5.33 and 5.64. Even the two verses concluding the BṛŚV chapter depict the same dialogue between guru and disciple found in the CŚV.[12] Only the names of the teacher and student differ.

When it comes to the particulars of Śaṅkara's time of birth there is a real divergence in the two texts. The BṛŚV devotes five verses to this matter. Three of these verses are very conspicuous in their absence from the CŚV. I will highlight in bold the verses common to the two works :

> **Then, in the 10th month [of her pregnancy], at a time which was replete with auspicious signs**, in the year 2631 of the Yudhiṣṭhira Śaka, in the auspicious year of Nandana; when the [sun's] rays were in Aries, on the fifth lunar day of the bright half of the splendid month of Vaiśākha, on Sunday; when the moon was in [the *nakṣatra*] Punarvasu, and the ascendant was in [the sign] known as Cancer, **at midday in the *muhūrta* known as Abhijit,** whose aspect was auspicious; when Jupiter, Saturn, Mars and the sun were in exaltation and also in *kendra*; when Venus was at its summit, and Mercury was in conjunction with the sun, **that good woman gave birth to a son, as Girijā [had given birth] to the six-faced one.**[13]

---

11 *Ibid*., pp. 272-275. His translation follows this (pp. 275-281).

12 Compare CŚV 5.64 and 5.65b / 4.55 cd with BṛŚV 31-32.

13 The Sanskrit text of the BṛŚV is as follows:

In addition to the material in bold type, the CŚV reads: "...on a day in the spring season when the five planets were in exaltation, when [the moon] was in conjunction with [the constellation] Ārdrā".[14] This latter detail, the identity of the constellation (*nakṣatra*) that the moon was in at the time of Śaṅkara's birth, is one point on which there is disagreement between the two texts. According to the BṛŚV it was Punarvasu, while Cidvilāsa says it was Ārdrā. With this one exception, the close relationship of the two accounts is readily apparent.

It is difficult to see how Cidvilāsa could have accurately reproduced some of the details of Śaṅkara's time of birth—and nearly all the remaining material from the one available BṛŚV chapter as well—but failed to cite the very verses which specify the exact time of the birth. In view of this, it hardly seems possible to maintain that Cidvilāsa could have composed his work on the basis of the BṛŚV. Rather, it is more likely that the BṛŚV is based on the CŚV, at least insofar as the description of Śaṅkara's birth is concerned. Indeed, none of the

---

(12) *tataḥ sā daśame māse sampūrṇa-śubha-lakṣaṇe / ṣaḍviṃśe śatake śrīmad-yudhiṣṭhira-śakasya vai //*

(13) *ekatriṃśe 'tha varṣe tu hāyane nandane śubhe / meṣa-rāśiṃ gate sūrye vaiśākhe māsi śobhane //*

(14) *śukla-pakṣe ca pañcamyāṃ tithyāṃ bhāskara-vāsare / punarvasu-gate candre lagne karkaṭāhvaye //*

(15) *madhyāhne cābhijin-nāma-muhūrte śubha-vīkṣite / svocca-sthe kendra-sthe ca gurau mande kuje ravau//*

(16) *nija-tuṅga-gate śukre raviṇā saṅgate budhe / prasūta tanaya sādhvī girijeva ṣaḍ-ānanam //*

14 The text of the CŚV concerning the time of Śaṅkara's birth reads:

(5.36cd) *tataḥ sā daśame māse sampūrṇa-śubha-lakṣaṇe //*

(5.37) *divase mādhavartau ca socca-sthe graha-pañcake / madhyāhne cābhijin-nāma-muhūrte cārdrayā yute //*

(5.38cd) *prasūta tanaya sādhvī girijeva ṣaḍ-ānanam //.*

hagiographers discussed here seem to know of the BṛŚV For we do not find the same date of birth (nor another one, for that matter) put forth in any of our eight texts. Neither is there evidence supporting the rest of the many specific dates, cited in the BṛŚV, on which the major incidents in Śaṅkara's life are said to have occurred. For this reason, I cannot help but be somewhat suspicious of the authenticity of this chapter and the remaining portions of the BrŚV.[15] Because of these doubts, and more especially, because of the lack of an available manuscript, I have excluded the BṛŚV from further consideration.

---

[15] I am unaware of any Hindu author, writing in Sanskrit, who provides specific dates of persons and events prior to Kalhaṇa's *Rājataraṅginī*, composed in the 12th century. Moreover, this work is a chronicle of kings. It is rare indeed to find an early Sanskrit text which supplies dates for persons other than kings. I would not like to suggest that Narayana Sastry (who was, incidentally, a high court *vakīl*) actually fabricated the BrŚV. I would prefer to assume that he found a fragment of a MS. he wrongly believed to be quite old. Considering the climate of the Madras region, one can readily imagine a MS. taking on an old appearance within a relatively short time. This "old" MS. might have been written as late as the beginning of the 19th century on the model of the CŚV. It should be noted that Narayana Sastry's primary concern is in seeking to demonstrate that Śaṅkara was born in 509 B.C. He tries to refute the range of dates accepted by most critical scholars and argues, in particular, against the identity of Candragupta Maurya and Sandracottus. His conclusion entails his pushing back the date of the Buddha to 1862 B.C. A number of other writers have carried on in a similar vein, in order to justify traditional dates. One recent publication in this genre is S. D. Kulkarni, *Adi Sankara: the saviour of mankind*, Bombay: Bhishma, 1987.

APPENDIX C

Sources for Verses Incorporated in Mādhava's ŚDV

CHAPTER I (98 verses)

29-32; 34-40	=TŚA 1.27-37
43ab; 44ab	=TŚA 1.38ab; 1.38cd
45-47; 55-97	=TŚA 1.39-84

CHAPTER II (93 verses)

6-46	=VŚV 1.2-42
47; 49-65	=VŚV 4.1; 4.3-19
66-70	=reworked RŚA 1.21-25
71-75	=VŚV 4.21-24
76	=reworked RŚA 1.27
78	=reworked TŚA 1.96
79-84	=VŚV 4.25-30
85-87	=reworked RŚA 1.31-33
88-91	=TŚA 2.9; 2.11; 1.101-102

CHAPTER III (83 verses)

1-7	=TŚA 2.1-7
10-77	=VŚV 6.9cd-77

CHAPTER IV (110 verses)

1-3	=VŚV 11.113-115
4-9; 10	=TŚA 2.12-17; 2.8
11-17	=VŚV 11.116-122
19	=AŚV p.3 (lines 3-7)
21-31	=TŚA 2.21-31
32	=reworked AŚV p.11 (lines 1-2)
33-37; 44-45	=TŚA 2.32-33; 35-39
48-53	=TŚA 2.40-45
62-64; 71-74	=TŚA 2.50-55; 2.57

98-99	=TŚA 2.61-62

CHAPTER V (172 verses)

1	=TŚA 2.66
2-4	=VŚV 11.124-125; 123
30-31	=TŚA 2.70-71
34	=VŚV 4.42
35-58	=TŚA 2.76-99
60-67	=VŚV 11.127-134
68-80	=VŚV 4.49-61
82	=TŚA 2.103
86	=VŚV 3.14d, 3.5d, 3.4cd
87; 90acd	=PC 8.18-19acd
91ab; 92-95	=PC 8.62cd-66
96-97	=TŚA 2.104-105
98-101	=PC 8.67-70
102-103	=TŚA 3.1-2
105-106	=VŚV 4.63-64
107-09;118-25	=TŚA 3.3-13
129-171	=TŚA 3.14-56

CHAPTER VI (107 verses)

1-5; 14	=VŚV 4.87-92
15	=RŚA 2.15
19-29	=TŚA 3.58-59 [varient]; 61-69
33-37; 39	=TŚA 3.70-74; 3.76
44-52	=TŚA 3.77-85 [3.77var.]
54bc; 55	=PC 8.45cd; 46
57-59ab	=PC 8.60-62ab
60-61	=RŚA 1.64 [var.]; 1.62
64	=VŚV 4.68
68-71	=RŚA 2.16-19
73-79; 102	=TŚA 3.99-105; 3.89

CHAPTER VII (121 verses)

11	=AŚV [var.] p.169 v.1

16-17	=RŚA 2.3-4
18-21	=TŚA 4.4;4.6-8
23-28	=VŚV 4.71-76
29-30	=RŚA 2.5; 2.7
32; 34	=TŚA 4.9; 4.11
39-40; 44-45	=VŚV 4.80-81; 4.82; 84
46ab; 47	=RŚA 2.11ab; 2.10
48; 54	=TŚA 4.12-13
55	=RŚA 2.12
56	=TŚA 4.15
57-58	=VŚV 4.85-86
59	=RŚA 2.13
60	=TŚA 4.16 [var.]
61	=RŚA 2.20
62	=TŚA 4.17
63	=RŚA 2.21
64	=VŚV 5.3
65	=RŚA 2.22
66	=VŚV 5.5
67-70	=RŚA 2.24-26; 29
72	=VŚV 5.9
73; 75-78	=TŚA 4.18 [var.]; 4.19-22
79	=RŚA 2.32ab / VŚV 5.10cd
80-100	=VŚV 5.11-31
101-103	=TŚA 4.25-27
104-107	=RŚA 2.33; 35-37
108	=TŚA 4.29
109-110	=RŚA 2.38 [var.]-39
111-113	=TŚA 4.30-32
114-115	=VŚV 5.35-36
116-118	=RŚA 2.41 [var.]-43
119	=TŚA 4.33
120abc	=RŚA 2.44abc

CHAPTER VIII (136 verses)

11-13;35-36ab	=TŚA 4.40-42; reworked 43; 44ab

45-48	=VŚV 6.84-87
49; 51; 58-59	=TŚA 4.45; 47-49
61-65	=VŚV 6.91-95
66	=RŚA 2.48
67-69	=VŚV 6.97-99
70-71	=TŚA 4.50-51
72-73	=VŚV 6.100-101
74-130	=TŚA 4.53-109
132cd; 133	=RŚA 2.49cd; reworked 2.50

CHAPTER IX (109 verses)

1-21; 23-24	=TŚA 5.1-23 [5.11varient]
29-30; 33-36	=TŚA 5.24-29
38; 43-68	=TŚA 5.30-56 [5.56 var.]
69-70	=VŚV 12.62-63
72-74	=TŚA 5.57-58[var.]; 5.76
75-86	=RŚA 4.34-45
87-89	=TŚA 5.60-62
90	=RŚA 4.47cd/48ab
92-104	=TŚA 5.63-75 [5.75var.]
105-106	=VŚV 12.66-67
107-109	=TŚA 5.78-80

CHAPTER X (119 verses)

1-8; 12-16	=TŚA 6.1-8; 27-31
17-18	=VŚV 12.70-71
19-22; 30-42	=TŚA 6.42-57; 59
44-56; 61-63	=TŚA 6.60-63; 65-72; 74; 78-80
64	=VŚV 6.103
65-72; 74	=TŚA 6.81-88; 90
75	=RŚA 2.51
76-103	=VŚV 6.104; 7.1-7.27
104	=TŚA 6.92
105	=RŚA 2.61
106-116	=TŚA 6.93-103

CHAPTER XI (75 verses)

1-13	=TŚA 7.1-13
14	=RŚA 4.66
15	=TŚA 7.14
16-17	=VŚV 9.39-40
18	=TŚA 7.15
19	=VŚV 9.41
20-21	=RŚA 4.64-65
22	=TŚA 7.16
23	=VŚV 9.38
24-26	=TŚA 7.17-19
27	=TŚA 7.20a / VŚV 9.42bcd
28-32	=VŚV 9.43-47
33-36	=TŚA 7.22-25
37; 38c	=VŚV 9.48; 9.49a
39-40	=TŚA 7.26-27
44	=VŚV 9.52
45-52	=RŚA 4.70-77
60-67	=VŚV 9.54-61
71-73	=RŚA 4.79-81
74	=VŚV 9.84

CHAPTER XII (89 verses)

1-37	=RŚA 4.1-2; 6-7; 14-33; 50-62
40-42; 44-62	=VŚV 12.24; 12.11-29
70-74	=VŚV 9.84-88
76-79	=TŚA 3.92-95
82	=RŚA 3.40
83	=reworked TŚA 3.96
84-85	=VŚV 9.95-96
86	=TŚA 3.97

CHAPTER XIII (75 verses)

2-4; 6-14	=VŚV 7.28-30; 37-45
21	=RŚA 2.53
40-48ab	=reworked VŚV 7.46; 7.47-54ab

49-50	=RŚA 2.54; reworked 2.55
51-61; 64-68	=VŚV 7.55-70 [7.56 varient]
69	=RŚA 2.57
70	=VŚV 7.71
71; 72acd; 73	=RŚA 2.58; 59acd; 60

CHAPTER XIV (175 verses)

1-26; 28ab	=VŚV 7.72-98ab
29	=RŚA 3.2
30; 35	=VŚV 4.95-96
39-41	=RŚA 3.5-7
42	=VŚV 4.99
45-47	=RŚA 3.15-17
48-49; 52	=VŚV 4.101-102; 9.14
56-71	=VŚV 7.99-101; reworked 7.102 and 8.1-2; 8.3-9; reworked 8.10;8.19-20
74-90; 92-105	=VŚV 8.36-39; reworked 8.40-41; 8.42-66
107-123	=VŚV 8.67-70; reworked 8.71-73; 8.74-83
124-25ab;126-33	=reworked VŚV 8.84; 85bc; 8.86-93
138cd-142	=VŚV 9.29cd-33
149-56; 159-62	=RŚA 3.19-30
166-68; 170-74	=RŚA 3.31-32; reworked 3.33; 3.34-38

CHAPTER XV no borrowed verses identified

CHAPTER XVI (107 verses)

3	=reworked RŚA 3.39
4-15;18-20	=VŚV 10.1-3; 5-12;11.93cd-96ab;
21cd-26	=VŚV 11.98ab-100ab; 11.101-103
28	=RŚA 3.41
55-60; 62-81	=VŚV 12.30-55
82ab	=RŚA 7.65cd
84-87ab	=reworked VŚV 12.79; 12.80-82ab
91-92	=RŚA 7.68-69

BIBLIOGRAPHY

Eight Sanskrit Hagiographies of Śaṅkara

AŚV *The Śaṅkaravijaya, or the life and polemics of Śaṅkara Āchāryya by Ānandagiri*. Edited by Jayanārāyaṇa Tarkapañcānana. Bibliotheca Indica Series, no. 46. Calcutta: Baptist Mission Press, 1868. Reprinted, Osnabrück: Biblio Verlag, 1982.

Śaṅkaravijaya by Ānandagiri. Edited by Jīvānanda Vidyāsāgara Bhaṭṭācārya. Calcutta: Sārasudhānidhi Press, 1881.

Śrī Śaṅkaravijaya. of Anantānandagiri. Edited by N. Veezhinathan. Madras: University of Madras, 1971.

CŚV *Śrī Śaṅkaravijayavilāsa by Cidvilāsa-muni*. Edited by W.R. Antarkar. *Bhāratīya Vidyā* 33 (1973), 1-92.

GŚC *Śrī Śaṅkarācāryacaritam by Govindanātha*. Edited by Narmadāśaṅkar Methā. Poona: Citraśāla Press, 1931.

GVK *Guruvaṃśakāvyam by Kāśī Lakṣmaṇa-Śāstrī*. Śrīraṅgam: Śrī Vāṇīvilās Press, 1966. [The same publisher brought out an earlier edition, edited by Kunigal Rama Sastrigal, Sri Vani Vilas Sanskrit Series no. 12, n. d. This contains only the first seven chapters but has a commentary by the author].

RŚA *Śrī Śaṅkarābhyudayam by Rājacūḍāmaṇi-Dīkṣita*. With a commentary by S.V. Rādhākṛṣṇa-Śāstrī. Srirangam: Śimili Śrī Veṅkaṭarāma-Śāstrī Trust, 1986. [The first printed edition appeared in *The Sanskrit Journal: Sahṛdayā* 17-18 {new series 5-6} (1914-15?), published in Srirangam].

ŚDV *Śrīmacchaṅkaradigvijaya by Vidyāraṇya. With the Diṇḍimā of Dhanapatisūri and the Advaitarājyalakṣmī [of Acyuta]*. Edited by Mahādeva Cimaṇājī Āpte. Ānandāsrama Sanskrit Series 22. Poona: Ānandāśrama Press, 1891.

Translations of the ŚDV:

Śrī Śaṅkaradigvijaya by Mādhavācārya. [Sanskrit text] with Hindi translation and commentary by Baldev Upādhyāy. [1943] 3d ed.; Haridvār: Śrī Śravaṇanāth Jñān-mandir, 1985.

Sankara-dig-vijaya: the traditional life of Sri Sankaracharya by Madhava-Vidyaranya. Translated by Swami Tapasyananda. Madras: Sri Ramakrishna Math, 1978.

Srimad Sankara digvijayam by Vidyaranya. [Sanskrit text] with English translation by K. Padmanaban. 2 vols., Madras: K. Padmanabhan, 1985/86.

TŚA *Śri Śaṅkarābhyudayamahākāvya by Tirumala-Dīkṣita.* Edited by W.R. Antarkar. *Journal of the University of Bombay* 34 (1965), 138-187.

VŚV *Śaṅkaravijaya by Vyāsācala.* Edited by T. Chandrasekharan. Madras Govern-ment Oriental Manuscripts Series 24. Madras: Government of Madras, 1954.

Other Śaṅkara Hagiographies

Printed Editions of Works Composed Before 1900

Acāryavijaya a/s Ācāryavijayākhyānam by Śrī Kavikaṇṭhīrava Parameśvara. Edited by W.R. Antarkar. *Journal of the University of Bombay* 37 (1968) 1-69.

Bṛhat-Śaṅkaravijaya. Lost text. See Sastry, T. S. Narayana. In *The Age of Śaṅkara,* Sastry states that he had a MS. of this work. It was apparently lost after his death in 1918. His book contains one chapter from this MS. (in Sanskrit, *devanāgarī* characters) and an English summary of the entire composition.

Patañjalicarita by Rāmabhadra-Dīkṣita. Edited by Śivadatta Śarmā. Kāvyamāla Series no.51, Bombay: Nirṇayasāgara Press, 1895. [Chapters 7 and 8 describe the life of Śaṅkara].

Prācīna-Śaṅkaravijaya. Lost text. 800 verses of this work are cited in Dhanapatisūri's commentary on *Śaṅkaradigvijaya,* in the Ānandāśrama edition of the ŚDV. These verses have been compiled and rearranged in an appendix to *The Śaṅkaravijaya of Anantānandagiri*, the Madras edition of the AŚV.

Śaṅkaradigvijayasāra by Sadānanda. Bombay: Nirṇayasāgara Press. [I have not sighted this work. The details are from W.R. Antarkar's thesis, "Śaṅkara-Vijayas: a comparative and critical study"].

Śaṅkarābhyudayakāvyam by Nīlakaṇṭha. Edited by W.R. Antarkar. *Journal of the University of Bombay* 33 (1964), 128-167.

Śaṅkaravijayasaṃgrahaḥ [Kūṣmāṇḍa-Śaṅkaravijaya] by Puruṣottama Bhāratī. Edited by W.R. Antarkar. *Oriental Thought* [Poona] 6 (1962), 1-16.

Works Composed Since 1900

Kāśikānanda Giri, Svāmī. *Saṃkṣipta Śaṅkaradigvijayaḥ: Śrīmadādyaśaṅkarācārya-caritam*. Vārāṇasī: Śrī Svāmī Kāśikānanda Trust, 1985.

Lakṣmaṇa Sūri. *Bhagavatpādābhyudayam*. [Title page missing, foreword dated 1927].

Madugulu, T.S. *The Ācārya: Śaṅkara of Kāladi. A story*. Delhi: Motilal Banarsidass, 1985. [A retelling of the *Śaṅkaradigvijaya*].

Nigamabodhatīrtha, Śrī Svāmī. *Śrī Śaṅkarācāryacaritam mahākāvyaṃ kusumāñjali ṭīkā saha*. Delhi: Parimal Publications, 1988.

Omkārānanda Giri, Svāmī. *Śrī Śaṅkara-caritāmṛta-kathāsāra yukta Saṃkṣipta-Śaṅkara-digvijaya*. Hośaṅgāvād Narmadāpura: Jñānasatra Prakāśan, 1987.

Rādhākṛṣṇa Śāstrī, S.V. *Śri Śaṅkaravijayamakaranda: compiled from all Śaṅkara vijayas and other sources of [the] life history of Śrī Śaṅkara Bhagavatpāda*. Trichy: Śimili Śrī Veṅkaṭarāma Śāstrī Trust, 1978.

Satyānanda Sarasvatī, Svāmī. *Śrī Śaṅkaradigvijaya*. Vārāṇasī: Govindamaṭha, *samvat* 2042 [=1984].

Subrahmaṇya Śāstrī, K.V. *Śrī Śaṅkarācāryacaritram*. Madhurā: E.M. Gopalakṛṣṇa, 1926.

Śaṅkara's Works

Brahmasūtra-Śaṅkarabhāṣyam. With the commentaries: Bhāṣyaratnaprabhā of Govindānanda, Bhāmatī of Vācaspatimiśra, Nyāya-Nirṇaya of Ānandagiri. Edited by J. L. Shastri, Delhi: Motilal Banarsidass, 1980.

Īśādidaśopaniṣadaḥ. Ten principal Upanishads with Śaṅkara-bhāṣya. Vol. I of *Śrī Śaṅkarācārya-granthāvalī. Works of Śaṅkarācārya.* Reprinted, Delhi: Motilal Banarsidass, 1978.

Śaṅkara's Upadeśasāhasrī. Critically edited with introduction by Sengaku Mayeda. Tokyo: Hokuseido Press, 1973.

Śrī Bhagavadgītā. Bhagavadgītā with Śaṅkarabhāṣya. Vol. II of *Works of Śaṅkarācārya.* [1929] Reprinted, Delhi: Motilal Banarsidass, 1981.

Śrī Śaṅkarācārya-viracita-prakaraṇa-granthāḥ. Minor works of Śrī Śaṅkarācārya. Edited by H. R. Bhagavat. Poona Oriental Series, no. 8. Poona: Oriental Book Agency, 1952. [Contains works traditionally ascribed to Śaṅkara].

Other Sanskrit Sources

Ānandarāghavam by Rājacūḍāmaṇi-Dīkṣita. Edited by P. M. Padmanābha-Śarmā. Tanjore Sarasvati Mahal Series no. 134. Tanjore: Maharaja Serfoji's Sarasvati Mahal Library, 1971.

Brahmāṇḍa-mahāpurāṇam. [Reprint of Veṅkateśvara Press edition]. With introduction and corrections by K.V. Sarma. Varanasi: Krishnadas Academy, 1983.

Brahmasiddhi by Acharya Maṇḍanamiśra with commentary by Śaṅkhapāṇi. Edited by S. Kuppuswami Sastri [Madras, 1937]. Reprinted Delhi, 1984.

Buddhacarita. See Johnston, E.H.

Gorakṣasiddhāntasaṃgraha. Edited by Gopī Nātha Kavirāja. Princess of Wales Sarasvati Bhavana Texts, no. 18. Benares: Vidya Vilas Press, 1925.

The Harṣa-carita of Bāṇa. See Cowell, E.B. and Thomas. F.W.

Jīvanmuktiviveka: liberation in life by Vidyāraṇya. Edited and translated by S. Subrahmanya Sastri and T. R. Srinivasa Ayyangar. [1935] Revised edition, Madras: Adyar Library, 1978.

Kṛtyakalpataru of Bhaṭṭa Lakṣmīdhara. [*Tīrthakāṇḍa*] Edited by K.V. Rangaswami Aiyangar, Gaekwad's Oriental Series XCVIII. Baroda: Oriental Institute, 1942.

Liṅgapurāṇa. Edited by J. L. Shastri. Delhi: Motilal Banarsidass, 1980.

Mahābharata: critical edition. Critically edited by V.S. Sukthankar et. al. 19 vols. Poona: Bhandarkar Oriental Institute, 1933-1971.

La Mahā Nārāyaṇa Upaniṣad. Edited by Jean Varenne. 2 vols.; Publications de l'Institut de Civilisation Indienne, Paris: Éditions E. de Boccard, 1960.

Maṇimañjarī by Nārāyaṇa-paṇḍita. Edited by T.R. Kṛṣṇācārya. Bombay: Nirṇaya-sāgara Press, *śaka* 1834 [=1912].

Naiṣkarmyasiddhi of Sureśvara. Edited with introduction, English translation, annotation and indices by R. Balasubramanian. Madras University Philosophical Series, no. 47. Madras: University of Madras, 1988.

Pañcapādikā by Padmapādācārya. [With five commentaries]. Edited by S. Śrīrāma Śāstrī and S.R. Krishnamurthi Śāstrī. Madras Government Oriental Series, no. 155. Madras: Government Oriental Manuscripts Library, 1958.

Pañcaviṃśa-Brāhmaṇa [Tāṇḍya-mahābrāhmaṇa]. The brāhmaṇa of twenty five chapters. Edited and translated by W. Caland. [Bibliotheca Indica, 1931] Reprinted, Delhi: Sri Satguru Publications, 1982.

Parāśara-smṛti. Parāśara-mādhava. With the gloss by Mādhava. [Bibliotheca Indica, 1893]. Reprinted in 2 vols. Calcutta: Asiatic Society, 1973-74.

Prapannāmṛtam by Anantācārya. Edited by Śrīnivāsa Nṛsiṃhācārya. Bombay: Śrī Veṇkaṭeśvara Steam Press, *śaka* 1829 [=1907].

Raghuvaṃśa of Kālidāsa with the commentary of Mallinātha. Edited and translated by Gopal Raghunath Nandargikar. [1897] Reprinted, Delhi: Motilal Banarsidass, 1982.

Saṃnyāsapaddhati of Rudradeva. Edited by Patrick Olivelle. Madras: Adyar Library, 1986.

Sarvadarśana-saṅgraha by Mādhavāchārya [Calcutta: Bibliotheca Indica, 1858] Reprinted Osnabrük: Biblio Verlag, 1981.

Sarva-Siddhānta-Saṅgraha of Śaṅkarācārya. Edited and translated by M. Raṅgācārya. [1909] Reprinted, New Delhi: Ajay Book Service, 1983.

Saurapurāṇaṃ by Vyāsa. Ānandāsrama Sanskrit Series, no. 18. 3d ed.; Poona: Ānandāśrama Press, 1980.

Siddhāntabindu by Madhusūdana Sarasvatī. Edited by Vasudev Shastri Abhyankar [1928] Reprinted, Poona: Bhandarkar Oriental Research Institute, 1962.

[Śivagītā] Śrīmatpadmapurāṇāntargata-Śivagītā with the commentary Bālānandinī by Lakṣmīnaraharisūnu. Bombay: Nirṇaya-sāgara, 1929.

Śivamahāpurāṇa. [Veṅkaṭeśvara Press edition]. Reprinted, 2 vols., Delhi: Nag, 1986.

Sumadhvavijaya by Nārāyaṇa-paṇḍita. Edited by T.R. Kṛṣṇācārya Bombay: Nirṇayasāgara Press, *śaka* 1834 [=1912].

Unpublished Upanishads. Edited by the Pandits of the Adyar Library under C. Kunhan Raja. Madras: Adyar Library, 1938. [Contains *Maṭhāmnāyopaniṣad*].

Vaiyāsikanyāyamālā by Bhāratītīrtha. [Published as the *Vyāsādhikaraṇamālā* in an appendix to the Bibliotheca Indica edition of the Brahmasūtras: *The aphorisms of the Vedānta by Bādarāyaṇa.* (Calcutta, 1863). Reprinted, Osnabrück: Biblio Verlag, 1981].

Vāyupurāṇa. [Veṅkaṭeśvara Press edition]. Reprinted, Delhi: Nag Publishers, 1983.

Yatidharmasaṃgrahaḥ by Viśveśvara Sarasvatī. Edited by V.S.R. Gokhale. Ānandāśrama Sanskrit Series no. 60. 2nd ed., Poona: Ānandāśrama, 1928.

Polemical literature arising from disputes between the *maṭhas*

Aiyar, R. Krishnaswamy and Venkatraman, K.R. *The Truth about the Kumbhakonam mutt*. [Publisher and place not identified], 1965.

Aiyer, A. Nataraja and Sastri, S. Lakshminarasimha. *The Traditional age of Sri Sankaracharya and the maths*. [1962] Reprinted, Madras: Rajan and Co., 1988.

Anantaanendra Sarasvati. *Sri Sankaracharya and Sankarite institutions*. Tiruchirapalli: Theni Printers, 1982.

Balasubramaniam, S. "Adi Sankara and courts: Sri Kamakoti Peetam and Sri Sringeri Peetam as respondents in one case", *Madras Law Journal*, vol. 170, nos. 13-14, 10 April, 1986, pp. 9-11.

Dave, Manjulal Sevaklal. *Shri Adya Shankaracharya: his maths and memorials*. [1963] Reprinted, Mysore: Sri Sharada Mudrana Prakashanalaya, 1976.

Iyengar, H.R. Rangaswami and Chakravarthi, R. *Śri Śaṅkara vijayam*. 2nd edition; Madras: Ganesh and Co., 1976.

Kuppuswami, A. *Śrī Śaṅkarācārya and his connection with Kāñcīpuram*. Madras: A. Kuppuswami, 1987.

Mariappan, M. "Adi Sankara and courts: a reply", *Madras Law Journal*, vol. 173, nos. 5-8, 26 February 1987, pp. 32-34.

Rama Sastrigal, Polagam Sri. *The Mutts founded by Sri Sankara Bhagavatpada*. Madras: B. G. Paul, 1973. [Originally published in Tamil, n.d.].

Reddiar, N. Krishnaswami *Some judicial references and administrative records regarding Sankaracharya Mutts*. Madras: D. Ramanathan Chettiar, 1987.

Śarmā, J.V Rāj Gopal. *Śrīmad jagadguru śaṅkaramaṭha vimarśa* [in Hindi].Vārāṇasī, 1963.

Sastry, Mudigonda Venkatarama. *Kāmakoṭi śatakoṭi: one hundred proofs exposing the spurious and concocted books depended by* [sic] *the Kanchi Mutt as its authorities.* [First published in Sanskrit, 1963]. Translated by Ramalingeswara Rao. Varanasi and Bangalore: Ganga-Tunga Prakashan, 1990.

Sharma, V. Raj Gopal. *Kanchi Kamakoti Math: a myth.* Varanasi: Ganga-tunga Prakashan, 1987.

Secondary Sources

Adi Shankara. [Comic book]. Amara Chitra Katha no. 60. Bombay: India Book House Education Trust, n.d.

Aiyar, R. Krishnaswamy. *Dialogues with the guru: talks with His Holiness Sri Chandrasekhara Bharati Swaminah late Sankaracharya of Sringeri Mutt.* 4th ed.; Bombay: Chetana, 1981.

Aiyer, C. N. Krishnaswami. *Sri Madhwa and Madhwaism: a short historic sketch.* Madras: G.A. Natesan, n.d. [191-?].

Alston, A.J. *Śaṃkara on the absolute. A Śaṃkara source-book.* Vol. 1, London: Shanti Sadan, 1980.

Antarkar, W.R. "Bṛhat-Śaṅkara-Vijaya of Citsukhācārya and Prācīna-Śaṅkara-Vijaya of Ānandagiri A/S Ānanda-Jñāna", *Journal of the University of Bombay* 29 (1960), 113-121.

———. "Śaṅkara-Vijaya of Anantānandagiri", *Journal of the University of Bombay* 30 (1961), 73-80.

———. "Śaṅkara-Vijayas: a comparative and critical study". Ph. D. thesis, University of Poona, 1960.

———. "Saṅkṣepa Śaṅkara Jaya of Mādhavācārya or Śaṅkara Digvijaya of Śrī Vidyāraṇyamuni", *Journal of the University of Bombay* 41 (1972), 1-23.

Appadurai, Arjun "The Puzzling status of Brahmin temple priests in Hindu India", *South Asian Anthropologist* 4 (1983), 43-52.

Auboyer, Jeannine. "The Symbolism of sovereignty in India according to iconography", *Indian Arts and Letters* 12 (1938), 26-36.

Bader, Jonathan. *Meditation in Śaṅkara's Vedānta*. Delhi: Aditya Prakashan, 1990.

Bailey, Greg. "Brahmā, Pṛthu and the theme of the earth-milker in Hindu mythology", *Indo-Iranian Journal* 23 (1981), 105-116.

———. *Materials for the study of ancient Indian ideologies;* pravṛtti *and* nivṛtti. Pubblicazioni di Indologica Taurinensia, no. 19. Torino: Istituto di Indologia, 1985.

Bareau, André. "The Superhuman personality of Buddha and its symbolism in the *Mahāparinirvāṇasūtra* of the Dharmaguptaka", in *Myths and symbols: studies in honor of Mircea Eliade*. Edited by Joseph M. Kitagawa and Charles H. Long. Chicago: University of Chicago, 1969, 9-21.

Belvalkar, S. K. *Shree Gopal Basu Mallik lectures on Vedānta philosophy*. Part 1: lectures 1-6. Poona: Bilvakuñja Publishing House, 1929.

Bharadwaj, Surinder Mohan. *Hindu places of pilgrimage in India: a study in cultural geography*. Berkeley: University of California, 1973.

Bharati, Agehananda. "*Mokṣa* and *devībhakti*: the (seeming) Śaṃkara paradox". [Chapter 2 of] *Hindu views and ways and the Hindu Muslim interface: an anthropological assessment*. New Delhi, 1981, 23-40.

———. "Pilgrimage in the Indian tradition", *History of Religions* 3 (1963), 135-167.

———. "Pilgrimage sites and Indian civilization", in *Chapters in Indian civilization*, Edited by Joseph W. Elder. 2nd ed., Dubuque: Kendall/Hunt, 1970, 83-126.

Bhatt, P. Gururaja. *Antiquities of South Kanara*. Udupi [n.p.], 1969.

The Biographical process: studies in the history and psychology of religion. Edited by Frank E. Reynolds and Donald Capps. The Hague: Mouton, 1976.

Bonazzoli, Giorgio. "Prayāga and its Kumbha Melā", *Purāṇa* 19 (1977), 81-179.

Briggs, George W. *Gorakhnāth and the Kānphaṭa Yogīs.* Calcutta: YMCA Publishing House, 1938.

Brown, C. Mackenzie, "Purāṇa as scripture: from sound to image of the holy word in the Hindu tradition", *History of Religions* 26 (1986), 68-86.

Candraśekharendra Sarasvatī [Śaṅkarācārya of Kānchipuram]. *Adi Śaṅkara: his life and times.* [First published in Tamil, 1933]. Translated by T. M. P. Mahadevan [1980]. Reprinted, Bombay: Bharatiya Vidya Bhavan, 1988.

———. *Aspects of our religion.* Bombay: Bharatiya Vidya Bhavan, 1988.

———. *Hindu dharma.* [Talks 1932-1957]. Translated from the Tamil by T.M.P. Mahadevan. Kumbhakonam: Sri Kamakoti Research Centre, 1988.

Carman, John Braisted. *The Theology of Rāmānuja: an essay in interreligious understanding.* New Haven: Yale University, 1974.

Cenker, William. *A Tradition of teachers: Śaṅkara and the Jagadgurus today.* Delhi: Motilal Banarsidass, 1983.

Chakraborti, Haripada. *Asceticism in ancient India.* Calcutta: Punthi Pustak, 1973.

Clothey, Fred W. *The Many faces of Murukan̲: the history and meaning of a south Indian god.* The Hague: Mouton Publishers, 1978.

Coburn, Thomas B. " 'Scripture' in India: towards a typology of the word in Hindu life", *Journal of the American Academy of Religion* 52 (1984), 435-459.

Coèdes, G. *Inscriptions du Cambodge.* Vol. 1. Collection de textes et documents sur l'Indochine III. Hanoi: École Française d'Extrême-Orient, 1937.

Cohen, Bernard S. "The Role of the Gosains in the economy of eighteenth and nineteenth century upper India", *Indian Economic and Social History Review* 1 (1964), 175-182.

Coomaraswamy, A. K. "The Pilgrim's way", *Journal of the Bihar Research Society* 23 (1937) 452-471.

———. *Yakṣas*. [1928-31] Reprinted, New Delhi: Munshiram Manoharlal, 1980.

Cowell, E.B. and Thomas. F.W. [translators]. *The Harṣa-carita of Bāṇa*. Reprinted. Delhi: Motilal Banarsidass, 1961.

Cox, Patricia. *Biography in late antiquity: a quest for the holy man*. Berkeley: University of California, 1983.

Das, R.K. *Temples of Tamil Nad*. Bombay: Bharatiya Vidya Bhavan, 1964.

Dave, J. H. *Immortal India*. 4 vols., Bombay: Bharatiya Vidya Bhavan, 1959-61.

Derrett, J. Duncan M. "Rājadharma", *Journal of Asian Studies* 35 (1976), 597-609.

Devasenapati, V.A. *Kāmakoṭṭam, Nāyanmārs and Ādi Śaṅkara*. Madras: University of Madras, 1975.

Dey, Nundo Lal. *The Geographical dictionary of ancient and medieval India*. [1927] Reprinted, New Delhi: Oriental Books Reprint, 1971.

Diehl, Carl Gustav. *Instrument and purpose: studies on rites and rituals in south India*. Lund: C W K Gleerup, 1956.

Dimock, Edward C. "On impersonality and Bengali religious biography", in *Sanskrit and Indian studies*. Edited by M. Nagatomi, B.K. Matilal, J.M. Masson and E. Dimock. Dordrecht: Reidel, 1980, 237-242.

———. "Religious biography in India: the 'Nectar of the acts' of Caitanya", in *The Biographical process: studies in the history and psychology of religion*. Edited by Frank Reynolds and Donald Capps. The Hague: Mouton, 1976, 109-117.

Dube, D.P. "Kumbha Mela: origin and historicity of India's greatest fair", *The National Geographical Journal of India* 33 (1987), 1-17 [=*Homage to David E. Sopher*, ed. R. L. Singh and Rana P. B. Singh, Varanasi, 1987].

Dumont, Louis. "World renunciation in Indian religions", *Contributions to Indian Sociology* 4 (1960), 33-62.

Eck, Diana L. *Banaras: city of light*, London: Routledge and Kegan Paul, 1983.

———. "India's *tīrthas*: 'crossings' in sacred geography", *History of Religions* 20 (1981), 323-344.

Edgerton, Franklin. *The Beginnings of Indian philosophy*. Cambridge, Mass.: Harvard University, 1970.

Eliade, Mircea. *The Myth of the eternal return or, cosmos and history*. Translated by Willard R. Trask. Bollingen Series XLVI. [1965] Reprinted, Princeton: Princeton University, 1971.

———. *Yoga: immortality and freedom*. Translated by Willard R. Trask. Bollingen Series LVI. Princeton: Princeton University, 1973.

Ensink, J. "Problems of the study of pilgrimage in India", *Indologica Taurinensia* 2 (1974), 57-79.

Farquhar, J. N. "The Organization of the Sannyasis of the Vedanta", *Journal of the Royal Asiatic Society*, 1925, 479-486.

Filliozat, Vasundhara. *L'Épigraphie de Vijayanagar du début à 1377*. Paris: École Française d' Extrême-Orient, 1973.

Fuller, C. J. *Servants of the goddess: the priests of a south Indian temple*. Cambridge: Cambridge University Press, 1984.

Gazetteer of India. Karnataka State Gazetteer. Chikmagalur District. Bangalore: Govt. of Karnataka, 1981.

———. *Shimoga District*. Bangalore: Govt. of Karnataka, 1975.

———. *South Kanara District*. Bangalore: Govt. of Karnataka, 1973.

Gerow, Edwin. "Some thoughts on Indian government policy as it affects Sanskrit education", in *Studies in the language and culture of South Asia*. Edited by E. Gerow and M. D. Lang. Seattle and London: University of Washington, 1973, 111-124.

Ghosh, Jogendra Chunder. *The Principles of Hindu law*. 3d ed., 2 vols.; Calcutta: S. C. Audy, 1917.

Ghurye, G. S. *Indian sadhus*. Bombay: Popular Book Depot, 1953.

Gold, Daniel. "Clan and lineage among the Sants: seed, substance, service", in *The Sants: studies in a devotional tradition of India.* Edited by Karine Schomer and W.H. McLeod. Delhi: Motilal Banarsidass, 1987, 305-27.

Gonda, J. *Ancient Indian kingship from the religious point of view.* [1966] Reprinted, Leiden: E.J. Brill, 1969.

———. *Change and continuity in Indian religion.* [1965] Reprinted, New Delhi: Munshiram Manoharlal, 1985.

———. *Viṣṇuism and Śivaism: a comparison.* [1970] Reprinted, New Delhi: Munshiram Manoharlal, 1976.

Goudriaan, Teun and Gupta, Sanjukta. *Hindu tantric and Śakta literature.* Vol. II, fasc. 2 of *A History of Indian literature.* Ed. J. Gonda. Wiesbaden: Harrassowitz, 1981.

Granoff, Phyllis. "Authority and innovation: a study of the use of similes in the biography of Hiravijaya to provide sanction for the monk at court", *Jinmanjari* [Ontario] 1 (1990), 48-60.

———. "The Biographies of Arya Khapatacarya: a preliminary investigation into the transmission and adaptation of biographical legends", in *Monks and magicians: religious biographies in Asia.* Edited by Phyllis Granoff and Koichi Shinohara. Oakville, Ontario: Mosaic Press, 1988, 67-98.

———. "The Biographies of Siddhasena: a study in the texture of allusion and the weavings of a group-image", *Journal of Indian Philosophy,* in two parts, 17 (1989), 329-384, and 18 (1990), 261-304.

———. "God as idol: the role of special images in sectarian conflict in mediaeval Vaiṣṇavism", *Saras Bulletin* [South Asian Religious Art Studies] 2-3 (1983), 12-25.

———. "Holy Warriors: a preliminary study of some biographies of saints and kings in the classical Indian tradition", *Journal of Indian Philosophy* 12 (1984), 291-303.

———."Jain biographies of Nagarjuna: notes on the composing of a biography in medieval India", in *Monks and magicians: religious biographies in Asia.* Edited by Phyllis Granoff and

Koichi Shinohara. Oakville, Ontario: Mosaic Press, 1988, 45-66.

———. "Jain lives of Haribhadra: an inquiry into the sources and logic of the legends", *Journal of Indian Philosophy* 17 (1989), 105-128.

———. "The Miracle of a hagiography without miracles: some comments on the Jain lives of the Pratyekabuddha Karakaṇḍa" *Journal of Indian Philosophy* 14 (1986), 389-403.

———. "Scholars and wonder workers: some remarks on the role of the supernatural in philosophical contests and Vedānta hagiographies", *Journal of the American Oriental Society* 105 (1985), 459-467.

Grierson, G. A. "Mādhvas, Mādhvāchārīs", in *Encyclopaedia of Religion and Ethics*. Edited by James Hastings, Edinburgh, 1908-26, vol. VIII, 232-235.

Grierson, G. A. "The Magadha pura of the Mahabharata", *Journal of the Bihar and Orissa Research Society* 2 (1916), 95-96.

Gussner, Robert E. "A Stylometric study of the authorship of seventeen Sanskrit hymns attributed to Śaṅkara"', *Journal of the American Oriental Society* 96 (1976), 259-267.

———. "Śaṅkara's crest jewel of discrimination: a stylometric approach to the question of authorship", *Journal of Indian Philosophy* 4 (1977), 265-278.

Hacker, Paul. "Eigentümlichkeiten der Lehre und Terminologie Śaṅkaras", *Zeitschrift der Deutschen Morgenländischen Gesellschaft* 100 (1950), 246-286.

———. "Relations of early Advaitins to Vaiṣṇavism", *Wiener Zeitschrift für die Kunde Süd- und Ostasiens* 9 (1965), 147-154.

———. "Śaṅkarācārya and Śaṅkarabhagavatpāda: preliminary remarks concerning the authorship problem", in *Paul Hacker: Kleine Schriften*. Edited by Lambert Schmithausen. Wiesbaden: Franz Steiner Verlag, 1978, 41-58.

———. "Śaṅkara der Yogin und Śaṅkara der Advaitin. Einige Beobachtungen", *Beiträge zur Geistesgeschichte Indiens. Festschrift für Erich Frauwallner.* Wien, 1968 [=*WZKSO* 12/13 (1968-69)] 119-148.

Hadas, Moses and Smith, Morton. *Heroes and gods: spiritual biographies in antiquity.* London: Routledge and Kegan Paul, 1965.

Halbfass, Wilhelm. *India and Europe: an essay in understanding.* Albany: State University of New York, 1988.

———. *Studies in Kumārila and Śaṅkara.* Studien zur Indologie und Iranistik, Monographie 9. Reinbek, 1983.

Hamāre pūrvaja. [Hindi reader for schools in U.P., 8th Standard] by Kṛṣṇadev Prasād Gauṛ. [Many reprintings] 3 vols.; Mathurā: Taiknīkal Prakāśan, 1980.

Hariścandra. *Bhāratendu granthāvalī.* Edited by Vrajaratnadāsa. Kāśī: Nāgarī-pracāriṇo Sabhā, *saṃvat* 2010 [=1953], vol. III, 42-50.

Heesterman, Johannes Cornelis. *The Ancient Indian royal consecration.* [Thesis, Utrecht]. The Hague: Mouton, 1957.

———. "Householder and wanderer", *Contributions to Indian Sociology* 15 (1981), 251-271.

———. *The Inner conflict of tradition: essays in Indian ritual, kingship, and society.* Chicago: University of Chicago, 1985.

Hiltebeitel, Alf. *The Ritual of battle: Krishna in the* Mahābhārata. Ithaca and London: Cornell University, 1976.

The Hindu (New Delhi edition). "Sri Jayendra Saraswati missing", 24-28 August 1987 (front pages); 9 September, p. 9 and 4 October 1987, p. 4.

The Hindu (International edition). "Kanchi acharyas ask P.M. to rehabilitate J & K Hindus", 5 January 1991, p. 2.

Hiriyanna, M. *Outlines of Indian philosophy.* [1932] Reprinted, London: George Allen & Unwin, 1968.

A Historical atlas of South Asia. Edited by Joseph Schwartzberg. Chicago: University of Chicago, 1978.

The History of Nataraja temple. Chidambaram, n.d.

Illustrated Weekly. "The curious case of the missing monk", 13 September 1987, pp. 9-17.

———."Letters", 11 October 1987, p. 4.

Imperial Gazetteer of India. Provincial Series: United Provinces of Agra and Oudh. Vol. II [1908]. Reprinted, New Delhi: Usha, 1984.

Inden, Ronald. *Imagining India.* Oxford and Cambridge Mass.: Basil Blackwell, 1990.

India Today (International edition). "The Swami returns" 30 September 1987, p. 96.

———."MGR's legacy: political vacuum", 15 January 1988, pp. 6-15; "Invoking legacies", 15 January 1989, pp. 24-26.

———."Hindu mutts: a changing outlook", 30 June 1988, p. 71.

———."Secular stand", 15 November 1989, p. 48.

———."Ram Janmabhoomi: acting tough", 31 May 1990, p. 29.

Indian Express (Madras edition). "Facts about Sringeri Mutt heads", 25 June 1989; 12 August; 26 August; 2 September and 7 October 1989.

Ingalls, Daniel H. H. "The Study of Śaṃkarācārya", *Annals of the Bhandarkar Oriental Research Institute* 33 (1952), 1-14.

———. "Śaṃkara's arguments against the Buddhists", *Philosophy East and West* 3 (1954) 291-306.

———. *An Anthology of Sanskrit court poetry: Vidyākara's "Subhāṣitaratnakośa".* Harvard Oriental Series, vol 44. Cambridge, Mass.: Harvard University, 1965.

Iyer, G. V. "Ādi Śaṅkarācārya". [Feature film in Sanskrit]. Production by N.F.D.C., Bombay, 1982-83.

Iyer, K.V. Subbarathnam. *Srimad Abhinava Vidyateertha Vijayam.* [Originally published in Tamil, 1975]. Translated by K. Mahadevan. Sringeri: Sri Sarada Trust, 1986.

The Jagadguru replies. [Talks with Śrī Abhinava Vidyātīrtha, originally published in Tamil]. Translated by P.N. Neelakantan. Sringeri: Sringeri Sarada Peetam [1983].

Jaini, Padmanabh S. *The Jaina path of purification.* Berkeley and Los Angeles: University of California, 1979.

Johnston, E. H. [translator]. *The Buddhacarita or, acts of the Buddha.* New Delhi: Oriental Reprints, 1972.

Jordens, J.T.F. "Orthodoxy and heresy: reflections of the 1881 Calcutta pandit council", in *World perspectives on Swami Dayananda Saraswati.* [Edited by] Ganga Ram Garg, New Delhi: Concept Publishing, 1984, 239-252.

Joshi, Hariprasad Shivprasad. *Origin and development of Dattātreya worship in India.* Baroda: University of Baroda, 1965.

Kane, P.V. *History of Dharmaśāstra: ancient and mediaeval religious and civil law.* 5 vols. in 8 parts. Poona : Bhandarkar Oriental Institute, 1962-75.

Kramrisch, Stella. *The Presence of Śiva.* Princeton: Princeton University, 1981.

Krishnamachariar, M. *History of Classical Sanskrit Literature* [1937] Reprinted, Delhi, 1974.

Kuiper, F.B.J. "The Ancient Indian verbal contest", *Indo-Iranian Journal* 4 (1960), 217-281.

Kulke, Hermann. *Cidambaramāhātmya: Eine Untersuchung der religions-geschichtlichen und historischen Hintergründe für die Enstehung der Tradition einer südindischen Tempelstadt.* Wiesbaden: Harrassowitz, 1970.

———. "Mahārājas, mahants and historians: reflections on the historiography of early Vijayanagara and Sringeri", in *Vijayanagara—city and empire: new currents of research.* Edited by A. L. Dallapiccola. 2 vols., Stuttgart: Steiner Verlag Wiesbaden, 1985, vol. I, 120-143.

Kunjunni Raja, K. *The Contribution of Kerala to Sanskrit literature.* Madras: University of Madras, 1958.

——— "On the date of Śaṅkarācārya and allied problems", *Adyar Library Bulletin* 24 (1960), 125-148.

Laine, James W. *Visions of God: narratives of theophany in the Mahābhārata.* Publications of the De Nobili Research

Library, vol. XVI. Vienna: Institute for Indology, University of Vienna, 1989.

Lariviere, Richard W. "Justices and *paṇḍitas*: some ironies in contemporary readings of the Hindu legal past", *The Journal of Asian Studies* 48 (1989), 757-769.

Law, Bimal Churn. *Historical geography of ancient India.* [1954] Reprinted, Delhi, Ess Ess Publications, 1976.

Lévi-Strauss, Claude. "The Structural study of myth", in *Structural anthropology*. Translated by C. Jacobson and B.G. Schoepy. London: Allen Lane, 1968, 289-302.

Lorenzen, David N. *The Kāpālikas and Kālāmukhas: two lost Śaiva sects*. New Delhi: Thompson Press, 1972.

———. "The Life of Śaṅkarācārya", in *Experiencing Śiva: encounters with a Hindu deity*. Edited by Fred W. Clothey and J. Bruce Long, Colombia, Mo.: South Asia Books, 1983, 155-175.

Lütt, Jürgen. "The Śaṅkarācārya of Puri", in *The Cult of Jagannath and the regional tradition of Orissa.* Edited by A. Eschmann, H. Kulke and G. C. Tripathi, Delhi: Manohar, 1978, 411-419.

Kulkarni, S.D. *Adi Sankara: the saviour of mankind.* Bombay: Bhishma Publications, 1987.

Kuppuswami, A. *Śri Bhagavatpāda Śaṅkarācārya.* Chowkamba Sanskrit Studies, no. 89. Varanasi: Chowkamba Sanskrit Series Office, 1972.

McGregor, R. S. *Hindi literature from its beginnings to the nineteenth century*. Vol. 8, fasc. 6 of *A History of Indian literature*. Edited by J. Gonda. Wiesbaden: Harrassowitz, 1984.

Madhusūdana Sarasvatī. See *Siddhāntabindu.*

Madhusudan Parvat v. Shree Madhav Teerth, The Indian Law Reports, Bombay Series, 33 (1909), 278-293; The Bombay Law Reporter, 11 (1909) 58-68.

Mahadevan, T.M.P. *Gauḍapāda: a study in early Advaita.* Madras: University of Madras, 1975.

———. *The Philosophy of Advaita with special reference to Bhāratītīrtha-Vidyāraṇya.* [1938] 4th ed.; New Delhi: Arnold-Heinemann, 1976.

———. *Ramana Maharshi: the sage of Aruṇācala.* London: Allen & Unwin, 1977.

———. *The Sage of Kanchi.* [1967]. Reprinted, Secunderabad: Sri Kanchi Kamakoti Sankar Mandir, 1983.

———. *Sankaracharya.* [1968] Reprinted, New Delhi: National Book Trust, 1977.

Majumdar, A.K. *Caitanya: his life and doctrine. A study in Vaiṣṇavism.* Bombay: Bharatiya Vidya Bhavan, 1969.

Masson, J. Moussaieff. "The Psychology of the ascetic", *Journal of Asian Studies* 35 (1976), 611-625.

Mayeda, Sengaku. "The Authenticity of the Bhagavadgītābhāṣya ascribed to Śaṅkara", *Wiener Zeitschrift für die Kunde Süd- und Ostasiens* 9 (1965), 155-197.

———."The Authenticity of the Upadeśasāhasrī ascribed to Śaṅkara", *Journal of the American Oriental Society* 85 (1965),178-196.

———. "On the author of the *Māṇḍūkyopaniṣad* and the *Gauḍapādīya-Bhāṣya*", *Adyar Library Bulletin* 31-32 (1967-68), 73-94.

———. "On Śaṅkara's authorship of the Kenopaniṣadbhāṣya", *Indo-Iranian Journal* 10 (1967), 33-55.

———. *A Thousand teachings: the Upadeśasāhasrī of Śaṅkara.* Tokyo: University of Tokyo, 1979.

Meyyappan, S. *Chidambaram: golden temple.* Chidambaram [n.p.] 1987.

Mines, Mattison and Gourishankar, Vijayalakshmi. "Leadership and individuality in south Asia: the case of the south Indian big-man", *Journal of Asian Studies* 49 (1990), 761-786.

Mudaliar, A. Devaraja. *Day by day with Bhagavan. From a diary [dated] March 16, 1945 to January 4, 1947.* 2nd ed.; Tiruvannamalai: Sri Ramanasramam, 1977.

Mysore Archaeological Department [R. Narasimhachar, Director]. *Annual Report for the year 1916*. Bangalore: Government Press, 1917.

———. *Annual report for the year 1928*. Bangalore: Government Press, 1928.

Nābhājī, Gosvāmī [Nābhādās]. *Śrī Bhaktmāl, with the commentary of Priyādās*. Lucknow: Tejkumār Press, 1962 [pp. 316-322 on Śaṅkara's life.].

Nakamura, Hajime. *A History of early Vedānta philosophy*. Translated by Trevor Leggett, Sengaku Mayeda, et. al. Part One, Delhi, 1983 [First published in Japanese, 1950-56].

Nandimath, S.C. *A Handbook of Vīraśaivism*. [1942] 2nd ed., Delhi: Motilal Banarsidass, 1979.

Nārāyaṇa-paṇḍita. See *Maṇimañjarī* and *Sumadhvavijaya*.

Nehru, Jawaharlal. *The Discovery of India*. [1946] Reprinted London: Meridian Books, 1956.

Oddie, G.A. "The Character, role and significance of non-brahmin Saivite maths in Tanjore District in the nineteenth century", in *Changing south Asia: religion and society*. Edited by Kenneth Ballhatchet and David Taylor. London: Centre of South Asian Studies, School of Oriental and African Studies, 1984, 37-49.

O'Flaherty, Wendy Doniger. *Asceticism and eroticism in the mythology of Śiva*. London and New York: Oxford University Press, 1973.

———. *The Origins of evil in Hindu mythology*. Berkeley and Los Angeles: University of California, 1976.

Olivelle, Patrick. " A definition of world renunciation", *Wiener Zeitschrift für die Kunde Südasiens* 19 (1975), 75-83.

———. " King and ascetic", *Adyar Library Bulletin* 51 (1978), 39-59.

———. *Renunciation in Hinduism: a medieval debate*. 2 vols.; Publications of the De Nobili Research Library, 13-14. Vienna: Institut für Indologie der Universität Wien, 1986-1987.

———. [Editor and translator]. *Vāsudevāśrama Yatidharmaprakāśa: a treatise on world renunciation.* 2 vols.; Publications of the De Nobili Research Library, vols. 3-4. Vienna: Institut für Indologie der Universität Wien, 1976-77.

Pargiter, F.E. *Ancient Indian historical traditions.* London: Oxford University, 1922.

Pathak, Vishwambhar Sharan. *Ancient historians of India: a study in historical biographies.* Bombay: Asia Publishing House, 1966.

———. *History of Śaiva cults in northern India from inscriptions.* Varanasi, 1960.

———. *Smārta religious traditions.* Meerut: Kusumanjali Prakashan, 1987.

Periya puranam: a Tamil classic on the great Saiva saints of south India by Sekkizhar. Condensed English version by G.Vanmikanathan, Madras: Sri Ramakrishna Math, 1985.

Petech, Luciano. *Mediaeval history of Nepal c. 750-1482.* 2nd ed.; Roma: Istituto Italiano per il Medio ed Estremo Oriente, 1984.

Piantelli, Mario. *Śaṅkara e la rinascita del Brāhmanismo.* Fossano: Editrice Esperienze, 1974.

Pollock, Sheldon. "The Divine king in the Indian epic", *Journal of the American Oriental Society* 104 (1984), 505-528.

———. "Mīmāṃsā and the problem of history in traditional India", *Journal of the American Oriental Society* 109 (1989), 603-610.

———. "The Theory of practice and the practice of theory in Indian intellectual history", *Journal of the American Oriental Society* 105 (1985), 499-519.

Potter, Karl H. [Editor]. *Encyclopedia of Indian Philosophies.* [Vol. 3] *Advaita Vedānta up to Śaṃkara and his pupils.* Princeton: Princeton University, 1981.

———. "Śaṃkarācārya: the myth and the man", *Journal of the American Academy of Religion. Thematic Studies*, XLVIII (1982), 111-125.

Presler, Franklin A. *Religion under bureaucracy: policy and administration for Hindu temples in south India.* Cambridge: Cambridge University, 1987.

Rajendran v. Govt. of Tamil Nadu, Madras Law Journal, vol.169, 1985, pp. 337-342; All Indian Reporter, Madras, vol. 72, 1985, pp. 44-49.

Ramakrishnananda, Swami. *Life of Sri Ramanuja.* Translated from Bengali by Swami Budhananda. [1959] 4th ed.; Mylapore: Sri Ramakrishna Math, 1986.

Rama Sastrigal, Polagam Sri. "The Six orthodox ways of worship", in *Sankara and Shanmata.* Souvenir of the conference on Sankara and Shanmata, Madras, June 1-9, 1969. Madras: Sankara and Shanmata conference committee [no details on the editor of the volume, unpaginated].

Rao, R. Rama. "Identity of Vidyāraṇya and Mādhavācārya", *Indian Historical Quarterly* 10 (1934), 801-810.

———. "Origin of the Mādhava-Vidyāraṇya theory", *Indian Historical Quarterly* 7 (1931), 78-92.

Renou, Louis. *Études Védiques et Pāṇinéennes.* 17 vols. (1955-1969), Paris: Éditions E. de Boccard, 1961.

Report of the Hindu Religious and Charitable Endowments Commission. United Provinces. Allahabad: Government Press, United Provinces, 1931.

Report of the Hindu Religious Endowments Commission. C.P. Ramaswami Aiyer, chairman. Government of India: Ministry of Law, 1960-1962.

Rocher, Ludo. *The Purāṇas.* Vol.2, Fasc. 3 of *A History of Indian literature.* Edited by J. Gonda. Wiesbaden: Harrassowitz, 1986.

———. "Śiva in the Purāṇas", in *Discourses on Śiva.* Edited by Michael W. Meister, Philadelphia, 1984, 202-211.

Ruegg, D. Seyfort. "Towards a chronology of the Madhyamaka school", in *Indological and Buddhist studies: volume in honour of J. W. de Jong*. Edited by L.A. Hercus et. al., Canberra: Australian National University, Faculty of Asian Studies, 1982, 505-530.

Sadānanda Giri, Swāmi. *Society and sannyāsin: a history of the daśnāmī sannyāsins*. Varanasi: Swāmi Sadānanda Giri, 1976.

Sadasivaiah, H. M. *A Comparative study of two Vīraśaiva monasteries*. Mysore: Prasaranga Manasa Gangotri, 1967.

Salomon, Richard. "*Tīrtha-pratyāmnāyāḥ*: ranking of Hindu pilgrimage sites in classical Sanskrit texts", *Zeitschrift der Deutschen Morgenländischen Gesellschaft* 129 (1979), 102-128.

Sankara and Shanmata. Souvenir of the conference on Sankara and Shanmata, Madras, June 1-9, 1969. Madras: Sankara and Shanmata Conference Committee [no details on the editor of the volume, unpaginated].

Sankara the missionary. Central Chinmaya Mission Trust: Bombay, 1978.

Sarda, Har Bilas. "The Prithviraja vijaya", *Journal of the Royal Asiatic Society*, 1913, 259-281.

Sarkar, Jadunath. *A History of dasnami naga sanyasis*. Allahabad: Sri Panchayati Akhara Mahanirvani, n.d..

Sastri, S.S. Suryanarayana. *The Life and teachings of Sri Sankara*. Madras: G.A. Natesan [1946].

———."Mandana and Suresvara", in *Collected papers of Professor S.S. Suryanarayana Sastri*. Edited by T.M.P. Mahadevan, Madras: University of Madras, 1961, 281-291.

———. [Editor and translator] *The Śivādvaita of Śrīkaṇṭha*. [1930] Reprinted, Madras: Madras: University of Madras, 1972.

Sastri, T. S. Kuppuswami. "Rāmabhadra-Dīkṣita and the southern poets of his time", *The Indian Antiquary* 33 (1904), 126-142 [continued on] 176-196.

Sastry, T. S. Narayana, *The Age of Śaṅkara.* [1916] Reprinted, Madras: B.G. Paul, 1971.

Satchidanandendra Saraswati, Swamy. *Misconceptions about Śaṅkara.* Holenarsipur: Adhyatma Prakasha Karyalaya, 1973.

Sawai, Yoshitsugu. "The Faith of ascetics and lay Smārtas: a study of the Śaṅkaran tradition of Śṛṅgerī". Ph.D. thesis. Harvard University, Cambridge, Mass., 1984.

———. "The Legend of Śaṅkara's birth", *Journal of Indian and Buddhist Studies* 36 (1987), 464-468.

———. "The Nature of faith in the Śaṅkara tradition", *Numen* 34 (1987), 18-44.

———. "On a legendary biography of Śaṅkara", *Journal of Indian and Buddhist Studies* 34 (1985), 454-459.

Scheuer, Jacques. *Śiva dans le Mahābhārata.* Paris: Presses Universitaires de France, 1982.

Schiefner, Anton. *Tāranātha's Geschichte des Buddhismus in Indien.* St. Petersburg, 1869.

Schmithausen, Lambert. *Ālayavijñāna: on the origin and early development of a central concept of Yogācāra philosophy.* Studia Philologica Buddhica Mono-graph Series IVa-b. Tokyo: International Institute for Buddhist Studies, 1987.

Shastri, Udayavir. *The Age of Shankara.* Translated by Lakshmi Datta Dikshit. Gaziabad: Virjanand Vedic Research Institute, 1981.

Shastry, A. K. *A History of Śriṅgeri.* Dharwad: Prasaranga, Karnatak University, 1982, pp. 16-21.

Shulman, David Dean. *The King and the clown in south Indian myth and polity.* Princeton: Princeton University, 1985.

———. "Terror of symbols and symbols of terror": notes on the myth of Śiva as Sthāṇu", *History of Religions* 26 (1986), 101-124.

Siegel, Lee. *Fires of love / waters of peace: passion and renunciation in Indian culture.* Honolulu: University of Hawaii, 1983.

Sircar, D. C. *Cosmography and geography in early Indian literature.* Calcutta: Indian Studies Past and Present, 1967.

———. *The Śākta pīṭhas.* 2nd ed., Delhi: Motilal Banarsidass, 1973.

Sivaramamurti, C. *Bhagavatpāda Śri Śaṅkarācārya.* New Delhi: Sankara Academy of Sanskrit Culture and Classical Arts, 1972.

Solomon, Esther A. *Indian dialectics: methods of philosophical discussion.* 2 vols., Ahmedabad: B.J. Institute of Learning and Research, 1976-78.

Sontheimer, Günther D. "Folk deities in the Vijayanagara empire: Narasiṃha and Mallaṇṇa/Mailār", in *Vijayanagara—city and empire: new currents of research.* Edited by A. L. Dallipiccola. 2 vols., Stuttgart: Franz Steiner Verlag Wiesbaden, 1985, vol. I., 144-158.

———. "God as the king for all: the Sanskrit *Mallāri Māhātmya* and its context", in *The History of sacred places in India as reflected in traditional literature.* Edited by Hans Bakker, Leiden: E. J. Brill, 1990, 103-130.

Sopher, David E. "The Message of place in Hindu pilgrimage", *The National Geographical Journal of India* 33 (1987), 1-17 [=*Homage to David E. Sopher,* ed. R. L. Singh and Rana P. B. Singh, Varanasi, 1987].

Sri Sunkur Bharti Swami v. Sidha Lingayah Charanti, Moore's Indian Appeals, vol. 3 (1841-46) 199-219 [pp. 125-37 in reprint, Allahabad: Law Publishers, 1989].

Stein, Burton. "Devī shrines and folk Hinduism in Medieval Tamilnad", in *Studies in the language and culture of South Asia.* Edited. E. Gerow and M. D. Lang, Seattle and London: University of Washington, 1973, 75-90.

Survey of India, State maps (1:1 million series).

Swaminathan, K. D. *The Nāyakas of Ikkeri.* Madras: P.Varadachary, 1957.

Swarup, Ram. *Ramakrishna Mission in search of a new identity.* New Delhi: Voice of India, 1986.

Tambiah, S.J. "The Renouncer: his individuality and his community", *Contributions to Indian Sociology* 15 (1981), 299-320.

Tāranātha. *History of Buddhism in India.* Translated by Lama Chimpa and Alaka Chattopadhyaya. Edited by Debiprasad Chattopadhyaya. Simla: Indian Institute of Advanced Study, 1970.

Tattvāloka [Sringerī] 13 (Dec./Jan 1991), p. 81 [report on Rajiv Gandhi's visit].

Telang, K.T. "The Śaṅkaravijaya of Ānandagiri", *Indian Antiquary* 5 (1876), 287-93.

Thapar, Romila. "Syndicated moksha?", *Seminar* 313 (1985), 14-22.

Thrasher, Allen Wright. "The Dates of Maṇḍana Miśra and Śaṃkara", *Wiener Zeitschrift für die Kunde Südasiens* 23 (1979), 117-139.

Turner, Victor. "The Centre out there: pilgrim's goal", *History of Religions* 12 (1973), 191-230.

Upādhyāy, Baldev. *Śrī Śaṅkarācārya: Śrī Śaṅkarācārya ke jīvancarit tathā upadeśoṃ kā prāmāṇik vivaraṇ.* Allahabad: Hindustani Academy, 1950.

Vaidyanathan, K. R. *Temples and legends of Kerala.* Bombay: Bharatiya Vidya, 1988.

van Buitenen, J. A. B. [Translator]. *The Mahābhārata.* 3 vols. Chicago: Chicago University, 1973-75-78.

———. "On the structure of the sabhāparvan of the Mahābhārata", in *India maior: congratulatory volume presented to J. Gonda.* Leiden: Brill, 1972, pp. 68-84.

Veeramani, K. *Kanchi Sankarachariar: saint or sectarian?* [First published in Tamil, 1985]. Madras: Dravidar Kazhagam, 1988.

Venkataraman, K.R. *Samkara and his Sarada pitha in Sringeri: a study in growth and integration.* Calcutta: Kalpa Printers, 1969.

———. *The Throne of transcendental wisdom: Śrī Śaṅkarācārya's Śāradā pīṭha in Sringeri.* Tiruchirapalli [n.p.], 1959.

Venkataraman, K.R; Iyer, M.K. Venkatarama; Srinivasan, K.R. *The Age of Vidyaranya.* Calcutta: Kalpa Publishers, 1976.

Vetter, Tilmann. *Studien zur Lehre und Entwicklung Śaṅkaras.* Publications of the De Nobili Research Library, 6. Vienna: Indological Institute, University of Vienna, 1979.

Vivekananda, Swami. *The complete works of Swami Vivekananda.* 6th ed., 7 vols. Mayavati: Advaita Ashrama, 1948.

Voice of Śaṅkara: Śaṅkara Bhāratī, 4 (1979) 87-90.

Warder, A. K. *Indian kāvya literature.* Vol. 5, Delhi: Motilal Banarsidass, 1988.

Watters, Thomas. *On Yuan Chwang's travels in India.* Edited by T.W. Rhys Davids and S.W. Bushell. 2 vols., London: Royal Asiatic Society, 1904-1905.

The Week. October 22, 1989, p. 16 [report on women's anti-Śaṅkarācārya rally].

Zvelebil, Kamil V. *The Poets of the powers.* London: Rider and Co., 1973.